CHAINMAIL BIKINI

THE ANTHOLOGY OF
WOMEN GAMERS

When putting together *Chainmail Bikini*, I had two goals. One was to collect comics by an outstanding group of female artists about games and what they mean to us. The other was to celebrate the experience of women gamers, at a time when our presence in gaming culture is consistently marginalized.

The term "gamer" encompasses players of all sorts of games, from video games to Dungeons & Dragons to LARPing. What ties all these games together, and separates them from games like checkers or football? In my view, the common element is that of taking on a character and entering another reality. The comics in *Chainmail Bikini* explore why we're drawn to these fantasy worlds, and what roles they serve in our real lives.

It shouldn't be controversial for women to have an equal say as players, makers, and critics of games. Too many men see these games as their exclusive domain, and act out the same old sexism that's already prevalent in the real world. To play a game is to voluntarily take on a challenge, for fun. No one should be additionally challenged because of their gender.

It has been my great pleasure to work with the cartoonists, writers, and illustrators who contributed their comics to *Chainmail Bikini*. This anthology encompasses what we love about games, and our ideas to make them better.

Hazel Newlevant, Editor

a CERTAIN KIND of STORY

by molly ostertag

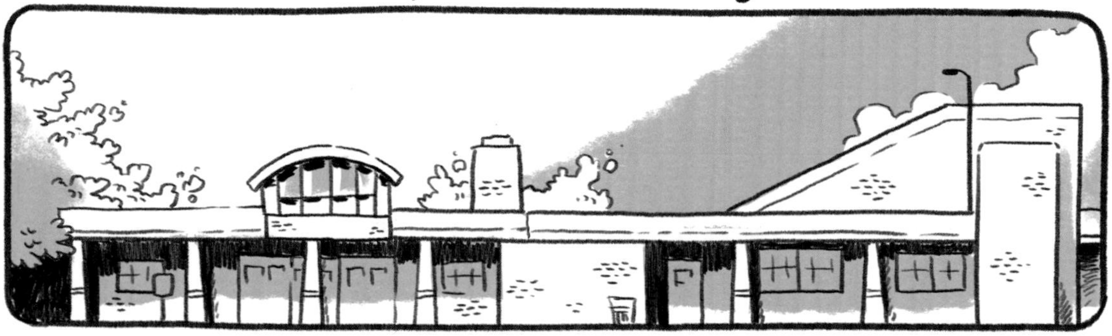

The stories I loved as a child always began somewhere small. A little town, a house in the country, a school with nothing out of the ordinary.

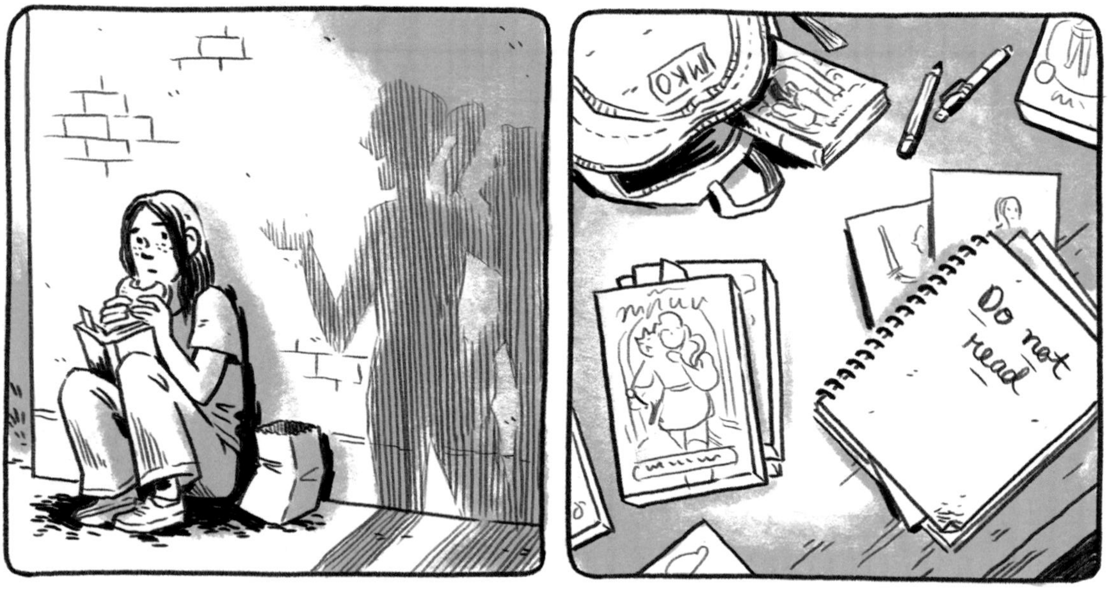
Do not read

The hero lived here in a kind of hibernation, waiting for her story to begin. She would be bit different from everyone else, a bit out of place.

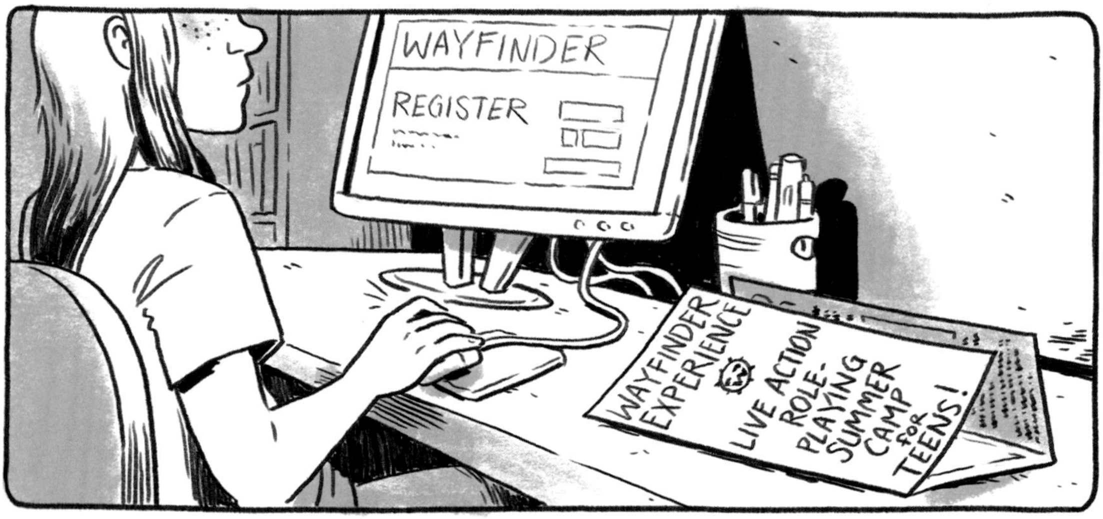
WAYFINDER
REGISTER
WAYFINDER EXPERIENCE
LIVE ACTION ROLE-PLAYING SUMMER CAMP for TEENS!

The story really began when a path appeared, leading to another world. The path would look strange, even dangerous, but she would plunge down it without a backwards glance.

It wasn't that the other world was a perfect, happy one. Often it was full of trials, and in the beginning she would fail at them.

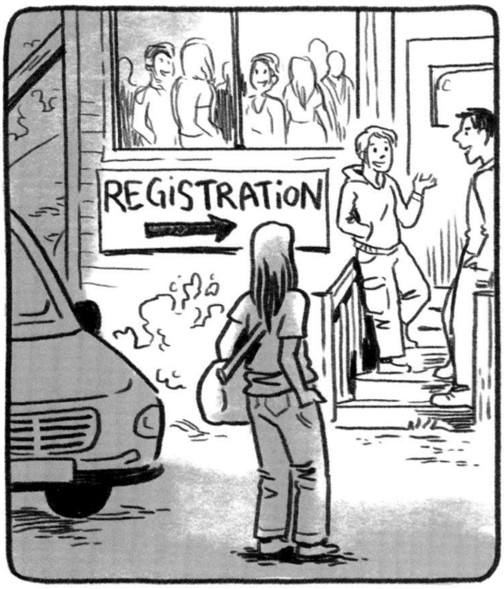
REGISTRATION

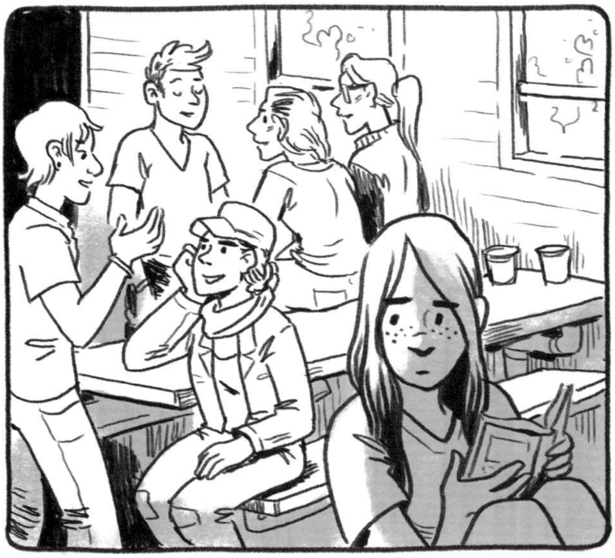

But it was a magical world, and that made all the difference. In a world like that, she would always triumph in the end, because she loved it too much to give up and walk away.

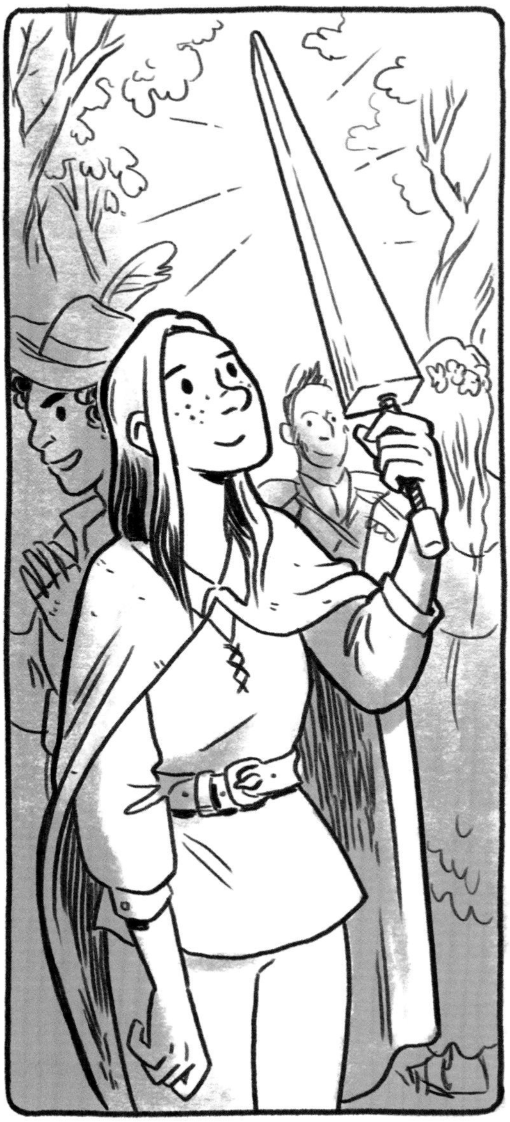

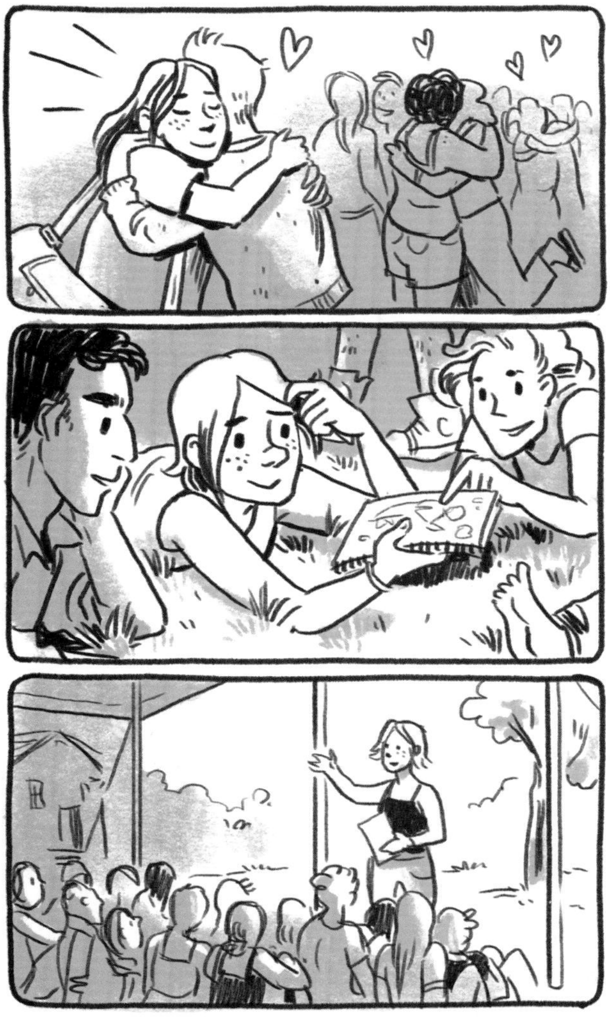

The hero would grow in power, gather companions, and be gifted with magic and weapons.

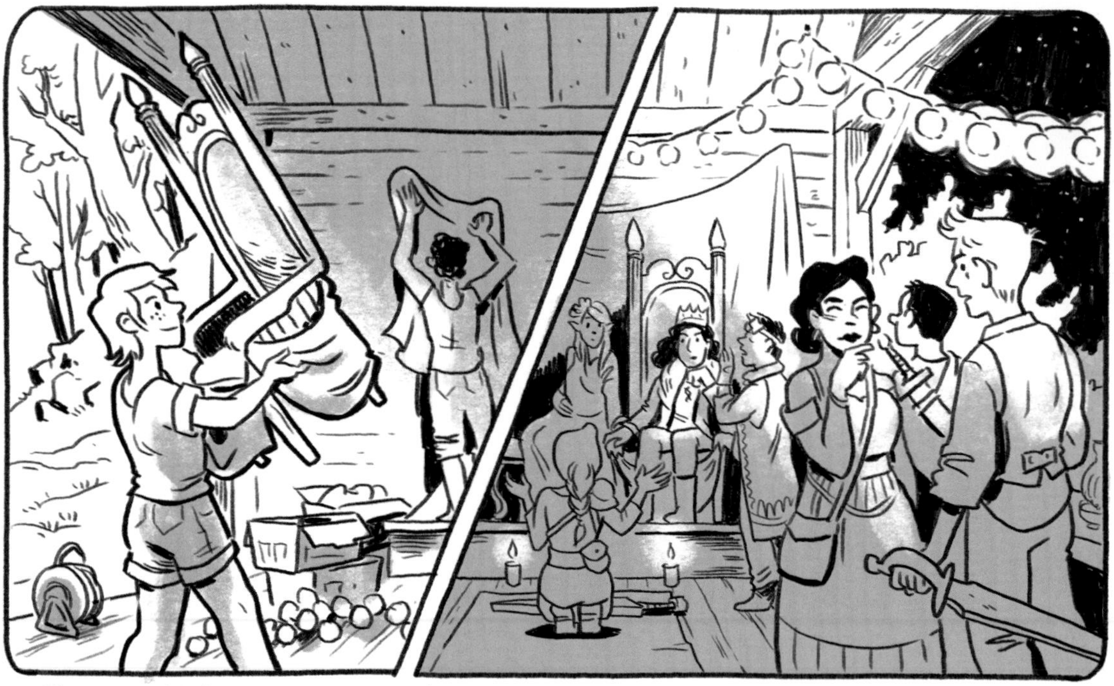

She would find a place in that world where she could do good. She had never been needed by others before, but now the fate of a kingdom rested on her shoulders, and she grew strong to bear the burden.

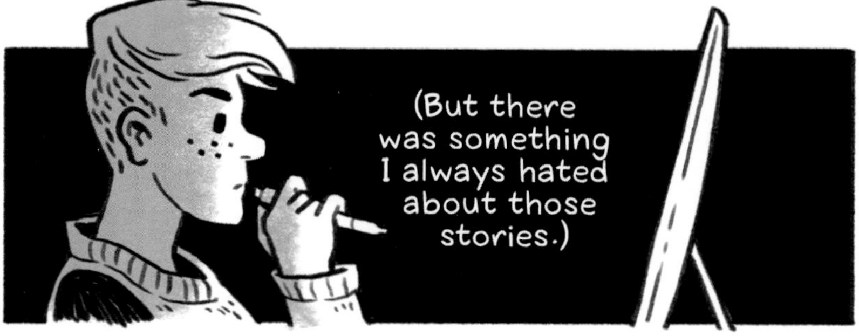
(But there was something I always hated about those stories.)

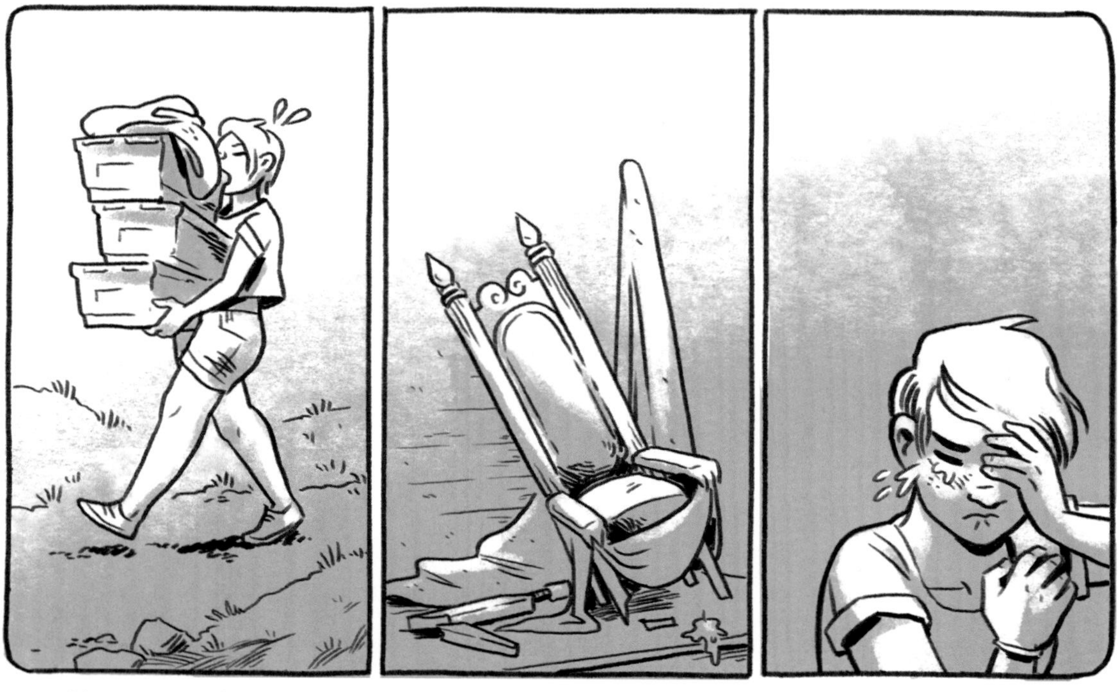

She would have to leave the world. The magic would stop working, and it would be revealed that her time there was only temporary.

So she would return to the mundane world, full of secrets and stories, this girl who had once slain dragons and saved a kingdom.

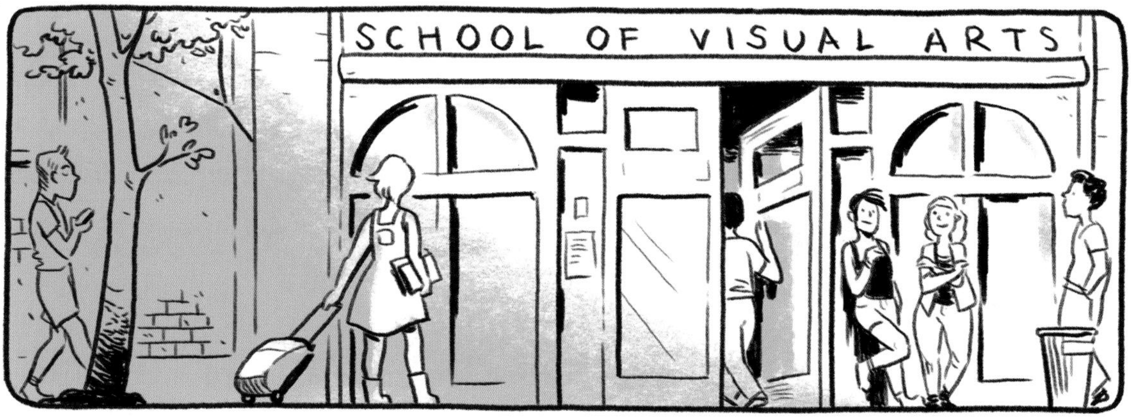
SCHOOL OF VISUAL ARTS

What I couldn't understand as a child was that she had been changed by the magical world until she no longer needed it.

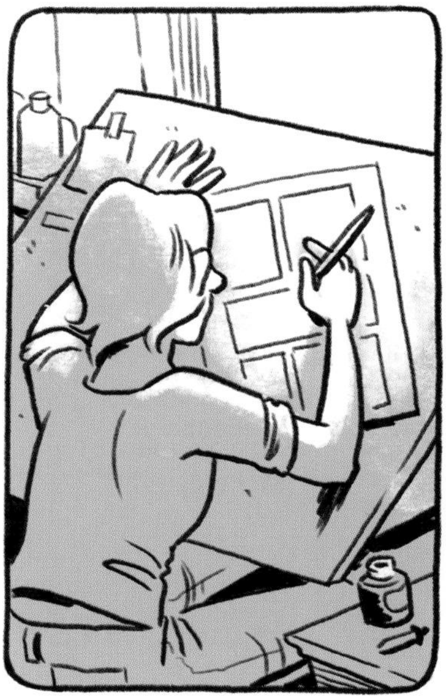

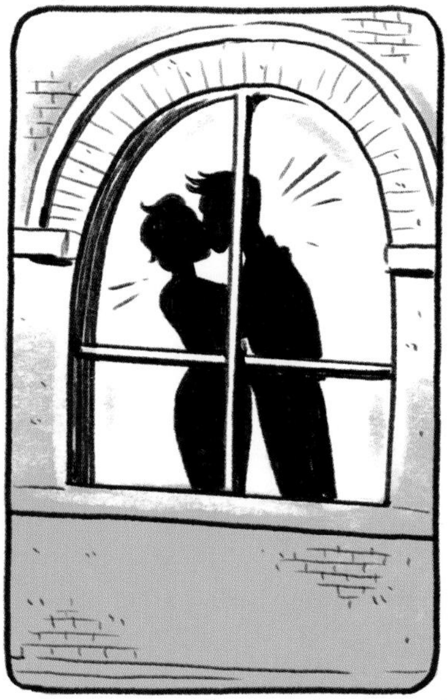

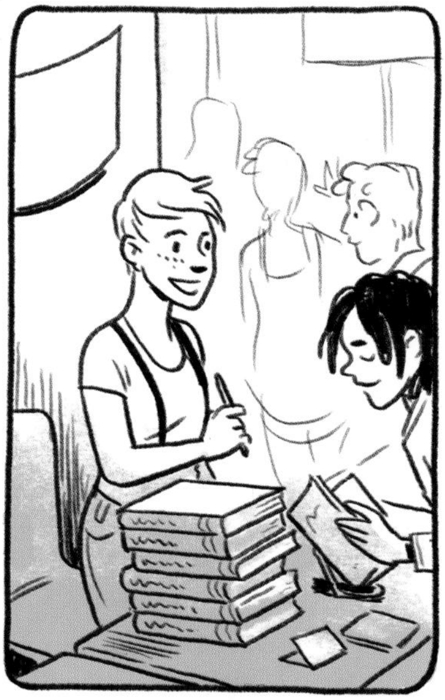

The pathway was closed to her, her weapons left behind, but the strength she had learned remained.

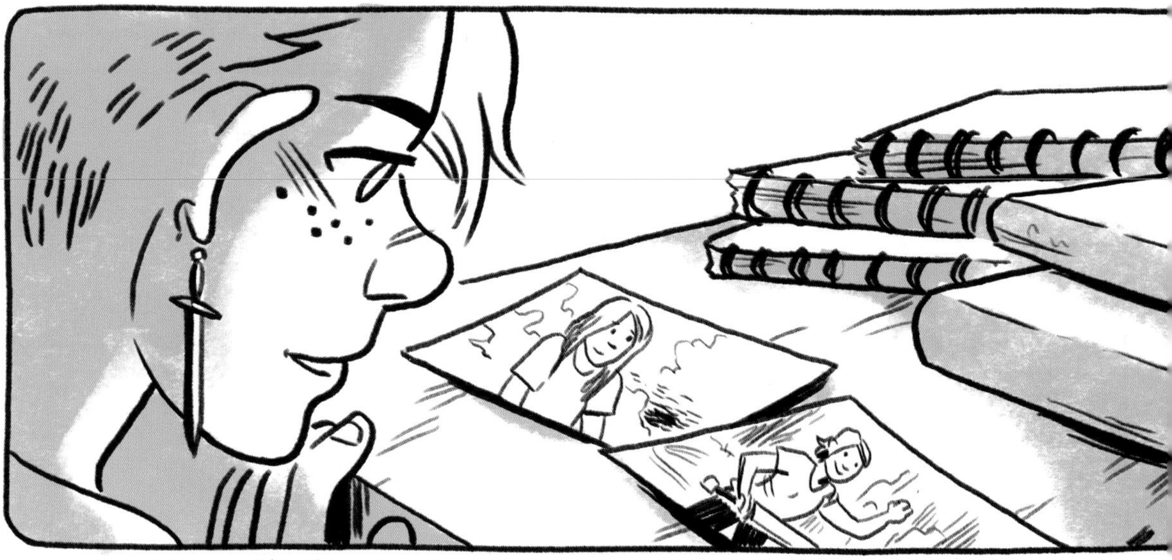

She had undergone a transformation, the only magic that kept working on her return. Her adventure (the first one, at least) was over, but she remained a hero.

LET ME DO IT

BY SARA GOETTER

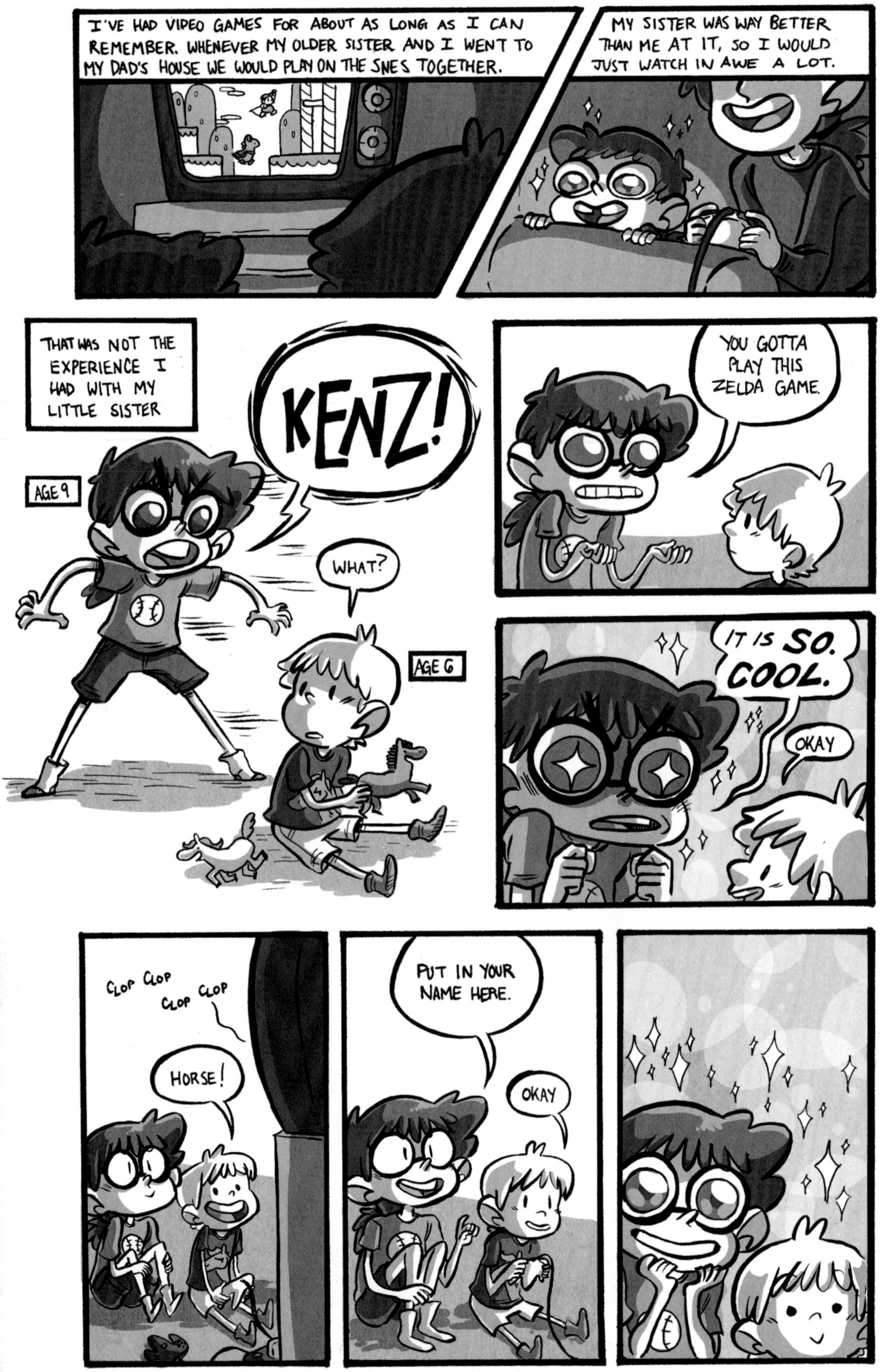

I'VE HAD VIDEO GAMES FOR ABOUT AS LONG AS I CAN REMEMBER. WHENEVER MY OLDER SISTER AND I WENT TO MY DAD'S HOUSE WE WOULD PLAY ON THE SNES TOGETHER.
MY SISTER WAS WAY BETTER THAN ME AT IT, SO I WOULD JUST WATCH IN AWE A LOT.
THAT WAS NOT THE EXPERIENCE I HAD WITH MY LITTLE SISTER
KENZ!
AGE 9
WHAT?
AGE 6
YOU GOTTA PLAY THIS ZELDA GAME.
IT IS SO. COOL.
OKAY
CLOP CLOP CLOP CLOP
HORSE!
PUT IN YOUR NAME HERE.
OKAY

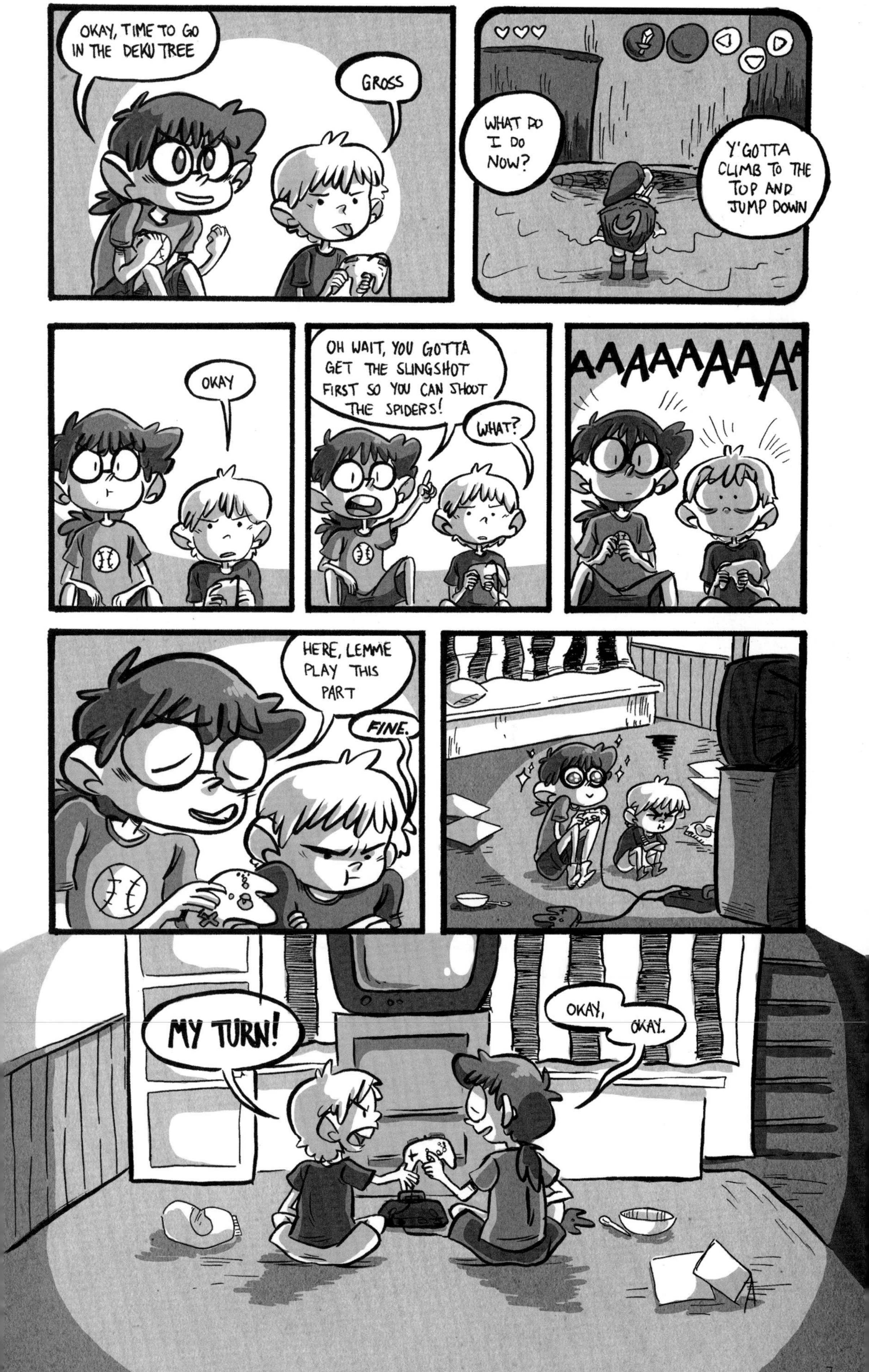
OKAY, TIME TO GO IN THE DEKU TREE
GROSS
WHAT DO I DO NOW?
Y'GOTTA CLIMB TO THE TOP AND JUMP DOWN
OKAY
OH WAIT, YOU GOTTA GET THE SLINGSHOT FIRST SO YOU CAN SHOOT THE SPIDERS!
WHAT?
AAAAAAAAA
HERE, LEMME PLAY THIS PART
FINE.
MY TURN!
OKAY, OKAY.

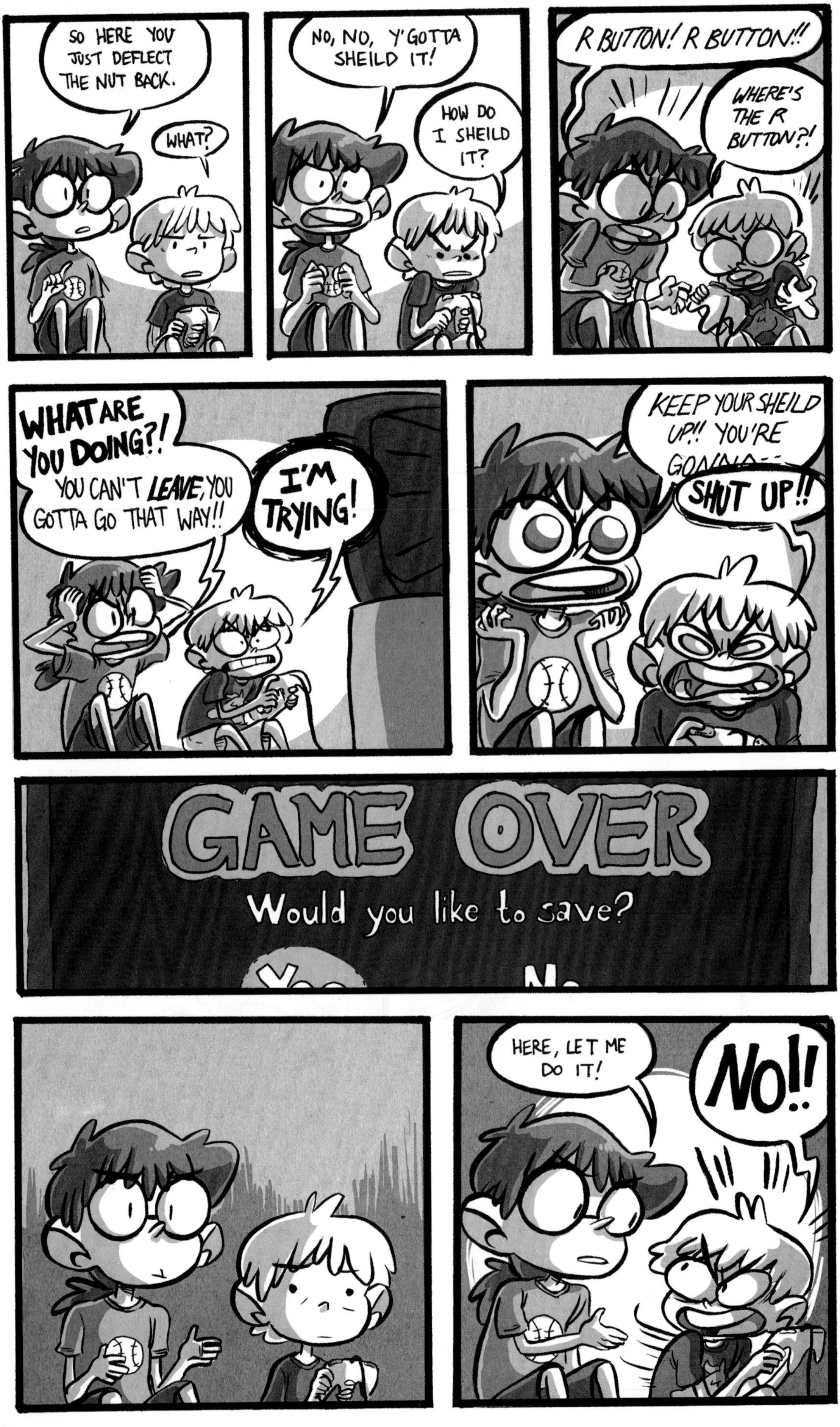

SO HERE YOU JUST DEFLECT THE NUT BACK.
WHAT?
NO, NO, Y'GOTTA SHEILD IT!
HOW DO I SHEILD IT?
R BUTTON! R BUTTON!!
WHERE'S THE R BUTTON?!
WHAT ARE YOU DOING?! YOU CAN'T LEAVE, YOU GOTTA GO THAT WAY!!
I'M TRYING!
KEEP YOUR SHEILD UP!! YOU'RE
SHUT UP!!
GAME OVER
Would you like to save?
HERE, LET ME DO IT!
NO!!

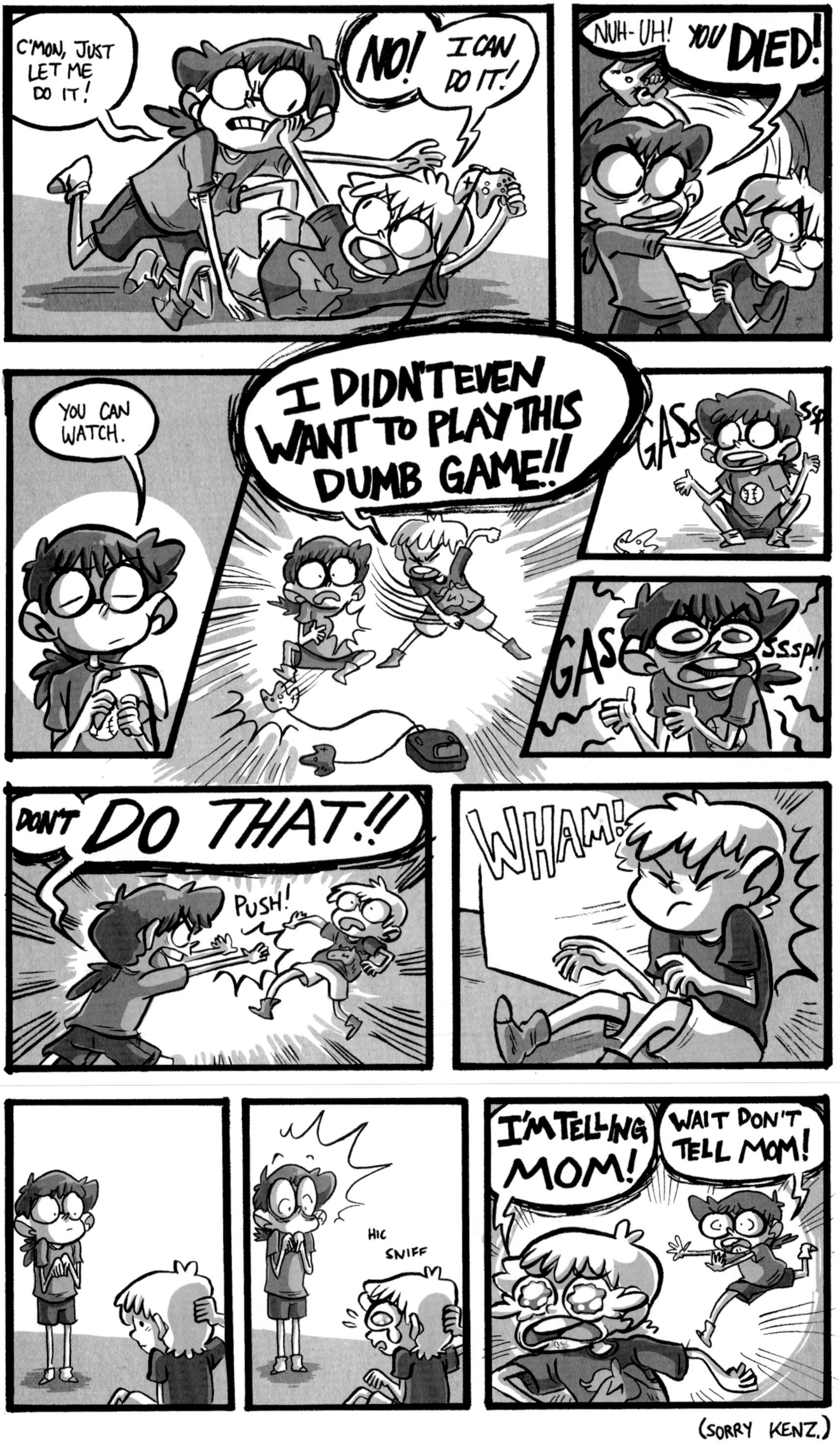
C'MON, JUST LET ME DO IT!
NO! I CAN DO IT!
NUH-UH! YOU DIED!
YOU CAN WATCH.
I DIDN'T EVEN WANT TO PLAY THIS DUMB GAME!!
GASSSP
GASSSP!!
DON'T DO THAT!!
PUSH!
WHAM!
HIC
SNIFF
I'M TELLING MOM!
WAIT DON'T TELL MOM!
(SORRY KENZ.)

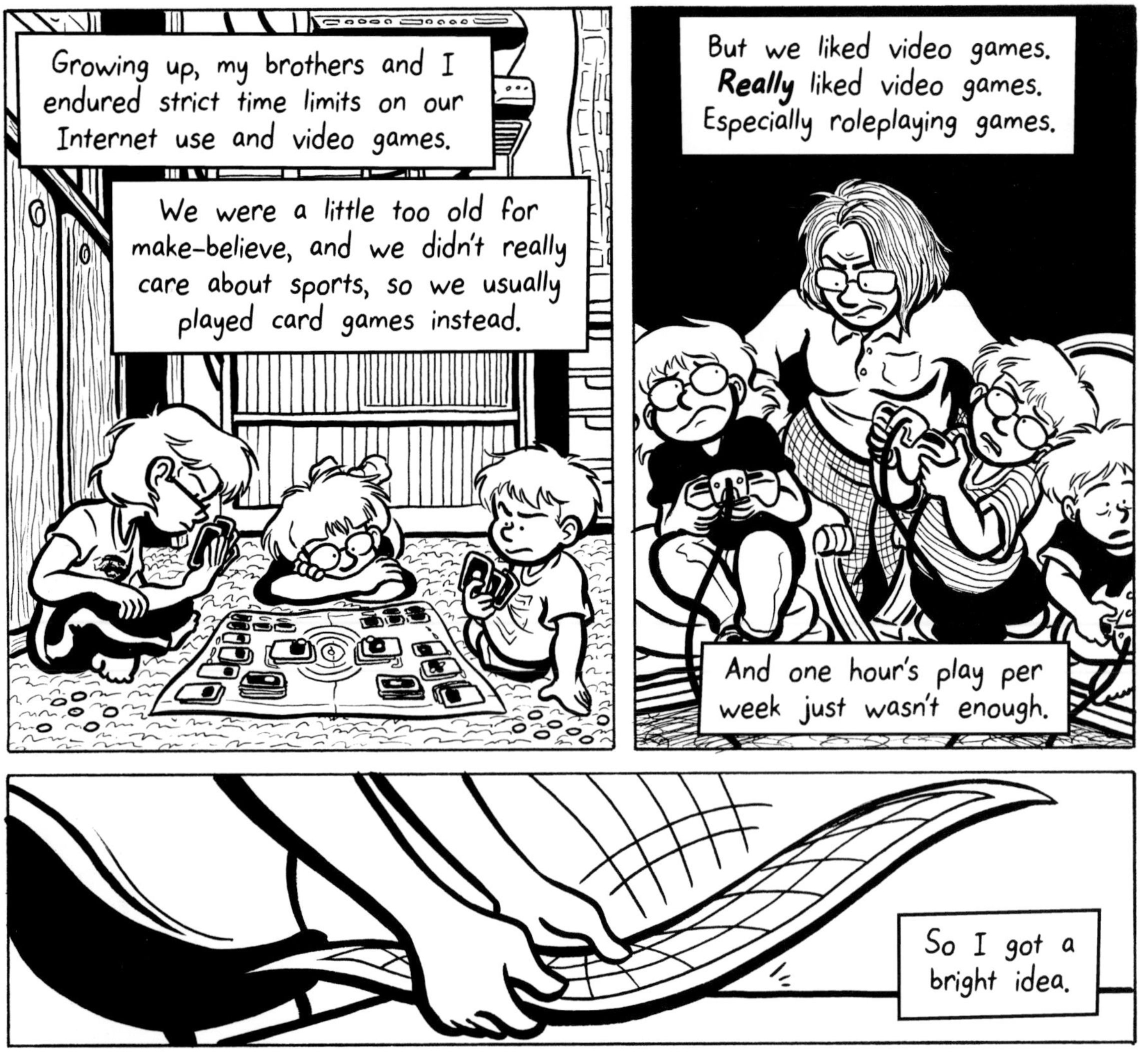
Growing up, my brothers and I endured strict time limits on our Internet use and video games.
We were a little too old for make-believe, and we didn't really care about sports, so we usually played card games instead.
But we liked video games. **Really** liked video games. Especially roleplaying games.
And one hour's play per week just wasn't enough.
So I got a bright idea.

Choose Your Own Adventure

by Rachel Ordway

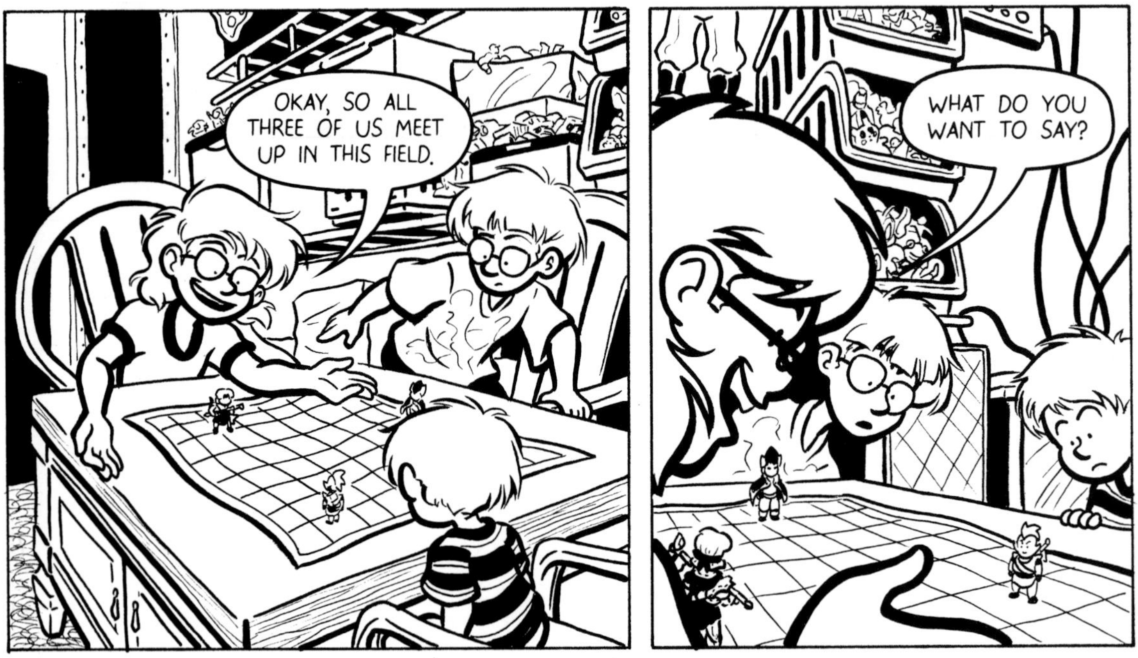
OKAY, SO ALL THREE OF US MEET UP IN THIS FIELD.
WHAT DO YOU WANT TO SAY?

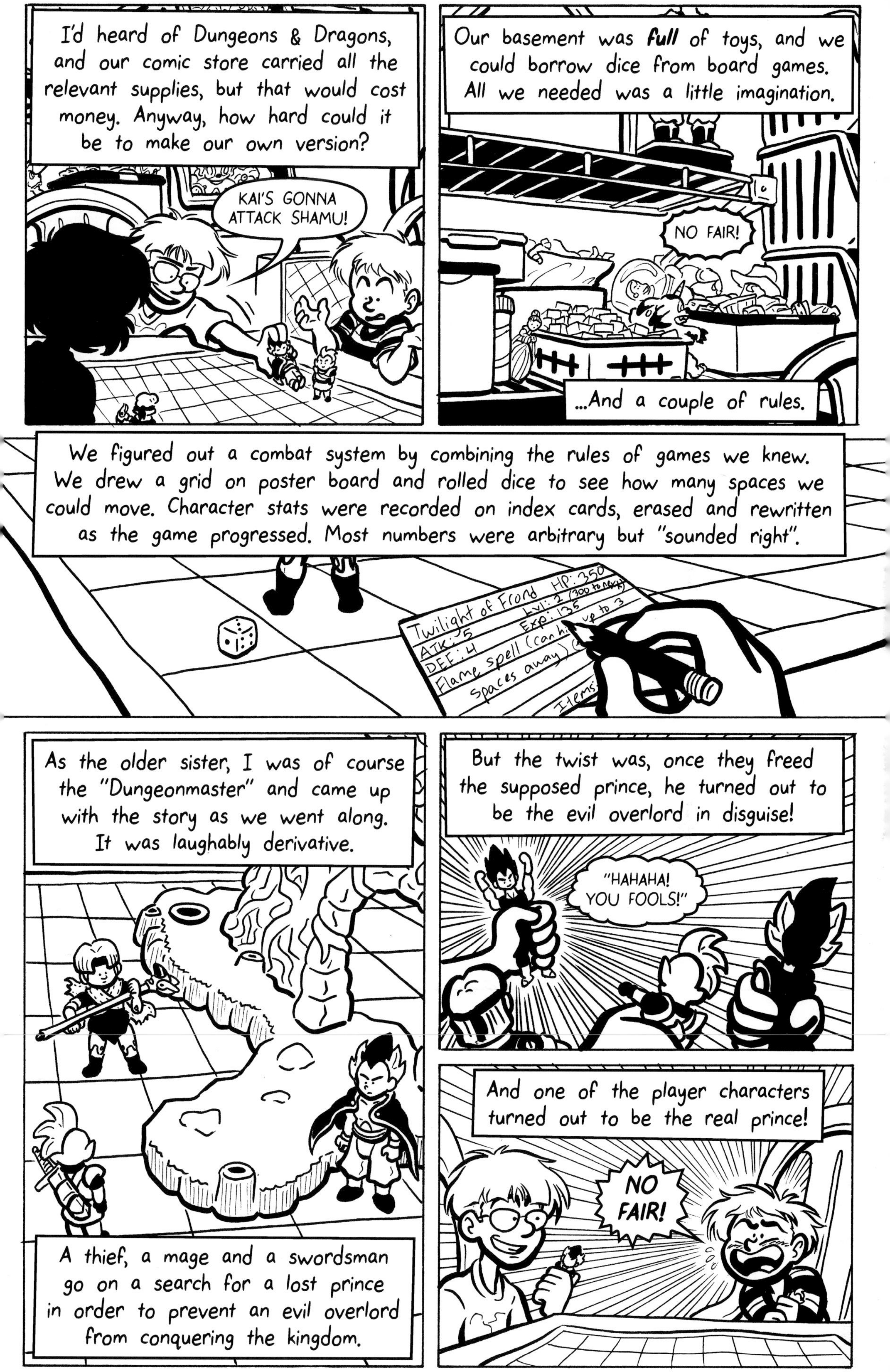
I'd heard of Dungeons & Dragons, and our comic store carried all the relevant supplies, but that would cost money. Anyway, how hard could it be to make our own version?
KAI'S GONNA ATTACK SHAMU!
Our basement was **full** of toys, and we could borrow dice from board games. All we needed was a little imagination.
NO FAIR!
...And a couple of rules.
We figured out a combat system by combining the rules of games we knew. We drew a grid on poster board and rolled dice to see how many spaces we could move. Character stats were recorded on index cards, erased and rewritten as the game progressed. Most numbers were arbitrary but "sounded right".
Twilight of Frond HP: 350
ATK: 5 Lvl: 2
DEF: 4 Exp: 135
Flame spell
spaces away)
As the older sister, I was of course the "Dungeonmaster" and came up with the story as we went along. It was laughably derivative.
A thief, a mage and a swordsman go on a search for a lost prince in order to prevent an evil overlord from conquering the kingdom.
But the twist was, once they freed the supposed prince, he turned out to be the evil overlord in disguise!
"HAHAHA! YOU FOOLS!"
And one of the player characters turned out to be the real prince!
NO FAIR!

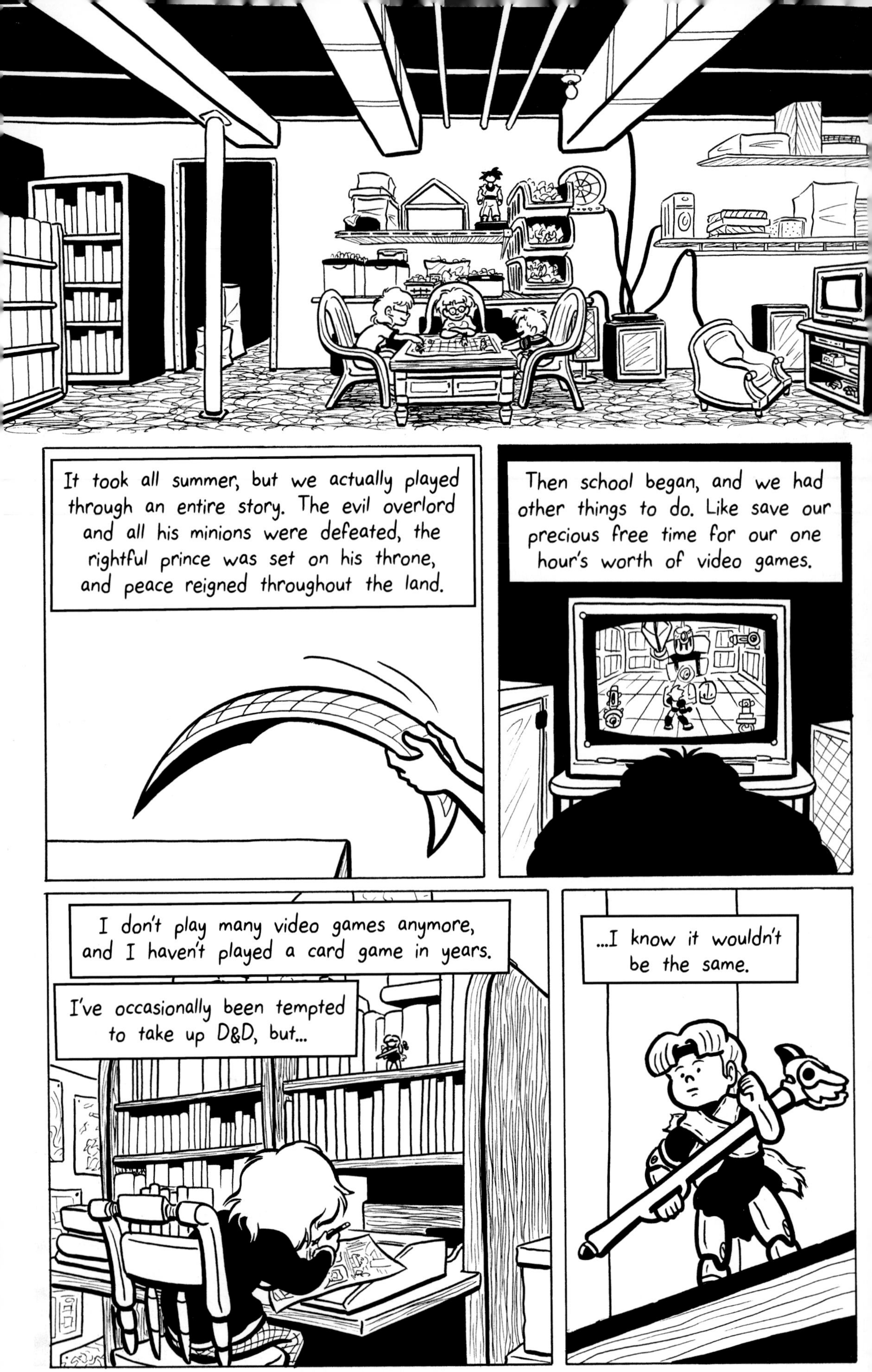
It took all summer, but we actually played through an entire story. The evil overlord and all his minions were defeated, the rightful prince was set on his throne, and peace reigned throughout the land.
Then school began, and we had other things to do. Like save our precious free time for our one hour's worth of video games.
I don't play many video games anymore, and I haven't played a card game in years.
I've occasionally been tempted to take up D&D, but...
...I know it wouldn't be the same.

Better Together

HAZEL NEWLEVANT

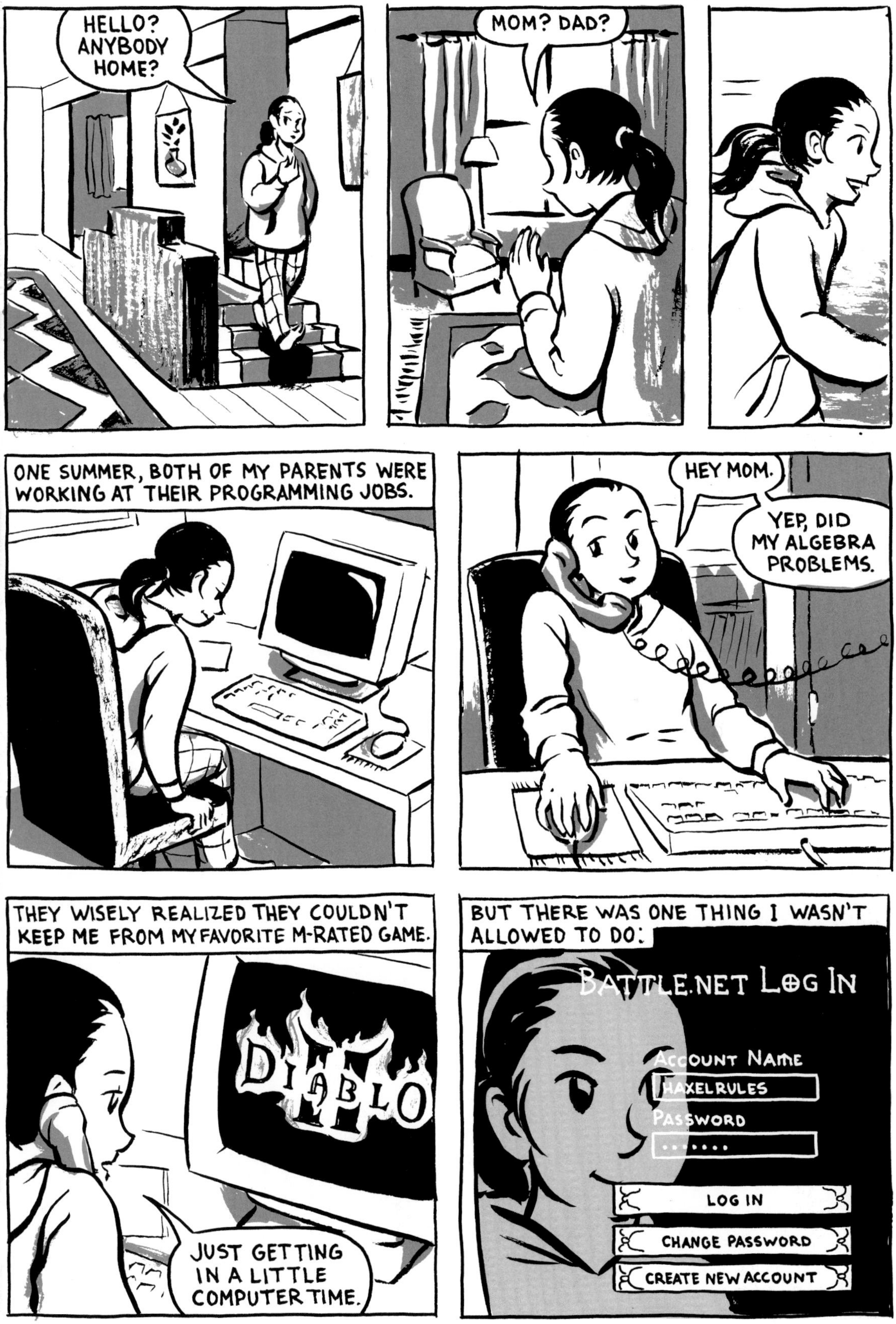
HELLO? ANYBODY HOME?
MOM? DAD?
ONE SUMMER, BOTH OF MY PARENTS WERE WORKING AT THEIR PROGRAMMING JOBS.
HEY MOM.
YEP, DID MY ALGEBRA PROBLEMS.
THEY WISELY REALIZED THEY COULDN'T KEEP ME FROM MY FAVORITE M-RATED GAME.
DIABLO II
JUST GETTING IN A LITTLE COMPUTER TIME.
BUT THERE WAS ONE THING I WASN'T ALLOWED TO DO:
BATTLE.NET LOG IN
ACCOUNT NAME
HAXELRULES
PASSWORD
LOG IN
CHANGE PASSWORD
CREATE NEW ACCOUNT

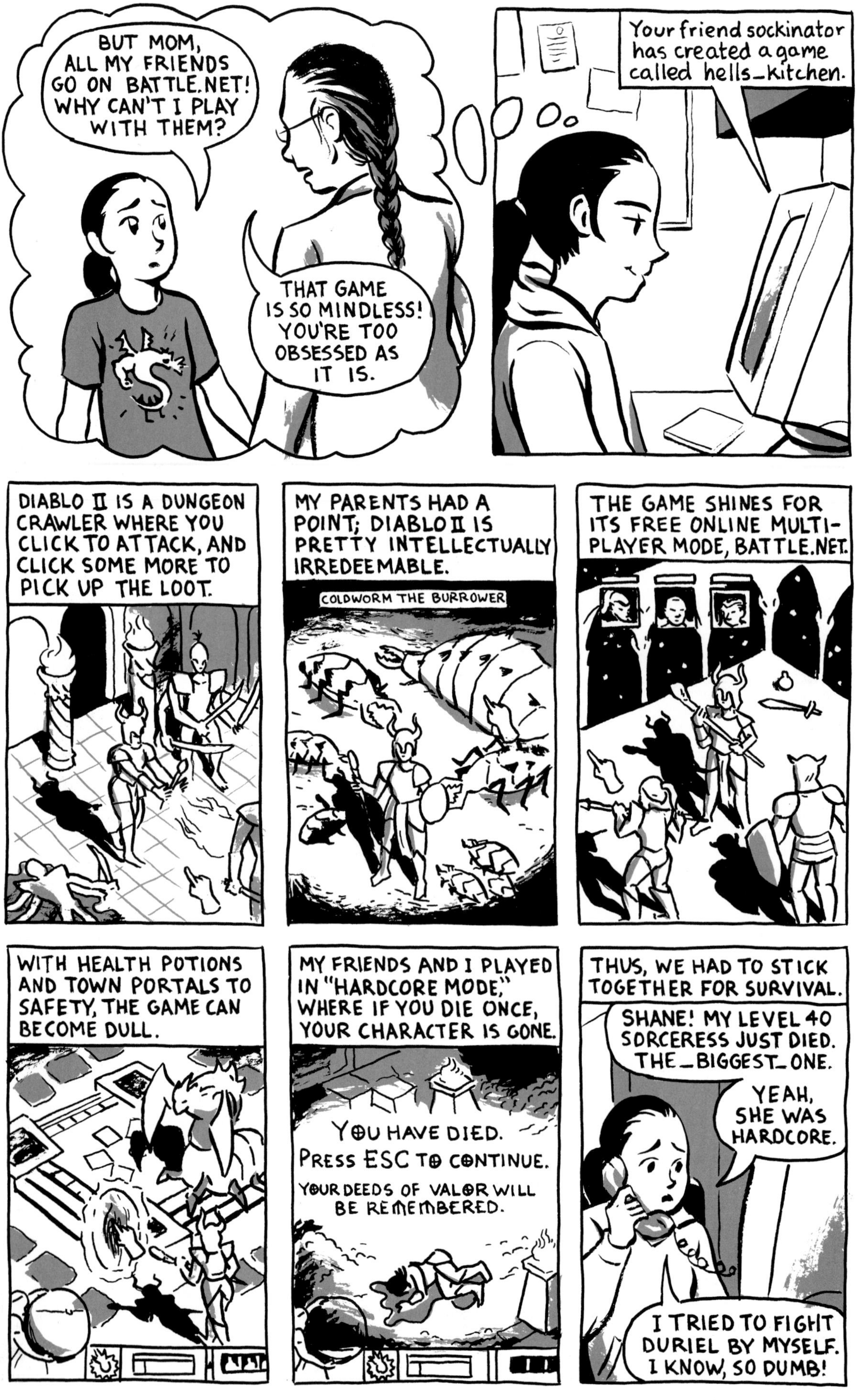
BUT MOM, ALL MY FRIENDS GO ON BATTLE.NET! WHY CAN'T I PLAY WITH THEM?
THAT GAME IS SO MINDLESS! YOU'RE TOO OBSESSED AS IT IS.
Your friend sockinator has created a game called hells_kitchen.
DIABLO II IS A DUNGEON CRAWLER WHERE YOU CLICK TO ATTACK, AND CLICK SOME MORE TO PICK UP THE LOOT.
MY PARENTS HAD A POINT; DIABLO II IS PRETTY INTELLECTUALLY IRREDEEMABLE.
COLDWORM THE BURROWER
THE GAME SHINES FOR ITS FREE ONLINE MULTI-PLAYER MODE, BATTLE.NET.
WITH HEALTH POTIONS AND TOWN PORTALS TO SAFETY, THE GAME CAN BECOME DULL.
MY FRIENDS AND I PLAYED IN "HARDCORE MODE," WHERE IF YOU DIE ONCE, YOUR CHARACTER IS GONE.
YOU HAVE DIED.
PRESS ESC TO CONTINUE.
YOUR DEEDS OF VALOR WILL BE REMEMBERED.
THUS, WE HAD TO STICK TOGETHER FOR SURVIVAL.
SHANE! MY LEVEL 40 SORCERESS JUST DIED. THE_BIGGEST_ONE.
YEAH, SHE WAS HARDCORE.
I TRIED TO FIGHT DURIEL BY MYSELF. I KNOW, SO DUMB!

WE MADE A PARTY OF HARDCORE PALADINS TO PLAY TOGETHER. A PALADIN'S SIGNATURE SKILLS ARE "AURAS"—PASSIVE ABILITIES THAT GIVE CERTAIN BONUSES, WHICH ARE SHARED BY ALL PARTY MEMBERS.
BY EACH SPECIALIZING IN A DIFFERENT AURA, WE WERE BETTER AS A TEAM!

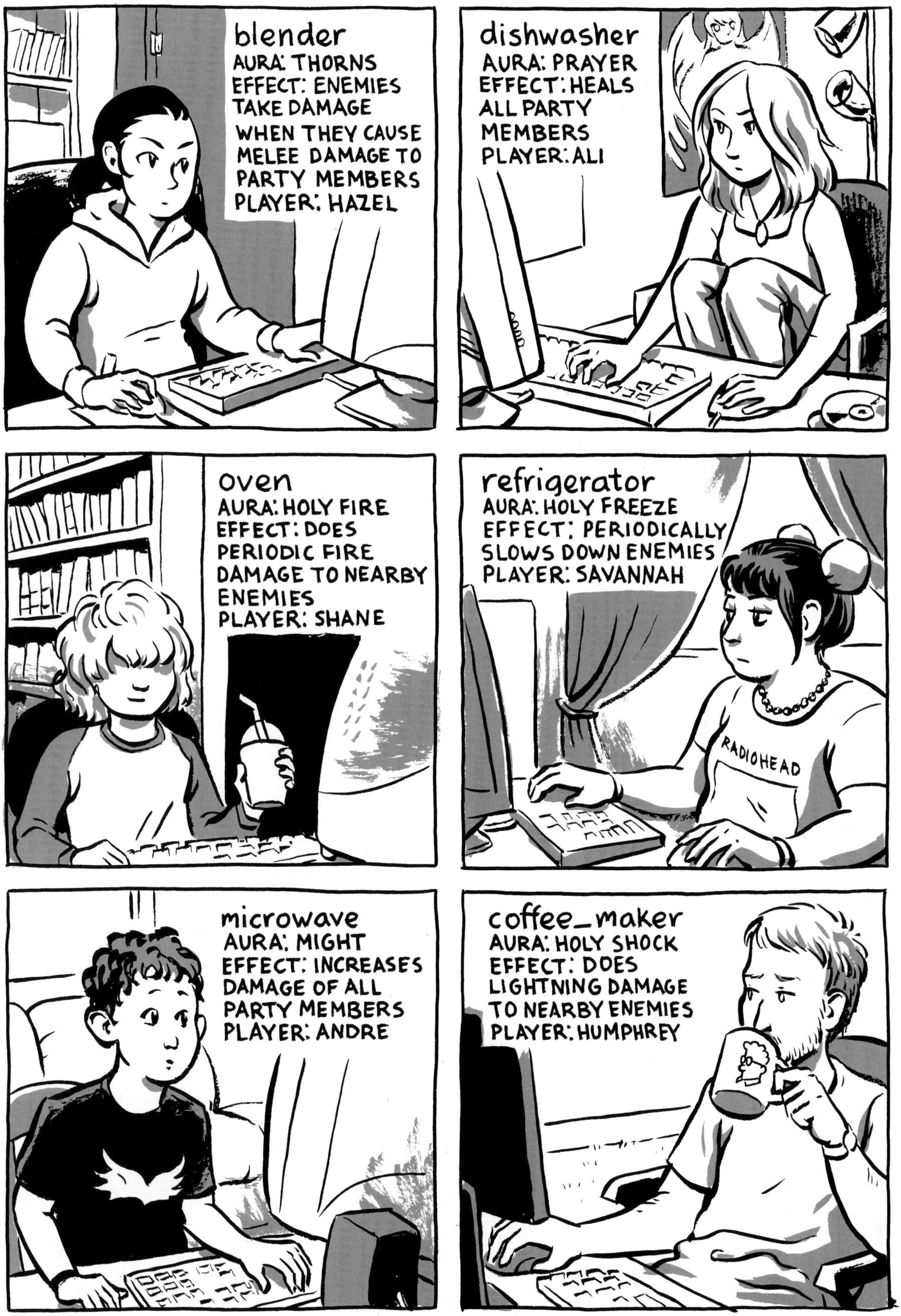
blender
AURA: THORNS
EFFECT: ENEMIES TAKE DAMAGE WHEN THEY CAUSE MELEE DAMAGE TO PARTY MEMBERS
PLAYER: HAZEL
dishwasher
AURA: PRAYER
EFFECT: HEALS ALL PARTY MEMBERS
PLAYER: ALI
oven
AURA: HOLY FIRE
EFFECT: DOES PERIODIC FIRE DAMAGE TO NEARBY ENEMIES
PLAYER: SHANE
refrigerator
AURA: HOLY FREEZE
EFFECT: PERIODICALLY SLOWS DOWN ENEMIES
PLAYER: SAVANNAH
RADIOHEAD
microwave
AURA: MIGHT
EFFECT: INCREASES DAMAGE OF ALL PARTY MEMBERS
PLAYER: ANDRE
coffee_maker
AURA: HOLY SHOCK
EFFECT: DOES LIGHTNING DAMAGE TO NEARBY ENEMIES
PLAYER: HUMPHREY

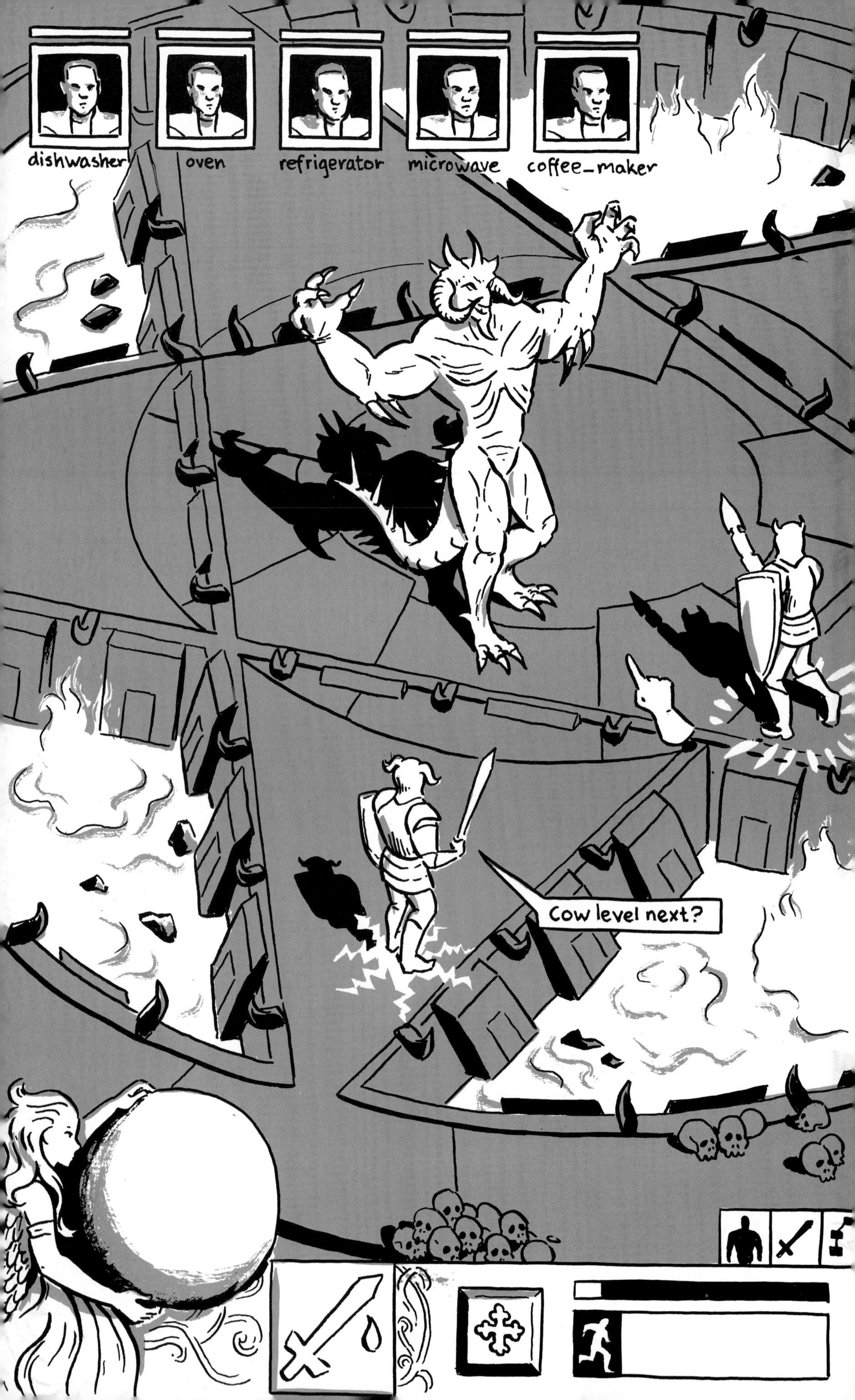
dishwasher
oven
refrigerator
microwave
coffee_maker
Cow level next?

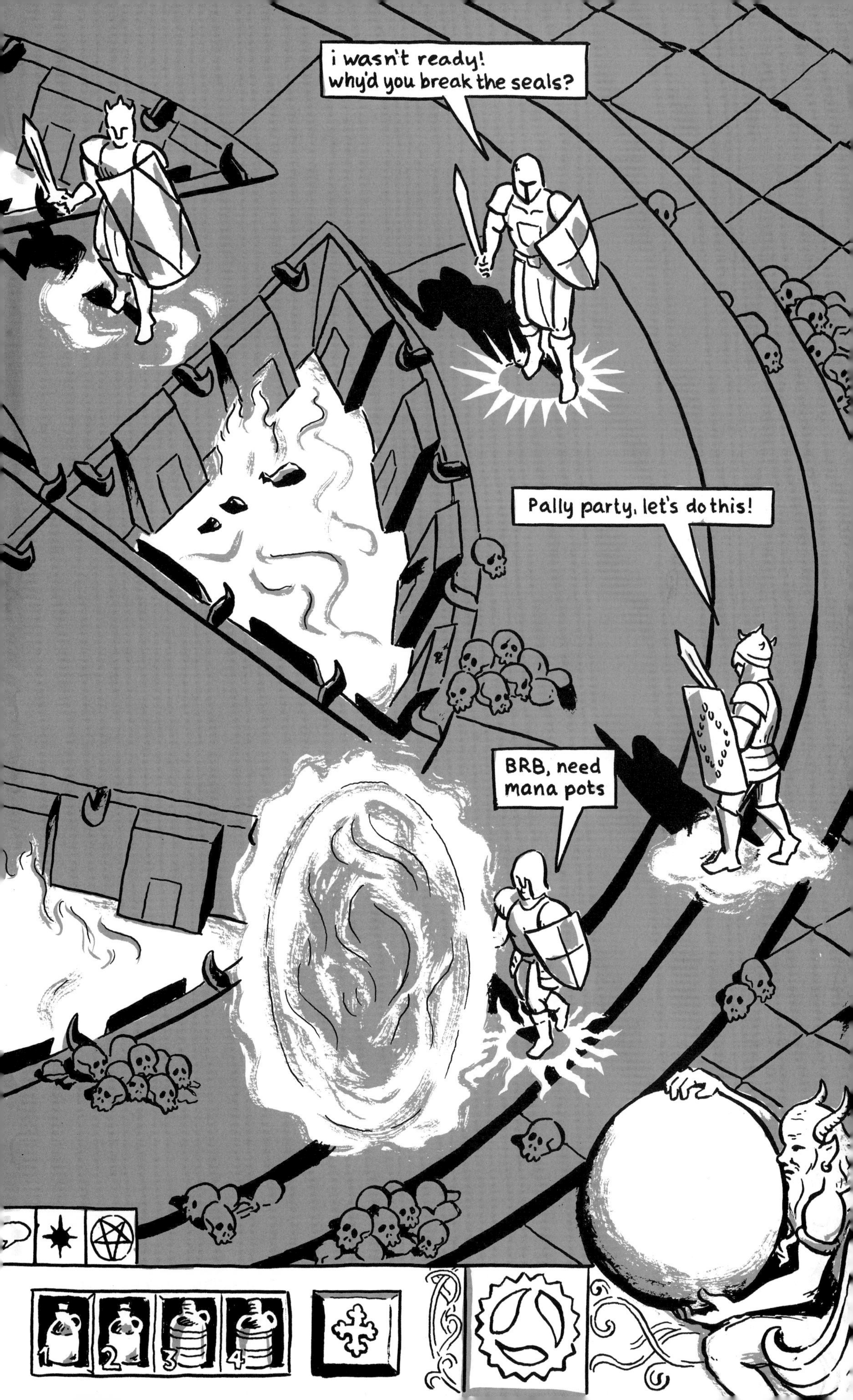
i wasn't ready!
why'd you break the seals?
Pally party, let's do this!
BRB, need
mana pots
1
2
3
4

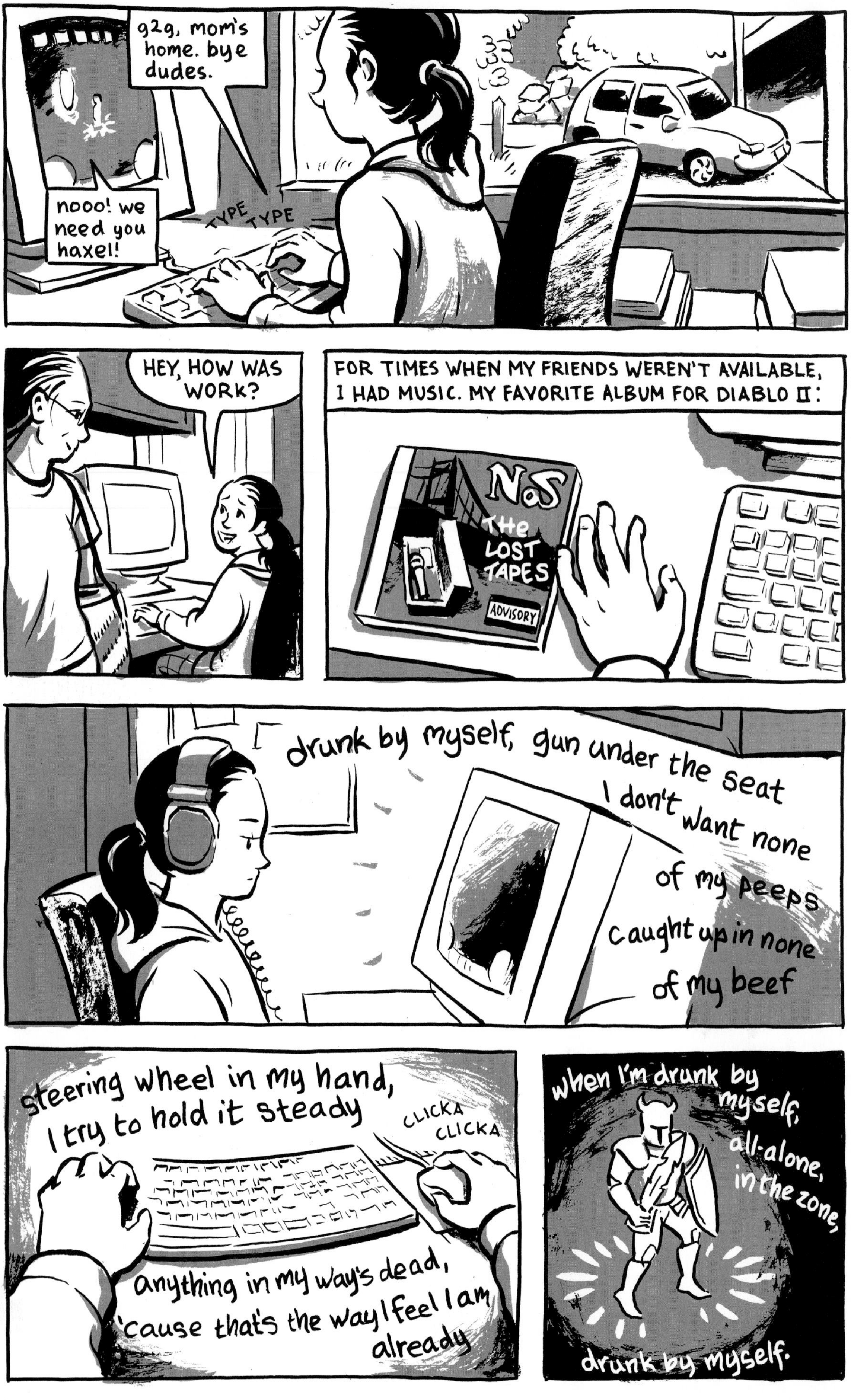
g2g, mom's home. bye dudes.
nooo! we need you haxel!
TYPE TYPE
HEY, HOW WAS WORK?
FOR TIMES WHEN MY FRIENDS WEREN'T AVAILABLE, I HAD MUSIC. MY FAVORITE ALBUM FOR DIABLO II:
NaS
THE LOST TAPES
ADVISORY
drunk by myself, gun under the seat
I don't want none of my peeps
caught up in none of my beef
steering wheel in my hand, I try to hold it steady
CLICKA CLICKA
anything in my way's dead, 'cause that's the way I feel I am already
when I'm drunk by myself, all alone, in the zone,
drunk by myself.

RETICULATING SPLINES

BY AMANDA SCURTI

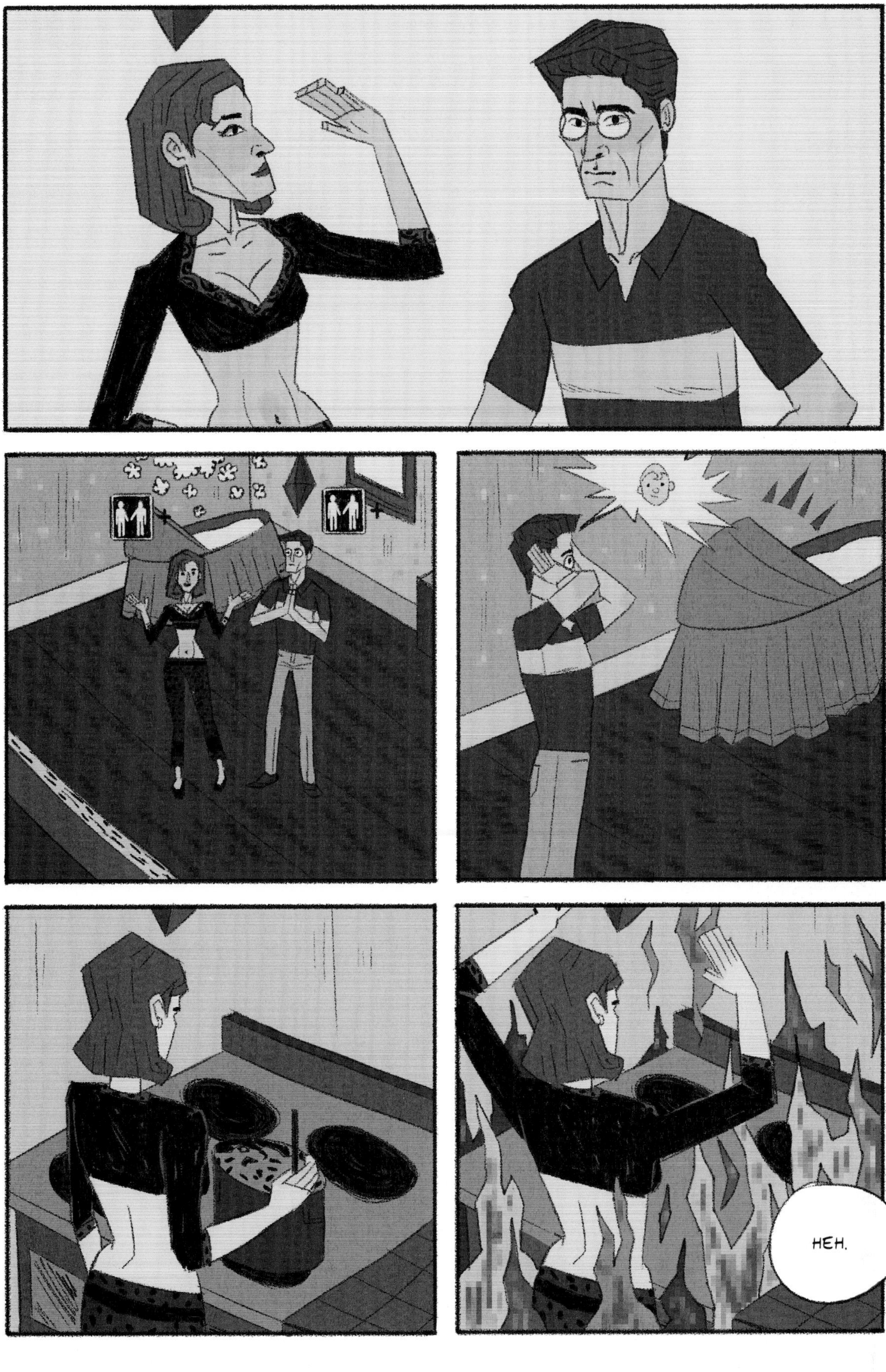
HEH.

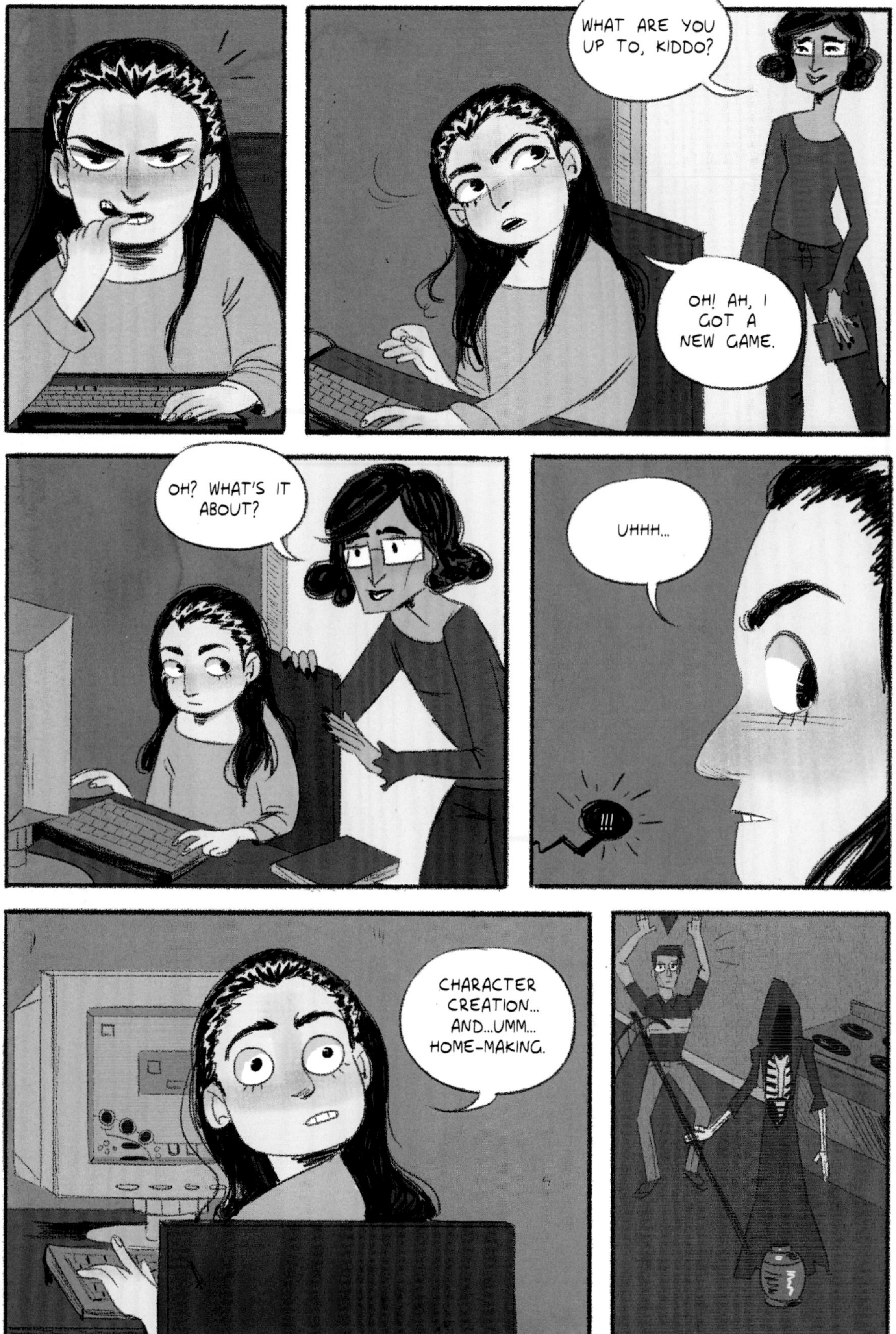
WHAT ARE YOU UP TO, KIDDO?
OH! AH, I GOT A NEW GAME.
OH? WHAT'S IT ABOUT?
UHHH...
!!!
CHARACTER CREATION... AND...UMM... HOME-MAKING.

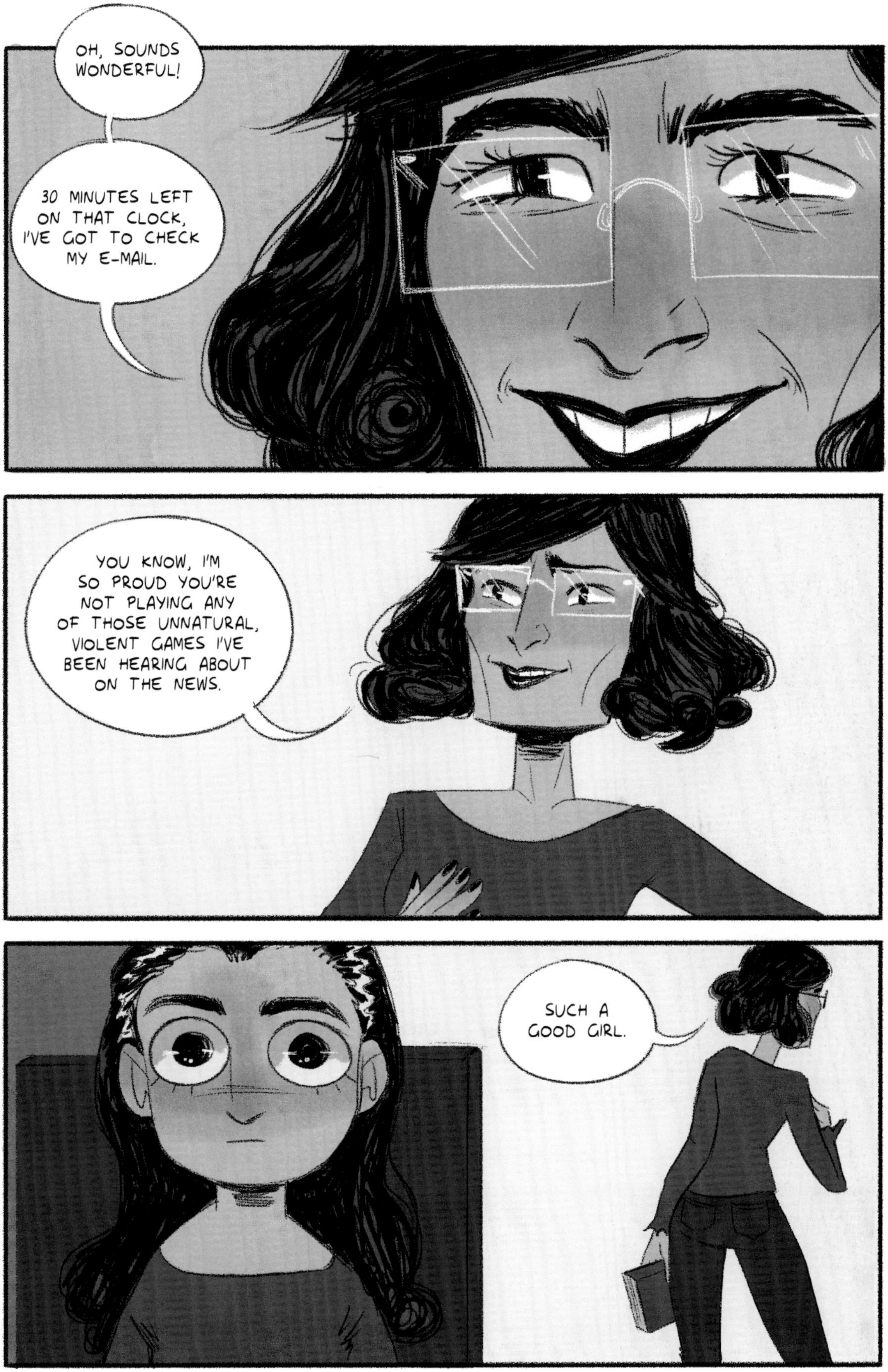
OH, SOUNDS WONDERFUL!
30 MINUTES LEFT ON THAT CLOCK, I'VE GOT TO CHECK MY E-MAIL.
YOU KNOW, I'M SO PROUD YOU'RE NOT PLAYING ANY OF THOSE UNNATURAL, VIOLENT GAMES I'VE BEEN HEARING ABOUT ON THE NEWS.
SUCH A GOOD GIRL.

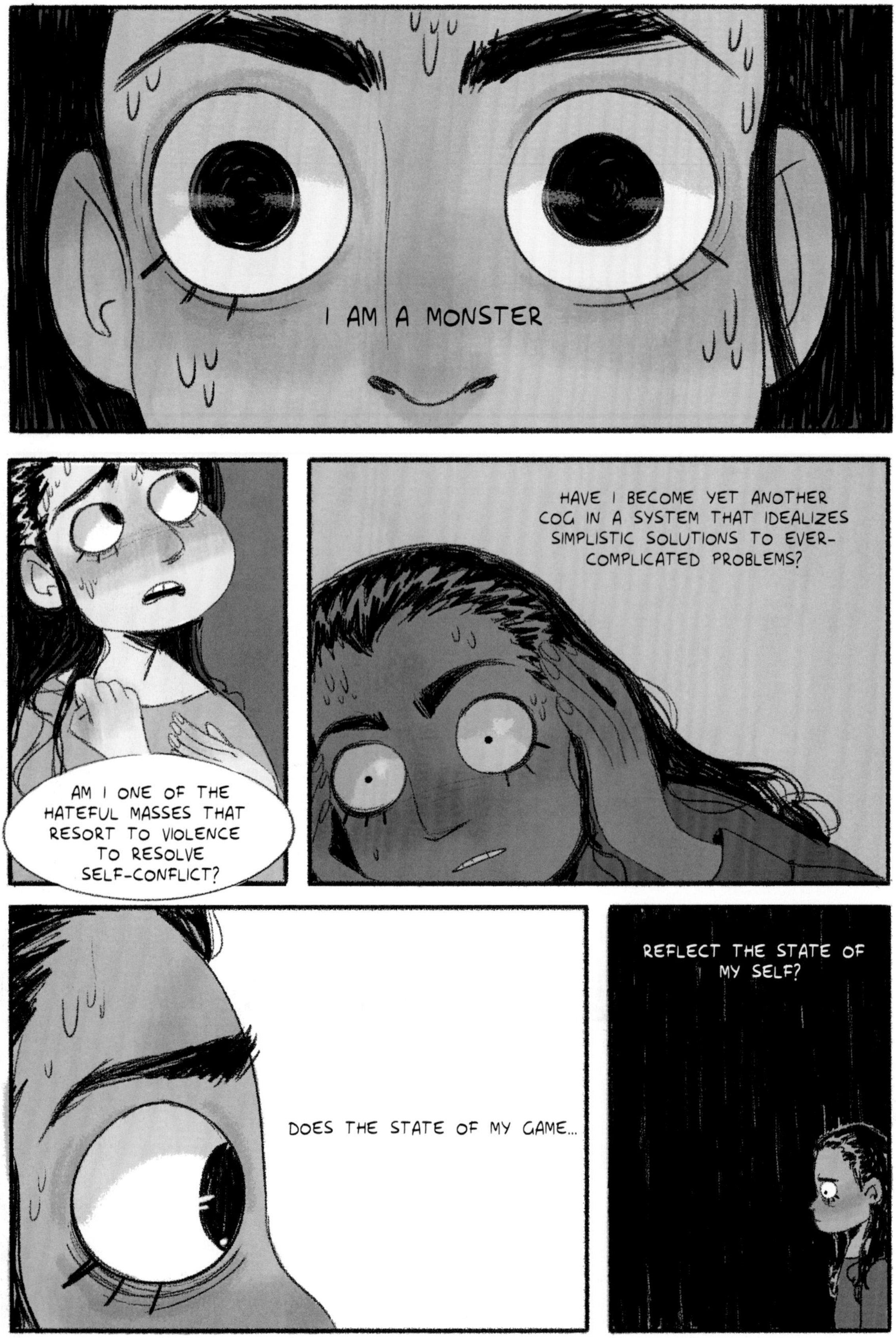
I AM A MONSTER
AM I ONE OF THE HATEFUL MASSES THAT RESORT TO VIOLENCE TO RESOLVE SELF-CONFLICT?
HAVE I BECOME YET ANOTHER COG IN A SYSTEM THAT IDEALIZES SIMPLISTIC SOLUTIONS TO EVER-COMPLICATED PROBLEMS?
DOES THE STATE OF MY GAME...
REFLECT THE STATE OF MY SELF?

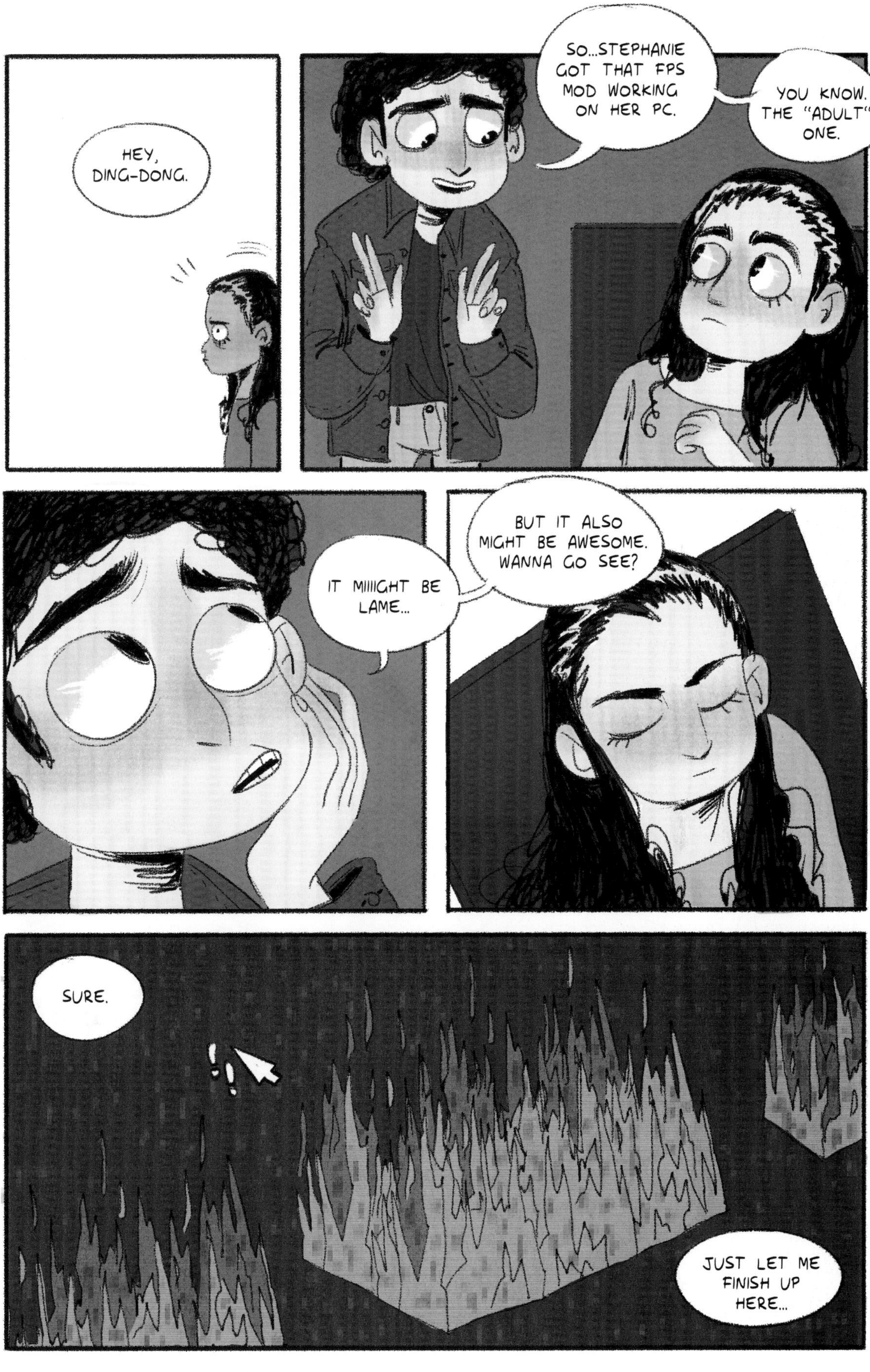
HEY, DING-DONG.
SO...STEPHANIE GOT THAT FPS MOD WORKING ON HER PC.
YOU KNOW. THE "ADULT" ONE.
IT MIIIIGHT BE LAME...
BUT IT ALSO MIGHT BE AWESOME. WANNA GO SEE?
SURE.
JUST LET ME FINISH UP HERE...

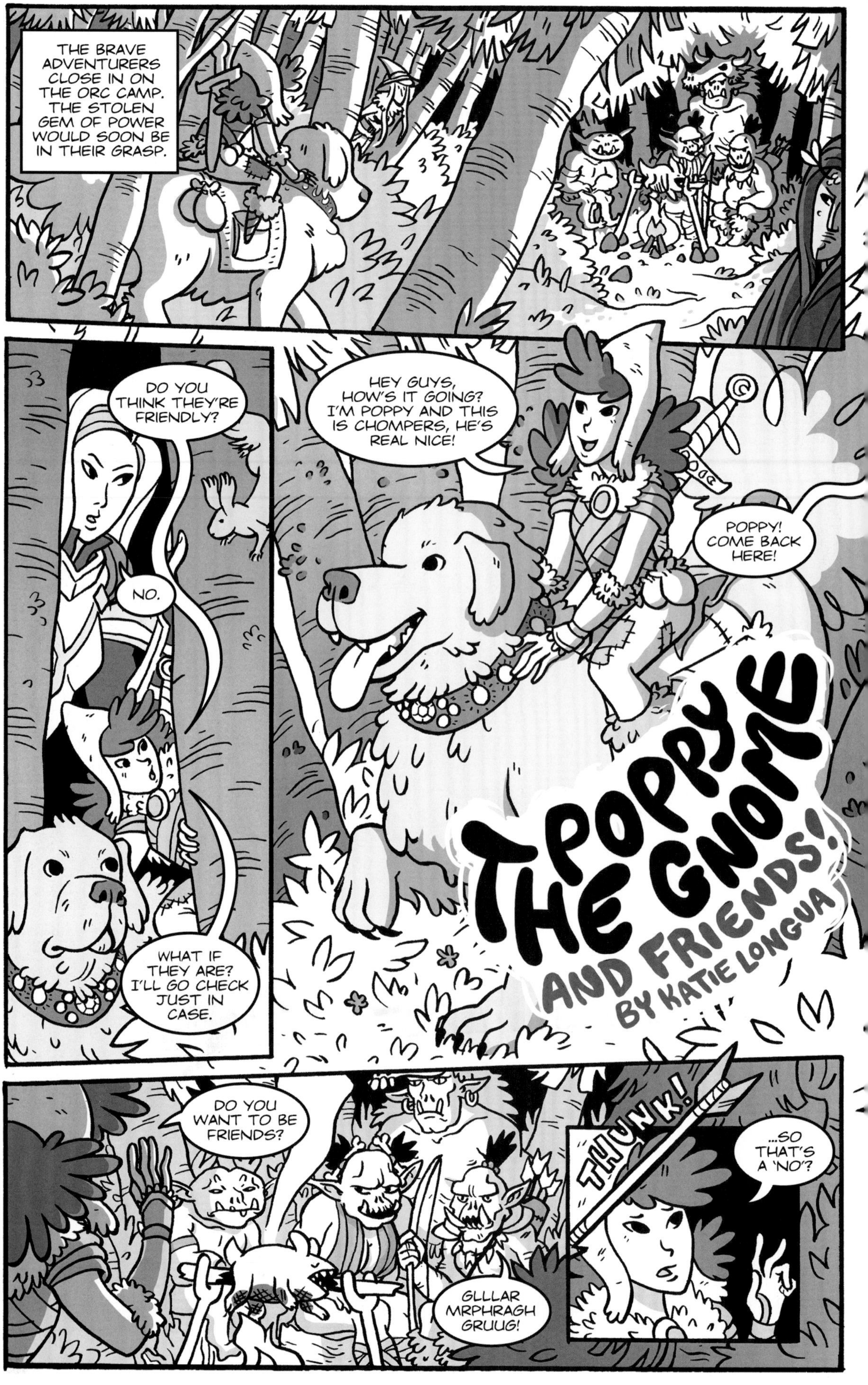
THE BRAVE ADVENTURERS CLOSE IN ON THE ORC CAMP. THE STOLEN GEM OF POWER WOULD SOON BE IN THEIR GRASP.
DO YOU THINK THEY'RE FRIENDLY?
NO.
WHAT IF THEY ARE? I'LL GO CHECK JUST IN CASE.
HEY GUYS, HOW'S IT GOING? I'M POPPY AND THIS IS CHOMPERS, HE'S REAL NICE!
POPPY! COME BACK HERE!
POPPY THE GNOME AND FRIENDS!
BY KATIE LONGUA
DO YOU WANT TO BE FRIENDS?
GLLLAR MRPHRAGH GRUUG!
THUNK!
...SO THAT'S A 'NO'?

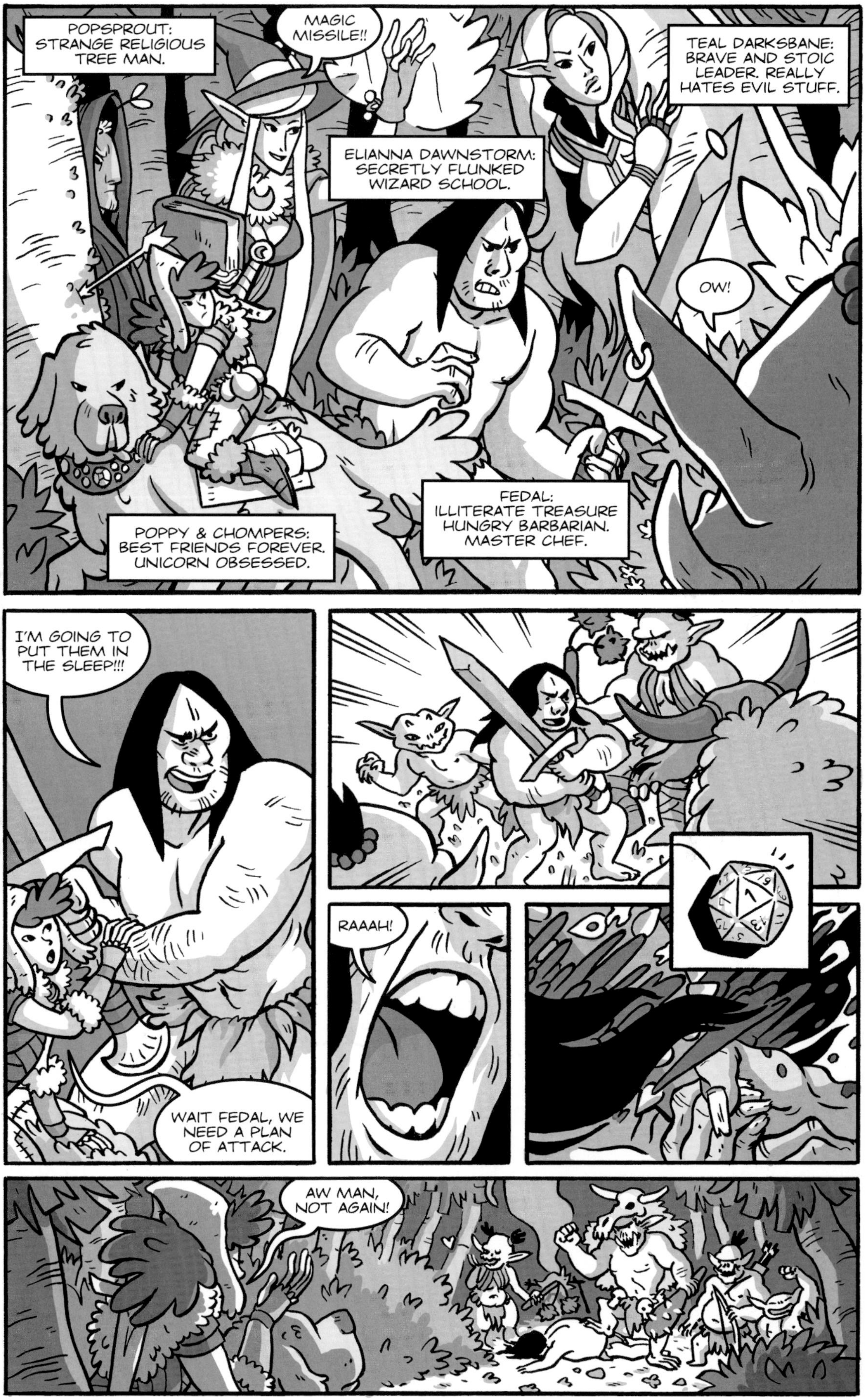
POPSPROUT: STRANGE RELIGIOUS TREE MAN.
MAGIC MISSILE!!
ELIANNA DAWNSTORM: SECRETLY FLUNKED WIZARD SCHOOL.
TEAL DARKSBANE: BRAVE AND STOIC LEADER. REALLY HATES EVIL STUFF.
OW!
POPPY & CHOMPERS: BEST FRIENDS FOREVER. UNICORN OBSESSED.
FEDAL: ILLITERATE TREASURE HUNGRY BARBARIAN. MASTER CHEF.
I'M GOING TO PUT THEM IN THE SLEEP!!!
WAIT FEDAL, WE NEED A PLAN OF ATTACK.
RAAAH!
AW MAN, NOT AGAIN!

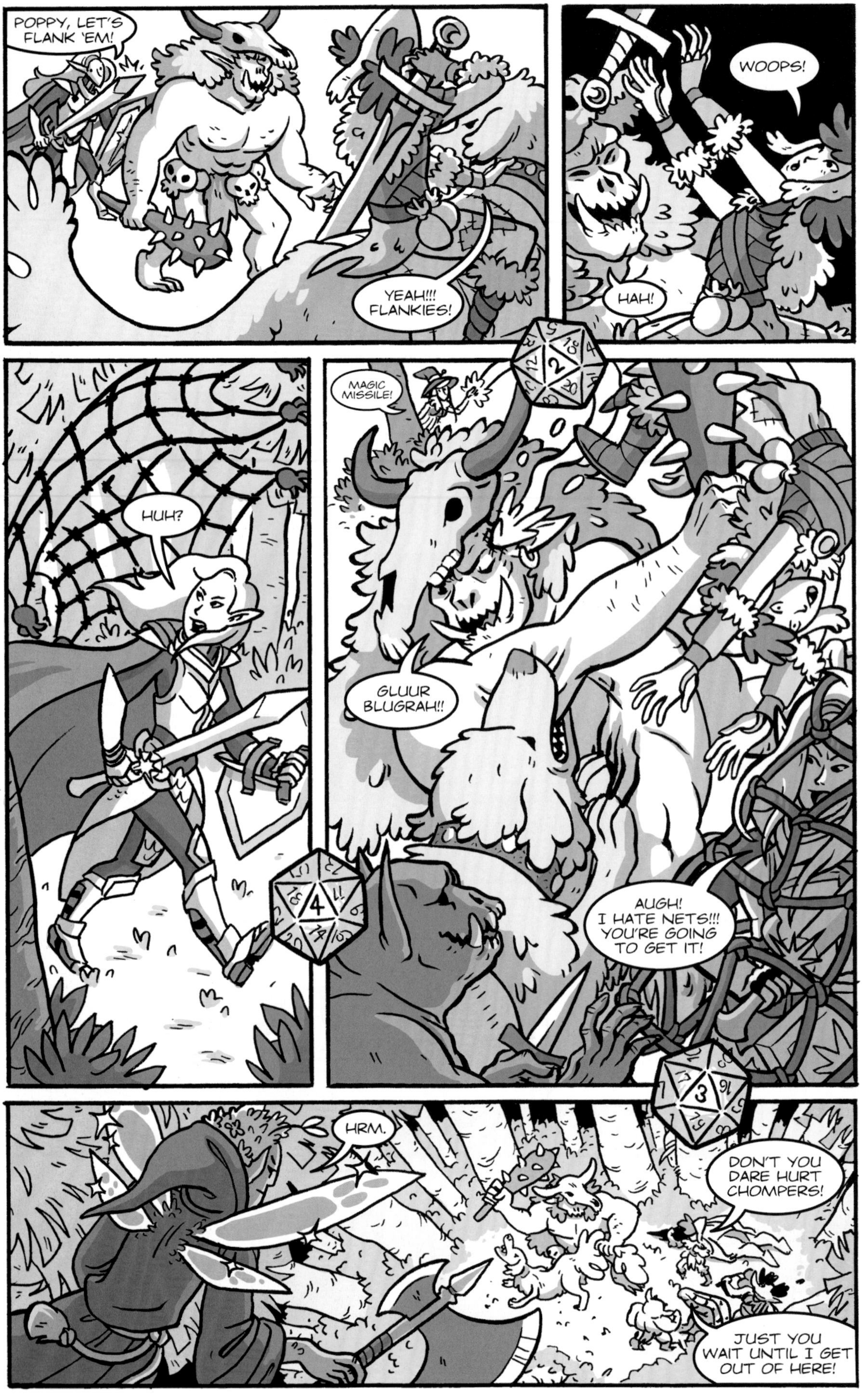
POPPY, LET'S FLANK 'EM!
YEAH!!! FLANKIES!
WOOPS!
HAH!
HUH?
MAGIC MISSILE!
GLUUR BLUGRAH!!
AUGH! I HATE NETS!!! YOU'RE GOING TO GET IT!
HRM.
DON'T YOU DARE HURT CHOMPERS!
JUST YOU WAIT UNTIL I GET OUT OF HERE!

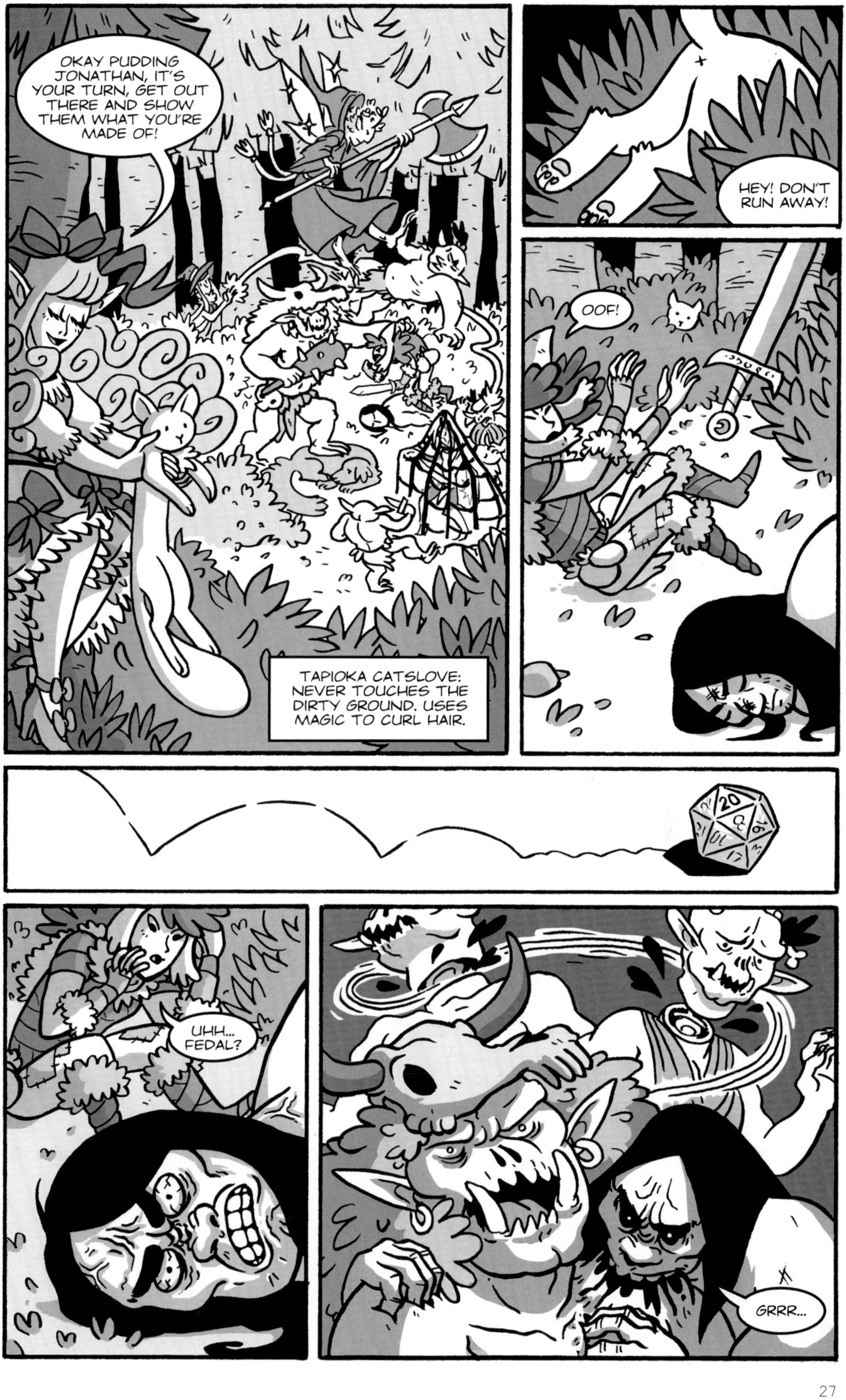
OKAY PUDDING JONATHAN, IT'S YOUR TURN, GET OUT THERE AND SHOW THEM WHAT YOU'RE MADE OF!
TAPIOKA CATSLOVE: NEVER TOUCHES THE DIRTY GROUND. USES MAGIC TO CURL HAIR.
HEY! DON'T RUN AWAY!
OOF!
20
UHH... FEDAL?
GRRR...

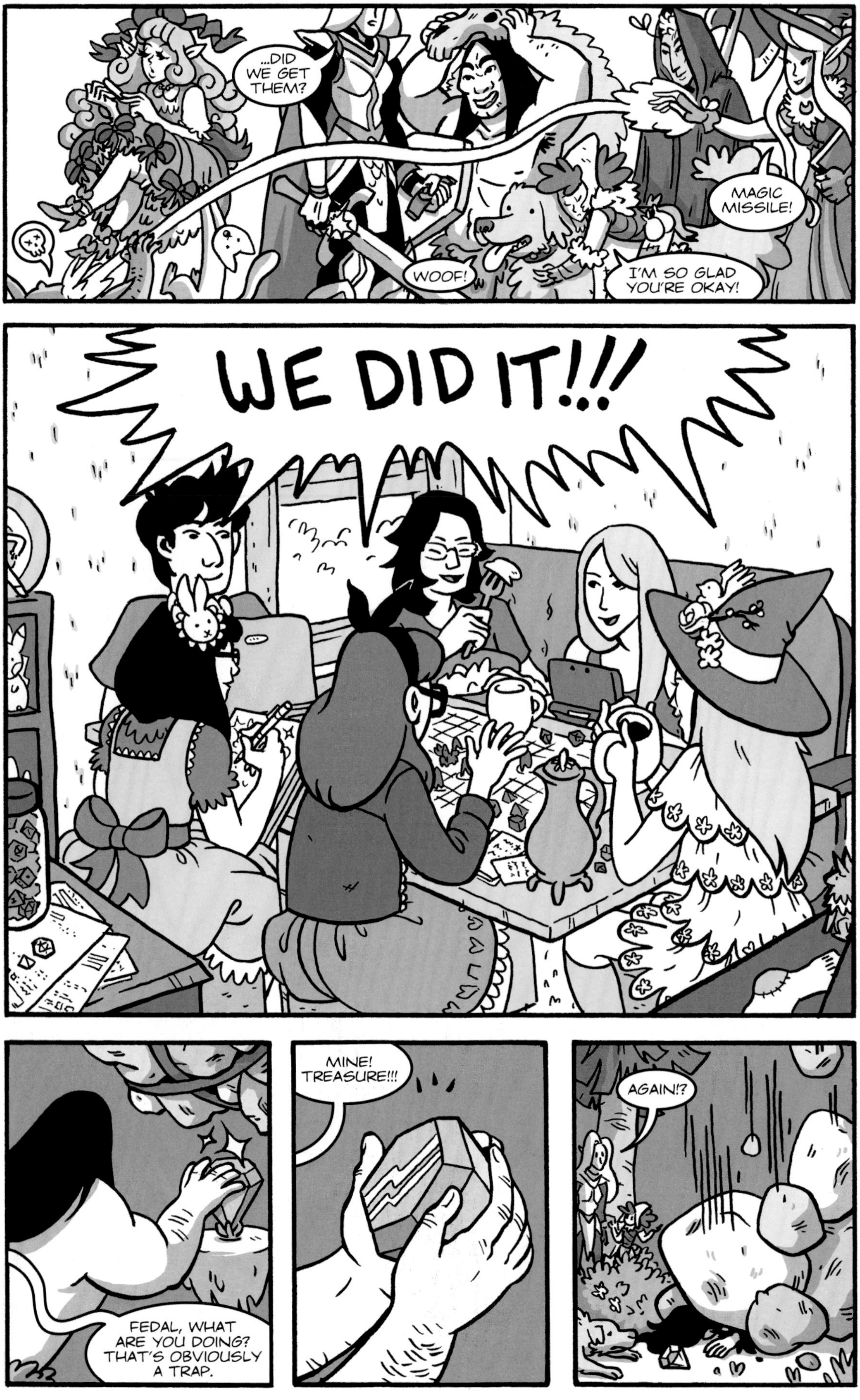
...DID WE GET THEM?
MAGIC MISSILE!
WOOF!
I'M SO GLAD YOU'RE OKAY!
WE DID IT!!!
FEDAL, WHAT ARE YOU DOING? THAT'S OBVIOUSLY A TRAP.
MINE! TREASURE!!!
AGAIN!?

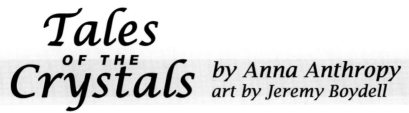

Tales OF THE Crystals

by Anna Anthropy
art by Jeremy Boydell

We are **four.**

Protector — Healer — Scribe — & Leader.

We are the guardians of the crystals, protectors of the land of Collingwood, and our task is no small one. The wicked Lady Morphia has done the unthinkable - she has captured and imprisoned a unicorn in her Castle of Dread.

The Castle is defended by enchantments and even the entrance is magically hidden - but the Protector's Crystal of True Sight should reveal it.

They say if you whisper a poem in a Unicorn's ear, you can charm it. For now, in our fort in the Secret Garden, we wait and plot, and come up with rhymes for "unicorn."

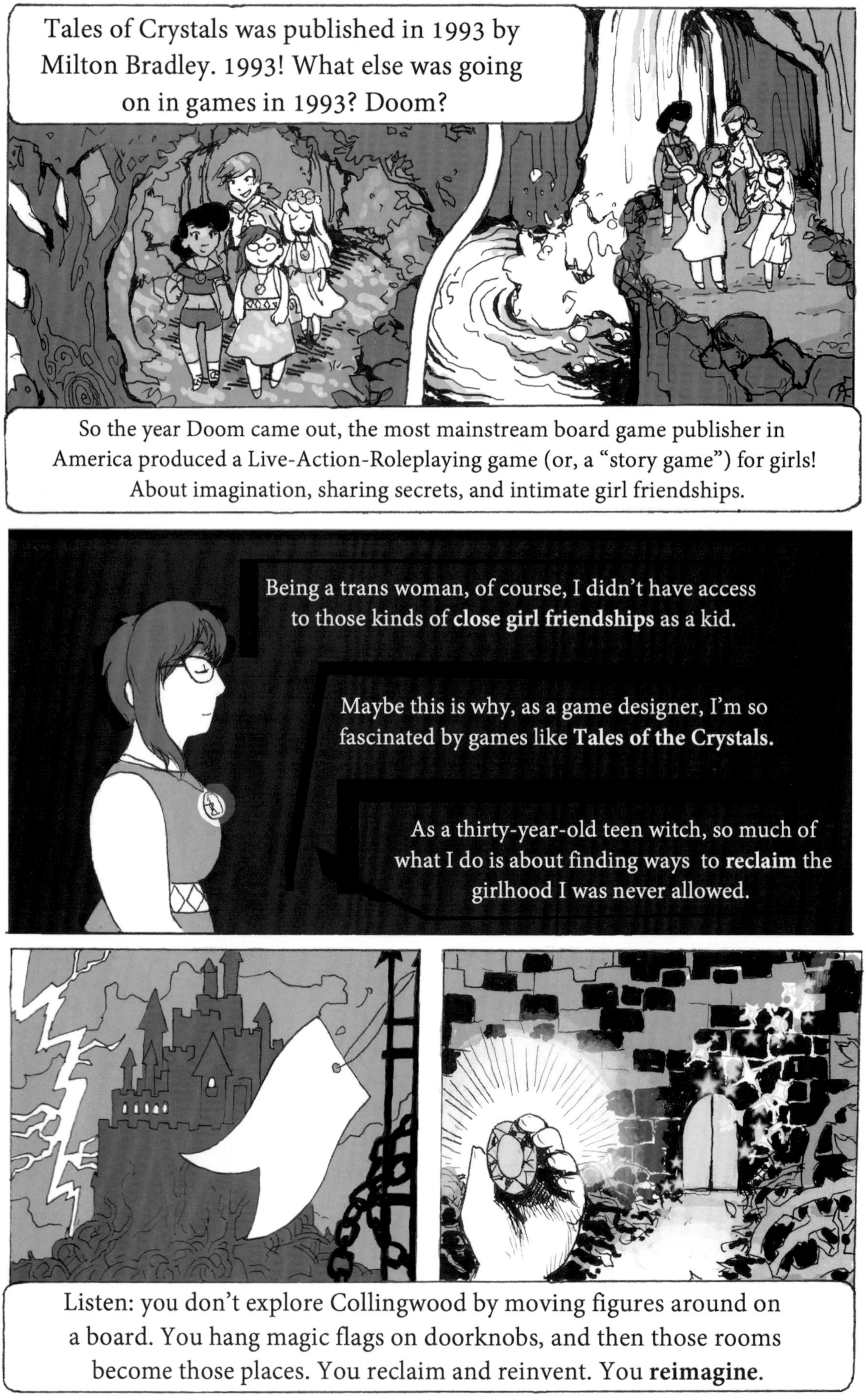
Tales of Crystals was published in 1993 by Milton Bradley. 1993! What else was going on in games in 1993? Doom?
So the year Doom came out, the most mainstream board game publisher in America produced a Live-Action-Roleplaying game (or, a "story game") for girls! About imagination, sharing secrets, and intimate girl friendships.
Being a trans woman, of course, I didn't have access to those kinds of **close girl friendships** as a kid.
Maybe this is why, as a game designer, I'm so fascinated by games like **Tales of the Crystals.**
As a thirty-year-old teen witch, so much of what I do is about finding ways to **reclaim** the girlhood I was never allowed.
Listen: you don't explore Collingwood by moving figures around on a board. You hang magic flags on doorknobs, and then those rooms become those places. You reclaim and reinvent. You **reimagine**.

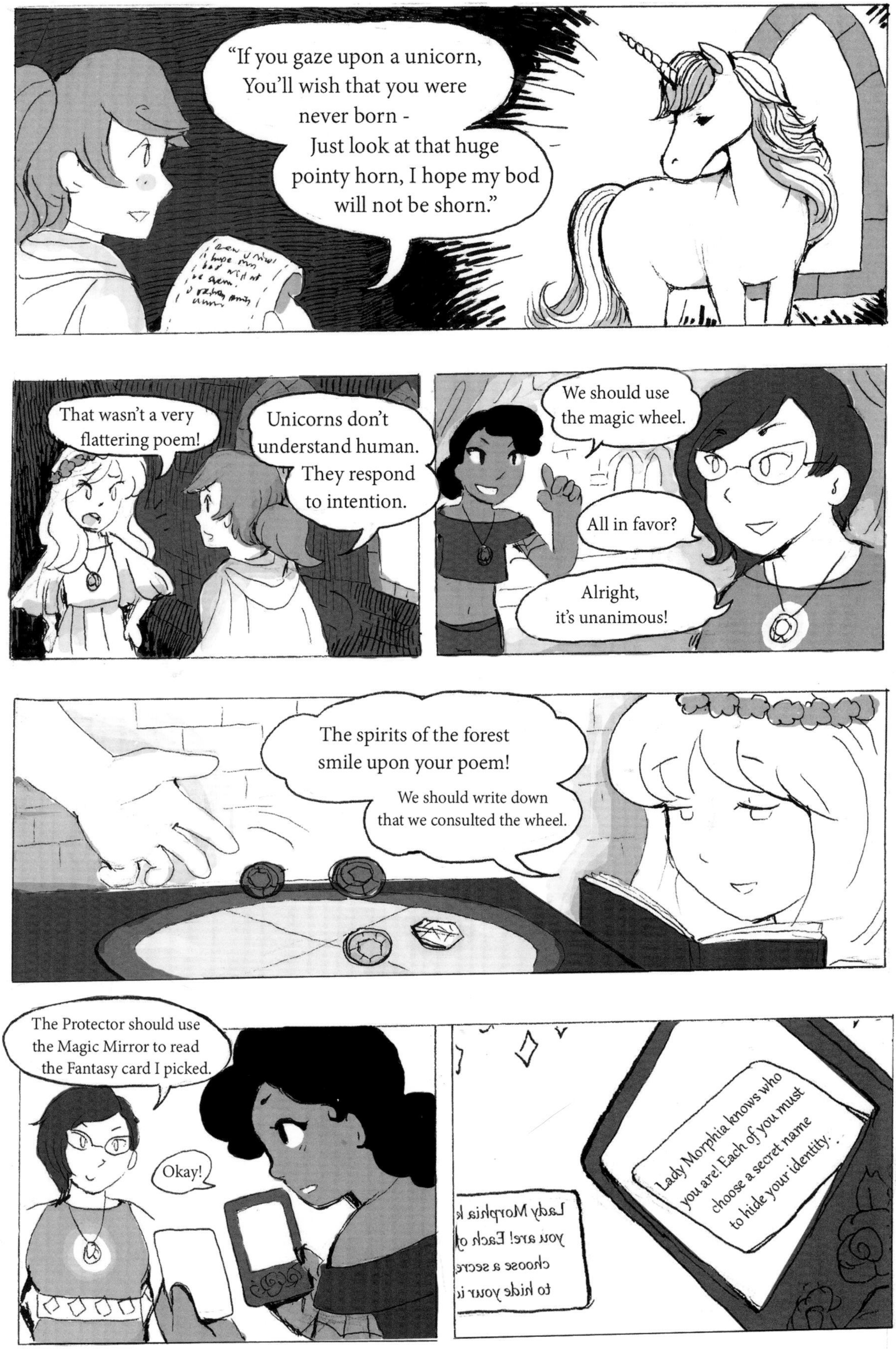
"If you gaze upon a unicorn, You'll wish that you were never born - Just look at that huge pointy horn, I hope my bod will not be shorn."
That wasn't a very flattering poem!
Unicorns don't understand human. They respond to intention.
We should use the magic wheel.
All in favor?
Alright, it's unanimous!
The spirits of the forest smile upon your poem!
We should write down that we consulted the wheel.
The Protector should use the Magic Mirror to read the Fantasy card I picked.
Okay!
Lady Morphia knows who you are! Each of you must choose a secret name to hide your identity.

Play is witchcraft.

Sometimes at night I like to light a single candle and write. A witch, crafting spells by candlelight.

I imagine I'm drawing from something deep and potent.

What else is magic other than the rituals we use to remind ourselves of our identities?

The power to reclaim our lives?

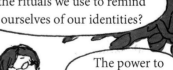

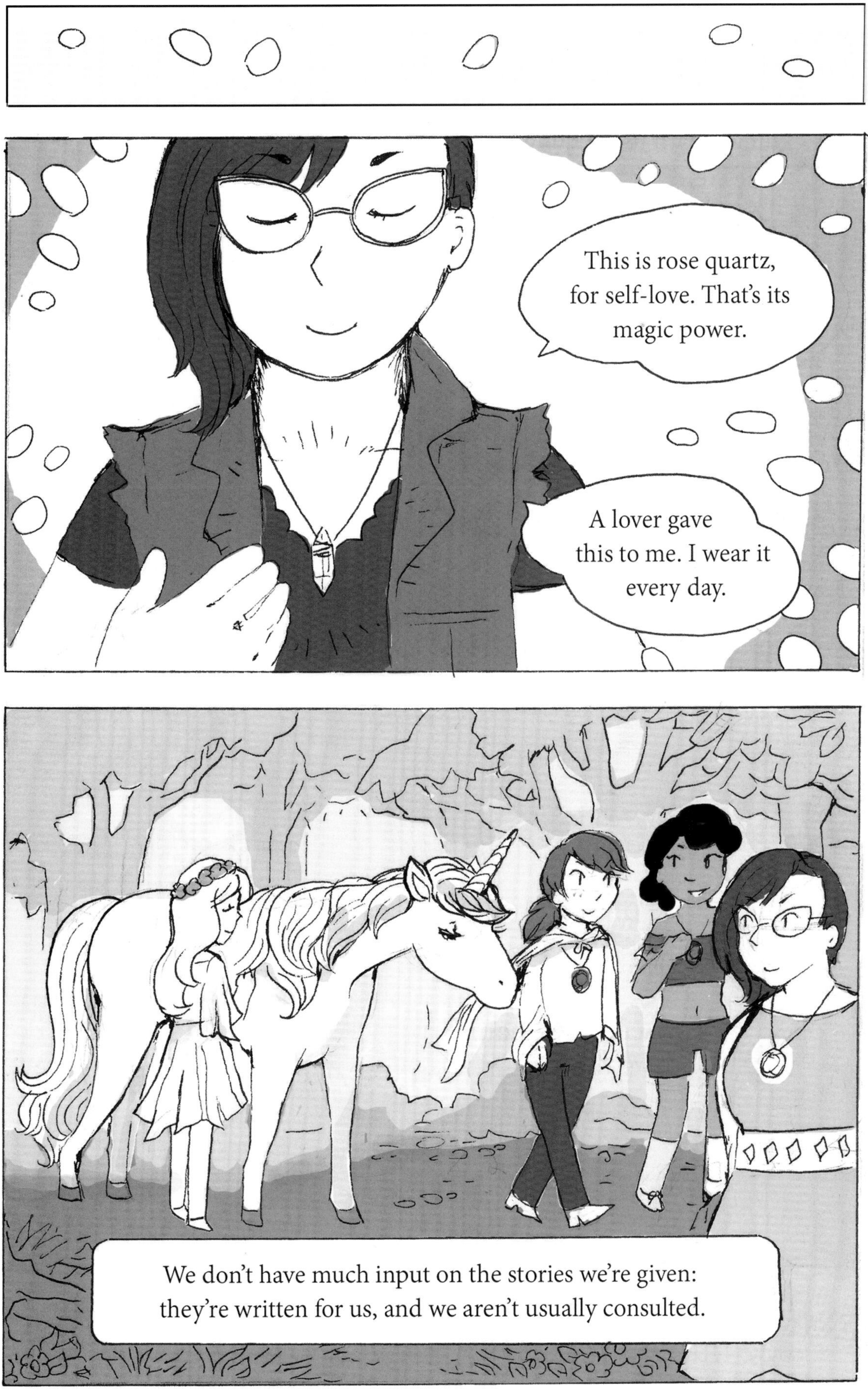
This is rose quartz, for self-love. That's its magic power.
A lover gave this to me. I wear it every day.
We don't have much input on the stories we're given: they're written for us, and we aren't usually consulted.

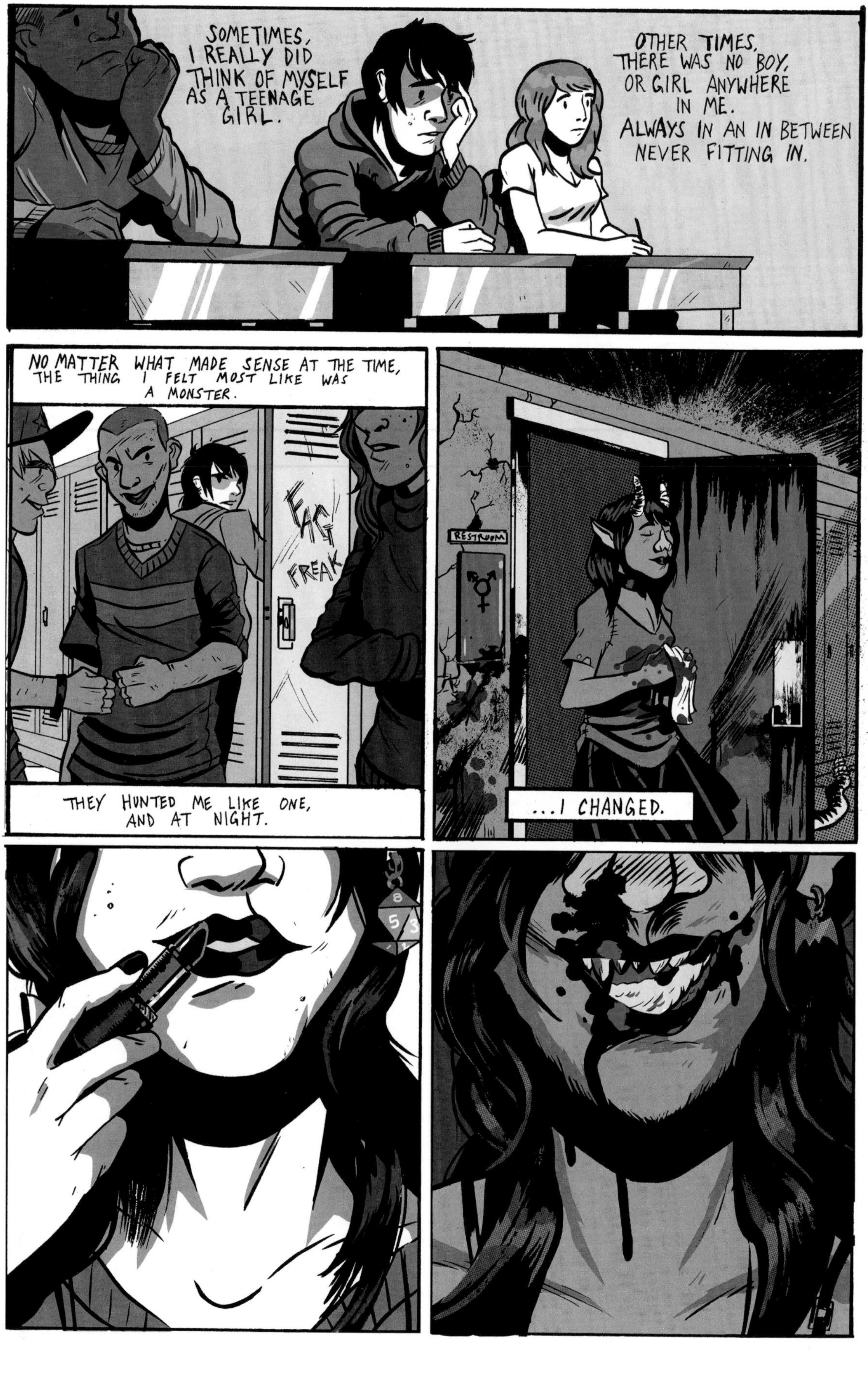
SOMETIMES, I REALLY DID THINK OF MYSELF AS A TEENAGE GIRL.
OTHER TIMES, THERE WAS NO BOY, OR GIRL ANYWHERE IN ME. ALWAYS IN AN IN BETWEEN NEVER FITTING IN.
NO MATTER WHAT MADE SENSE AT THE TIME, THE THING I FELT MOST LIKE WAS A MONSTER.
FAG
FREAK
THEY HUNTED ME LIKE ONE, AND AT NIGHT.
RESTROOM
...I CHANGED.

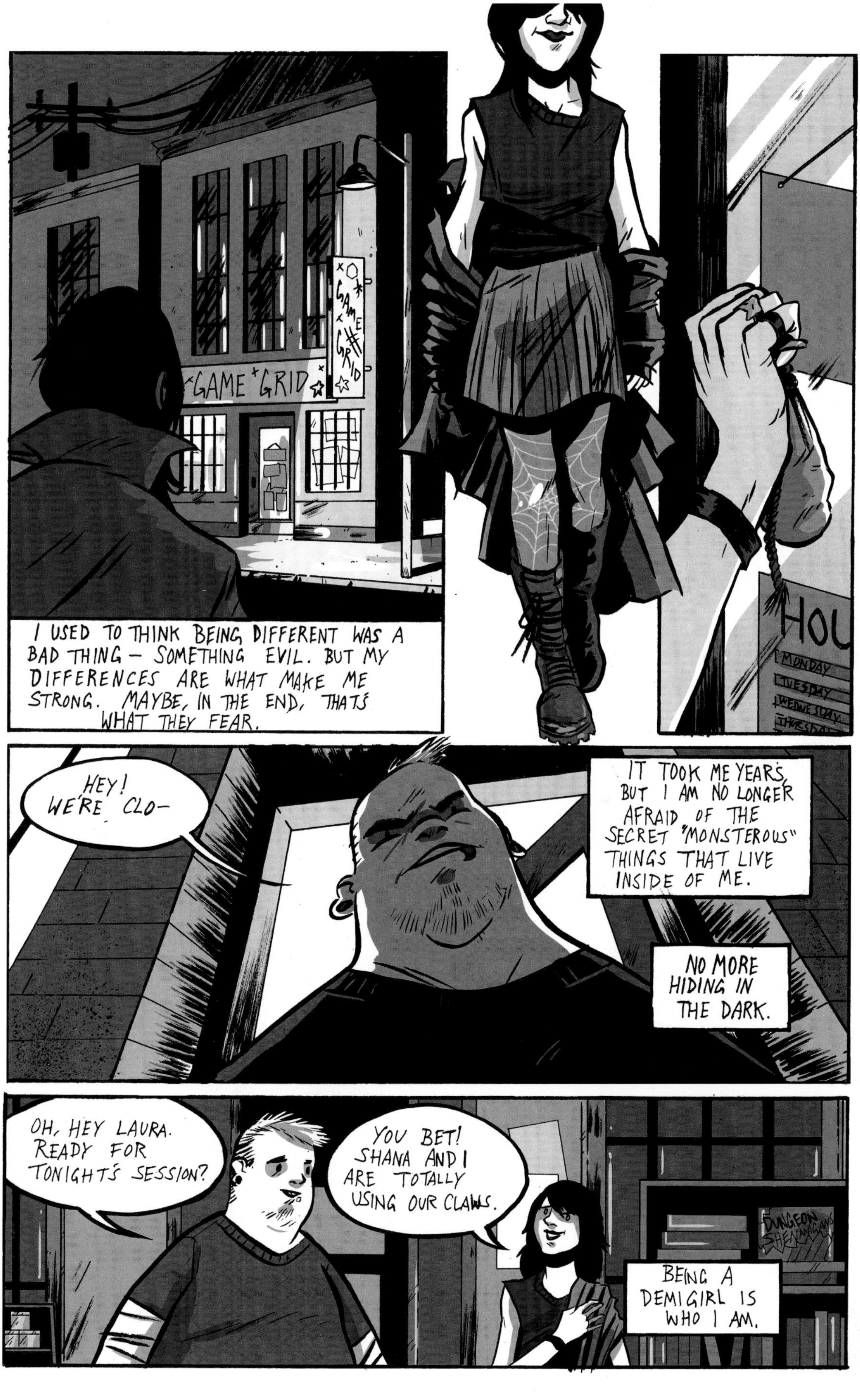

GAME GRID
GAME GRID
I USED TO THINK BEING DIFFERENT WAS A BAD THING – SOMETHING EVIL. BUT MY DIFFERENCES ARE WHAT MAKE ME STRONG. MAYBE, IN THE END, THAT'S WHAT THEY FEAR.
MONDAY
TUESDAY
WEDNESDAY
HEY! WE'RE CLO–
IT TOOK ME YEARS, BUT I AM NO LONGER AFRAID OF THE SECRET "MONSTEROUS" THINGS THAT LIVE INSIDE OF ME.
NO MORE HIDING IN THE DARK.
OH, HEY LAURA. READY FOR TONIGHT'S SESSION?
YOU BET! SHANA AND I ARE TOTALLY USING OUR CLAWS.
DUNGEON SHENANIGANS
BEING A DEMIGIRL IS WHO I AM.

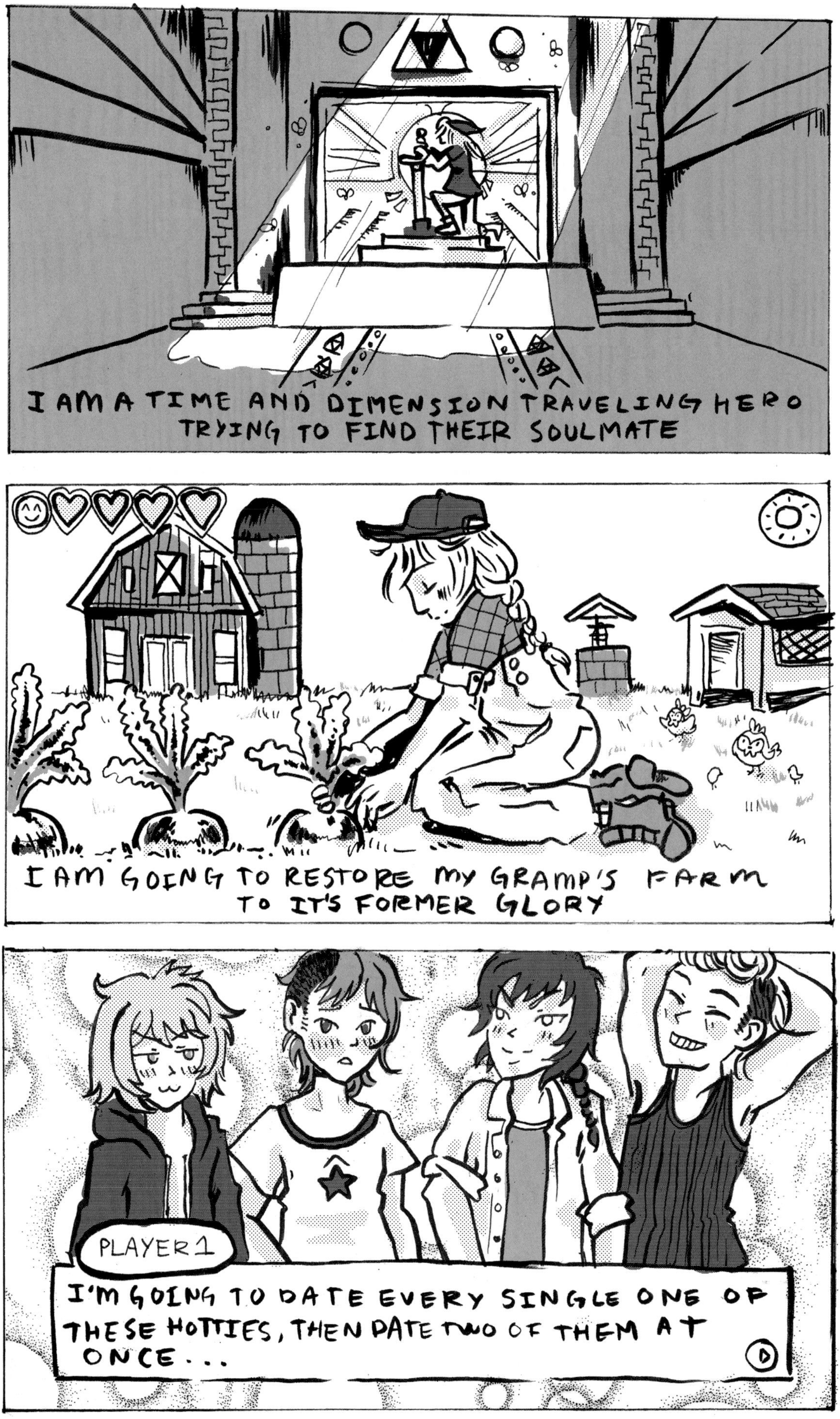
I AM A TIME AND DIMENSION TRAVELING HERO TRYING TO FIND THEIR SOULMATE
I AM GOING TO RESTORE MY GRAMP'S FARM TO IT'S FORMER GLORY
PLAYER 1
I'M GOING TO DATE EVERY SINGLE ONE OF THESE HOTTIES, THEN DATE TWO OF THEM AT ONCE...

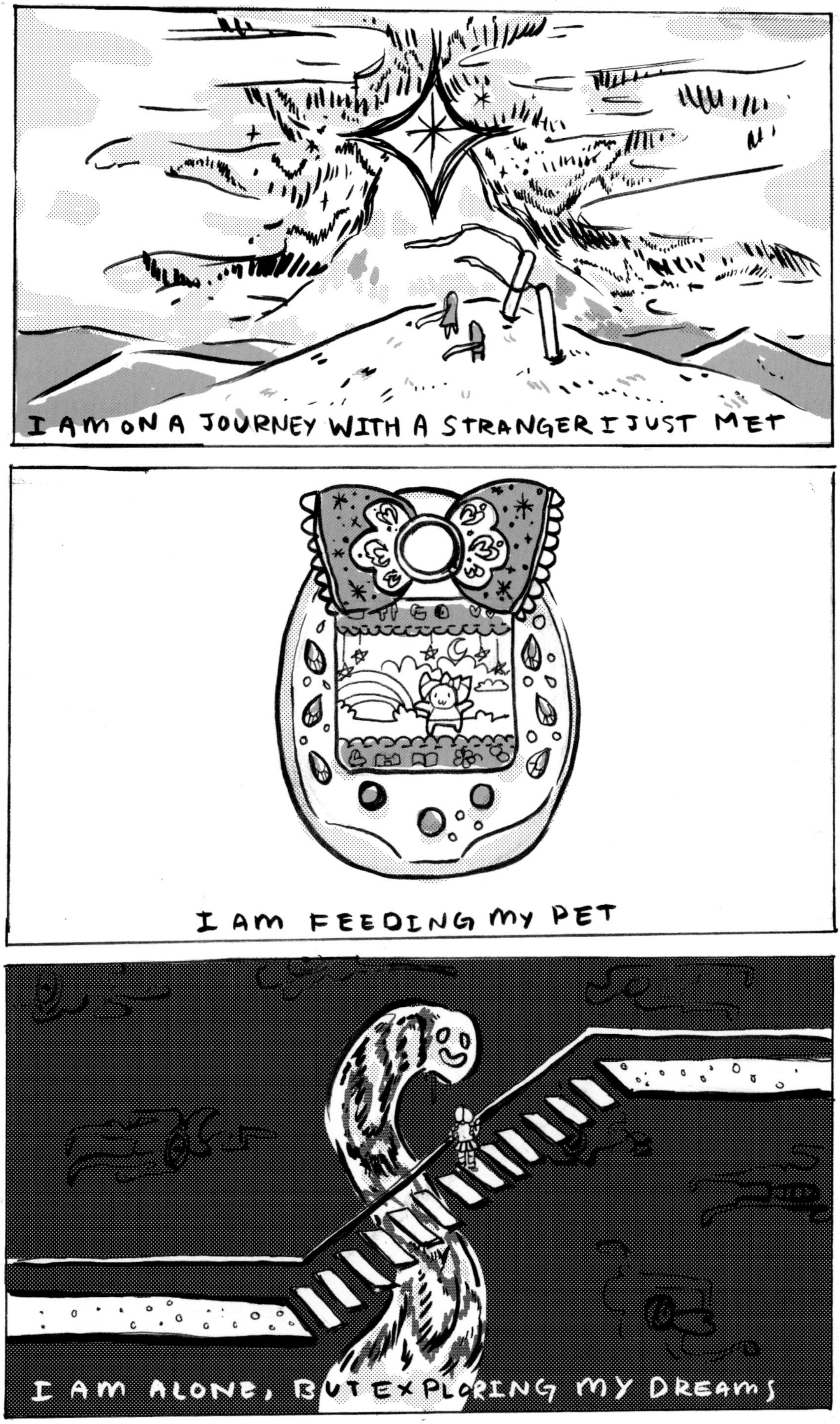
I AM ON A JOURNEY WITH A STRANGER I JUST MET
I AM FEEDING MY PET
I AM ALONE, BUT EXPLORING MY DREAMS

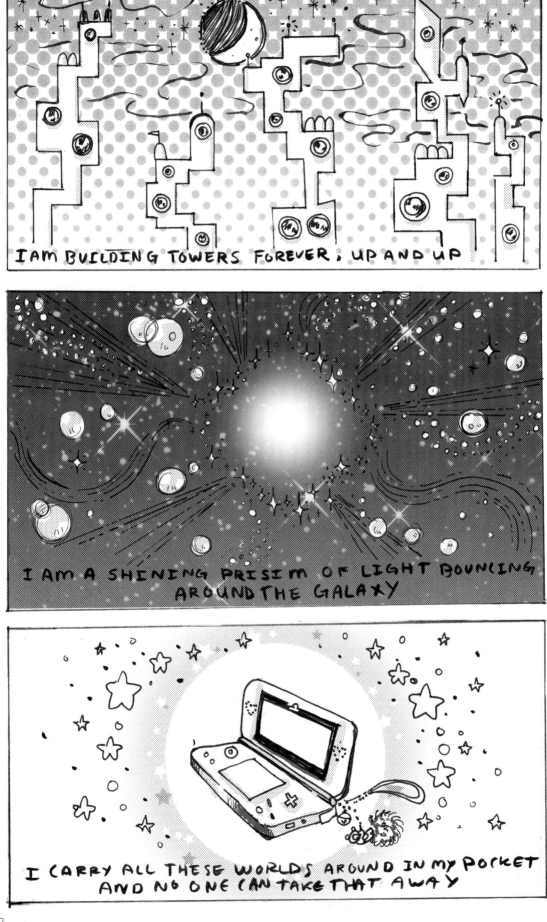

I AM BUILDING TOWERS FOREVER, UP AND UP

I AM A SHINING PRISM OF LIGHT BOUNCING AROUND THE GALAXY

I CARRY ALL THESE WORLDS AROUND IN MY POCKET AND NO ONE CAN TAKE THAT AWAY

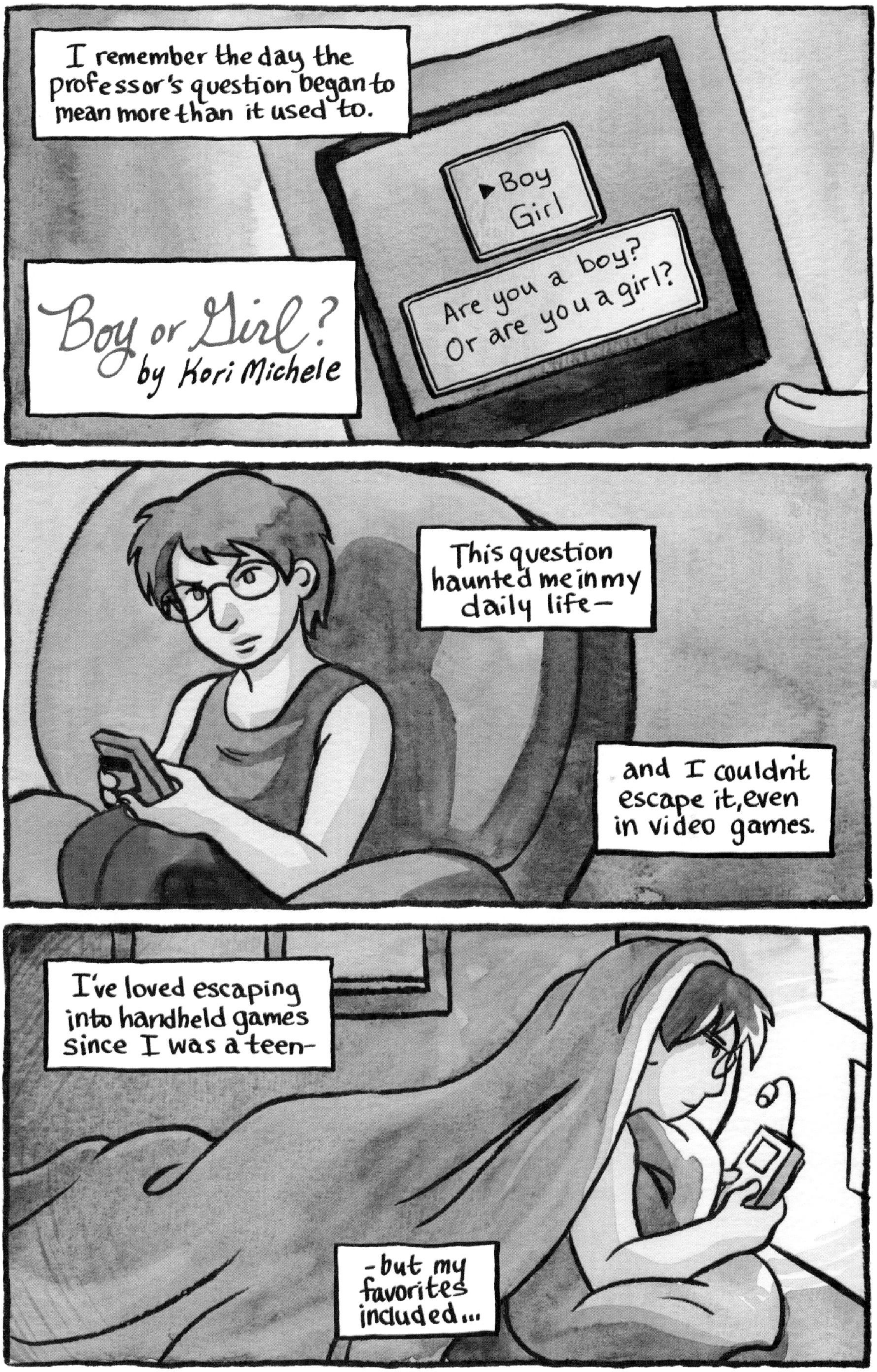
I remember the day the professor's question began to mean more than it used to.
▶Boy
Girl
Are you a boy? Or are you a girl?
Boy or Girl?
by Kori Michele
This question haunted me in my daily life–
and I couldn't escape it, even in video games.
I've loved escaping into handheld games since I was a teen–
–but my favorites included...

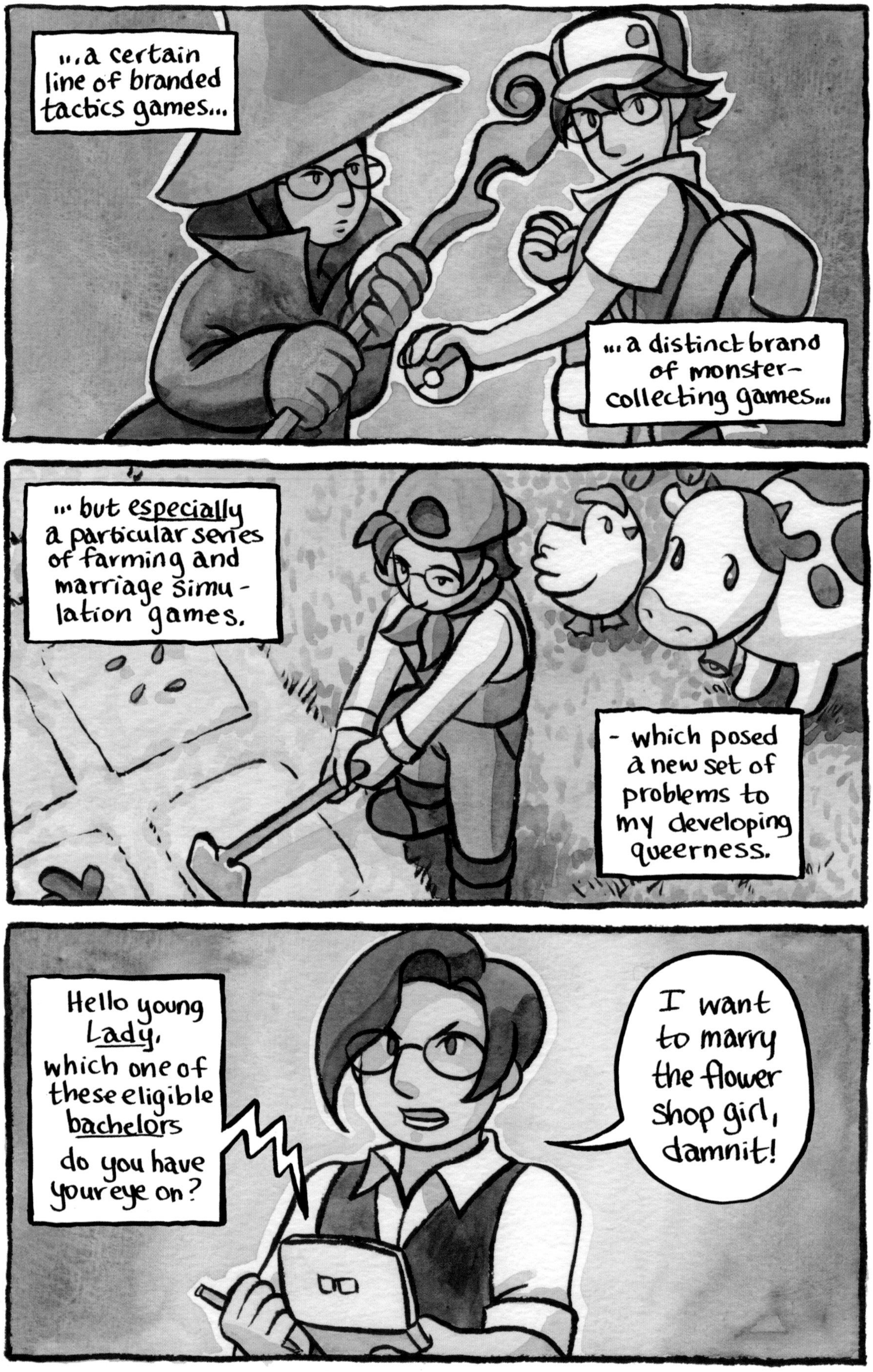
...a certain line of branded tactics games...
...a distinct brand of monster-collecting games...
...but especially a particular series of farming and marriage simu-lation games.
- which posed a new set of problems to my developing queerness.
Hello young Lady, which one of these eligible bachelors do you have your eye on?
I want to marry the flower shop girl, damnit!

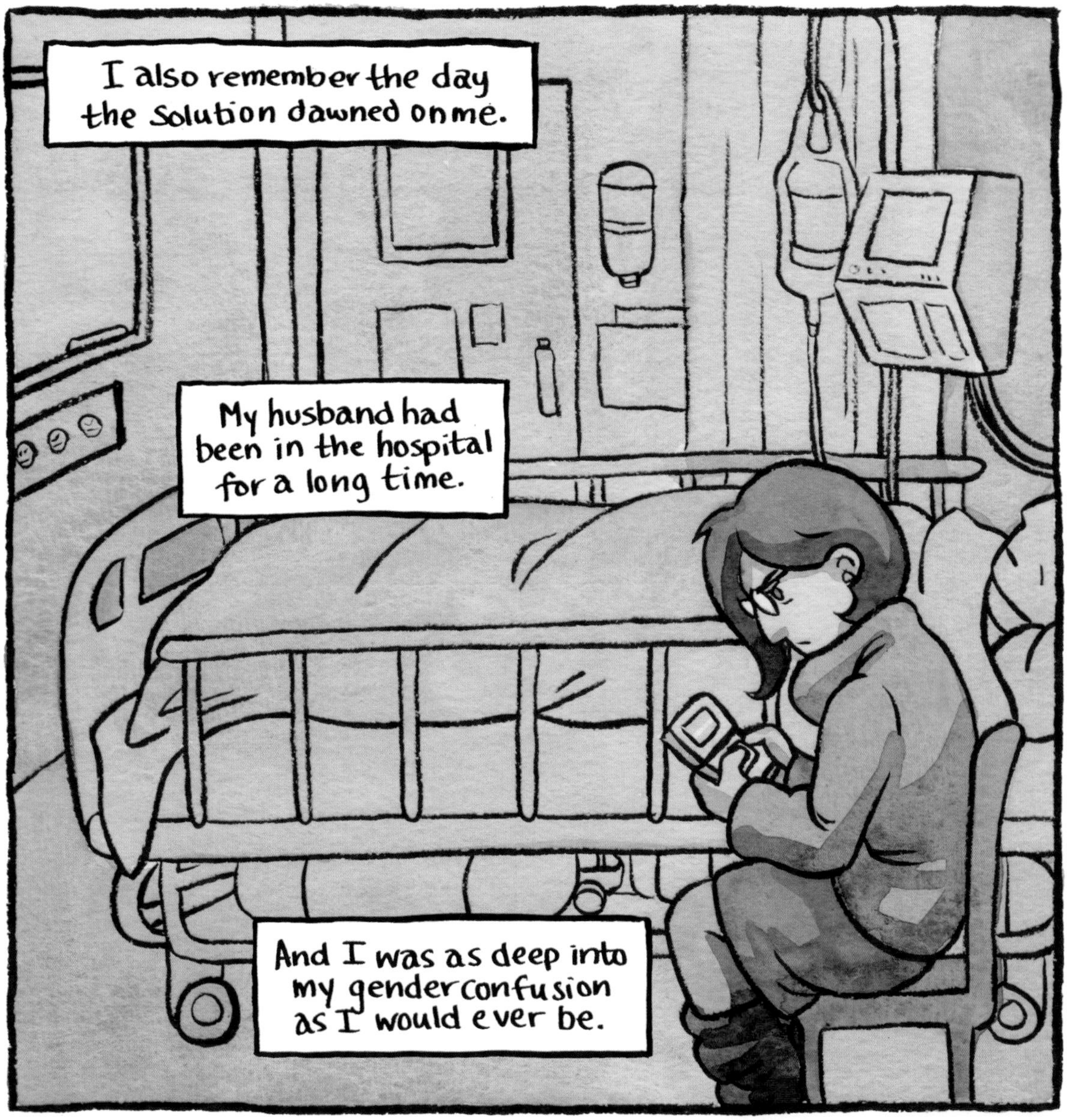
I also remember the day the solution dawned on me.
My husband had been in the hospital for a long time.
And I was as deep into my gender confusion as I would ever be.

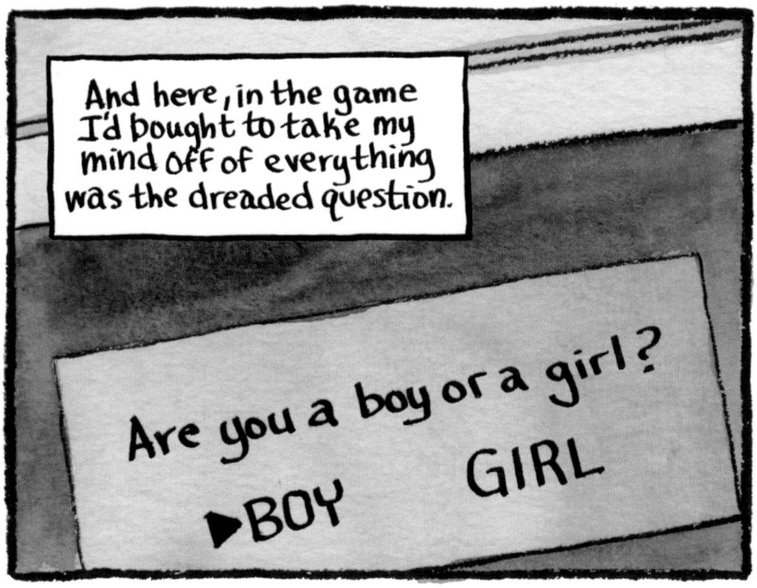
And here, in the game I'd bought to take my mind off of everything was the dreaded question.
Are you a boy or a girl?
▶BOY
GIRL

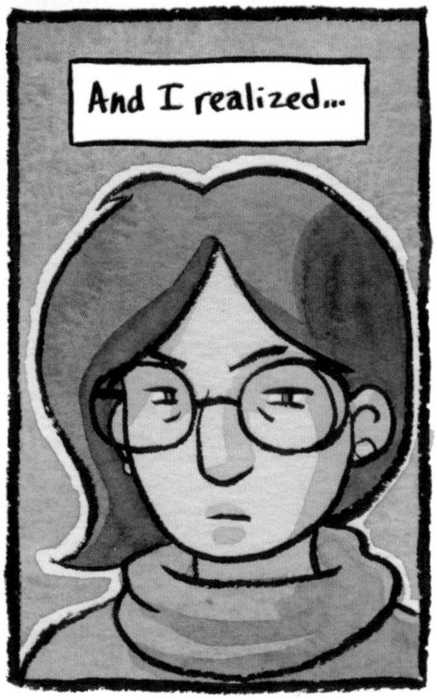
And I realized...

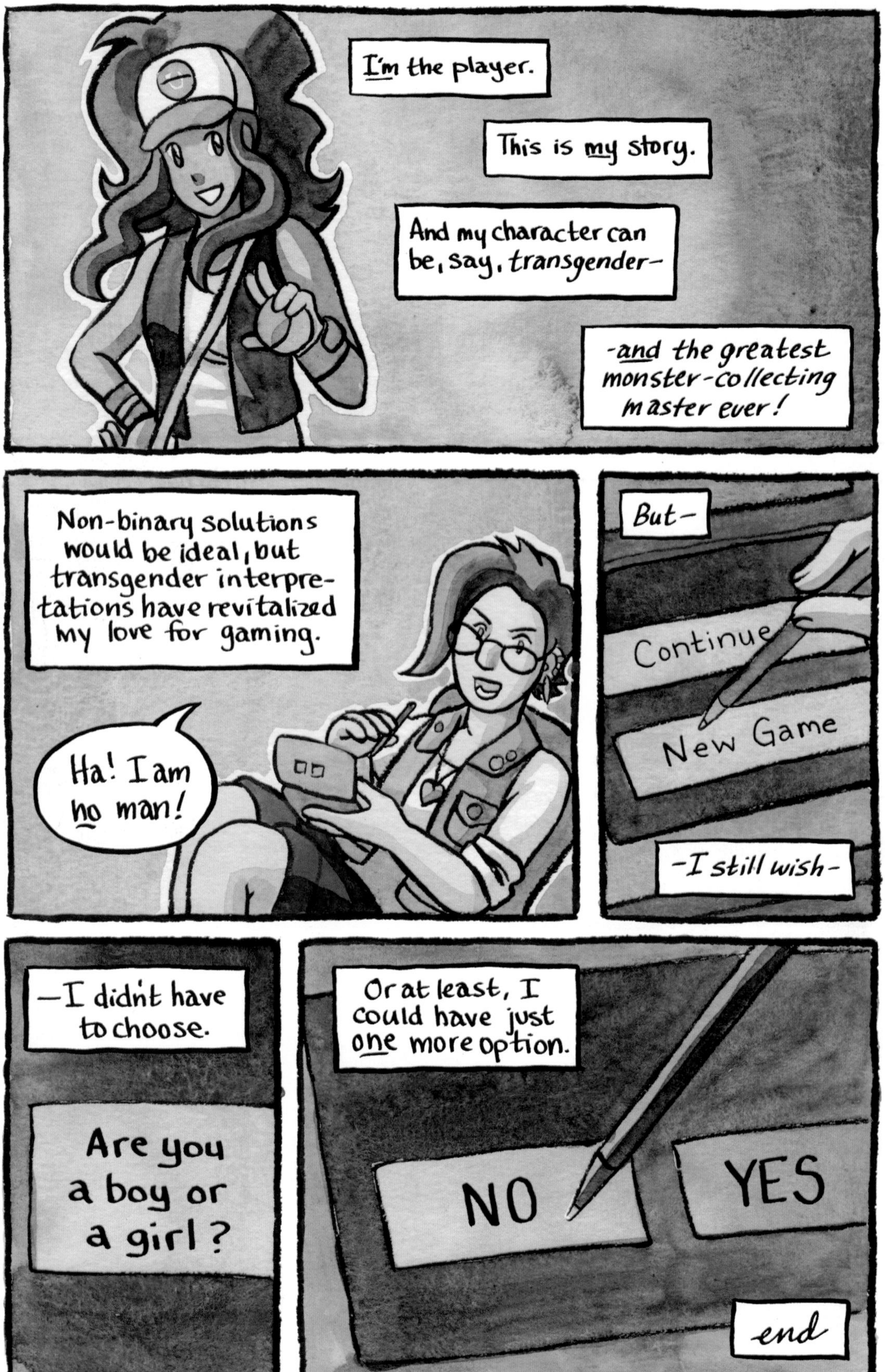
I'm the player.
This is my story.
And my character can be, say, transgender-
-and the greatest monster-collecting master ever!
Non-binary solutions would be ideal, but transgender interpretations have revitalized my love for gaming.
Ha! I am no man!
But-
Continue
New Game
-I still wish-
—I didn't have to choose.
Are you a boy or a girl?
Or at least, I could have just one more option.
NO
YES
end

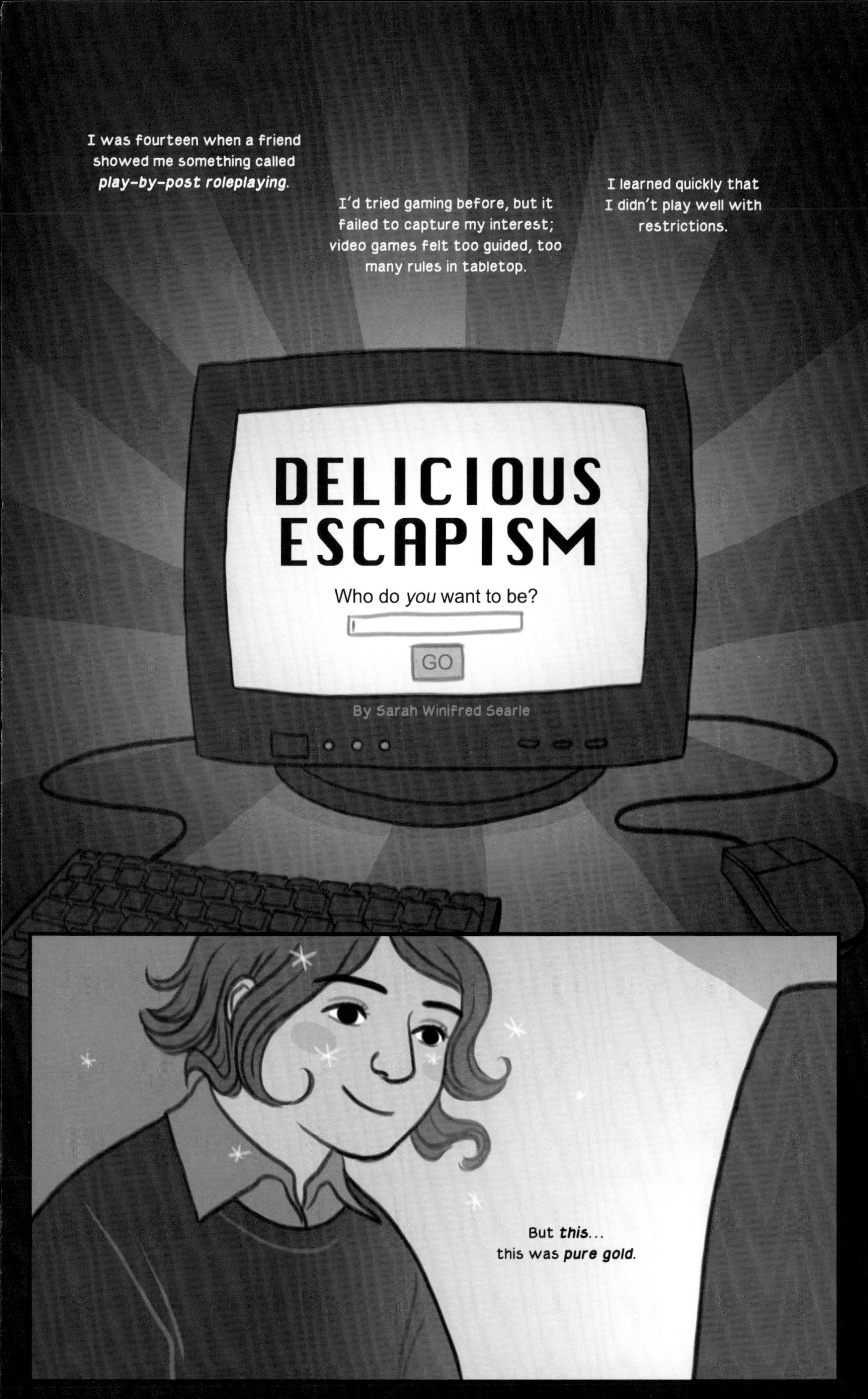

I was fourteen when a friend showed me something called *play-by-post roleplaying*.
I'd tried gaming before, but it failed to capture my interest; video games felt too guided, too many rules in tabletop.
I learned quickly that I didn't play well with restrictions.
DELICIOUS ESCAPISM
Who do *you* want to be?
GO
By Sarah Winifred Searle
But ***this***...
this was ***pure gold***.

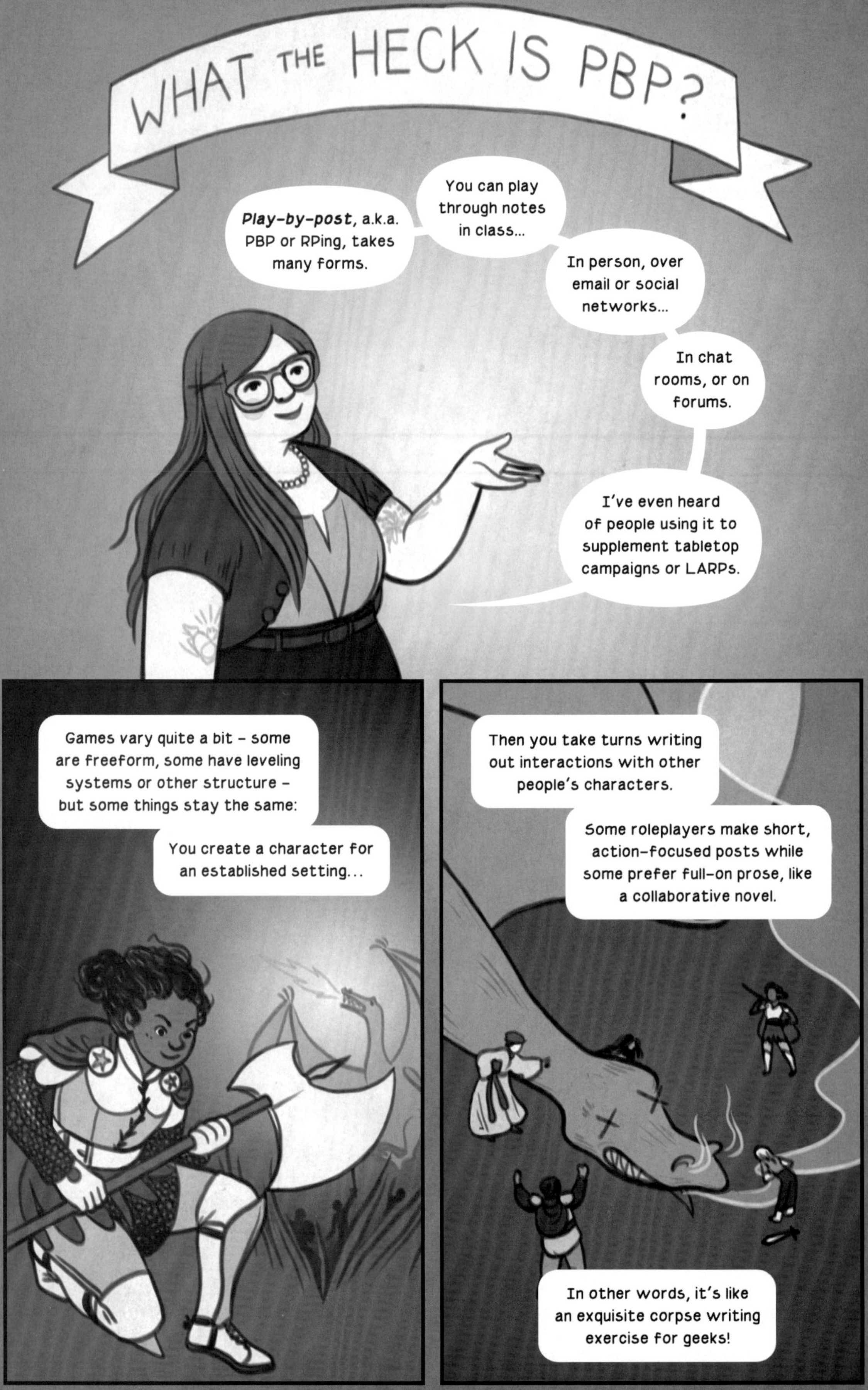
WHAT THE HECK IS PBP?
Play-by-post, a.k.a. PBP or RPing, takes many forms.
You can play through notes in class...
In person, over email or social networks...
In chat rooms, or on forums.
I've even heard of people using it to supplement tabletop campaigns or LARPs.
Games vary quite a bit – some are freeform, some have leveling systems or other structure – but some things stay the same:
You create a character for an established setting...
Then you take turns writing out interactions with other people's characters.
Some roleplayers make short, action-focused posts while some prefer full-on prose, like a collaborative novel.
In other words, it's like an exquisite corpse writing exercise for geeks!

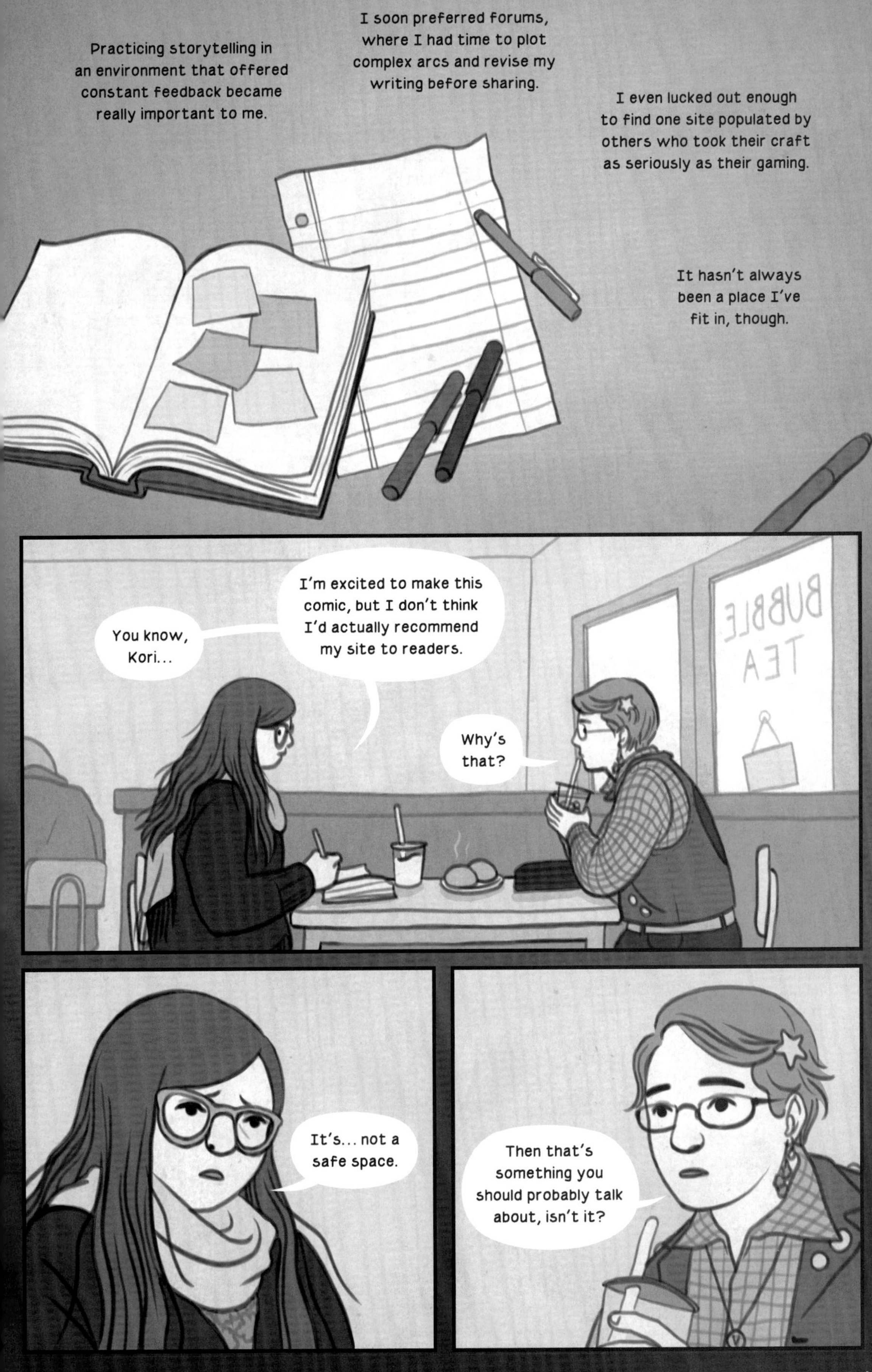
Practicing storytelling in an environment that offered constant feedback became really important to me.
I soon preferred forums, where I had time to plot complex arcs and revise my writing before sharing.
I even lucked out enough to find one site populated by others who took their craft as seriously as their gaming.
It hasn't always been a place I've fit in, though.
You know, Kori...
I'm excited to make this comic, but I don't think I'd actually recommend my site to readers.
BUBBLE TEA
Why's that?
It's... not a safe space.
Then that's something you should probably talk about, isn't it?

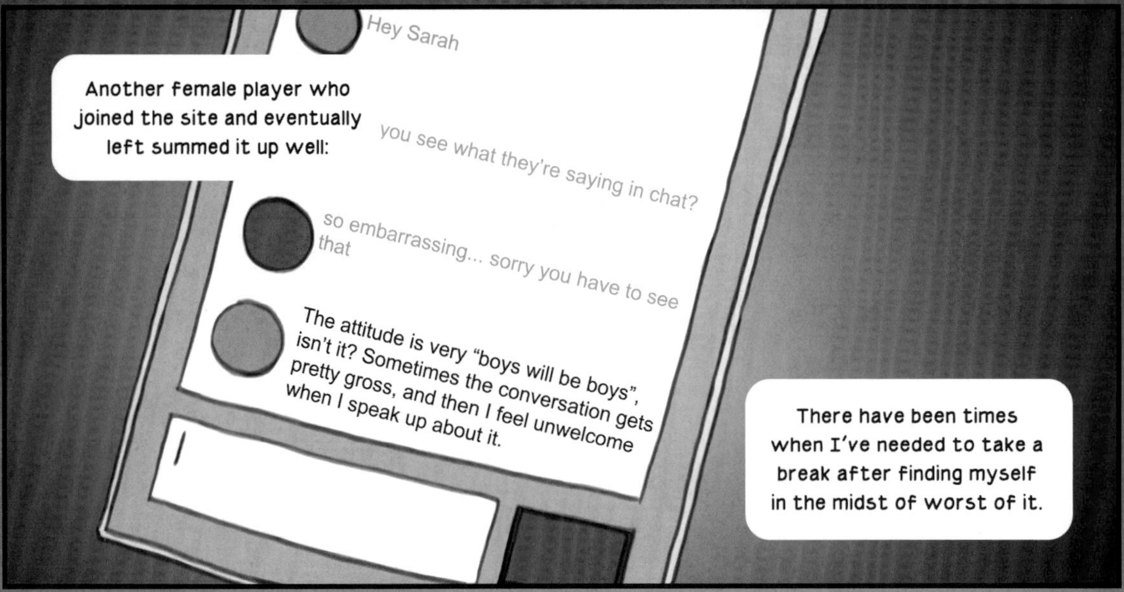
Another female player who joined the site and eventually left summed it up well:
Hey Sarah
you see what they're saying in chat?
so embarrassing... sorry you have to see that
The attitude is very "boys will be boys", isn't it? Sometimes the conversation gets pretty gross, and then I feel unwelcome when I speak up about it.
There have been times when I've needed to take a break after finding myself in the midst of worst of it.

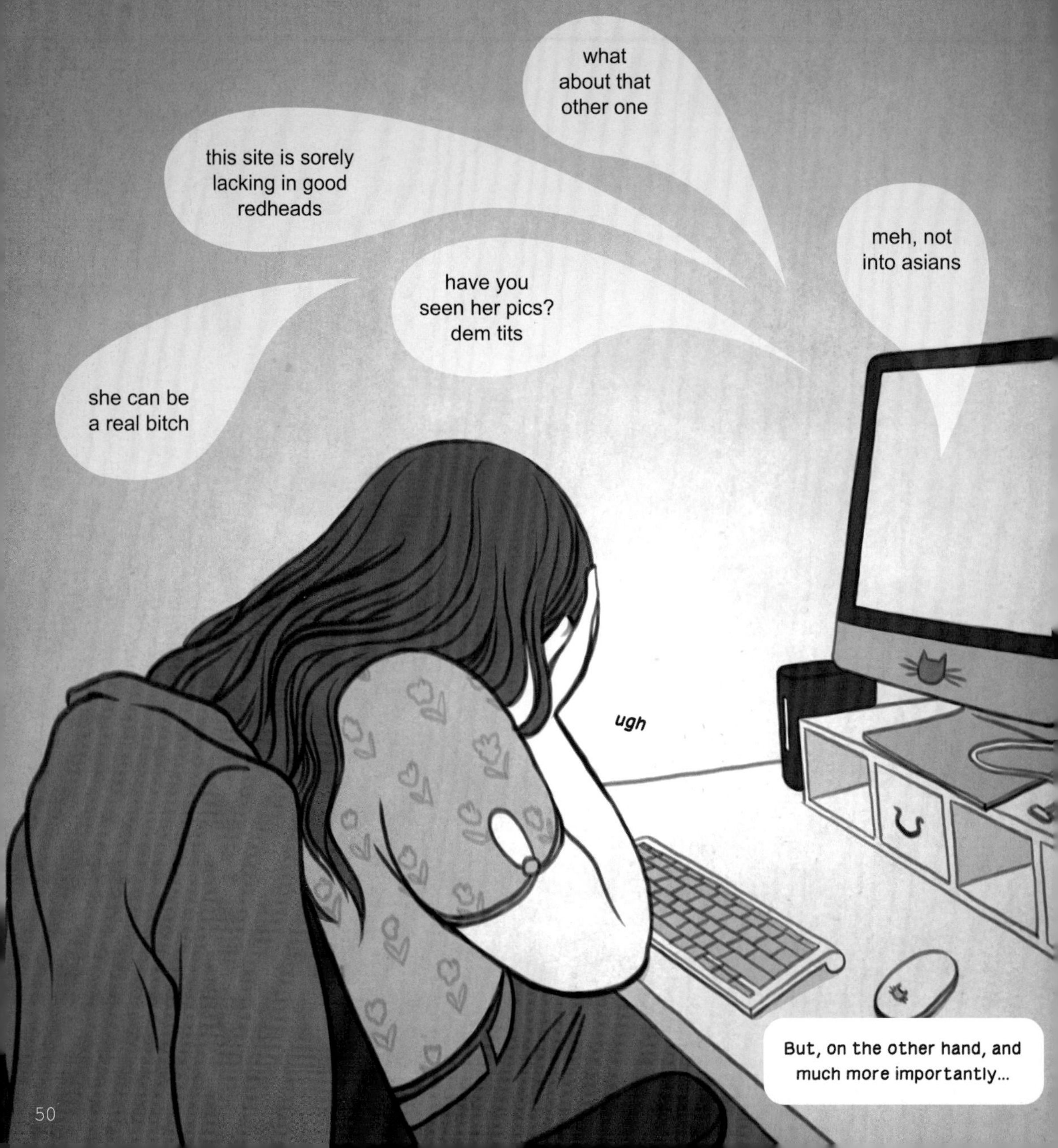
what about that other one
this site is sorely lacking in good redheads
meh, not into asians
have you seen her pics? dem tits
she can be a real bitch
ugh
But, on the other hand, and much more importantly...

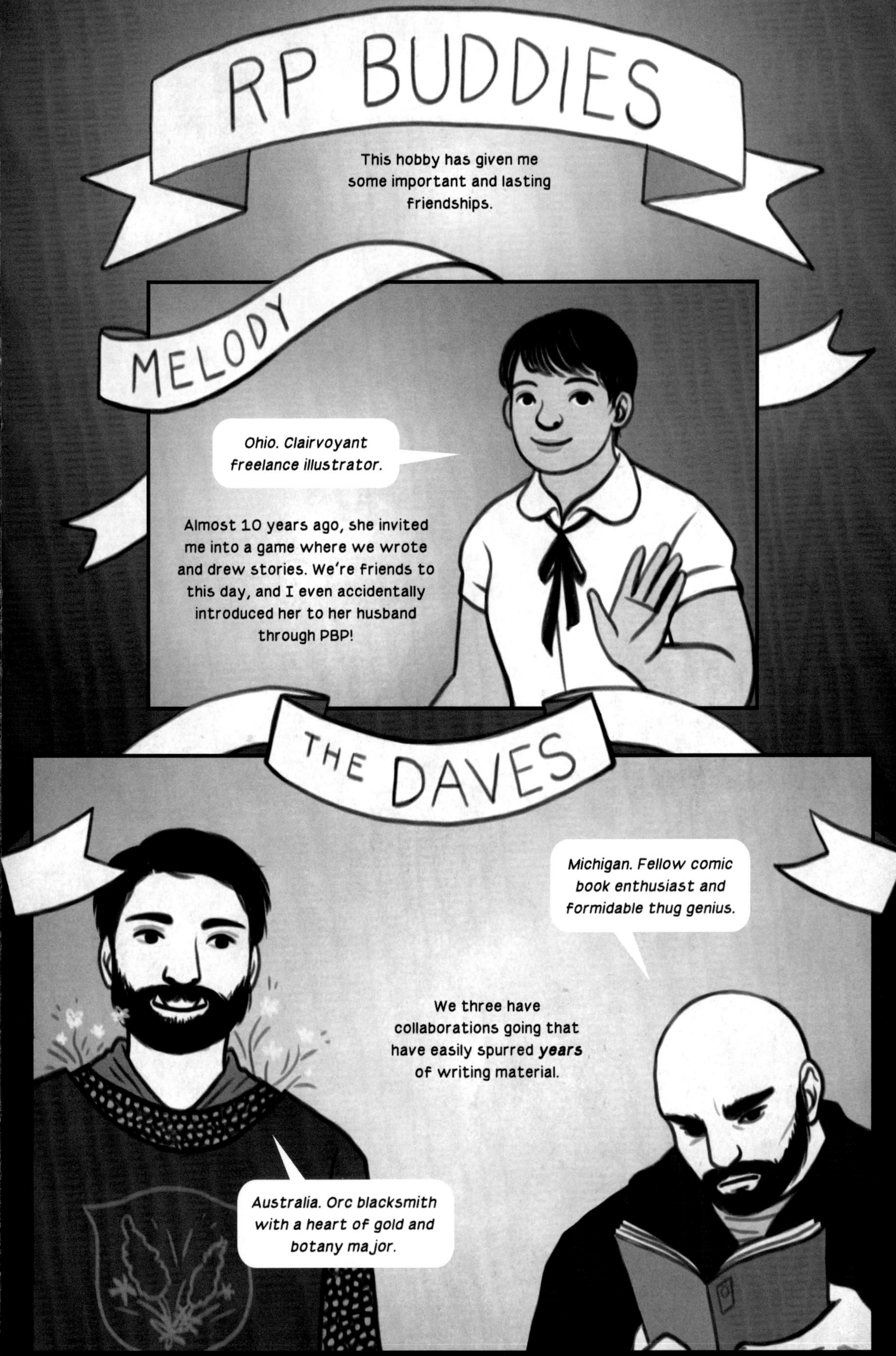
RP BUDDIES
This hobby has given me some important and lasting friendships.
MELODY
Ohio. Clairvoyant freelance illustrator.
Almost 10 years ago, she invited me into a game where we wrote and drew stories. We're friends to this day, and I even accidentally introduced her to her husband through PBP!
THE DAVES
Michigan. Fellow comic book enthusiast and formidable thug genius.
We three have collaborations going that have easily spurred *years* of writing material.
Australia. Orc blacksmith with a heart of gold and botany major.

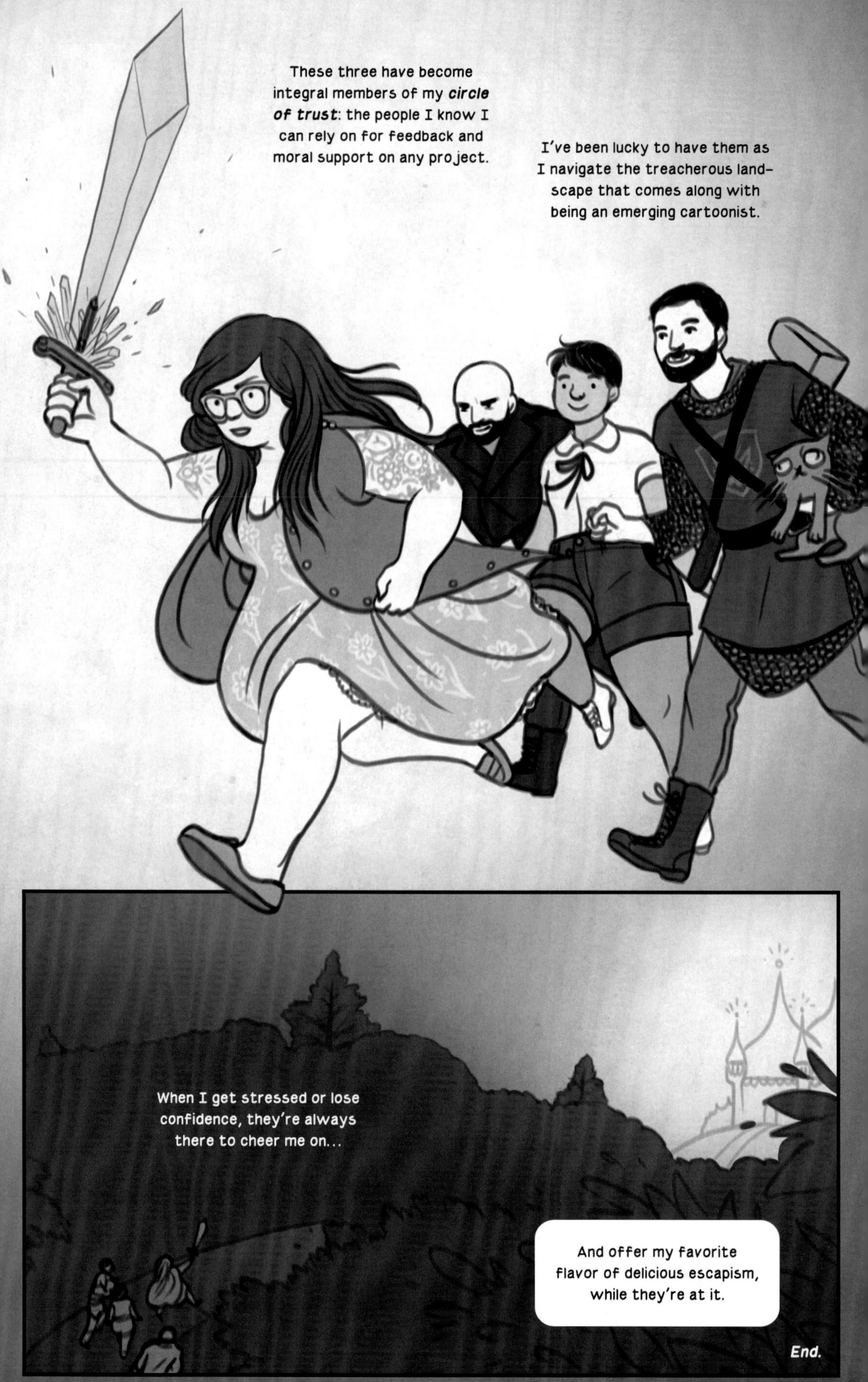
These three have become integral members of my ***circle of trust***: the people I know I can rely on for feedback and moral support on any project.
I've been lucky to have them as I navigate the treacherous land-scape that comes along with being an emerging cartoonist.
When I get stressed or lose confidence, they're always there to cheer me on...
And offer my favorite flavor of delicious escapism, while they're at it.
End.

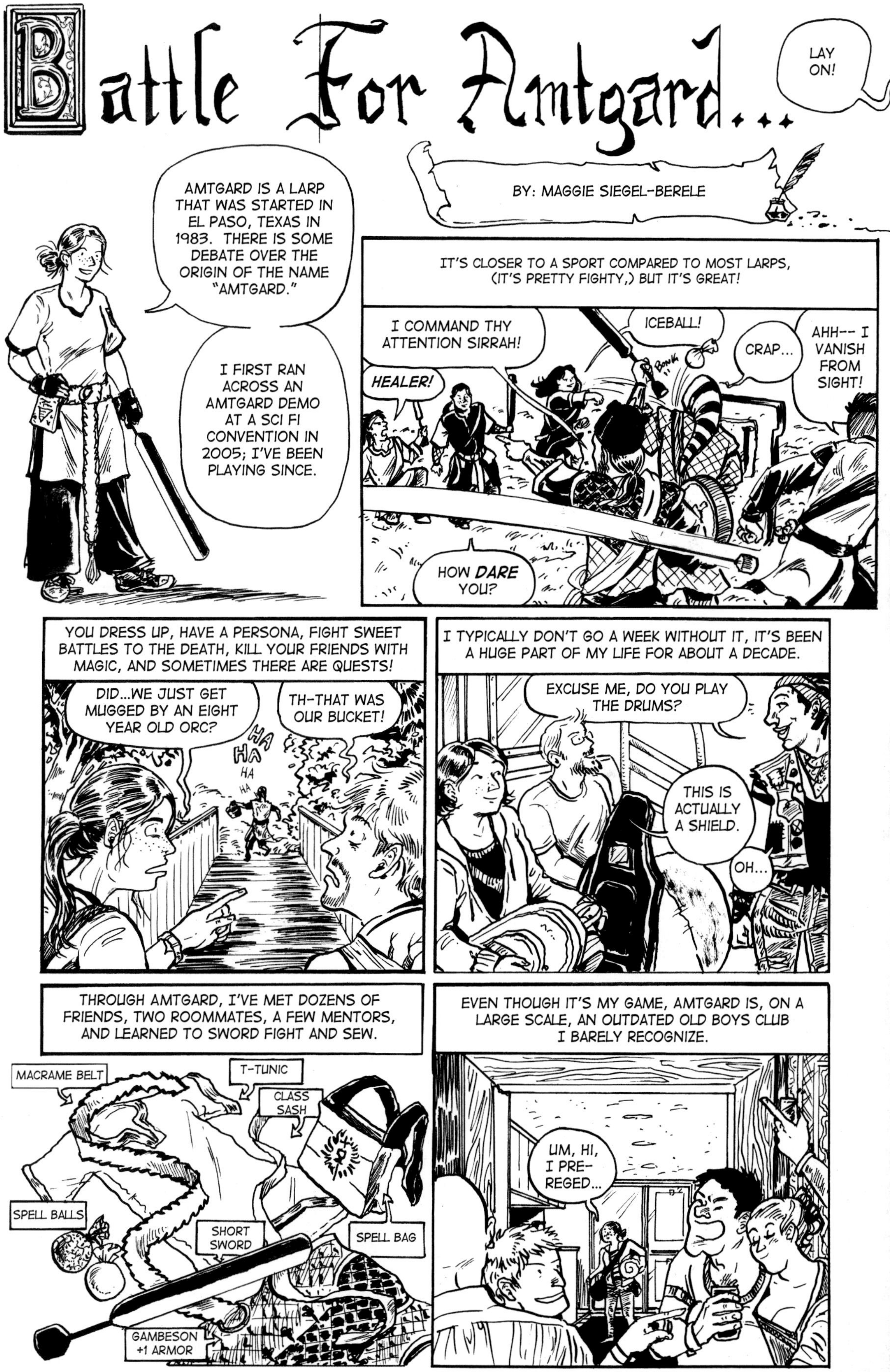
Battle For Amtgard...
LAY ON!
BY: MAGGIE SIEGEL-BERELE
AMTGARD IS A LARP THAT WAS STARTED IN EL PASO, TEXAS IN 1983. THERE IS SOME DEBATE OVER THE ORIGIN OF THE NAME "AMTGARD."
I FIRST RAN ACROSS AN AMTGARD DEMO AT A SCI FI CONVENTION IN 2005; I'VE BEEN PLAYING SINCE.
IT'S CLOSER TO A SPORT COMPARED TO MOST LARPS, (IT'S PRETTY FIGHTY,) BUT IT'S GREAT!
I COMMAND THY ATTENTION SIRRAH!
HEALER!
ICEBALL!
CRAP...
AHH-- I VANISH FROM SIGHT!
HOW DARE YOU?
YOU DRESS UP, HAVE A PERSONA, FIGHT SWEET BATTLES TO THE DEATH, KILL YOUR FRIENDS WITH MAGIC, AND SOMETIMES THERE ARE QUESTS!
DID...WE JUST GET MUGGED BY AN EIGHT YEAR OLD ORC?
TH-THAT WAS OUR BUCKET!
HA HA HA HA
I TYPICALLY DON'T GO A WEEK WITHOUT IT, IT'S BEEN A HUGE PART OF MY LIFE FOR ABOUT A DECADE.
EXCUSE ME, DO YOU PLAY THE DRUMS?
THIS IS ACTUALLY A SHIELD.
OH...
THROUGH AMTGARD, I'VE MET DOZENS OF FRIENDS, TWO ROOMMATES, A FEW MENTORS, AND LEARNED TO SWORD FIGHT AND SEW.
MACRAME BELT
T-TUNIC
CLASS SASH
SPELL BALLS
SHORT SWORD
SPELL BAG
GAMBESON +1 ARMOR
EVEN THOUGH IT'S MY GAME, AMTGARD IS, ON A LARGE SCALE, AN OUTDATED OLD BOYS CLUB I BARELY RECOGNIZE.
UM, HI, I PRE-REGED...

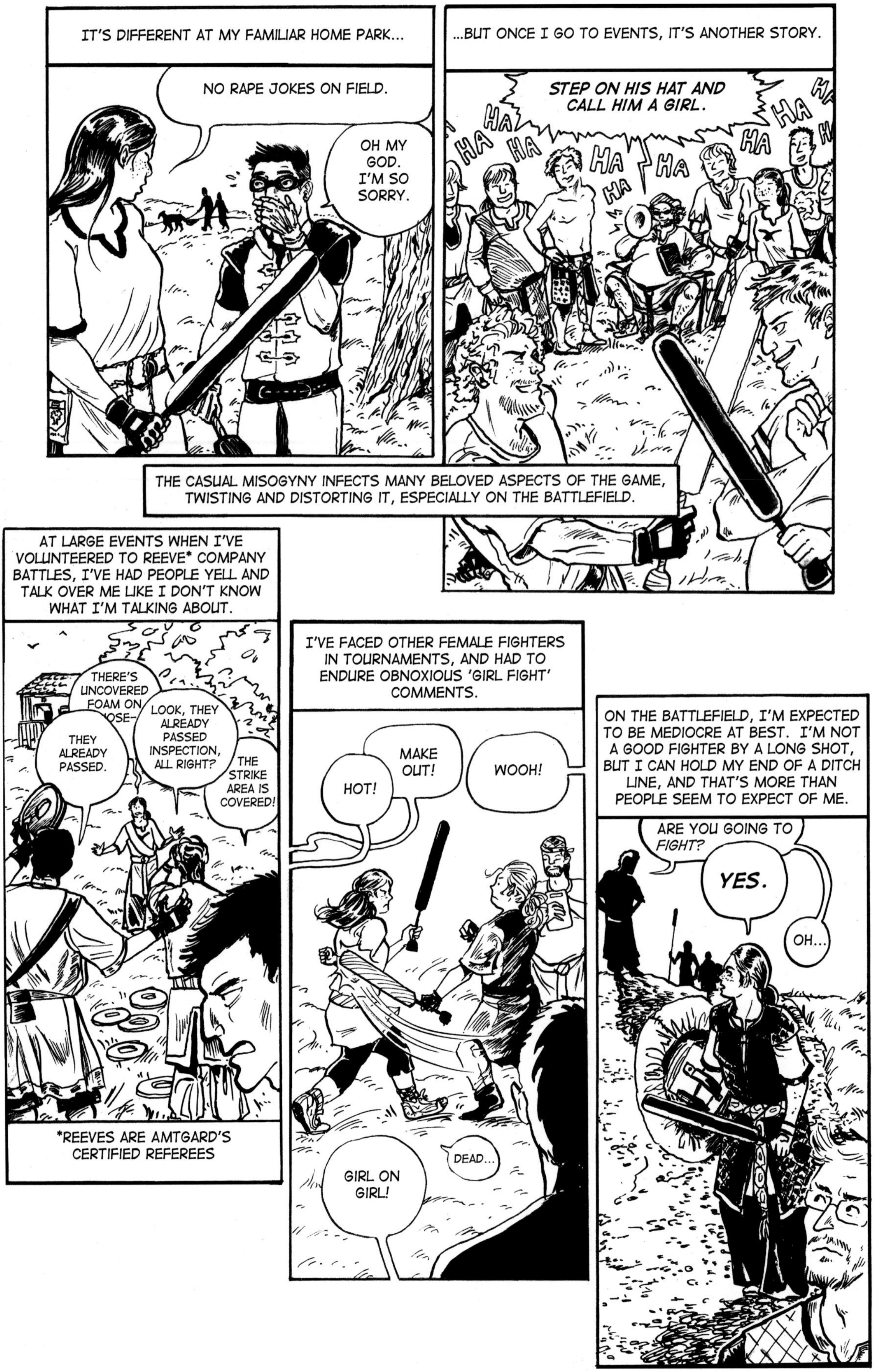
IT'S DIFFERENT AT MY FAMILIAR HOME PARK...
NO RAPE JOKES ON FIELD.
OH MY GOD. I'M SO SORRY.
...BUT ONCE I GO TO EVENTS, IT'S ANOTHER STORY.
STEP ON HIS HAT AND CALL HIM A GIRL.
HA HA HA HA HA HA HA HA HA HA
THE CASUAL MISOGYNY INFECTS MANY BELOVED ASPECTS OF THE GAME, TWISTING AND DISTORTING IT, ESPECIALLY ON THE BATTLEFIELD.
AT LARGE EVENTS WHEN I'VE VOLUNTEERED TO REEVE* COMPANY BATTLES, I'VE HAD PEOPLE YELL AND TALK OVER ME LIKE I DON'T KNOW WHAT I'M TALKING ABOUT.
THERE'S UNCOVERED FOAM ON
THEY ALREADY PASSED.
LOOK, THEY ALREADY PASSED INSPECTION, ALL RIGHT?
THE STRIKE AREA IS COVERED!
*REEVES ARE AMTGARD'S CERTIFIED REFEREES
I'VE FACED OTHER FEMALE FIGHTERS IN TOURNAMENTS, AND HAD TO ENDURE OBNOXIOUS 'GIRL FIGHT' COMMENTS.
HOT!
MAKE OUT!
WOOH!
GIRL ON GIRL!
DEAD...
ON THE BATTLEFIELD, I'M EXPECTED TO BE MEDIOCRE AT BEST. I'M NOT A GOOD FIGHTER BY A LONG SHOT, BUT I CAN HOLD MY END OF A DITCH LINE, AND THAT'S MORE THAN PEOPLE SEEM TO EXPECT OF ME.
ARE YOU GOING TO FIGHT?
YES.
OH...

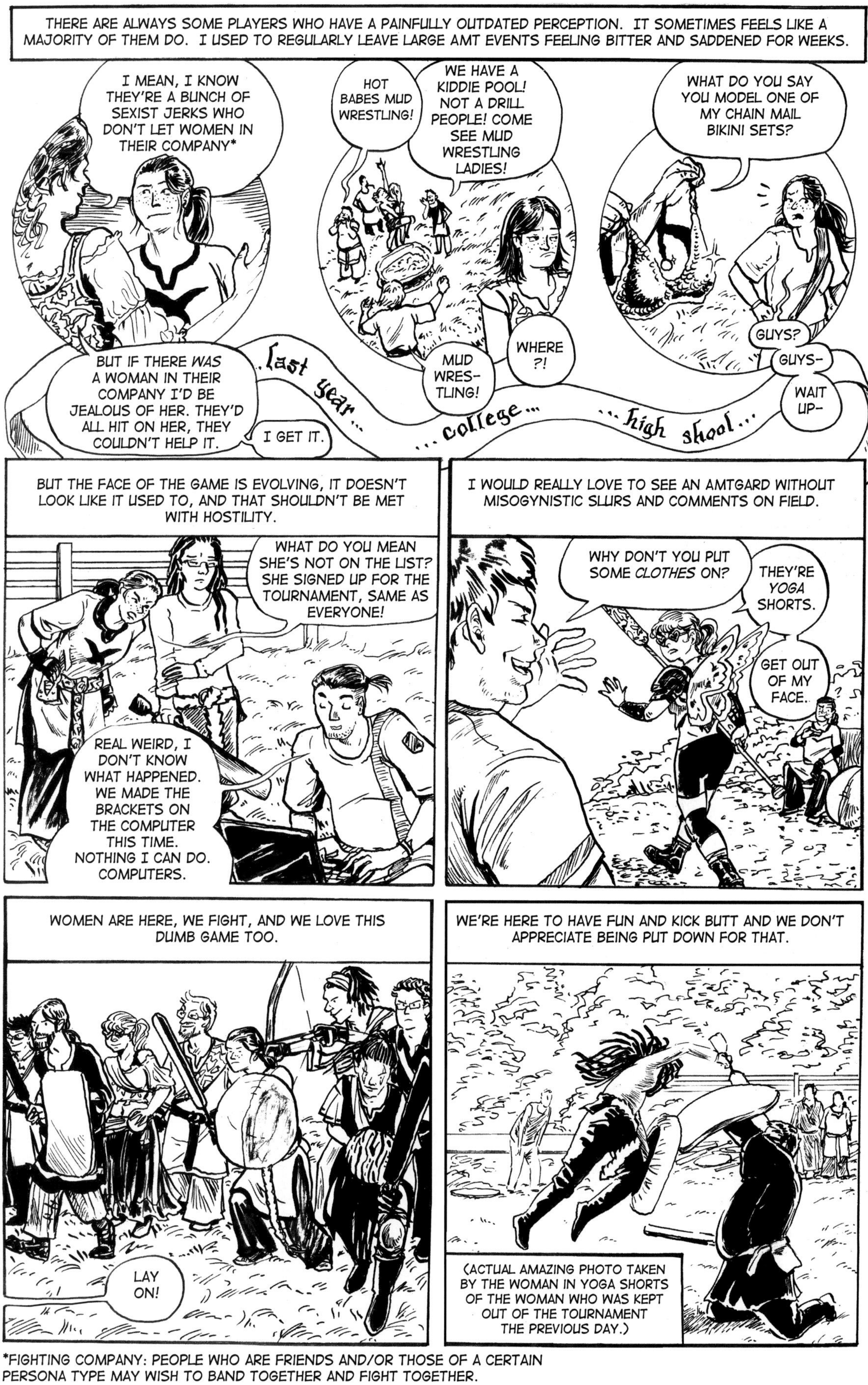
THERE ARE ALWAYS SOME PLAYERS WHO HAVE A PAINFULLY OUTDATED PERCEPTION. IT SOMETIMES FEELS LIKE A MAJORITY OF THEM DO. I USED TO REGULARLY LEAVE LARGE AMT EVENTS FEELING BITTER AND SADDENED FOR WEEKS.
I MEAN, I KNOW THEY'RE A BUNCH OF SEXIST JERKS WHO DON'T LET WOMEN IN THEIR COMPANY*
BUT IF THERE *WAS* A WOMAN IN THEIR COMPANY I'D BE JEALOUS OF HER. THEY'D ALL HIT ON HER, THEY COULDN'T HELP IT.
I GET IT.
...last year...
HOT BABES MUD WRESTLING!
WE HAVE A KIDDIE POOL! NOT A DRILL PEOPLE! COME SEE MUD WRESTLING LADIES!
MUD WRES-TLING!
WHERE ?!
...college...
WHAT DO YOU SAY YOU MODEL ONE OF MY CHAIN MAIL BIKINI SETS?
GUYS?
GUYS-
WAIT UP-
...high shool...
BUT THE FACE OF THE GAME IS EVOLVING, IT DOESN'T LOOK LIKE IT USED TO, AND THAT SHOULDN'T BE MET WITH HOSTILITY.
WHAT DO YOU MEAN SHE'S NOT ON THE LIST? SHE SIGNED UP FOR THE TOURNAMENT, SAME AS EVERYONE!
REAL WEIRD, I DON'T KNOW WHAT HAPPENED. WE MADE THE BRACKETS ON THE COMPUTER THIS TIME. NOTHING I CAN DO. COMPUTERS.
I WOULD REALLY LOVE TO SEE AN AMTGARD WITHOUT MISOGYNISTIC SLURS AND COMMENTS ON FIELD.
WHY DON'T YOU PUT SOME *CLOTHES* ON?
THEY'RE *YOGA* SHORTS.
GET OUT OF MY FACE.
WOMEN ARE HERE, WE FIGHT, AND WE LOVE THIS DUMB GAME TOO.
LAY ON!
WE'RE HERE TO HAVE FUN AND KICK BUTT AND WE DON'T APPRECIATE BEING PUT DOWN FOR THAT.
(ACTUAL AMAZING PHOTO TAKEN BY THE WOMAN IN YOGA SHORTS OF THE WOMAN WHO WAS KEPT OUT OF THE TOURNAMENT THE PREVIOUS DAY.)

*FIGHTING COMPANY: PEOPLE WHO ARE FRIENDS AND/OR THOSE OF A CERTAIN PERSONA TYPE MAY WISH TO BAND TOGETHER AND FIGHT TOGETHER.

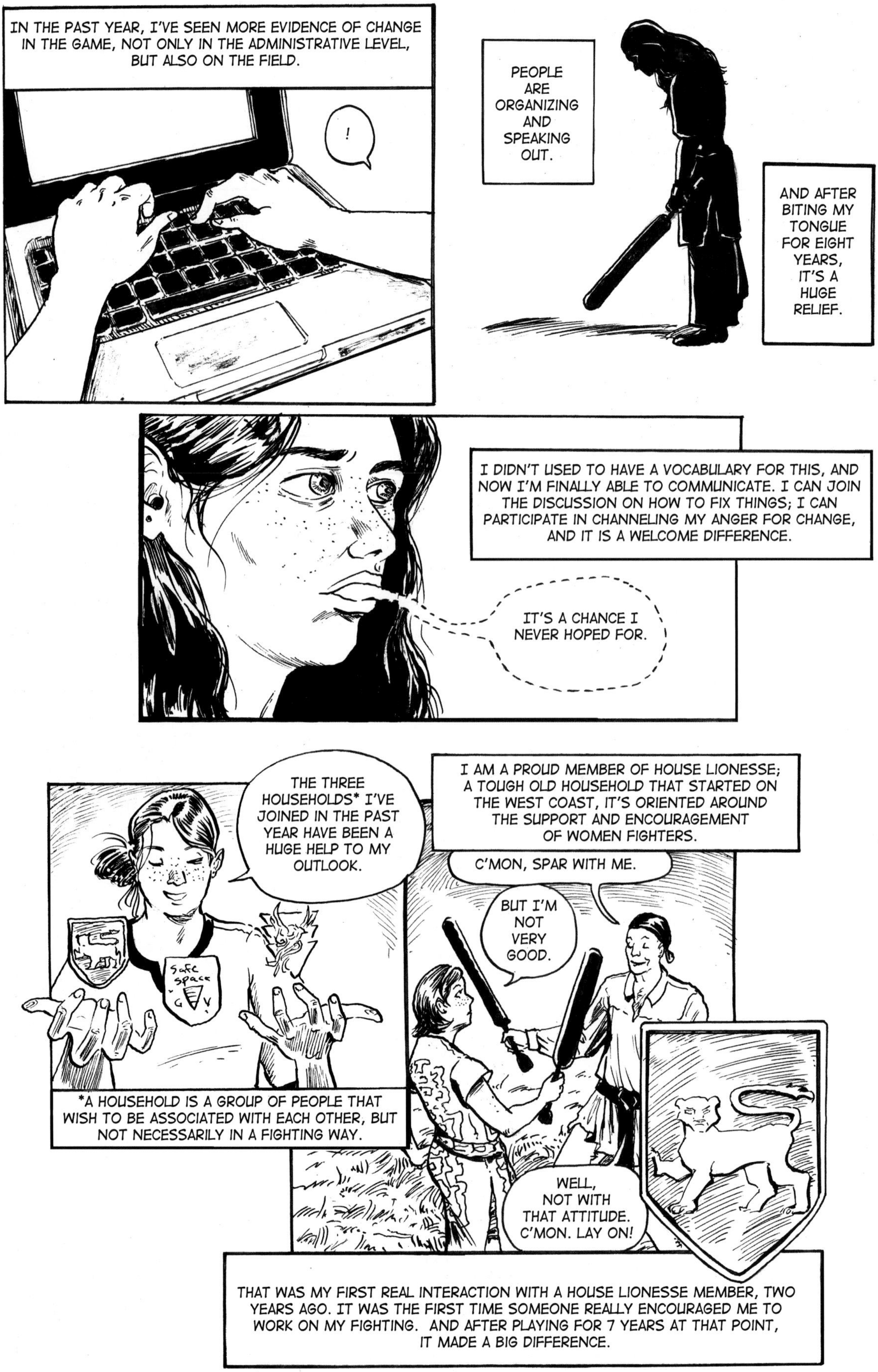
IN THE PAST YEAR, I'VE SEEN MORE EVIDENCE OF CHANGE IN THE GAME, NOT ONLY IN THE ADMINISTRATIVE LEVEL, BUT ALSO ON THE FIELD.
!
PEOPLE ARE ORGANIZING AND SPEAKING OUT.
AND AFTER BITING MY TONGUE FOR EIGHT YEARS, IT'S A HUGE RELIEF.
I DIDN'T USED TO HAVE A VOCABULARY FOR THIS, AND NOW I'M FINALLY ABLE TO COMMUNICATE. I CAN JOIN THE DISCUSSION ON HOW TO FIX THINGS; I CAN PARTICIPATE IN CHANNELING MY ANGER FOR CHANGE, AND IT IS A WELCOME DIFFERENCE.
IT'S A CHANCE I NEVER HOPED FOR.
THE THREE HOUSEHOLDS* I'VE JOINED IN THE PAST YEAR HAVE BEEN A HUGE HELP TO MY OUTLOOK.
*A HOUSEHOLD IS A GROUP OF PEOPLE THAT WISH TO BE ASSOCIATED WITH EACH OTHER, BUT NOT NECESSARILY IN A FIGHTING WAY.
I AM A PROUD MEMBER OF HOUSE LIONESSE; A TOUGH OLD HOUSEHOLD THAT STARTED ON THE WEST COAST, IT'S ORIENTED AROUND THE SUPPORT AND ENCOURAGEMENT OF WOMEN FIGHTERS.
C'MON, SPAR WITH ME.
BUT I'M NOT VERY GOOD.
WELL, NOT WITH THAT ATTITUDE. C'MON. LAY ON!
THAT WAS MY FIRST REAL INTERACTION WITH A HOUSE LIONESSE MEMBER, TWO YEARS AGO. IT WAS THE FIRST TIME SOMEONE REALLY ENCOURAGED ME TO WORK ON MY FIGHTING. AND AFTER PLAYING FOR 7 YEARS AT THAT POINT, IT MADE A BIG DIFFERENCE.

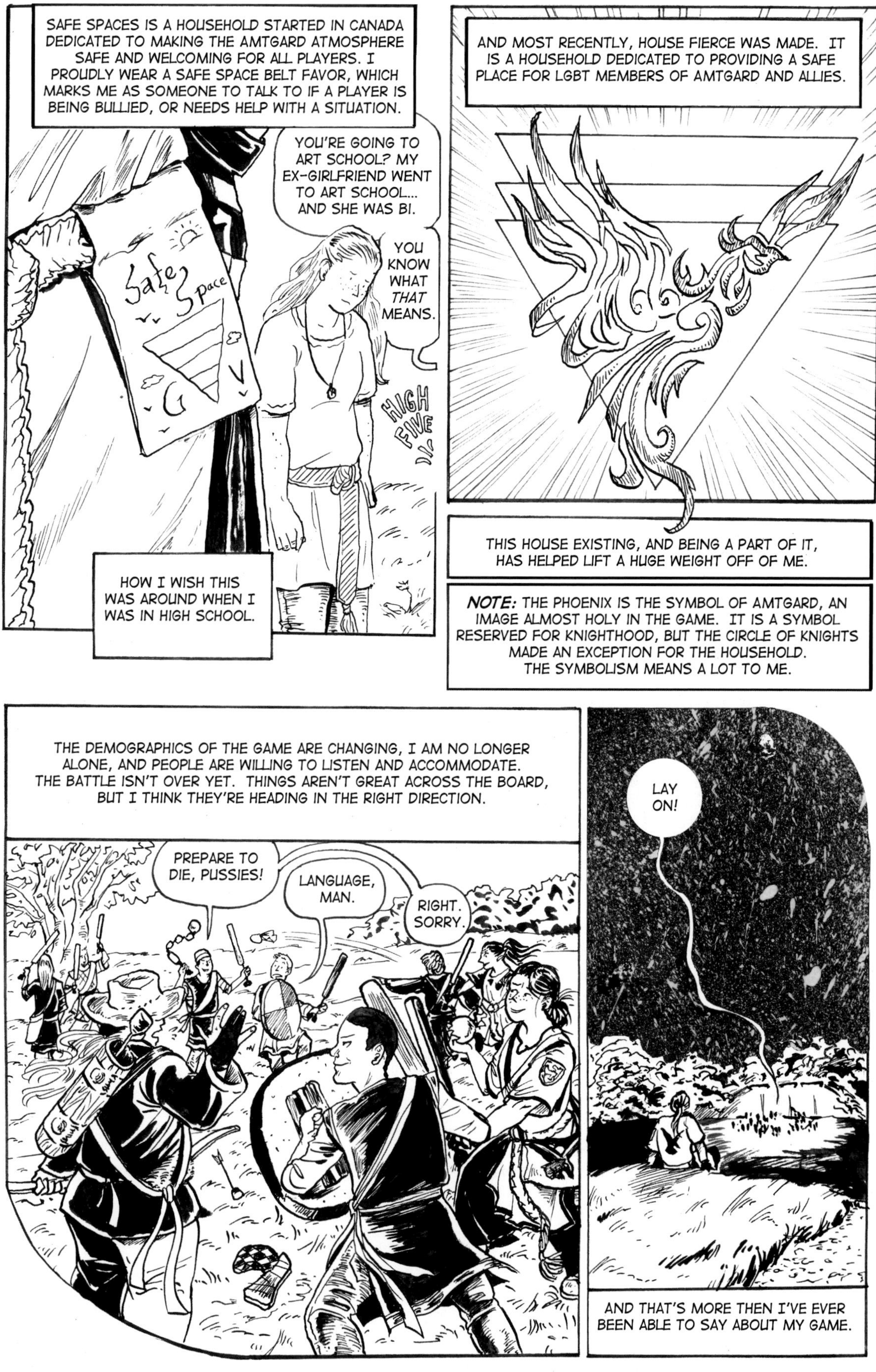

SAFE SPACES IS A HOUSEHOLD STARTED IN CANADA DEDICATED TO MAKING THE AMTGARD ATMOSPHERE SAFE AND WELCOMING FOR ALL PLAYERS. I PROUDLY WEAR A SAFE SPACE BELT FAVOR, WHICH MARKS ME AS SOMEONE TO TALK TO IF A PLAYER IS BEING BULLIED, OR NEEDS HELP WITH A SITUATION.
YOU'RE GOING TO ART SCHOOL? MY EX-GIRLFRIEND WENT TO ART SCHOOL... AND SHE WAS BI.
YOU KNOW WHAT *THAT* MEANS.
Safe Space
HIGH FIVE
HOW I WISH THIS WAS AROUND WHEN I WAS IN HIGH SCHOOL.
AND MOST RECENTLY, HOUSE FIERCE WAS MADE. IT IS A HOUSEHOLD DEDICATED TO PROVIDING A SAFE PLACE FOR LGBT MEMBERS OF AMTGARD AND ALLIES.
THIS HOUSE EXISTING, AND BEING A PART OF IT, HAS HELPED LIFT A HUGE WEIGHT OFF OF ME.
NOTE: THE PHOENIX IS THE SYMBOL OF AMTGARD, AN IMAGE ALMOST HOLY IN THE GAME. IT IS A SYMBOL RESERVED FOR KNIGHTHOOD, BUT THE CIRCLE OF KNIGHTS MADE AN EXCEPTION FOR THE HOUSEHOLD. THE SYMBOLISM MEANS A LOT TO ME.
THE DEMOGRAPHICS OF THE GAME ARE CHANGING, I AM NO LONGER ALONE, AND PEOPLE ARE WILLING TO LISTEN AND ACCOMMODATE. THE BATTLE ISN'T OVER YET. THINGS AREN'T GREAT ACROSS THE BOARD, BUT I THINK THEY'RE HEADING IN THE RIGHT DIRECTION.
PREPARE TO DIE, PUSSIES!
LANGUAGE, MAN.
RIGHT. SORRY.
LAY ON!
AND THAT'S MORE THEN I'VE EVER BEEN ABLE TO SAY ABOUT MY GAME.

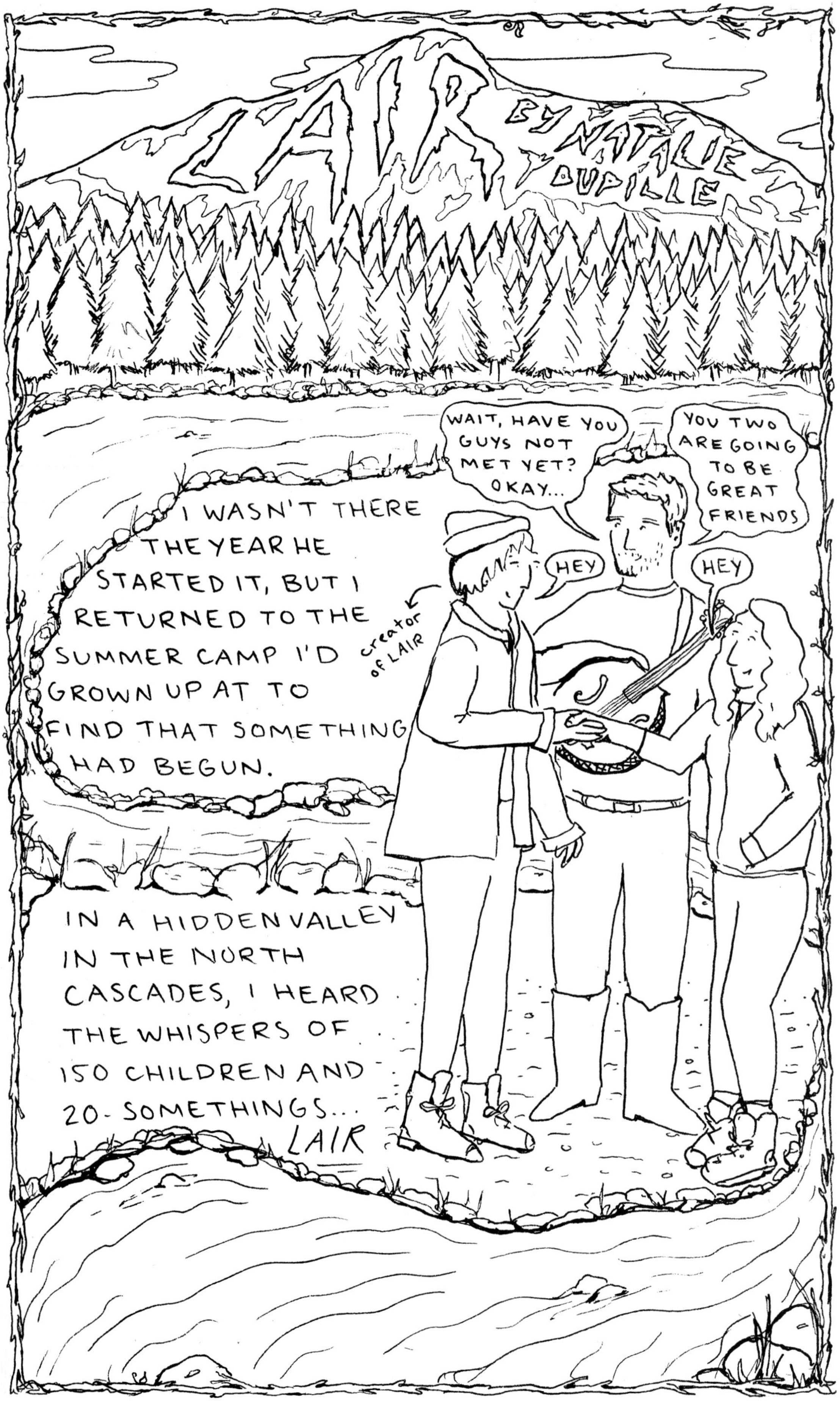
LAIR
BY NATALIE DUPILLE
I WASN'T THERE THE YEAR HE STARTED IT, BUT I RETURNED TO THE SUMMER CAMP I'D GROWN UP AT TO FIND THAT SOMETHING HAD BEGUN.
WAIT, HAVE YOU GUYS NOT MET YET? OKAY...
YOU TWO ARE GOING TO BE GREAT FRIENDS
HEY
HEY
creator of LAIR
IN A HIDDEN VALLEY IN THE NORTH CASCADES, I HEARD THE WHISPERS OF 150 CHILDREN AND 20-SOMETHINGS... LAIR

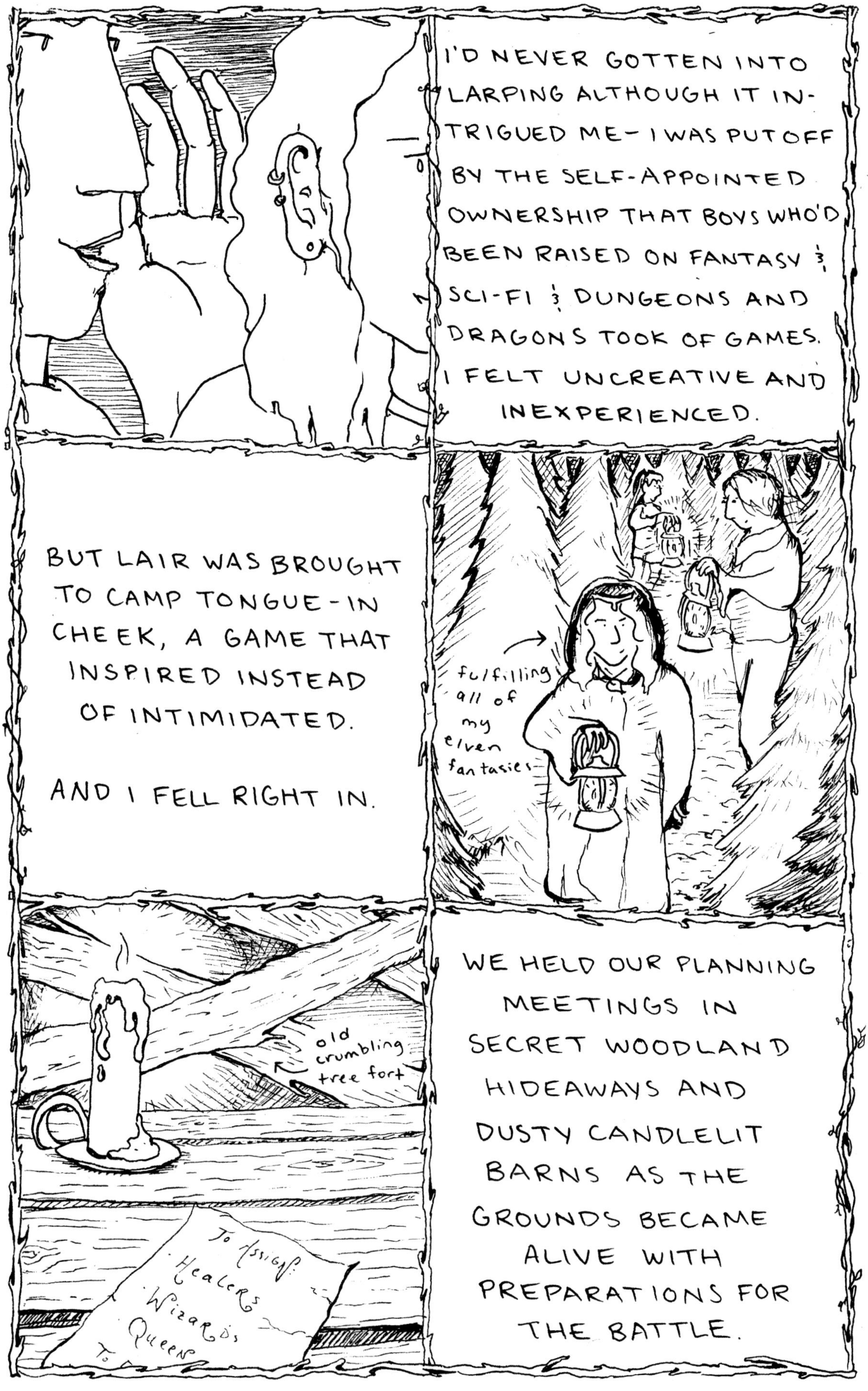
I'D NEVER GOTTEN INTO LARPING ALTHOUGH IT INTRIGUED ME – I WAS PUT OFF BY THE SELF-APPOINTED OWNERSHIP THAT BOYS WHO'D BEEN RAISED ON FANTASY & SCI-FI & DUNGEONS AND DRAGONS TOOK OF GAMES. I FELT UNCREATIVE AND INEXPERIENCED.
BUT LAIR WAS BROUGHT TO CAMP TONGUE-IN CHEEK, A GAME THAT INSPIRED INSTEAD OF INTIMIDATED.
AND I FELL RIGHT IN.
fulfilling all of my elven fantasies
old crumbling tree fort
To Assign:
Healers
Wizards
Queen
WE HELD OUR PLANNING MEETINGS IN SECRET WOODLAND HIDEAWAYS AND DUSTY CANDLELIT BARNS AS THE GROUNDS BECAME ALIVE WITH PREPARATIONS FOR THE BATTLE.

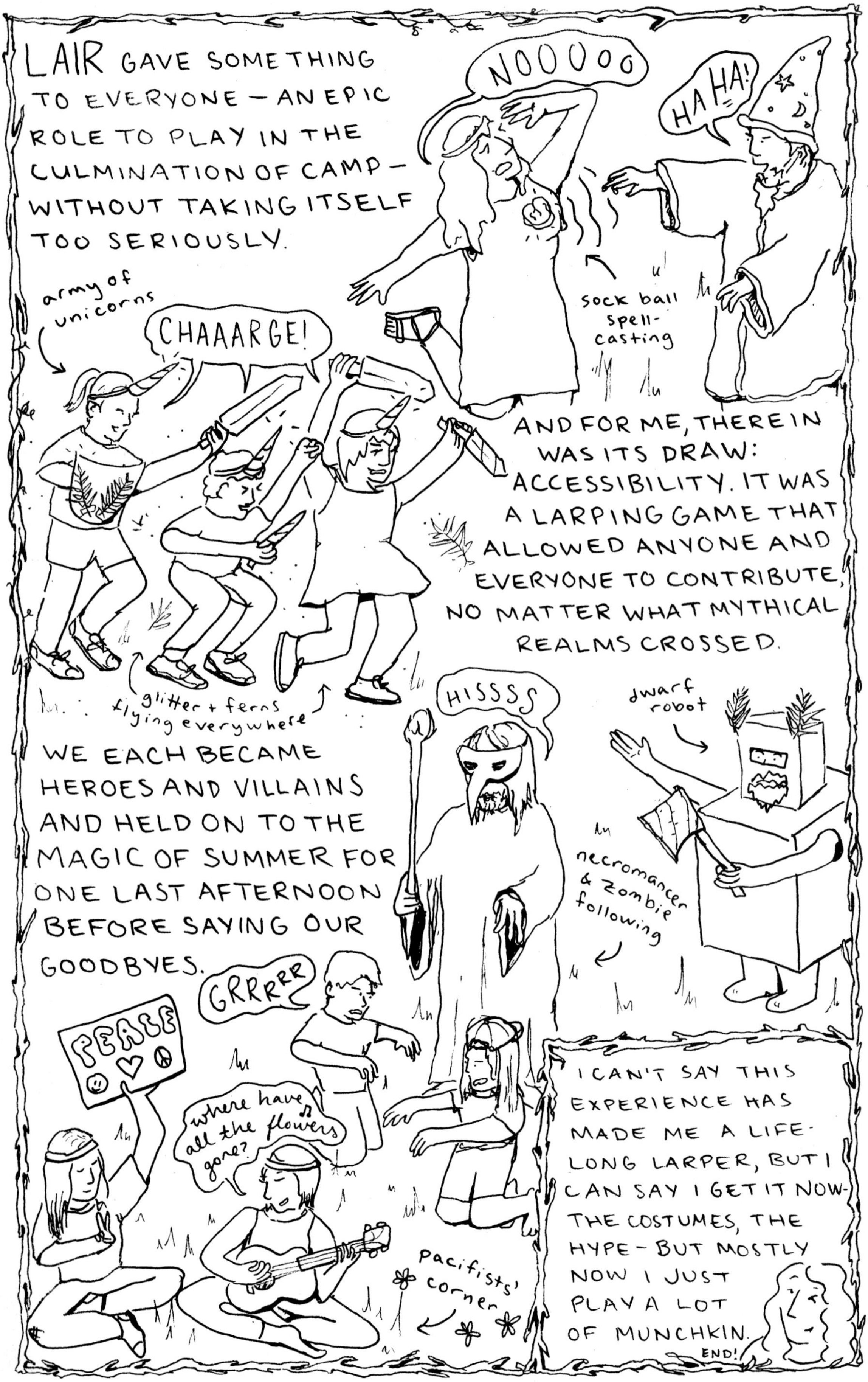
LAIR GAVE SOMETHING TO EVERYONE—AN EPIC ROLE TO PLAY IN THE CULMINATION OF CAMP—WITHOUT TAKING ITSELF TOO SERIOUSLY.
NOOOOO
HAHA!
sock ball spell-casting
army of unicorns
CHAAARGE!
AND FOR ME, THEREIN WAS ITS DRAW: ACCESSIBILITY. IT WAS A LARPING GAME THAT ALLOWED ANYONE AND EVERYONE TO CONTRIBUTE, NO MATTER WHAT MYTHICAL REALMS CROSSED.
glitter + ferns flying everywhere
HISSSS
dwarf robot
WE EACH BECAME HEROES AND VILLAINS AND HELD ON TO THE MAGIC OF SUMMER FOR ONE LAST AFTERNOON BEFORE SAYING OUR GOODBYES.
necromancer & zombie following
GRRRRR
PEACE
where have all the flowers gone?
pacifists' corner
I CAN'T SAY THIS EXPERIENCE HAS MADE ME A LIFE-LONG LARPER, BUT I CAN SAY I GET IT NOW—THE COSTUMES, THE HYPE—BUT MOSTLY NOW I JUST PLAY A LOT OF MUNCHKIN.
END!

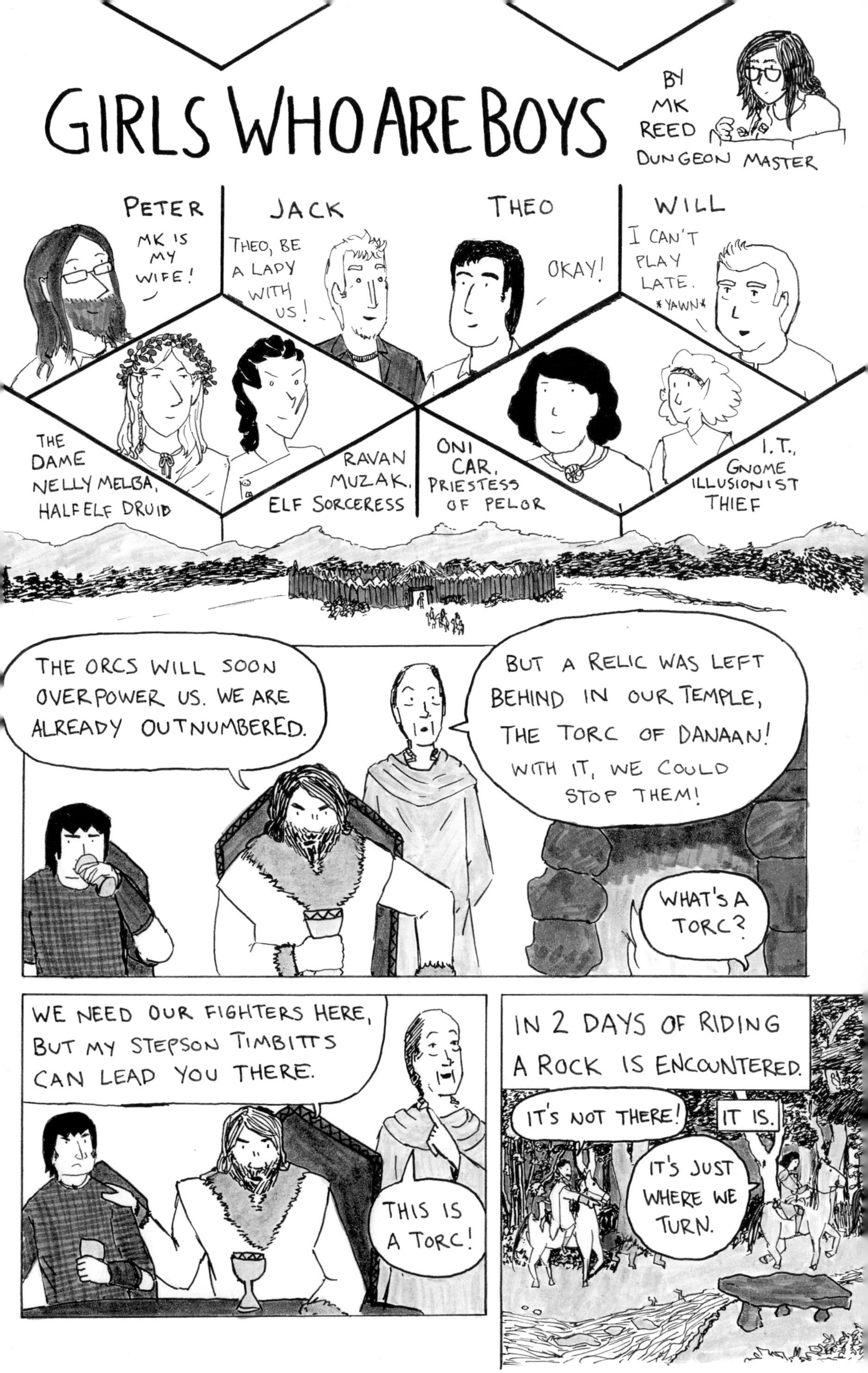
GIRLS WHO ARE BOYS
BY MK REED
DUNGEON MASTER
PETER
MK IS MY WIFE!
JACK
THEO, BE A LADY WITH US!
THEO
OKAY!
WILL
I CAN'T PLAY LATE.
YAWN
THE DAME NELLY MELBA, HALFELF DRUID
RAVAN MUZAK, ELF SORCERESS
ONI CAR, PRIESTESS OF PELOR
I.T., GNOME ILLUSIONIST THIEF
THE ORCS WILL SOON OVERPOWER US. WE ARE ALREADY OUTNUMBERED.
BUT A RELIC WAS LEFT BEHIND IN OUR TEMPLE, THE TORC OF DANAAN! WITH IT, WE COULD STOP THEM!
WHAT'S A TORC?
WE NEED OUR FIGHTERS HERE, BUT MY STEPSON TIMBITTS CAN LEAD YOU THERE.
THIS IS A TORC!
IN 2 DAYS OF RIDING A ROCK IS ENCOUNTERED.
IT'S NOT THERE!
IT IS.
IT'S JUST WHERE WE TURN.

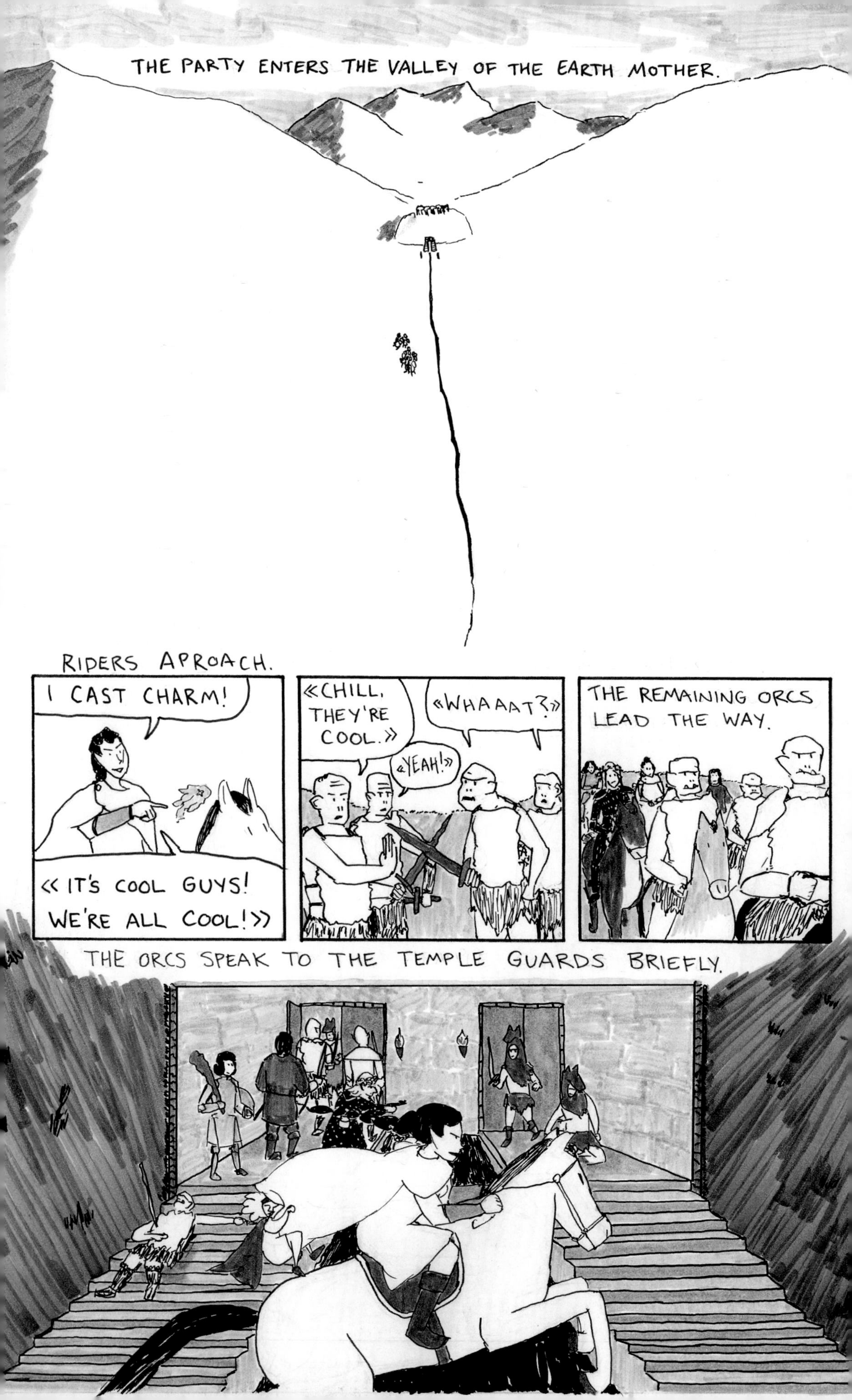
THE PARTY ENTERS THE VALLEY OF THE EARTH MOTHER.
RIDERS APROACH.
I CAST CHARM!
«IT'S COOL GUYS! WE'RE ALL COOL!»
«CHILL, THEY'RE COOL.»
«YEAH!»
«WHAAAT?»
THE REMAINING ORCS LEAD THE WAY.
THE ORCS SPEAK TO THE TEMPLE GUARDS BRIEFLY.

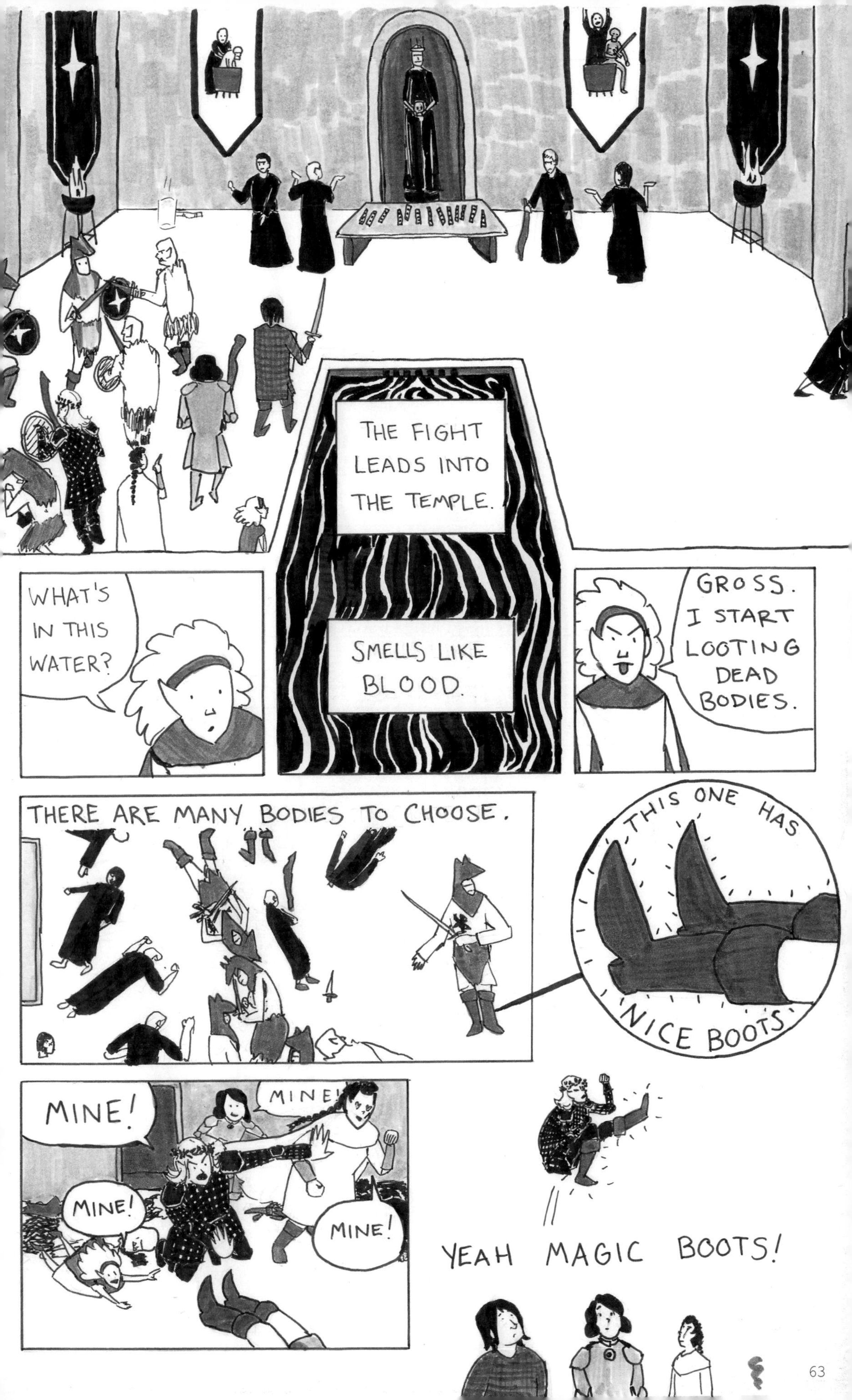
THE FIGHT LEADS INTO THE TEMPLE.
WHAT'S IN THIS WATER?
SMELLS LIKE BLOOD.
GROSS. I START LOOTING DEAD BODIES.
THERE ARE MANY BODIES TO CHOOSE.
THIS ONE HAS NICE BOOTS
MINE!
MINE!
MINE!
MINE!
YEAH MAGIC BOOTS!

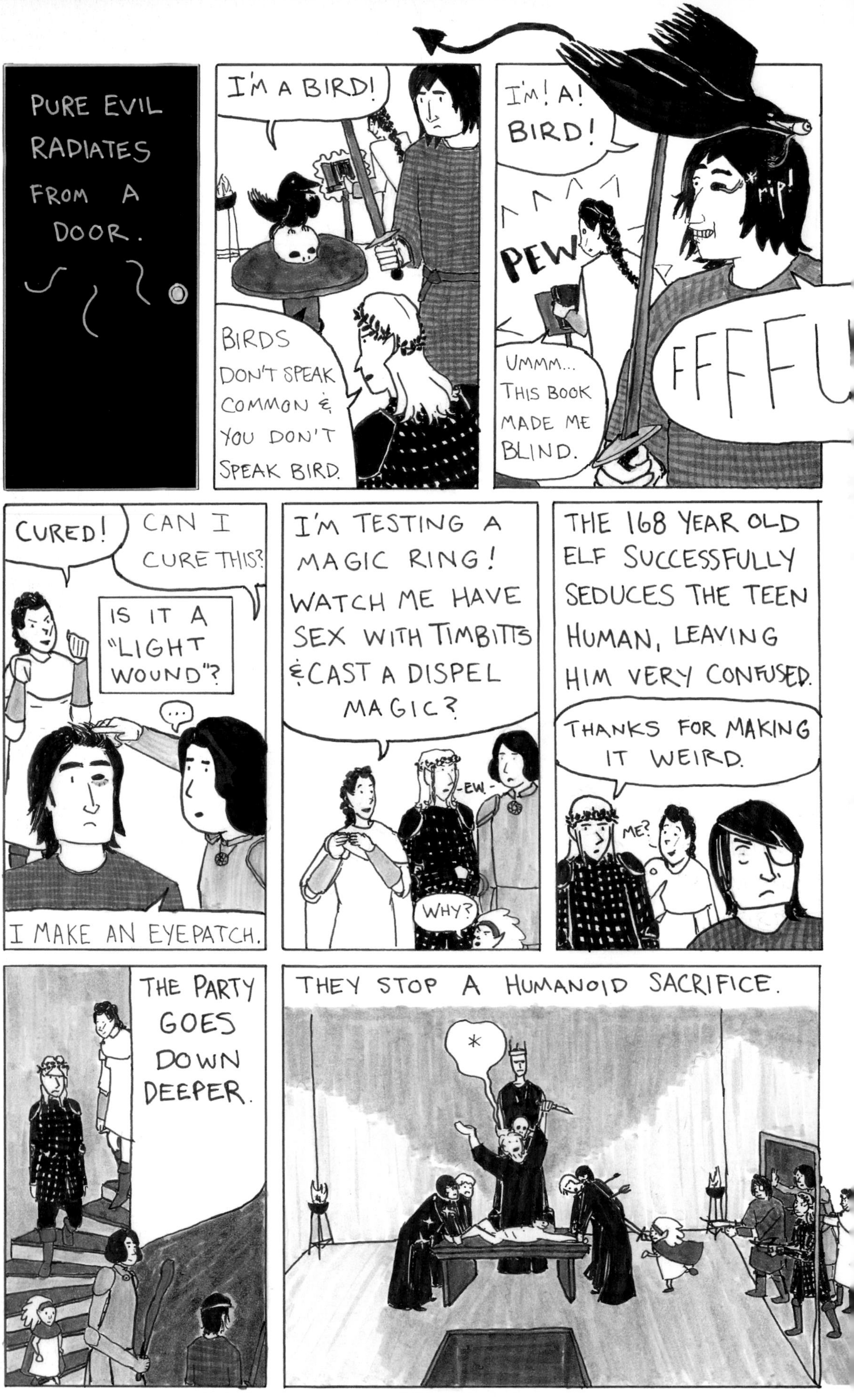
PURE EVIL RADIATES FROM A DOOR.
I'M A BIRD!
BIRDS DON'T SPEAK COMMON & YOU DON'T SPEAK BIRD.
I'M! A! BIRD!
PEW
UMMM... THIS BOOK MADE ME BLIND.
*rip!
FFFFU
CURED!
CAN I CURE THIS?
IS IT A "LIGHT WOUND"?
...
I MAKE AN EYEPATCH.
I'M TESTING A MAGIC RING! WATCH ME HAVE SEX WITH TIMBITTS & CAST A DISPEL MAGIC?
-EW!-
WHY?
THE 168 YEAR OLD ELF SUCCESSFULLY SEDUCES THE TEEN HUMAN, LEAVING HIM VERY CONFUSED.
THANKS FOR MAKING IT WEIRD.
ME?
THE PARTY GOES DOWN DEEPER.
THEY STOP A HUMANOID SACRIFICE.
*

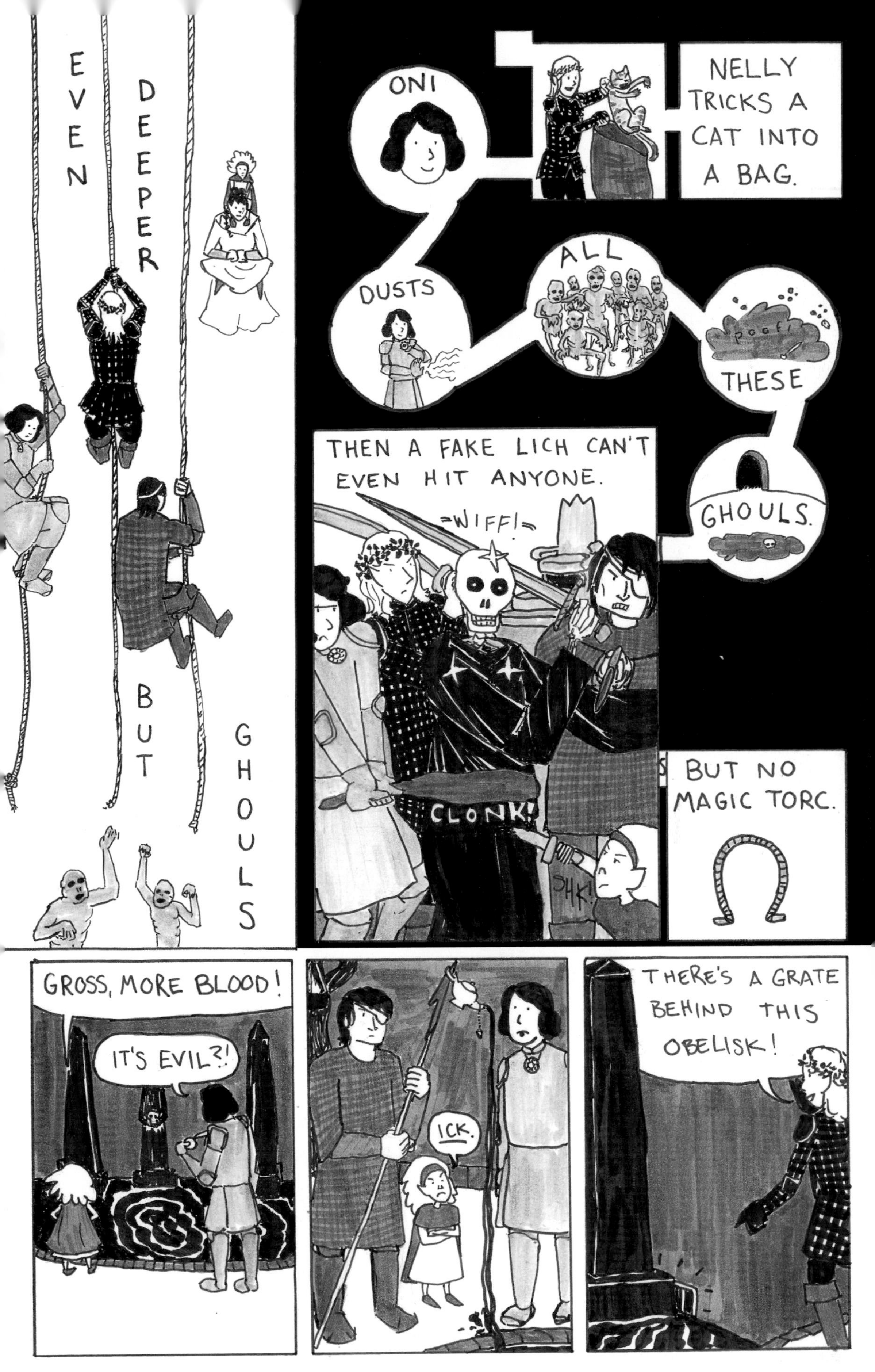

EVEN DEEPER
BUT GHOULS
NELLY TRICKS A CAT INTO A BAG.
ONI
DUSTS
ALL
POOF!
THESE
GHOULS.
THEN A FAKE LICH CAN'T EVEN HIT ANYONE.
=WIFF!=
CLONK!
SHK!
BUT NO MAGIC TORC.
GROSS, MORE BLOOD!
IT'S EVIL?!
ICK.
THERE'S A GRATE BEHIND THIS OBELISK!

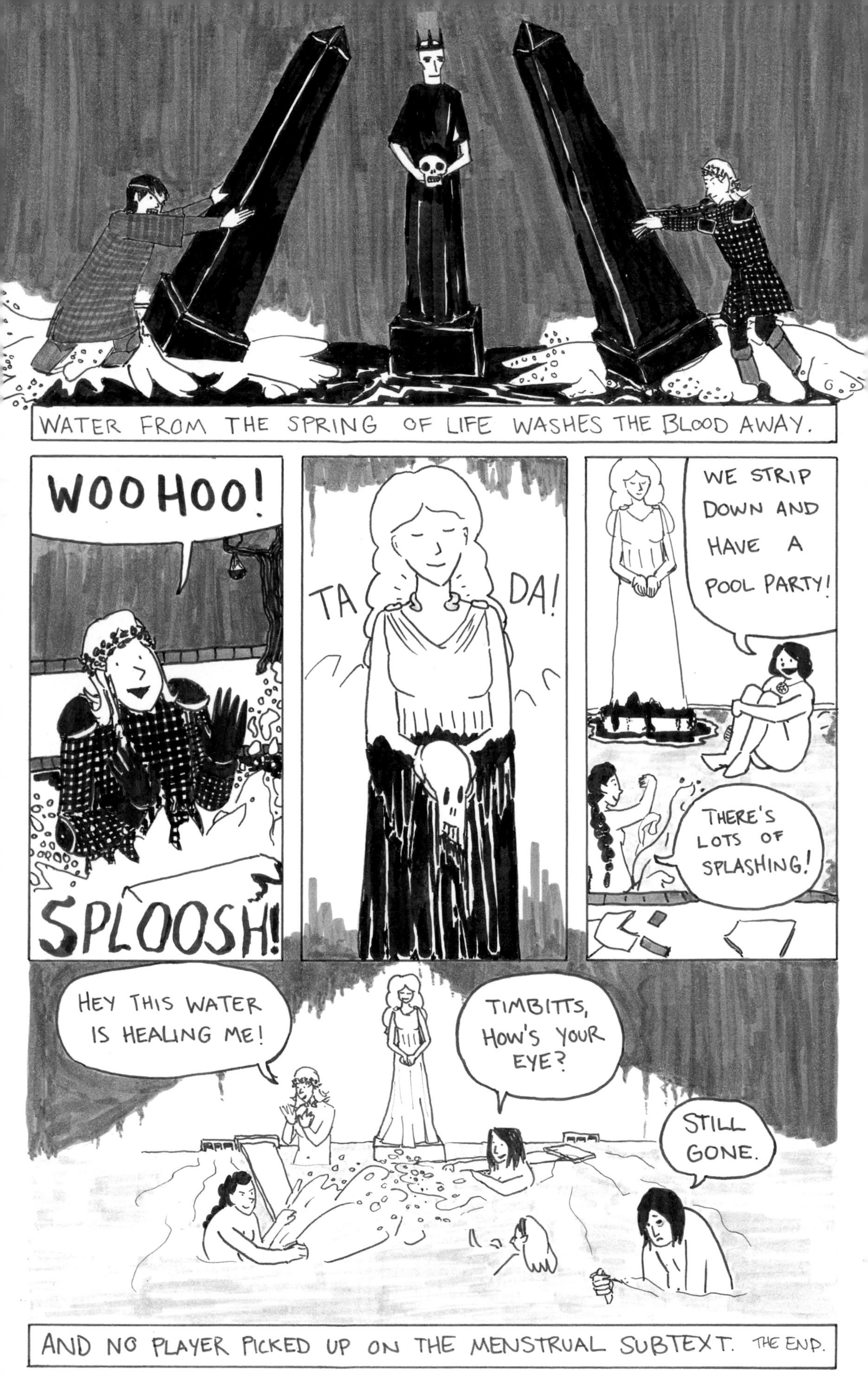
WATER FROM THE SPRING OF LIFE WASHES THE BLOOD AWAY.
WOOHOO!
SPLOOSH!
TA DA!
WE STRIP DOWN AND HAVE A POOL PARTY!
THERE'S LOTS OF SPLASHING!
HEY THIS WATER IS HEALING ME!
TIMBITTS, HOW'S YOUR EYE?
STILL GONE.
AND NO PLAYER PICKED UP ON THE MENSTRUAL SUBTEXT. THE END.

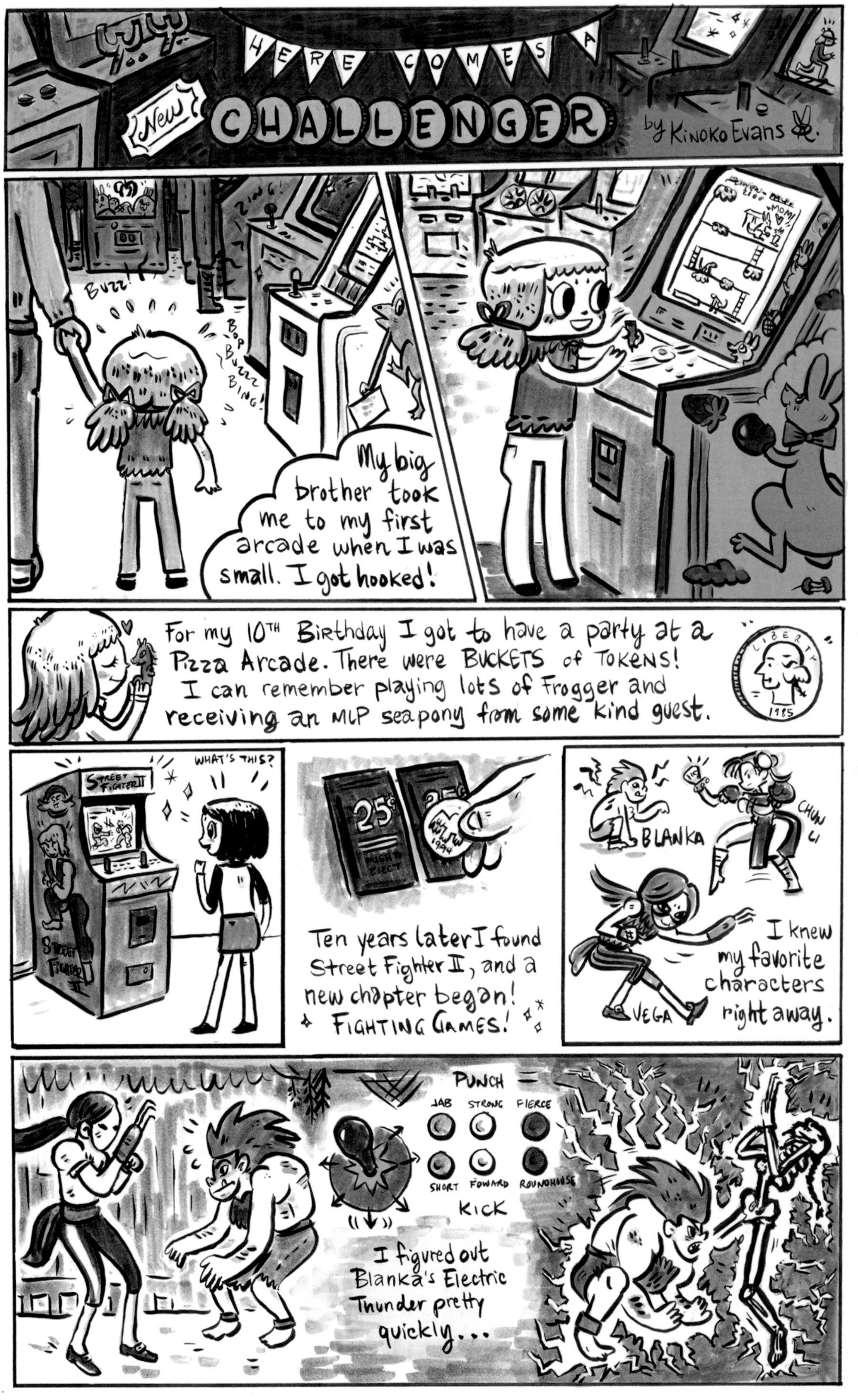
HERE COMES A
New
CHALLENGER
by Kinoko Evans
ZING!
BUZZ!
BOOP BUZZZ BING!
My big brother took me to my first arcade when I was small. I got hooked!
MOM!
For my 10TH Birthday I got to have a party at a Pizza Arcade. There were BUCKETS of TOKENS! I can remember playing lots of Frogger and receiving an MLP seapony from some kind guest.
LIBERTY
1985
STREET FIGHTER II
WHAT'S THIS?
STREET FIGHTER II
25¢
PUSH TO EJECT
1994
Ten years later I found Street Fighter II, and a new chapter began! FIGHTING GAMES!
BLANKA
CHUN LI
VEGA
I knew my favorite characters right away.
PUNCH
JAB
STRONG
FIERCE
SHORT
FOWARD
ROUNDHOUSE
KICK
I figured out Blanka's Electric Thunder pretty quickly...

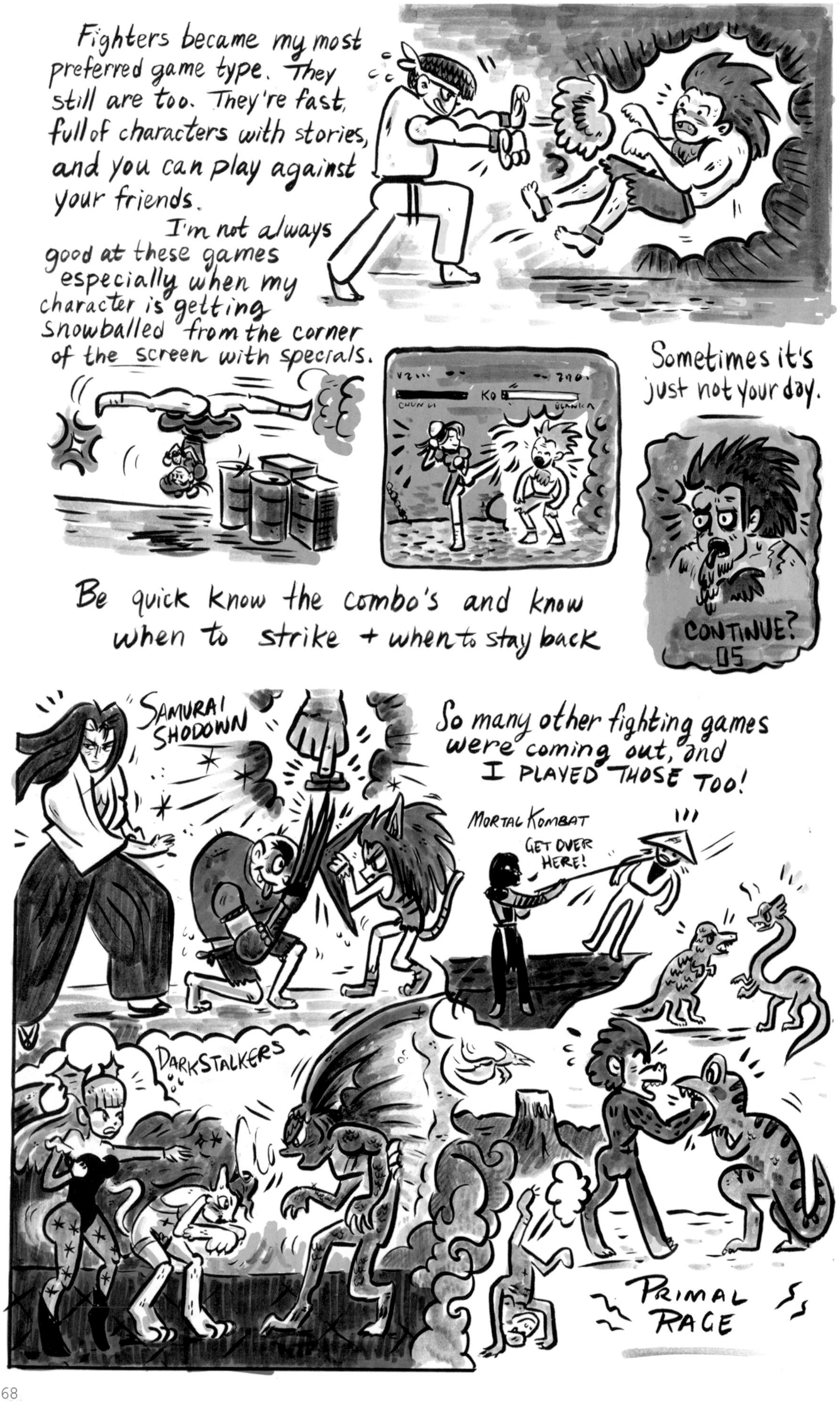
Fighters became my most preferred game type. They still are too. They're fast, full of characters with stories, and you can play against your friends.
I'm not always good at these games especially when my character is getting snowballed from the corner of the screen with specials.
KO
CHUN LI
BLANKA
Sometimes it's just not your day.
CONTINUE?
05
Be quick know the combo's and know when to strike + when to stay back
SAMURAI SHODOWN
So many other fighting games were coming out, and I PLAYED THOSE TOO!
MORTAL KOMBAT
GET OVER HERE!
DARKSTALKERS
PRIMAL RAGE

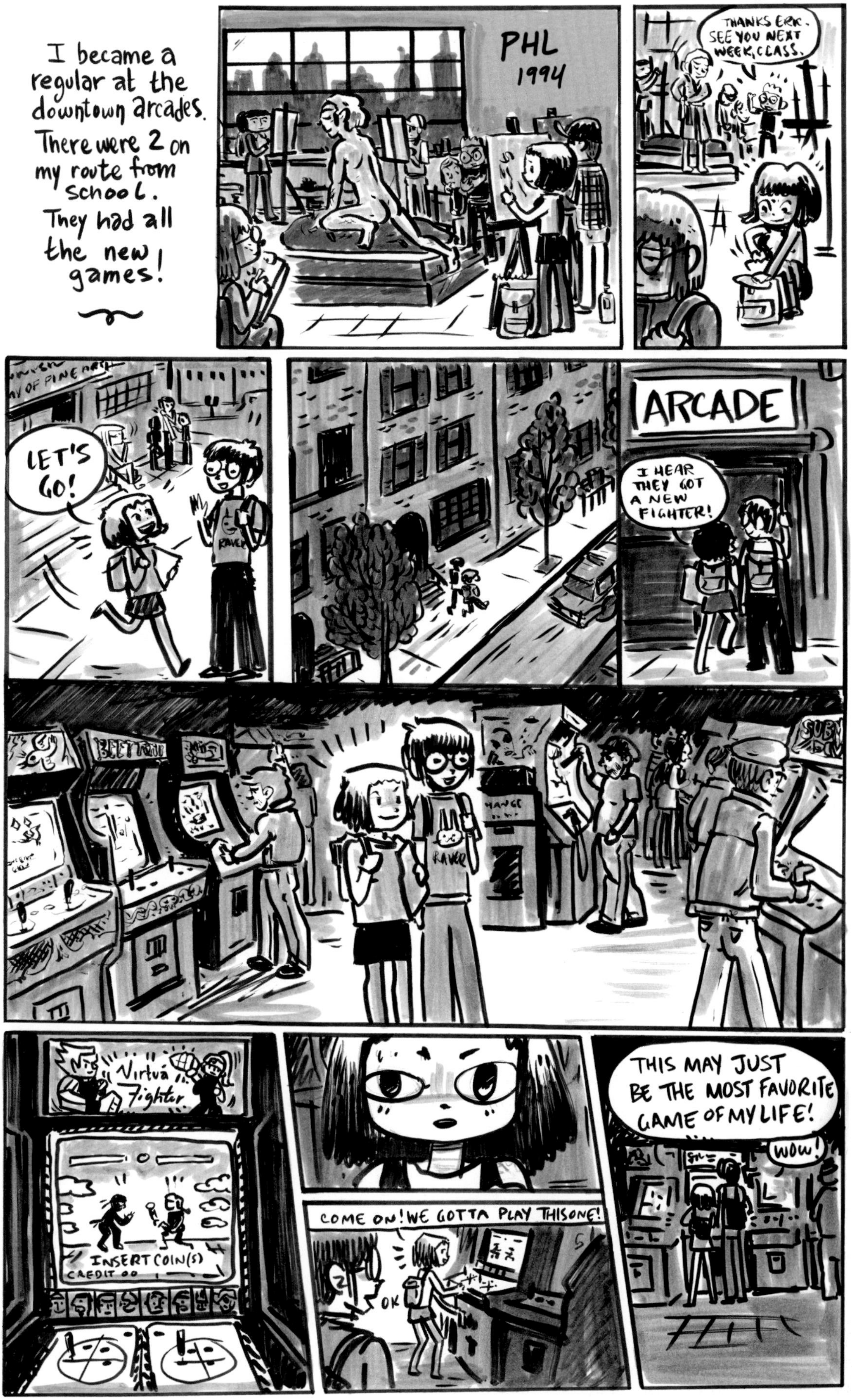
I became a regular at the downtown arcades. There were 2 on my route from school. They had all the new games!
PHL 1994
THANKS ERIC. SEE YOU NEXT WEEK, CLASS.
LET'S GO!
RAVER
I HEAR THEY GOT A NEW FIGHTER!
ARCADE
RAVER
Virtua Fighter
INSERT COIN(S)
COME ON! WE GOTTA PLAY THIS ONE!
OK
THIS MAY JUST BE THE MOST FAVORITE GAME OF MY LIFE!
WOW!

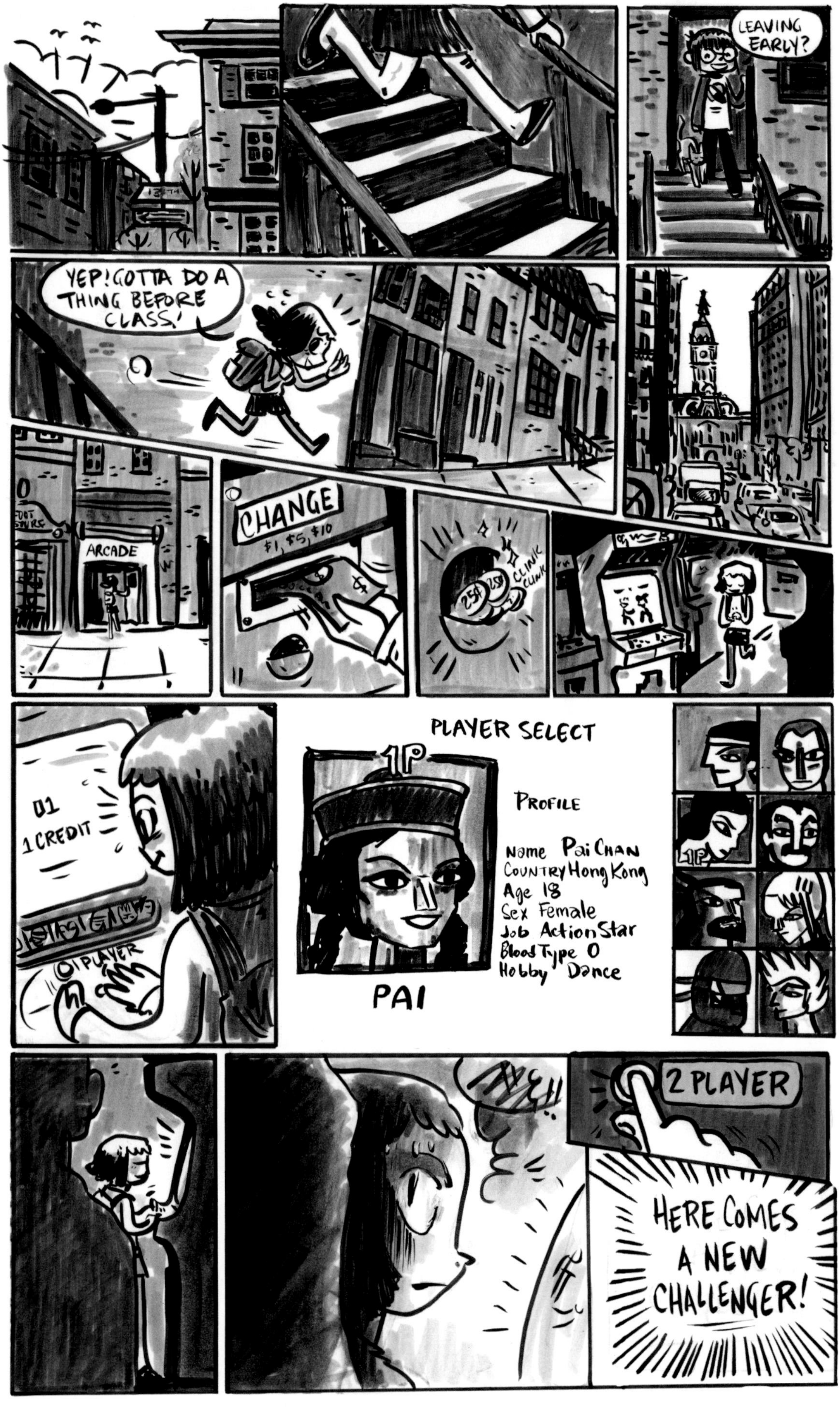
13TH
LEAVING EARLY?
YEP! GOTTA DO A THING BEFORE CLASS!
ARCADE
CHANGE
$1, $5, $10
25¢
25¢
CLINK
CLINK
01
1 CREDIT
1 PLAYER
PLAYER SELECT
1P
PAI
PROFILE
Name Pai Chan
Country Hong Kong
Age 18
Sex Female
Job Action Star
Blood Type O
Hobby Dance
1P
2 PLAYER
HERE COMES A NEW CHALLENGER!

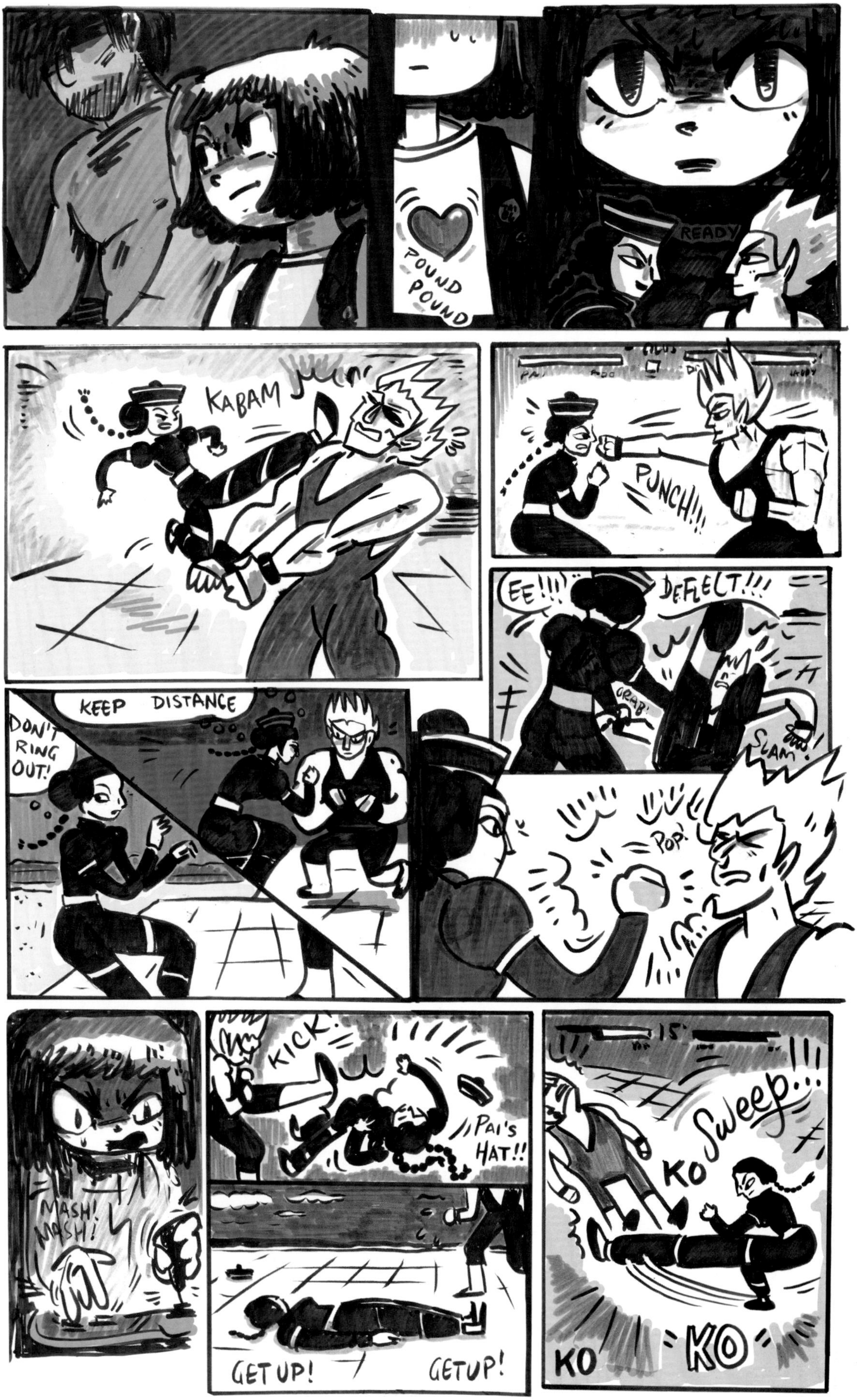

POUND
POUND
READY
KABAM
PUNCH!!!
EE!!!
DEFLECT!!!
GRAB!
SLAM!
KEEP DISTANCE
DON'T RING OUT!
POP!
MASH! MASH!
KICK!
PAI'S HAT!!
GET UP!
GETUP!
15
Sweep...
KO
KO
KO

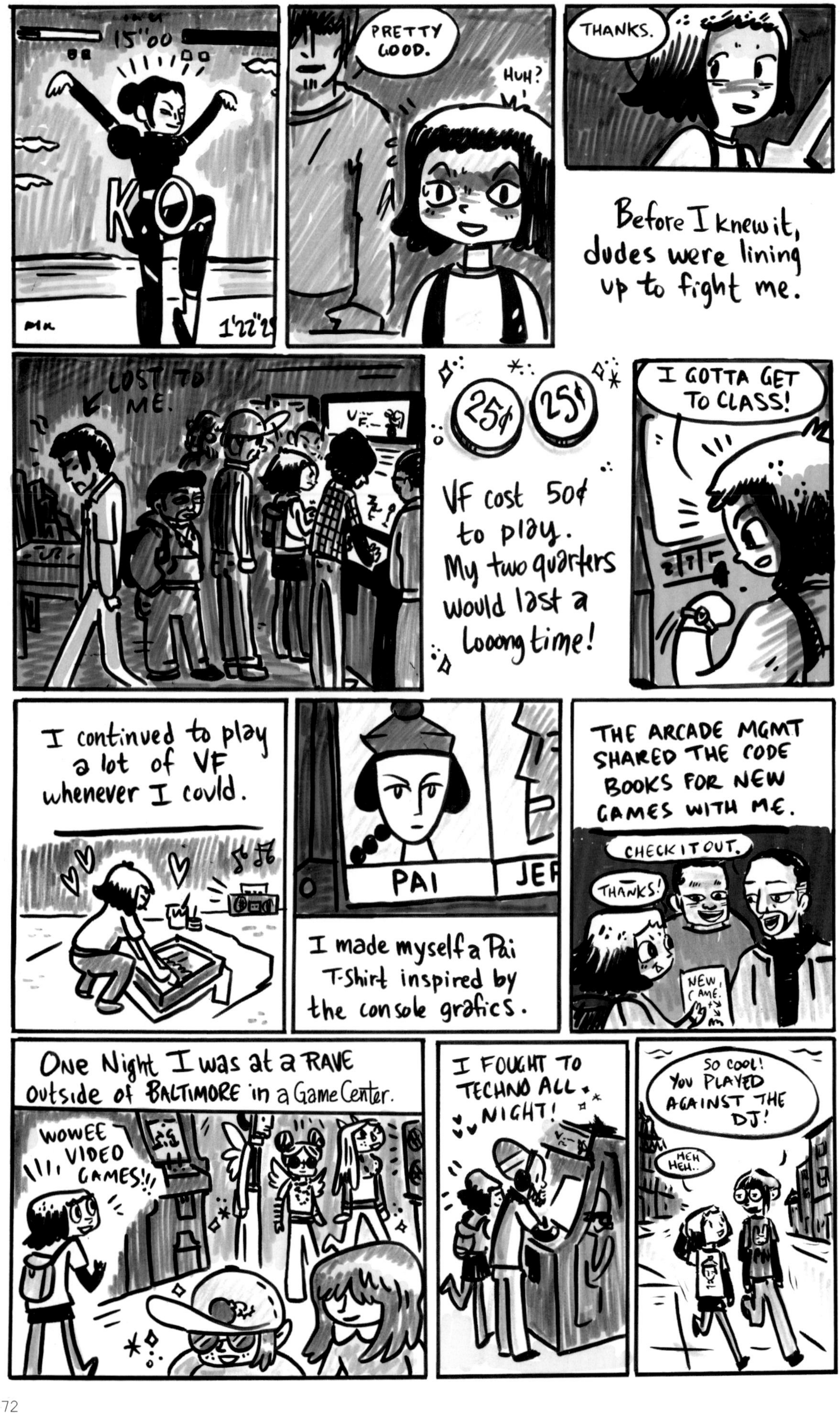
15"00
KO
1'22"29
PRETTY GOOD.
HUH?
THANKS.
Before I knew it, dudes were lining up to fight me.
LOST TO ME.
25¢
25¢
VF cost 50¢ to play. My two quarters would last a looong time!
I GOTTA GET TO CLASS!
I continued to play a lot of VF whenever I could.
PAI
I made myself a Pai T-Shirt inspired by the console grafics.
THE ARCADE MGMT SHARED THE CODE BOOKS FOR NEW GAMES WITH ME.
CHECK IT OUT.
THANKS!
NEW GAME.
One Night I was at a RAVE outside of BALTIMORE in a Game Center.
WOWEE VIDEO GAMES!!
I FOUGHT TO TECHNO ALL NIGHT!
SO COOL! YOU PLAYED AGAINST THE DJ!
HEH HEH..

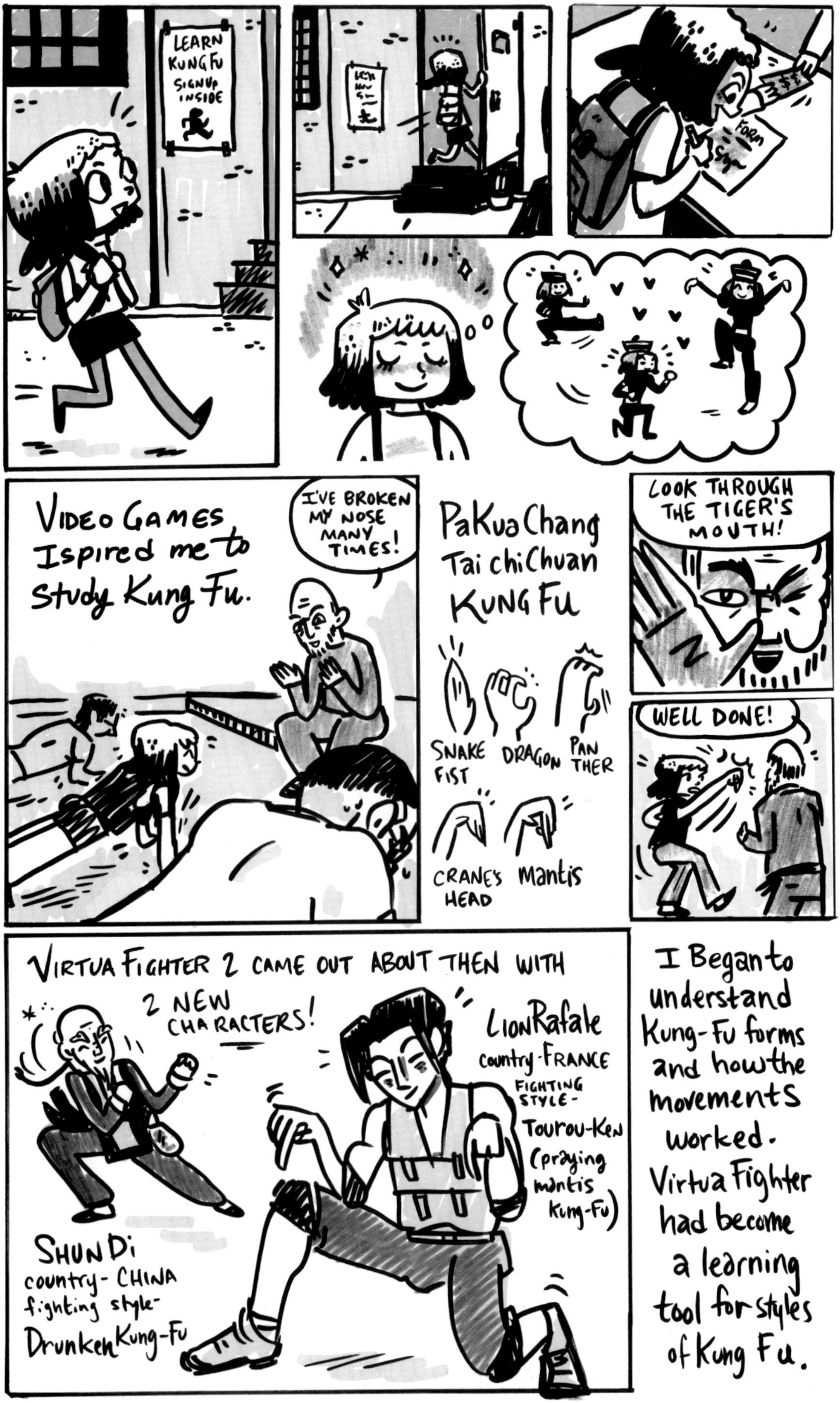
LEARN KUNG FU SIGNUP INSIDE
FORM
Sign
VIDEO GAMES Ispired me to study Kung Fu.
I'VE BROKEN MY NOSE MANY TIMES!
PaKua Chang
Tai chi Chuan
KUNG FU
SNAKE FIST
DRAGON
PAN THER
CRANE'S HEAD
Mantis
LOOK THROUGH THE TIGER'S MOUTH!
WELL DONE!
VIRTUA FIGHTER 2 CAME OUT ABOUT THEN WITH
2 NEW CHARACTERS!
Lion Rafale
country - FRANCE
FIGHTING STYLE -
Tourou-Ken (praying mantis Kung-Fu)
SHUN Di
country - CHINA
fighting style -
Drunken Kung-Fu
I Began to understand Kung-Fu forms and how the movements worked. Virtua Fighter had become a learning tool for styles of Kung Fu.

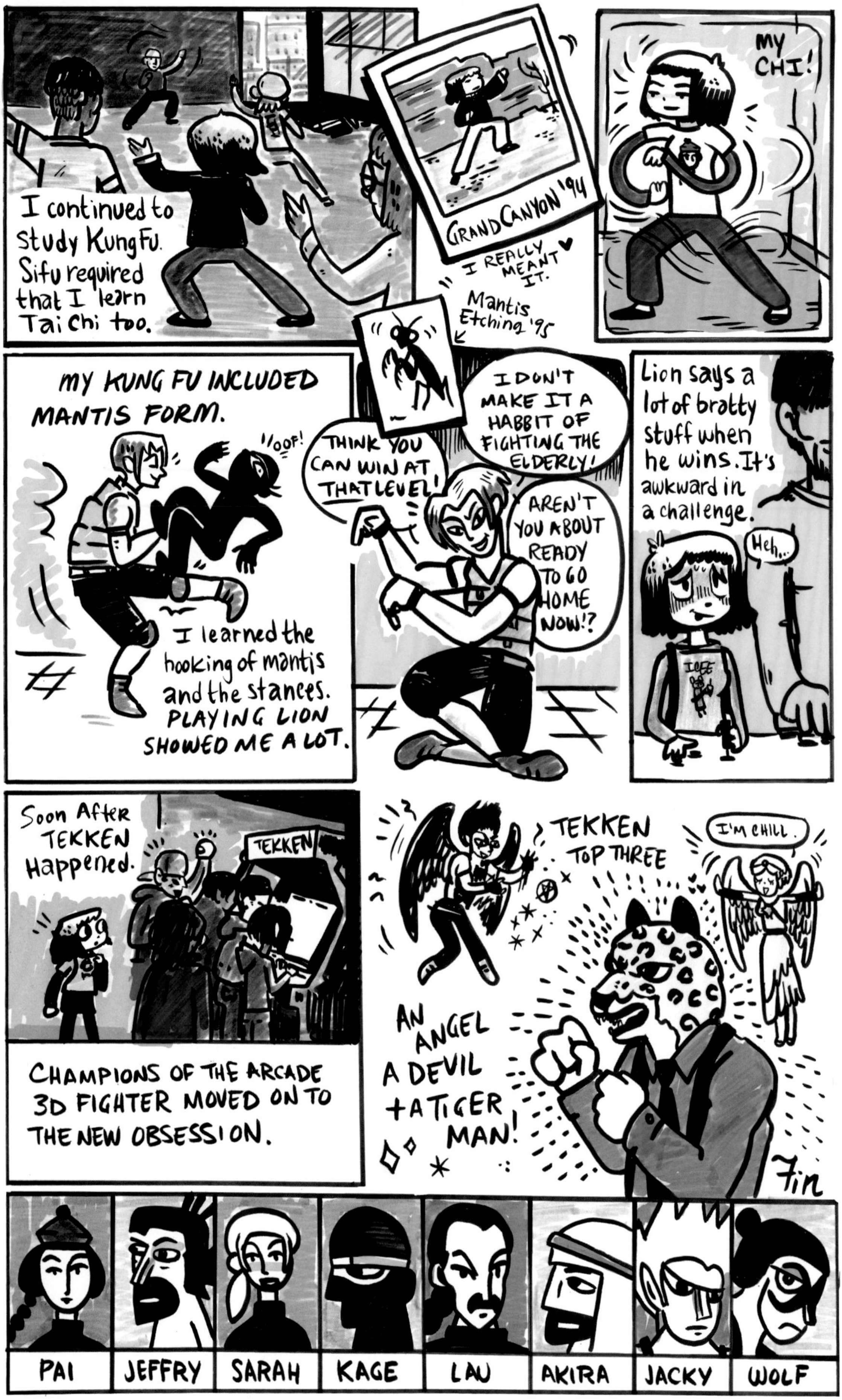
I continued to study Kung Fu. Sifu required that I learn Tai Chi too.
GRAND CANYON '94
I REALLY MEANT IT. ♥
MY CHI!
Mantis Etching '95
MY KUNG FU INCLUDED MANTIS FORM.
OOF!
I learned the hooking of mantis and the stances. PLAYING LION SHOWED ME A LOT.
THINK YOU CAN WIN AT THAT LEVEL!
I DON'T MAKE IT A HABBIT OF FIGHTING THE ELDERLY!
AREN'T YOU ABOUT READY TO GO HOME NOW!?
Lion says a lot of bratty stuff when he wins. It's awkward in a challenge.
Heh...
Soon After TEKKEN Happened.
TEKKEN
CHAMPIONS OF THE ARCADE 3D FIGHTER MOVED ON TO THE NEW OBSESSION.
TEKKEN TOP THREE
I'M CHILL.
AN ANGEL A DEVIL + A TIGER MAN!
Fin
PAI
JEFFRY
SARAH
KAGE
LAU
AKIRA
JACKY
WOLF

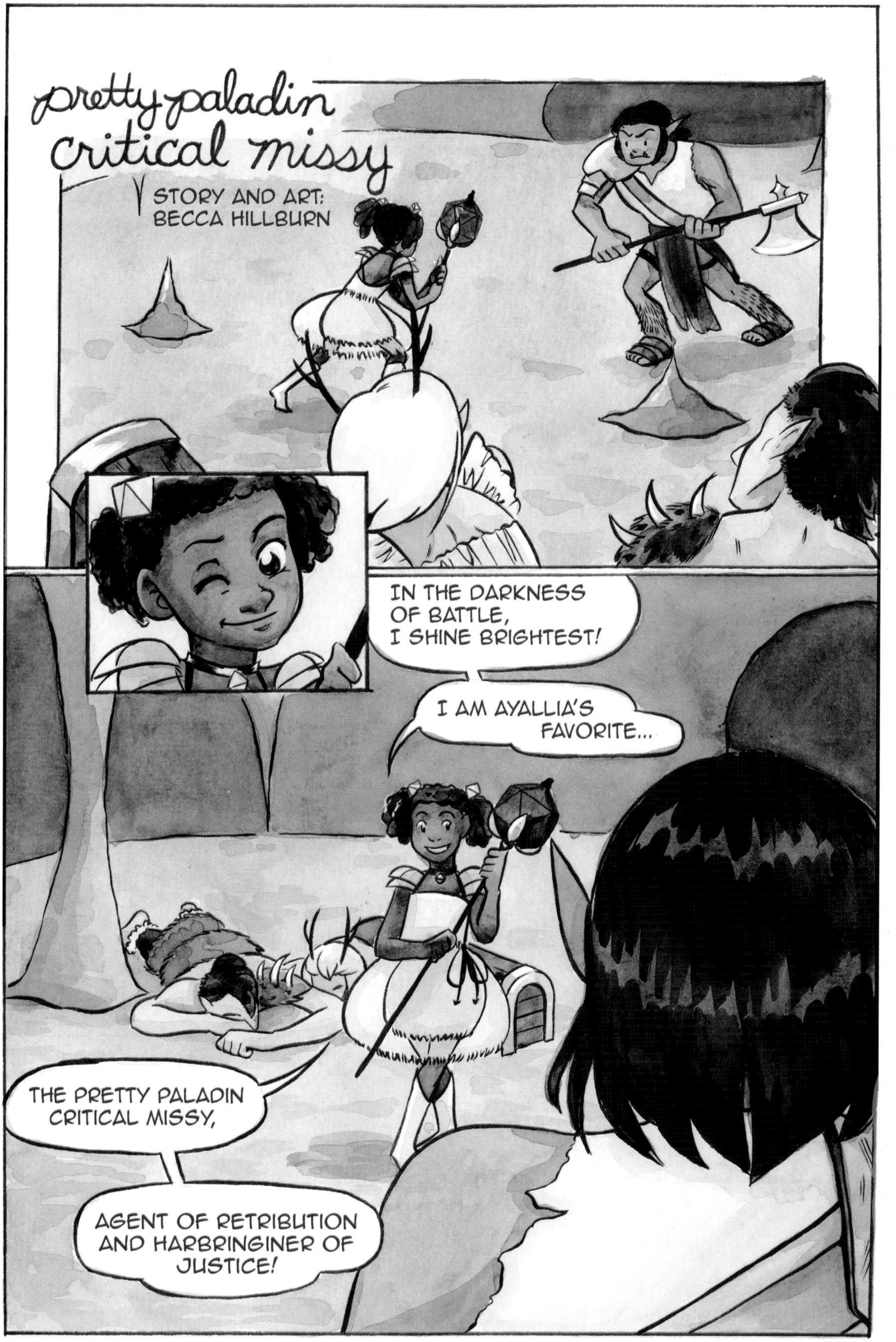
pretty paladin critical missy
STORY AND ART: BECCA HILLBURN
IN THE DARKNESS OF BATTLE, I SHINE BRIGHTEST!
I AM AYALLIA'S FAVORITE...
THE PRETTY PALADIN CRITICAL MISSY,
AGENT OF RETRIBUTION AND HARBRINGINER OF JUSTICE!

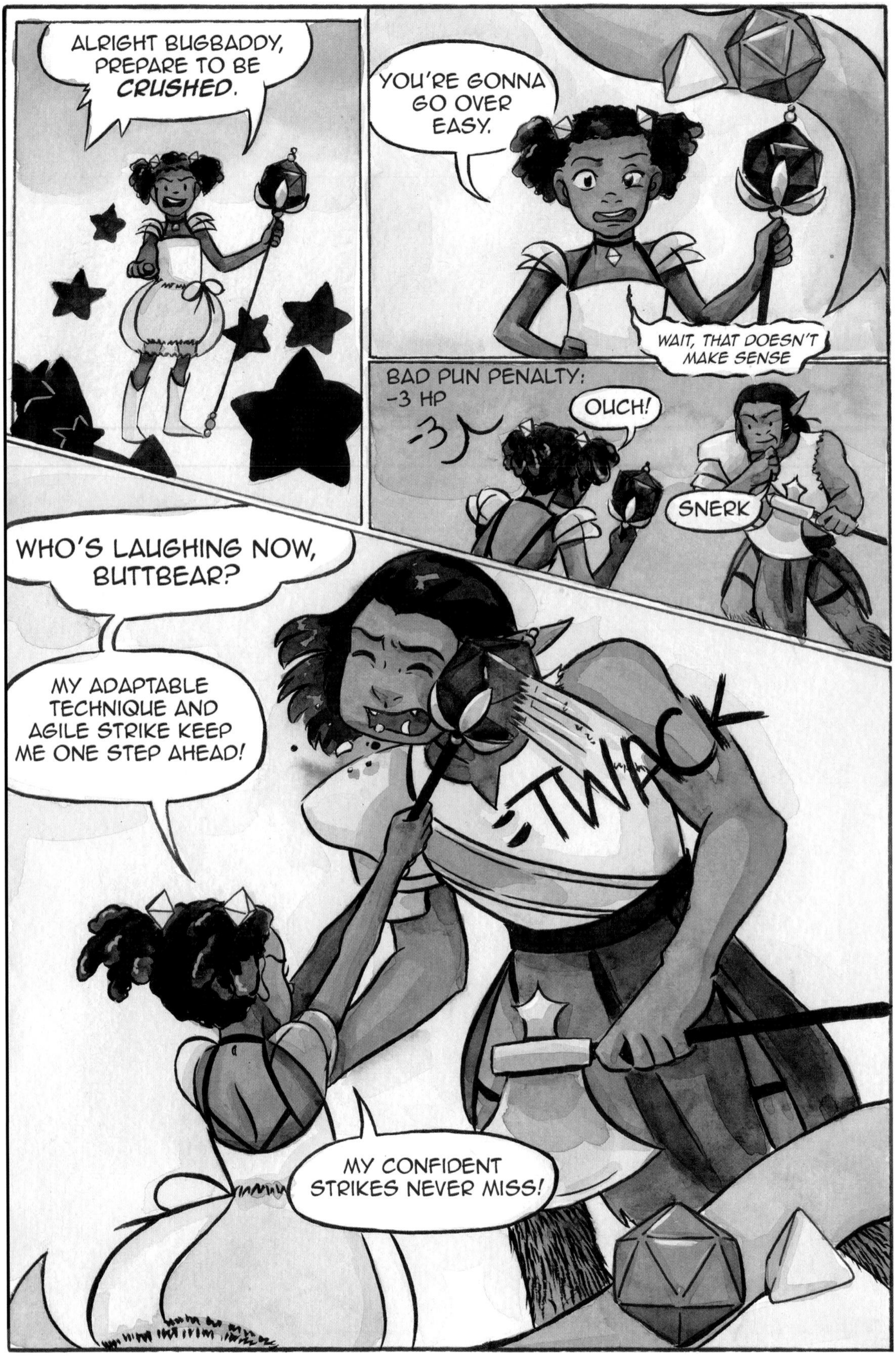
ALRIGHT BUGBADDY, PREPARE TO BE CRUSHED.
YOU'RE GONNA GO OVER EASY.
WAIT, THAT DOESN'T MAKE SENSE
BAD PUN PENALTY: -3 HP
OUCH!
SNERK
WHO'S LAUGHING NOW, BUTTBEAR?
MY ADAPTABLE TECHNIQUE AND AGILE STRIKE KEEP ME ONE STEP AHEAD!
TWACK
MY CONFIDENT STRIKES NEVER MISS!

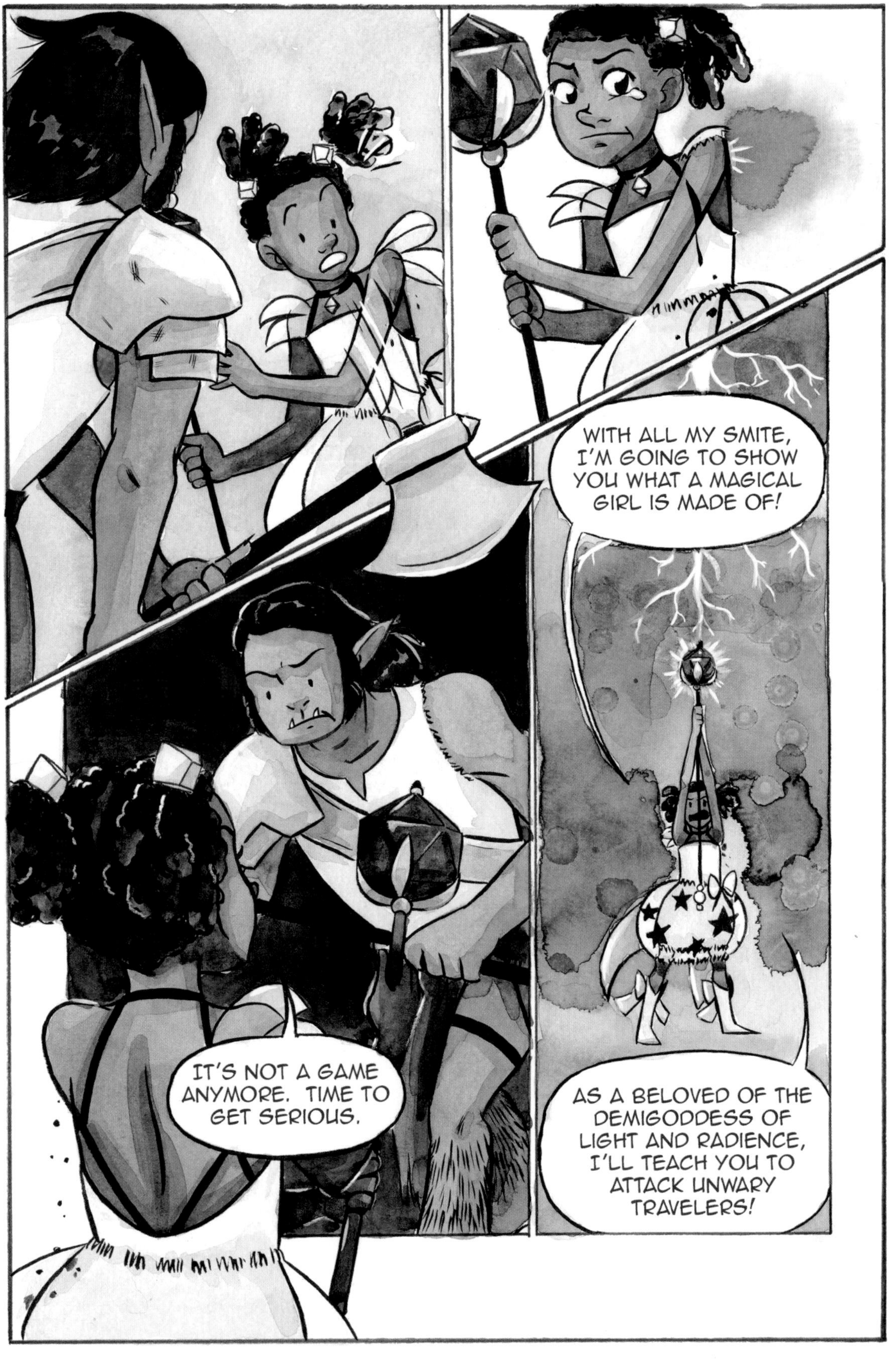
WITH ALL MY SMITE, I'M GOING TO SHOW YOU WHAT A MAGICAL GIRL IS MADE OF!
IT'S NOT A GAME ANYMORE. TIME TO GET SERIOUS.
AS A BELOVED OF THE DEMIGODDESS OF LIGHT AND RADIENCE, I'LL TEACH YOU TO ATTACK UNWARY TRAVELERS!

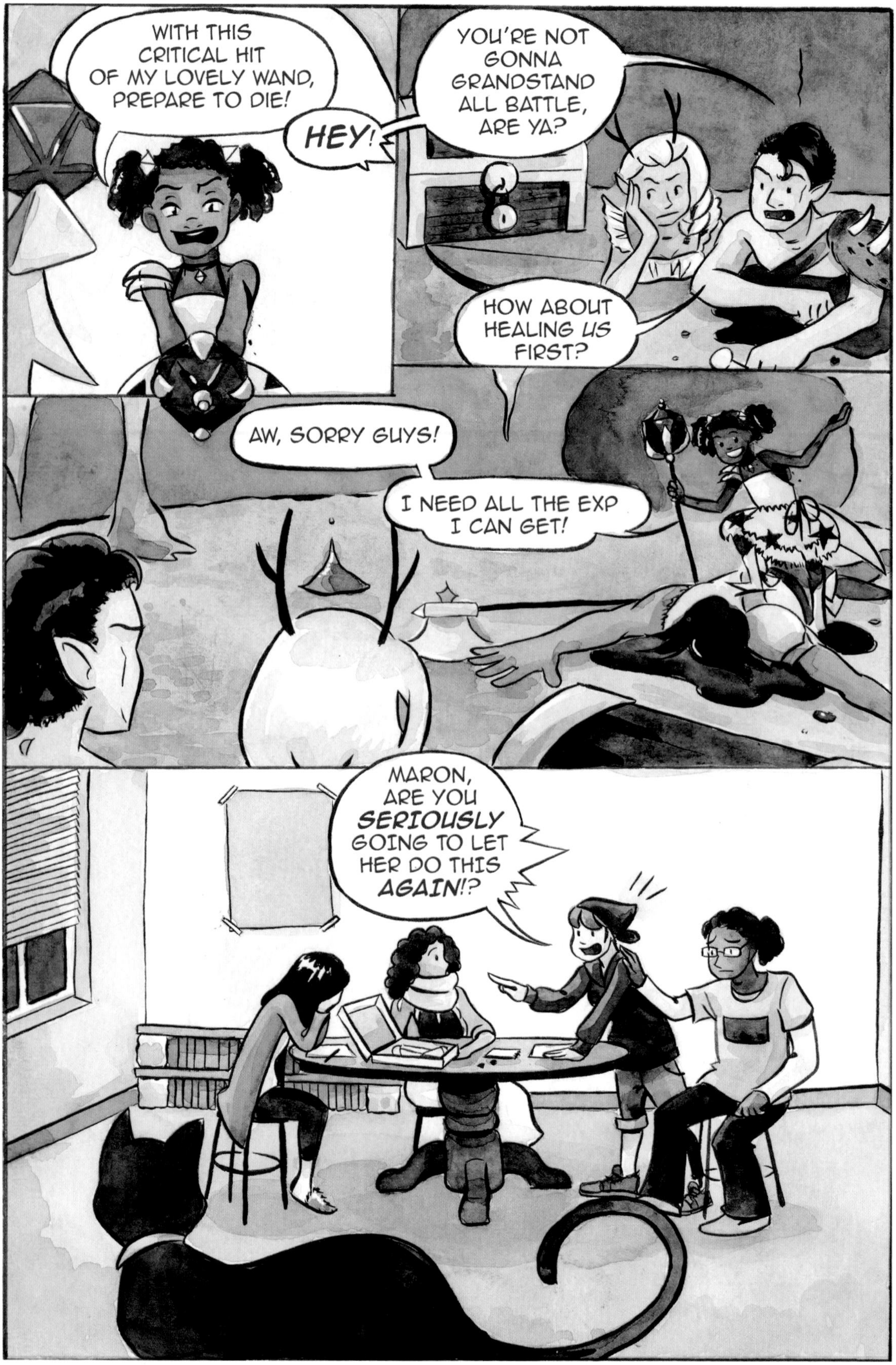
WITH THIS CRITICAL HIT OF MY LOVELY WAND, PREPARE TO DIE!
HEY!
YOU'RE NOT GONNA GRANDSTAND ALL BATTLE, ARE YA?
HOW ABOUT HEALING US FIRST?
AW, SORRY GUYS!
I NEED ALL THE EXP I CAN GET!
MARON, ARE YOU SERIOUSLY GOING TO LET HER DO THIS AGAIN!?

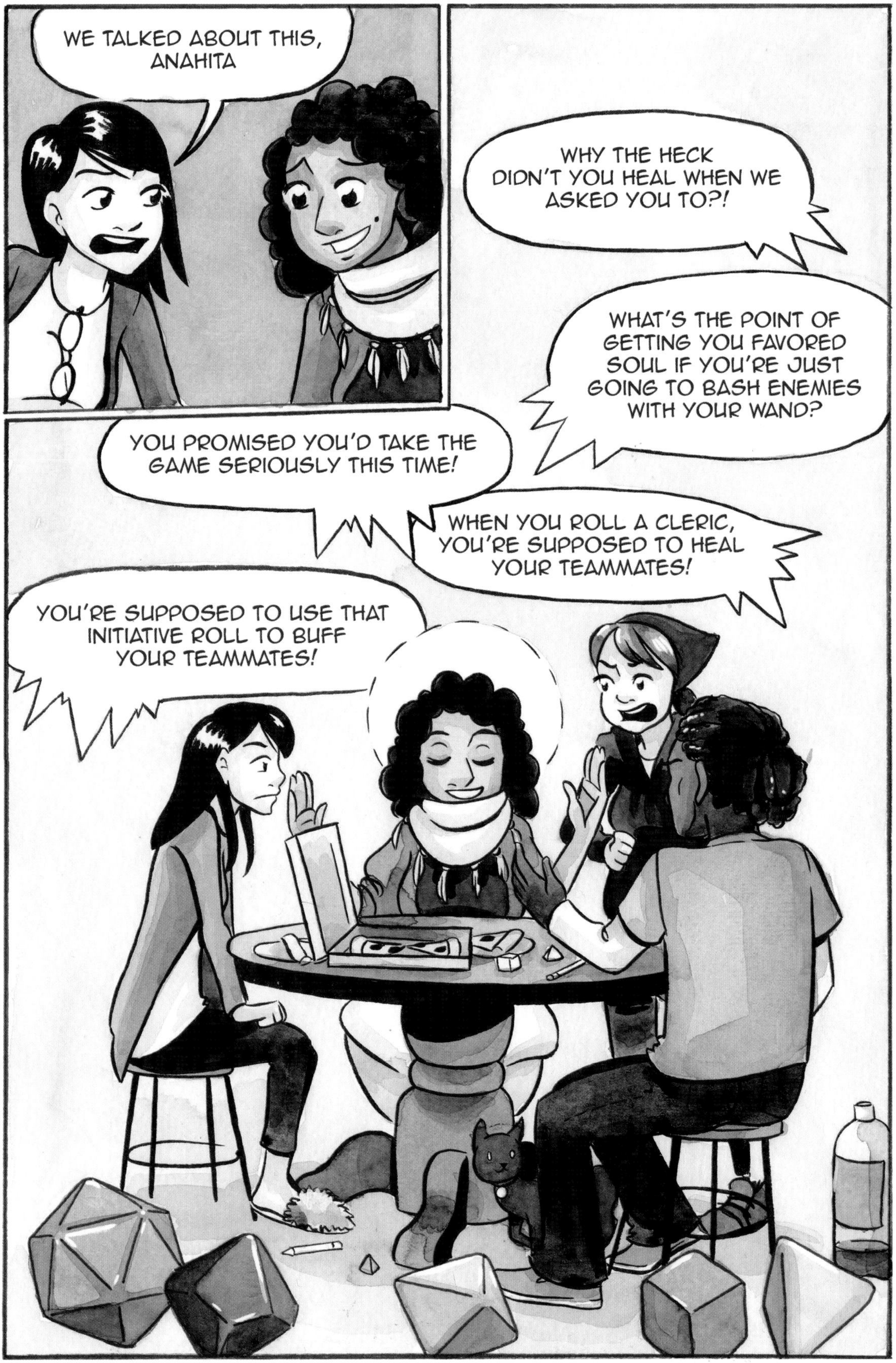
WE TALKED ABOUT THIS, ANAHITA
WHY THE HECK DIDN'T YOU HEAL WHEN WE ASKED YOU TO?!
WHAT'S THE POINT OF GETTING YOU FAVORED SOUL IF YOU'RE JUST GOING TO BASH ENEMIES WITH YOUR WAND?
YOU PROMISED YOU'D TAKE THE GAME SERIOUSLY THIS TIME!
WHEN YOU ROLL A CLERIC, YOU'RE SUPPOSED TO HEAL YOUR TEAMMATES!
YOU'RE SUPPOSED TO USE THAT INITIATIVE ROLL TO BUFF YOUR TEAMMATES!

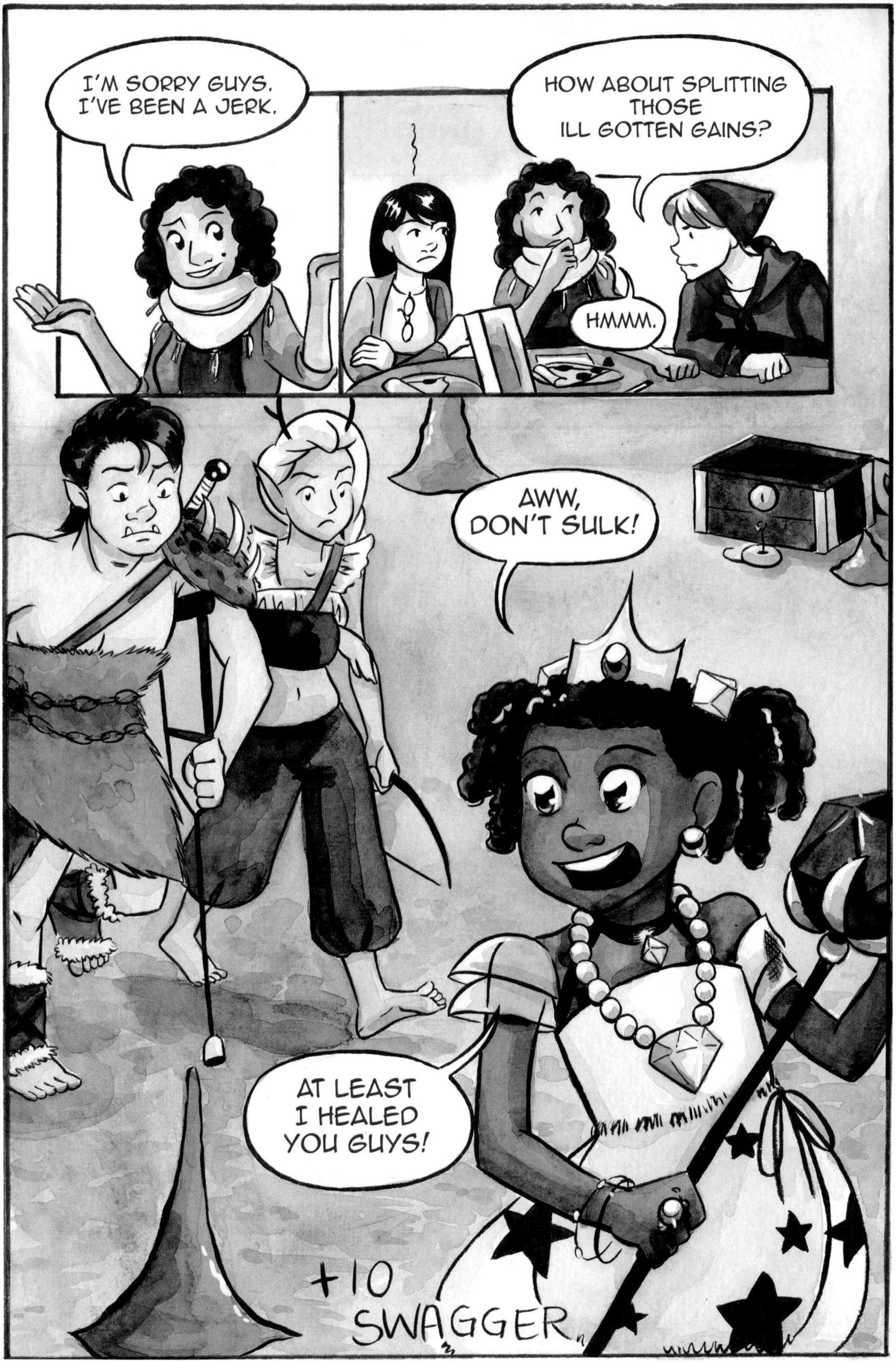
I'M SORRY GUYS. I'VE BEEN A JERK.
HOW ABOUT SPLITTING THOSE ILL GOTTEN GAINS?
HMMM.
AWW, DON'T SULK!
AT LEAST I HEALED YOU GUYS!
+10 SWAGGER

Rush of Blood by Hazel Newlevant

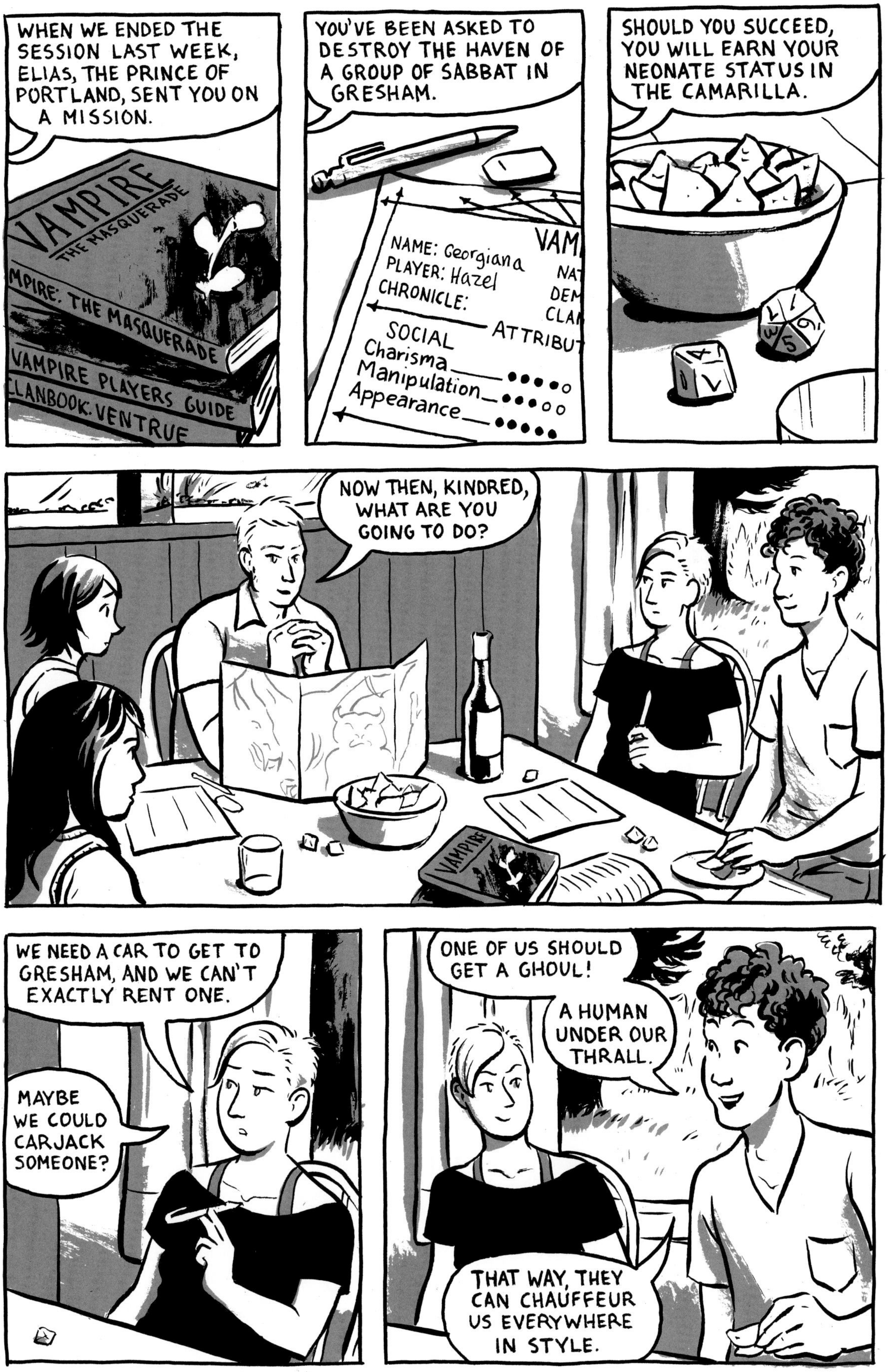

WHEN WE ENDED THE SESSION LAST WEEK, ELIAS, THE PRINCE OF PORTLAND, SENT YOU ON A MISSION.
VAMPIRE THE MASQUERADE
MPIRE: THE MASQUERADE
VAMPIRE PLAYERS GUIDE
LANBOOK: VENTRUE
YOU'VE BEEN ASKED TO DESTROY THE HAVEN OF A GROUP OF SABBAT IN GRESHAM.
NAME: Georgiana
PLAYER: Hazel
CHRONICLE:
ATTRIBUT
SOCIAL
Charisma
Manipulation
Appearance
SHOULD YOU SUCCEED, YOU WILL EARN YOUR NEONATE STATUS IN THE CAMARILLA.
NOW THEN, KINDRED, WHAT ARE YOU GOING TO DO?
VAMPIRE
WE NEED A CAR TO GET TO GRESHAM, AND WE CAN'T EXACTLY RENT ONE.
MAYBE WE COULD CARJACK SOMEONE?
ONE OF US SHOULD GET A GHOUL!
A HUMAN UNDER OUR THRALL.
THAT WAY, THEY CAN CHAUFFEUR US EVERYWHERE IN STYLE.

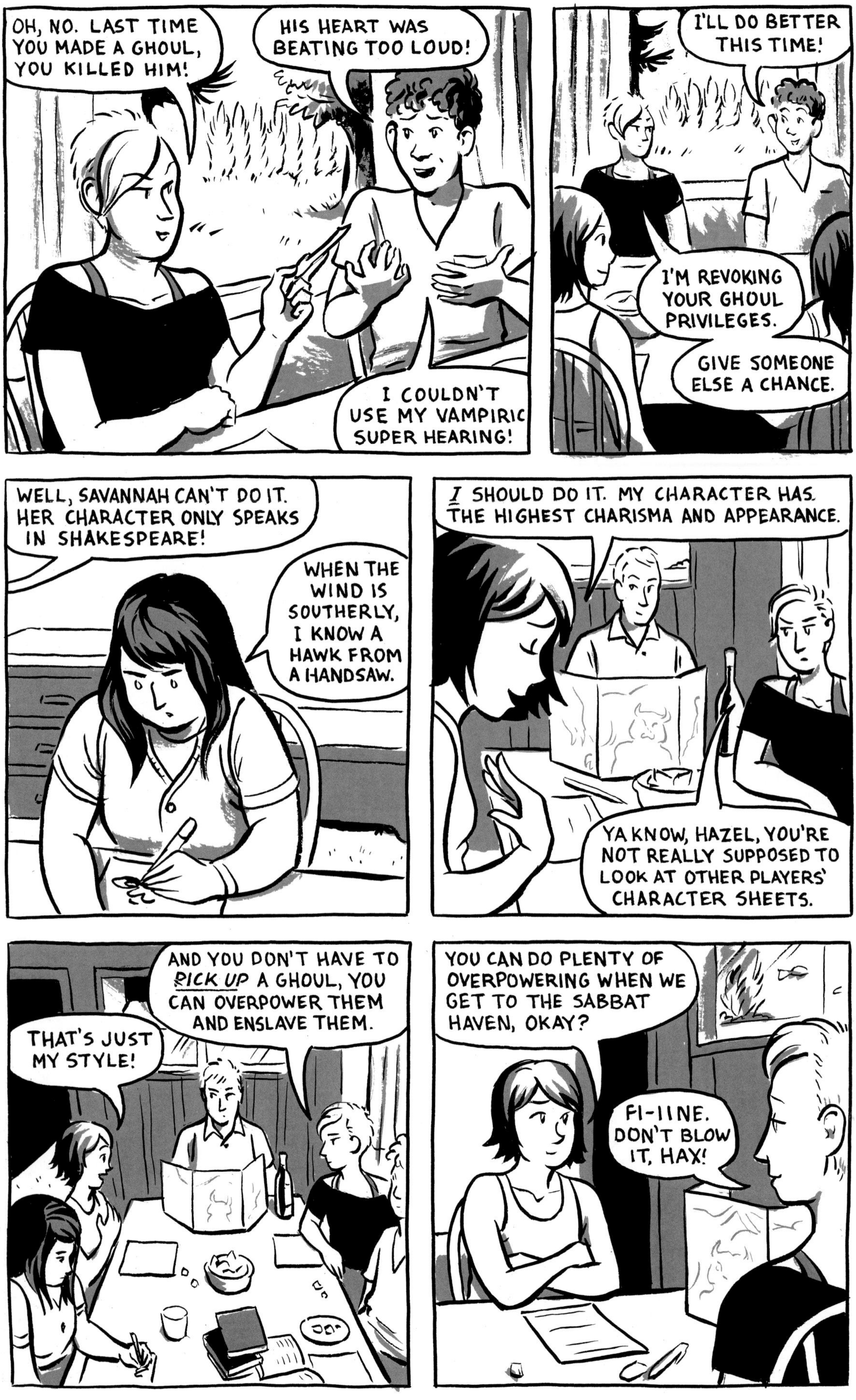

OH, NO. LAST TIME YOU MADE A GHOUL, YOU KILLED HIM!
HIS HEART WAS BEATING TOO LOUD!
I COULDN'T USE MY VAMPIRIC SUPER HEARING!
I'LL DO BETTER THIS TIME!
I'M REVOKING YOUR GHOUL PRIVILEGES.
GIVE SOMEONE ELSE A CHANCE.
WELL, SAVANNAH CAN'T DO IT. HER CHARACTER ONLY SPEAKS IN SHAKESPEARE!
WHEN THE WIND IS SOUTHERLY, I KNOW A HAWK FROM A HANDSAW.
I SHOULD DO IT. MY CHARACTER HAS THE HIGHEST CHARISMA AND APPEARANCE.
YA KNOW, HAZEL, YOU'RE NOT REALLY SUPPOSED TO LOOK AT OTHER PLAYERS' CHARACTER SHEETS.
AND YOU DON'T HAVE TO PICK UP A GHOUL, YOU CAN OVERPOWER THEM AND ENSLAVE THEM.
THAT'S JUST MY STYLE!
YOU CAN DO PLENTY OF OVERPOWERING WHEN WE GET TO THE SABBAT HAVEN, OKAY?
FI-IINE. DON'T BLOW IT, HAX!

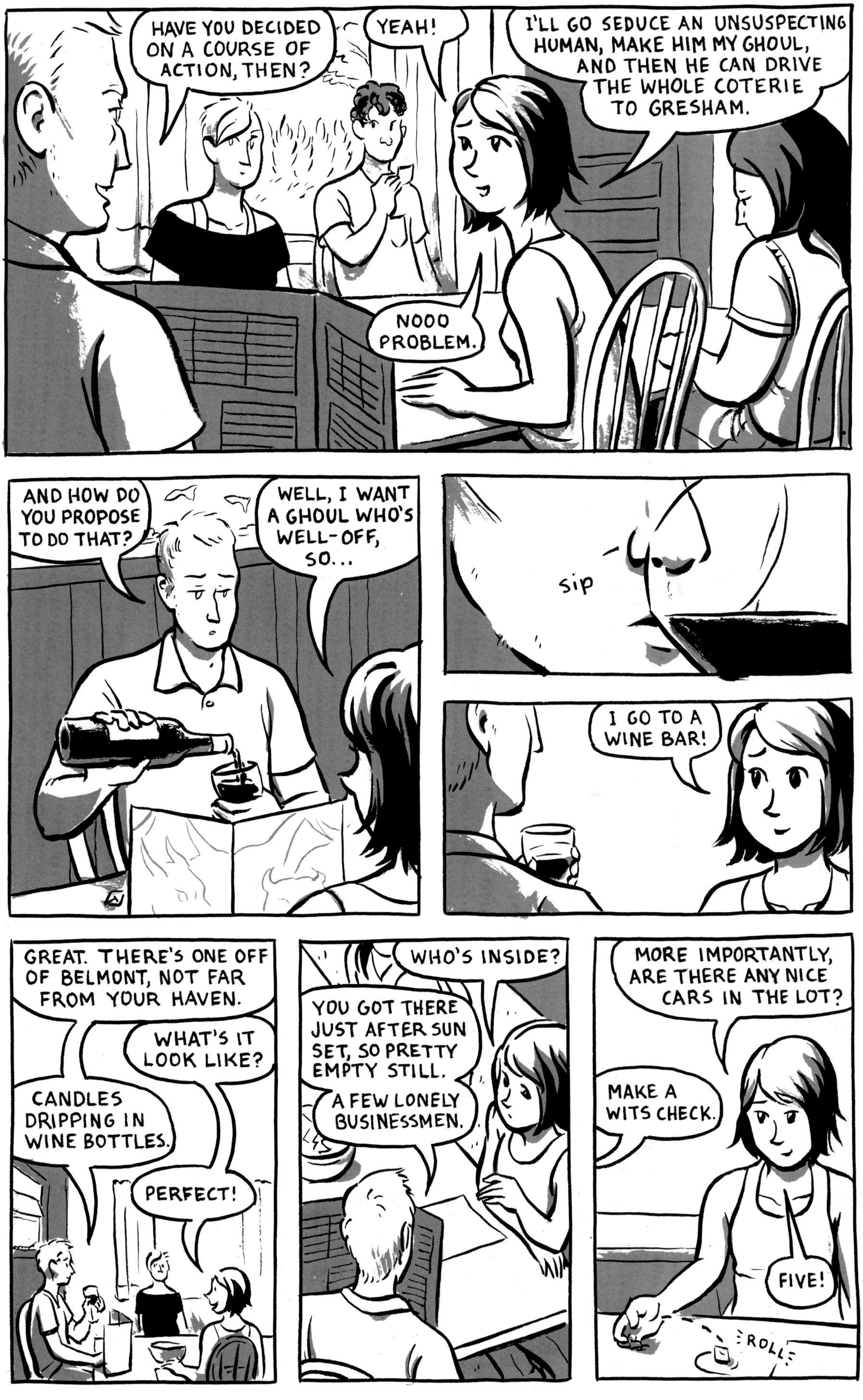
HAVE YOU DECIDED ON A COURSE OF ACTION, THEN?
YEAH!
I'LL GO SEDUCE AN UNSUSPECTING HUMAN, MAKE HIM MY GHOUL, AND THEN HE CAN DRIVE THE WHOLE COTERIE TO GRESHAM.
NOOO PROBLEM.
AND HOW DO YOU PROPOSE TO DO THAT?
WELL, I WANT A GHOUL WHO'S WELL-OFF, SO...
sip
I GO TO A WINE BAR!
GREAT. THERE'S ONE OFF OF BELMONT, NOT FAR FROM YOUR HAVEN.
WHAT'S IT LOOK LIKE?
CANDLES DRIPPING IN WINE BOTTLES.
PERFECT!
WHO'S INSIDE?
YOU GOT THERE JUST AFTER SUN SET, SO PRETTY EMPTY STILL.
A FEW LONELY BUSINESSMEN.
MORE IMPORTANTLY, ARE THERE ANY NICE CARS IN THE LOT?
MAKE A WITS CHECK.
FIVE!
ROLL

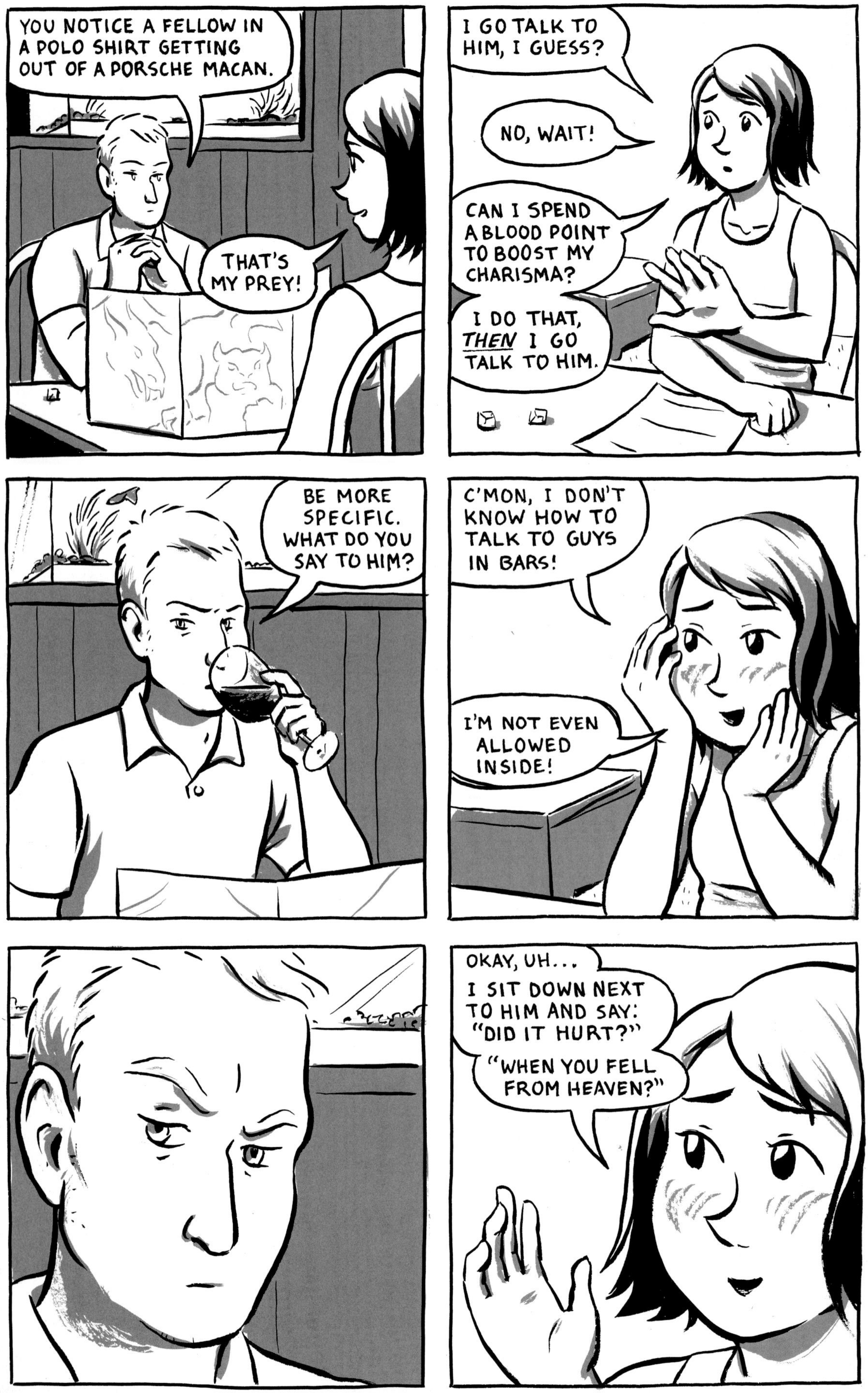
YOU NOTICE A FELLOW IN A POLO SHIRT GETTING OUT OF A PORSCHE MACAN.
THAT'S MY PREY!
I GO TALK TO HIM, I GUESS?
NO, WAIT!
CAN I SPEND A BLOOD POINT TO BOOST MY CHARISMA?
I DO THAT, THEN I GO TALK TO HIM.
BE MORE SPECIFIC. WHAT DO YOU SAY TO HIM?
C'MON, I DON'T KNOW HOW TO TALK TO GUYS IN BARS!
I'M NOT EVEN ALLOWED INSIDE!
OKAY, UH...
I SIT DOWN NEXT TO HIM AND SAY: "DID IT HURT?"
"WHEN YOU FELL FROM HEAVEN?"

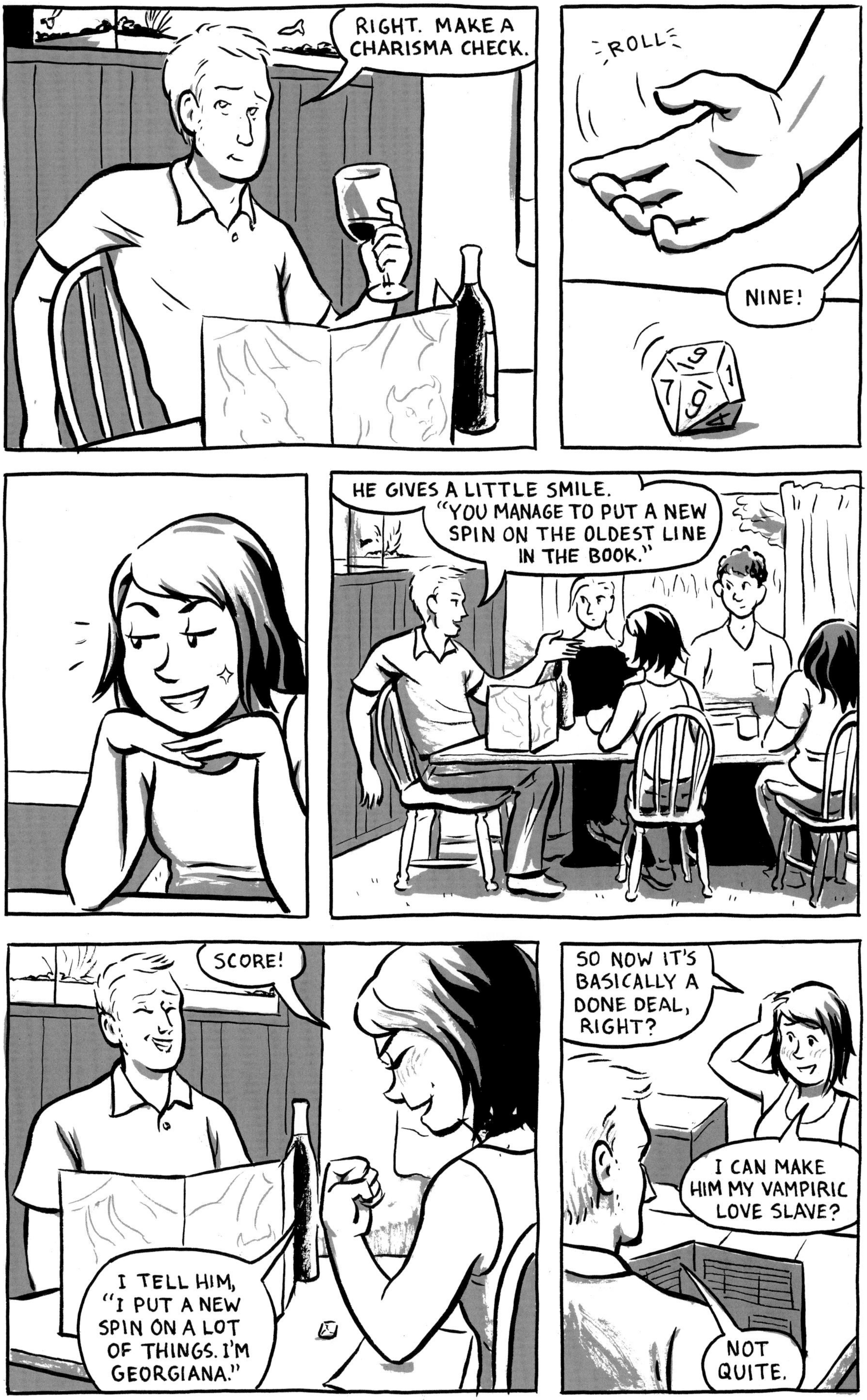
RIGHT. MAKE A CHARISMA CHECK.
ROLL
NINE!
HE GIVES A LITTLE SMILE. "YOU MANAGE TO PUT A NEW SPIN ON THE OLDEST LINE IN THE BOOK."
SCORE!
I TELL HIM, "I PUT A NEW SPIN ON A LOT OF THINGS. I'M GEORGIANA."
SO NOW IT'S BASICALLY A DONE DEAL, RIGHT?
I CAN MAKE HIM MY VAMPIRIC LOVE SLAVE?
NOT QUITE.

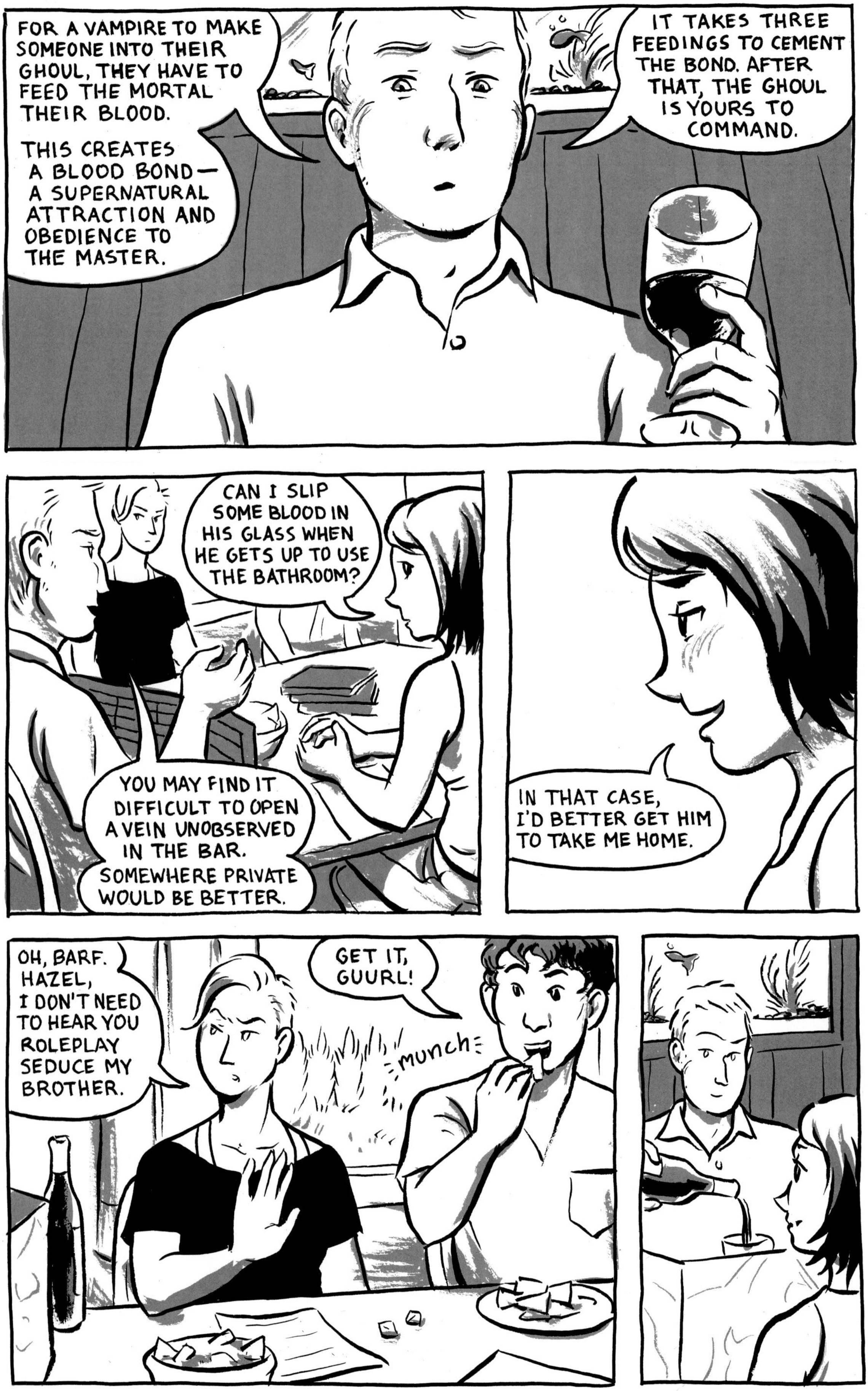
FOR A VAMPIRE TO MAKE SOMEONE INTO THEIR GHOUL, THEY HAVE TO FEED THE MORTAL THEIR BLOOD.
THIS CREATES A BLOOD BOND— A SUPERNATURAL ATTRACTION AND OBEDIENCE TO THE MASTER.
IT TAKES THREE FEEDINGS TO CEMENT THE BOND. AFTER THAT, THE GHOUL IS YOURS TO COMMAND.
CAN I SLIP SOME BLOOD IN HIS GLASS WHEN HE GETS UP TO USE THE BATHROOM?
YOU MAY FIND IT DIFFICULT TO OPEN A VEIN UNOBSERVED IN THE BAR.
SOMEWHERE PRIVATE WOULD BE BETTER.
IN THAT CASE, I'D BETTER GET HIM TO TAKE ME HOME.
OH, BARF. HAZEL, I DON'T NEED TO HEAR YOU ROLEPLAY SEDUCE MY BROTHER.
GET IT, GUURL!
munch

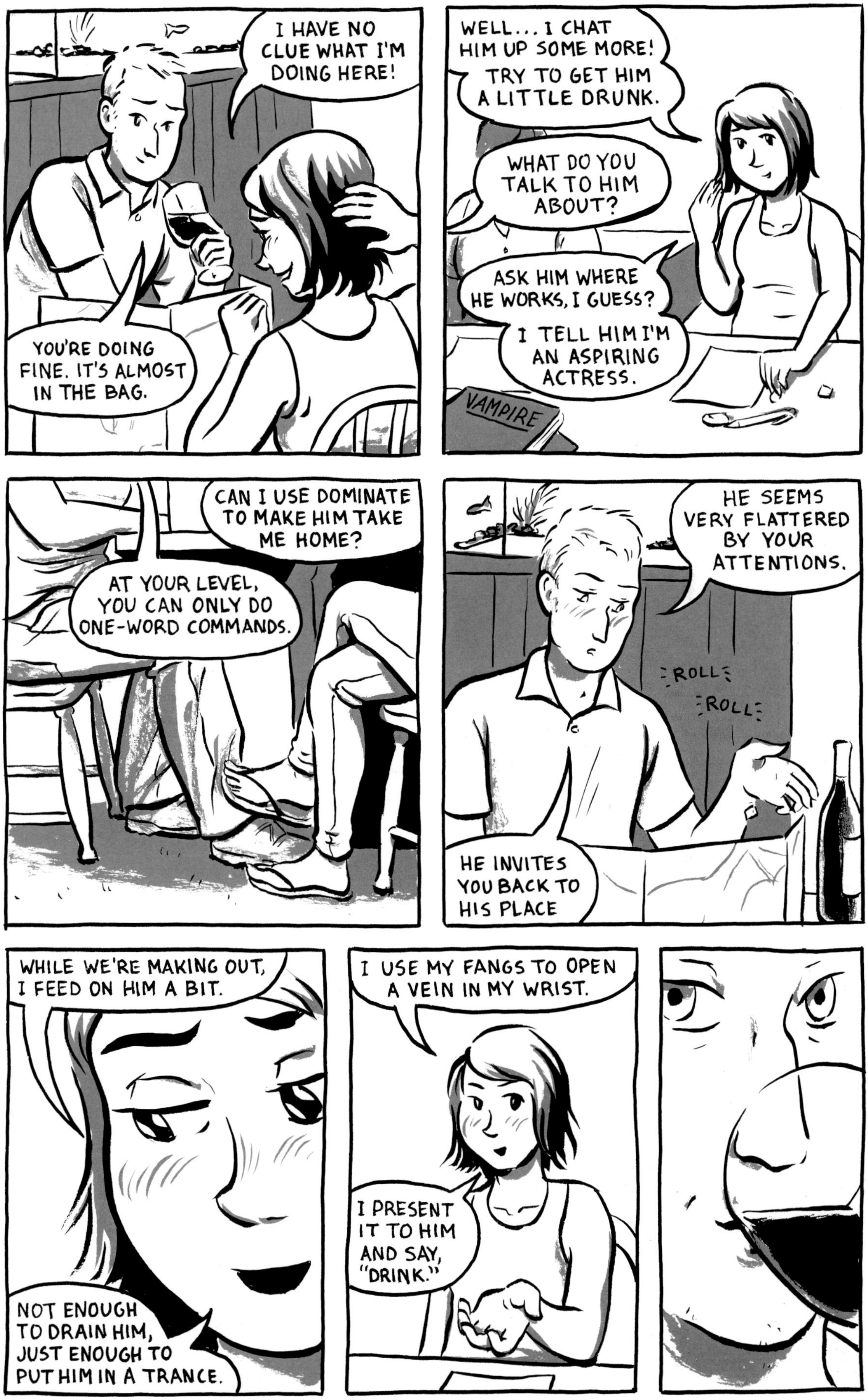
I HAVE NO CLUE WHAT I'M DOING HERE!
YOU'RE DOING FINE. IT'S ALMOST IN THE BAG.
WELL... I CHAT HIM UP SOME MORE!
TRY TO GET HIM A LITTLE DRUNK.
WHAT DO YOU TALK TO HIM ABOUT?
ASK HIM WHERE HE WORKS, I GUESS?
I TELL HIM I'M AN ASPIRING ACTRESS.
VAMPIRE
CAN I USE DOMINATE TO MAKE HIM TAKE ME HOME?
AT YOUR LEVEL, YOU CAN ONLY DO ONE-WORD COMMANDS.
HE SEEMS VERY FLATTERED BY YOUR ATTENTIONS.
ROLL
ROLL
HE INVITES YOU BACK TO HIS PLACE
WHILE WE'RE MAKING OUT, I FEED ON HIM A BIT.
NOT ENOUGH TO DRAIN HIM, JUST ENOUGH TO PUT HIM IN A TRANCE.
I USE MY FANGS TO OPEN A VEIN IN MY WRIST.
I PRESENT IT TO HIM AND SAY, "DRINK."

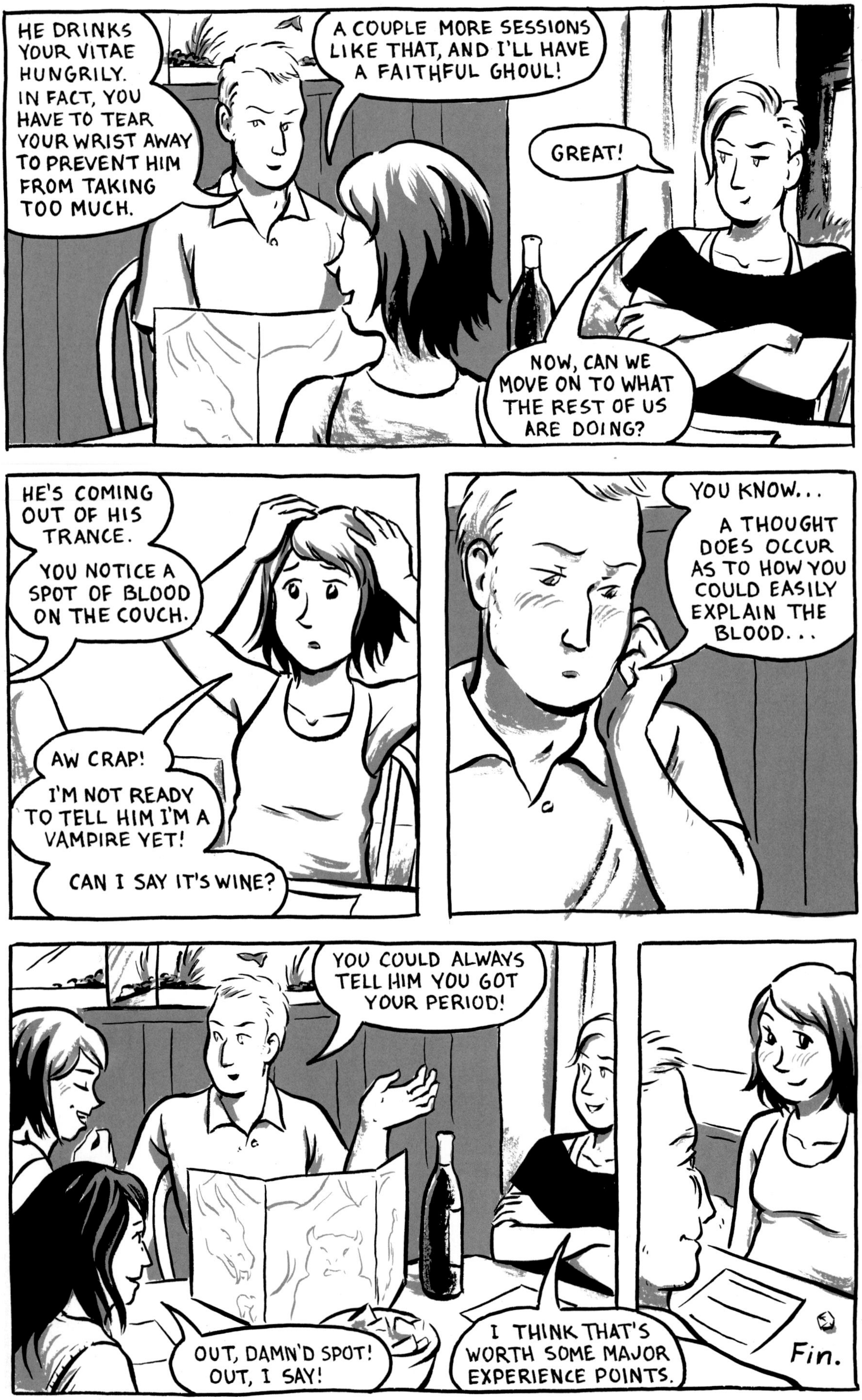
HE DRINKS YOUR VITAE HUNGRILY.
IN FACT, YOU HAVE TO TEAR YOUR WRIST AWAY TO PREVENT HIM FROM TAKING TOO MUCH.
A COUPLE MORE SESSIONS LIKE THAT, AND I'LL HAVE A FAITHFUL GHOUL!
GREAT!
NOW, CAN WE MOVE ON TO WHAT THE REST OF US ARE DOING?
HE'S COMING OUT OF HIS TRANCE.
YOU NOTICE A SPOT OF BLOOD ON THE COUCH.
AW CRAP!
I'M NOT READY TO TELL HIM I'M A VAMPIRE YET!
CAN I SAY IT'S WINE?
YOU KNOW...
A THOUGHT DOES OCCUR AS TO HOW YOU COULD EASILY EXPLAIN THE BLOOD...
YOU COULD ALWAYS TELL HIM YOU GOT YOUR PERIOD!
OUT, DAMN'D SPOT! OUT, I SAY!
I THINK THAT'S WORTH SOME MAJOR EXPERIENCE POINTS.
Fin.

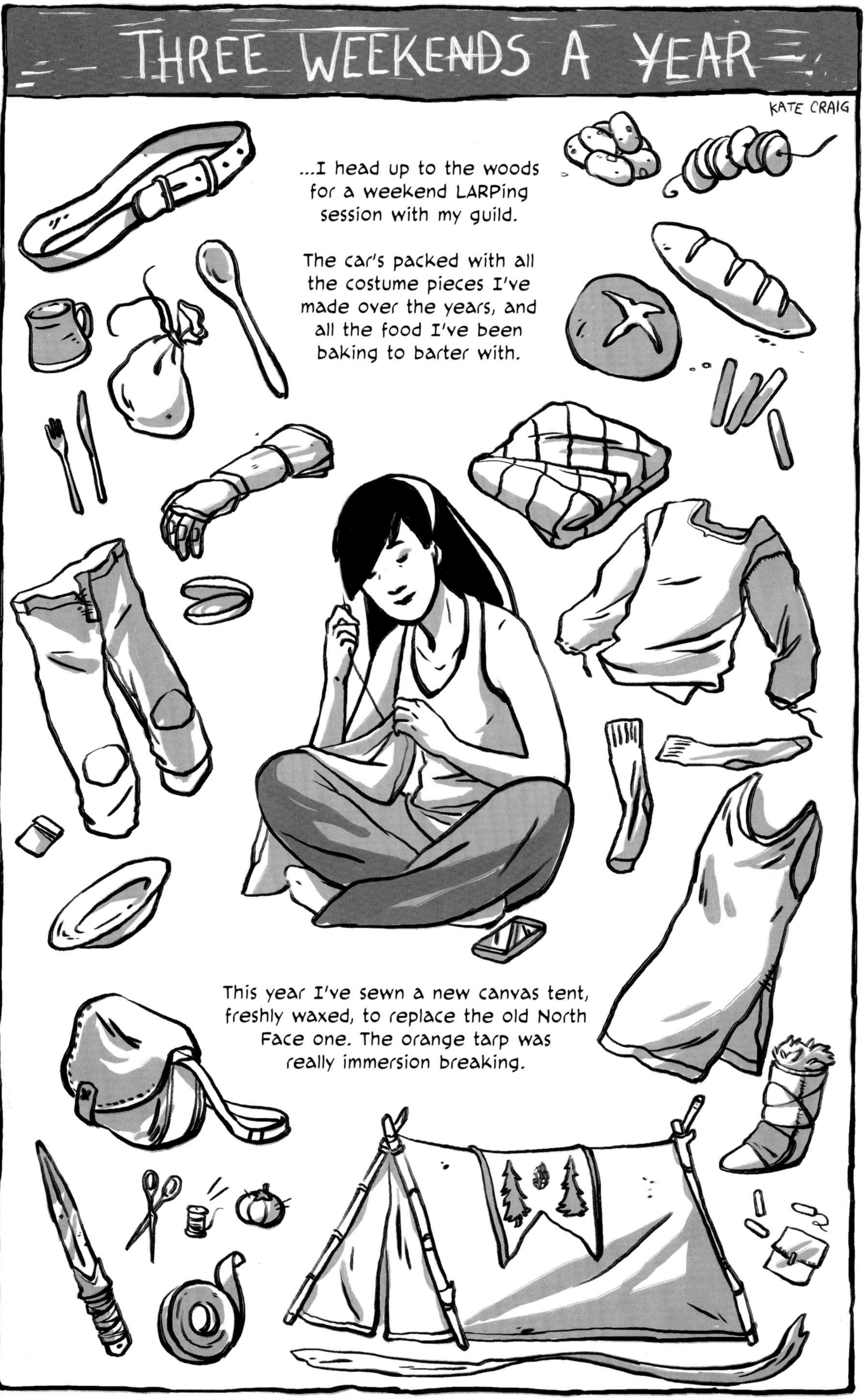
THREE WEEKENDS A YEAR
KATE CRAIG
...I head up to the woods for a weekend LARPing session with my guild.
The car's packed with all the costume pieces I've made over the years, and all the food I've been baking to barter with.
This year I've sewn a new canvas tent, freshly waxed, to replace the old North Face one. The orange tarp was really immersion breaking.

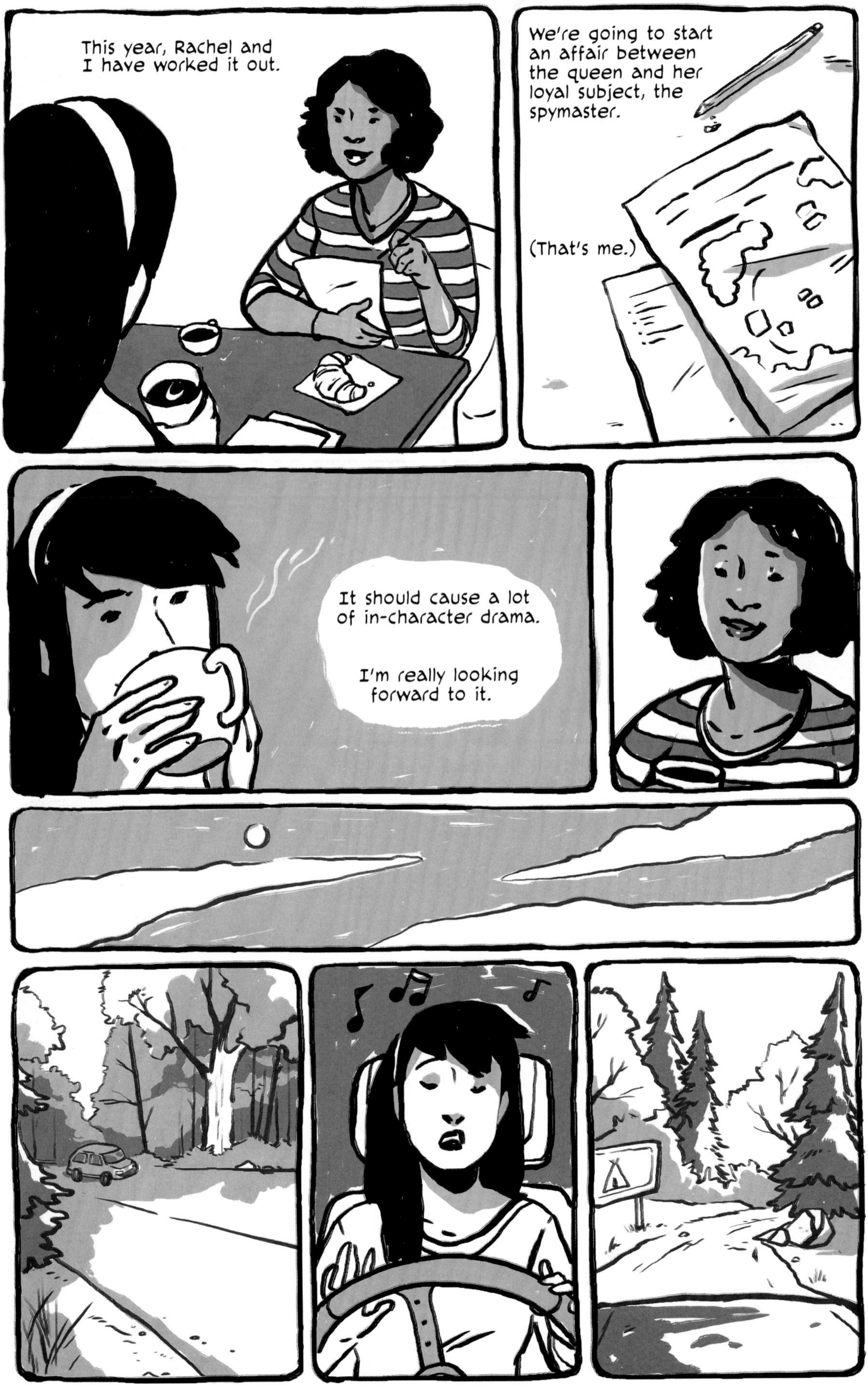
This year, Rachel and I have worked it out.
We're going to start an affair between the queen and her loyal subject, the spymaster.
(That's me.)
It should cause a lot of in-character drama.
I'm really looking forward to it.

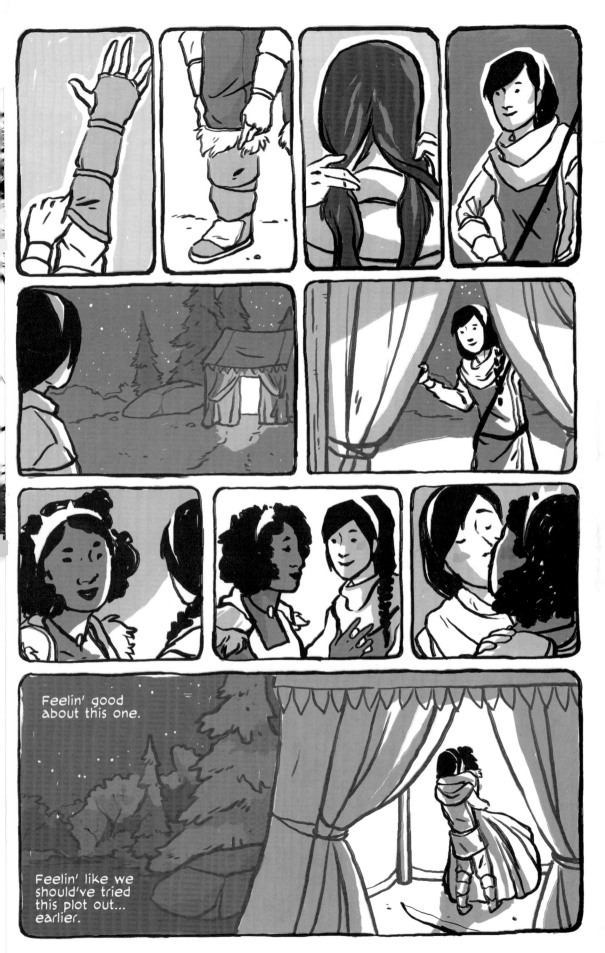

Feelin' good about this one.

Feelin' like we should've tried this plot out... earlier.

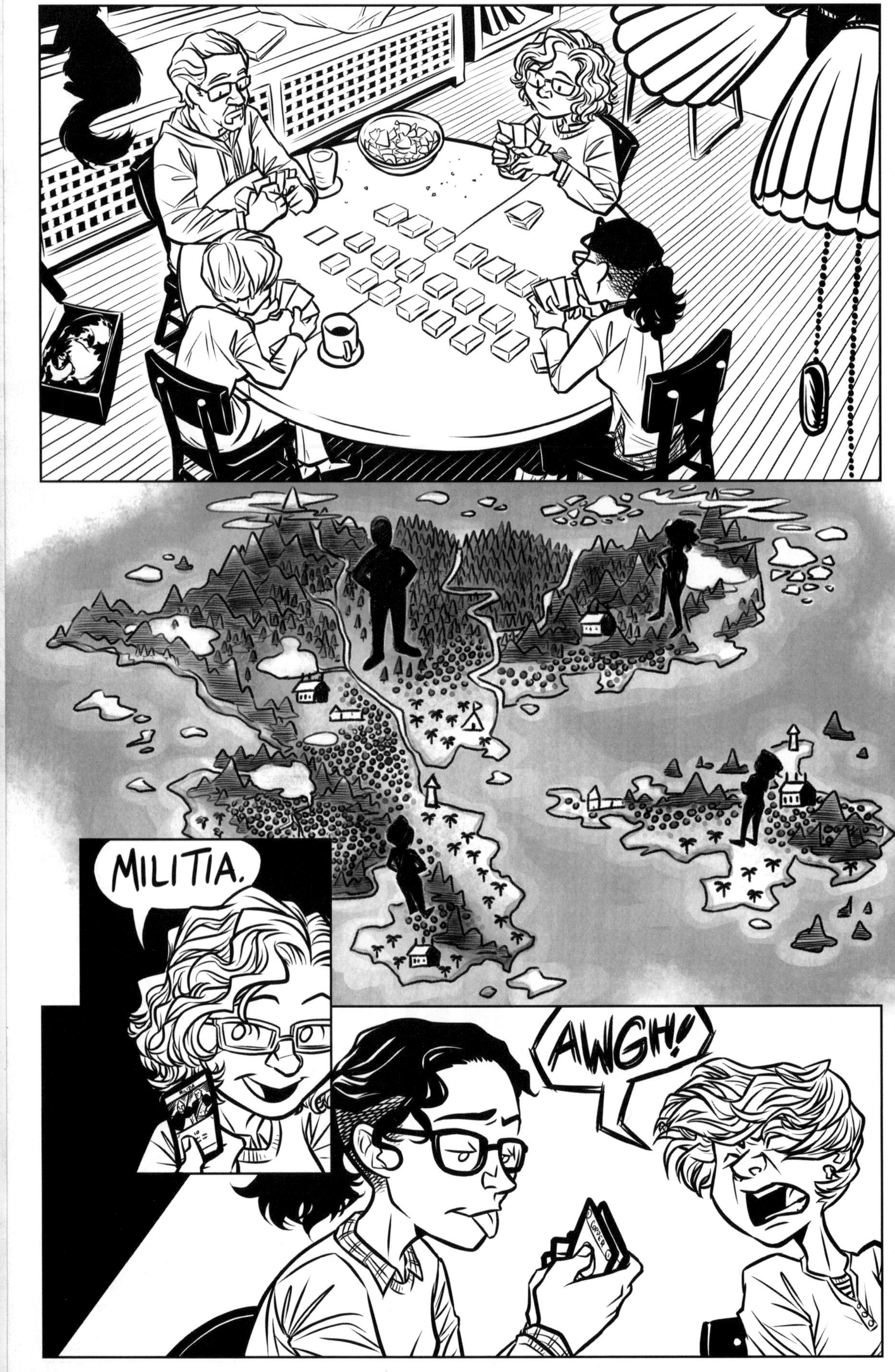
MILITIA.
AWGH!

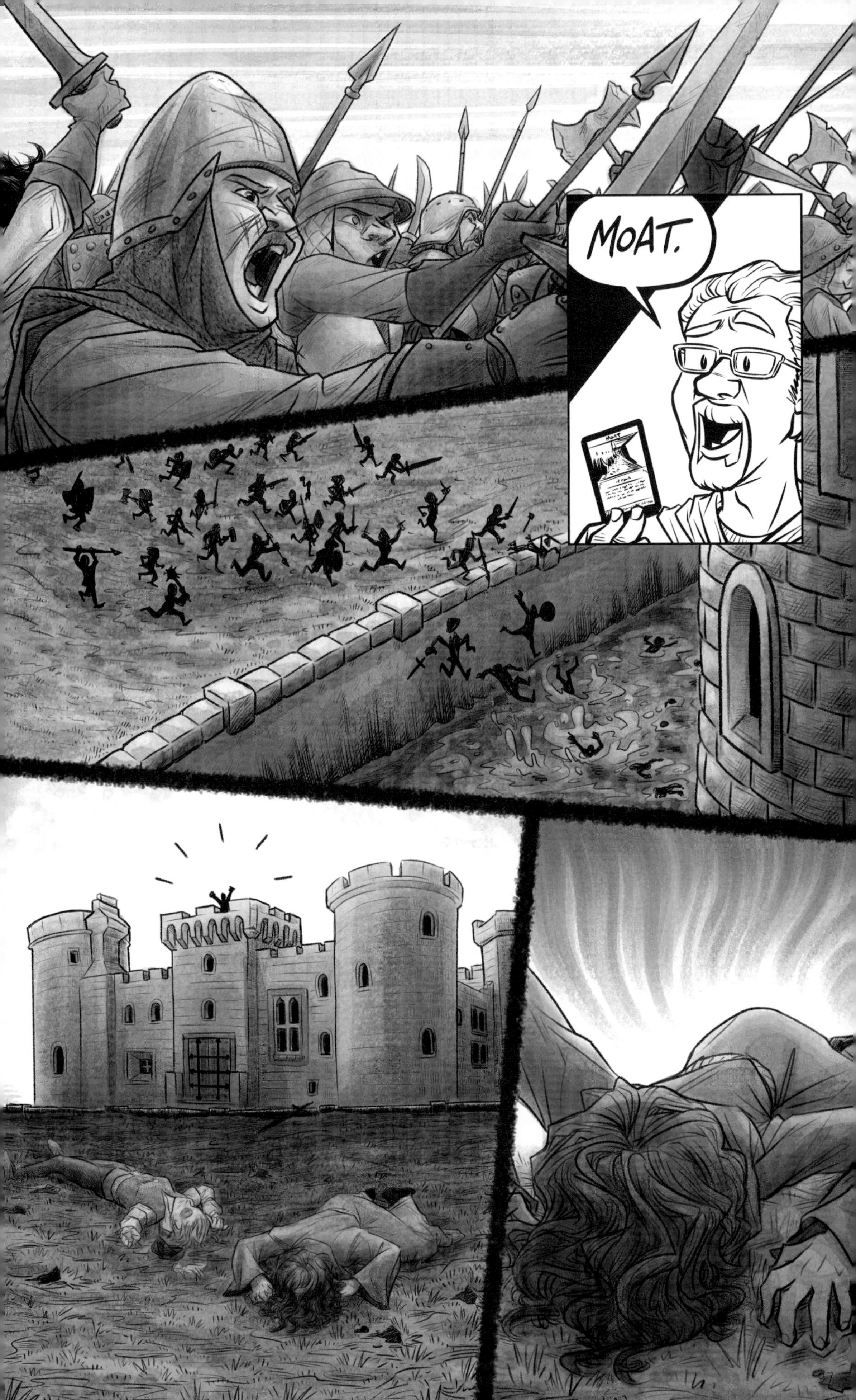
MOAT.

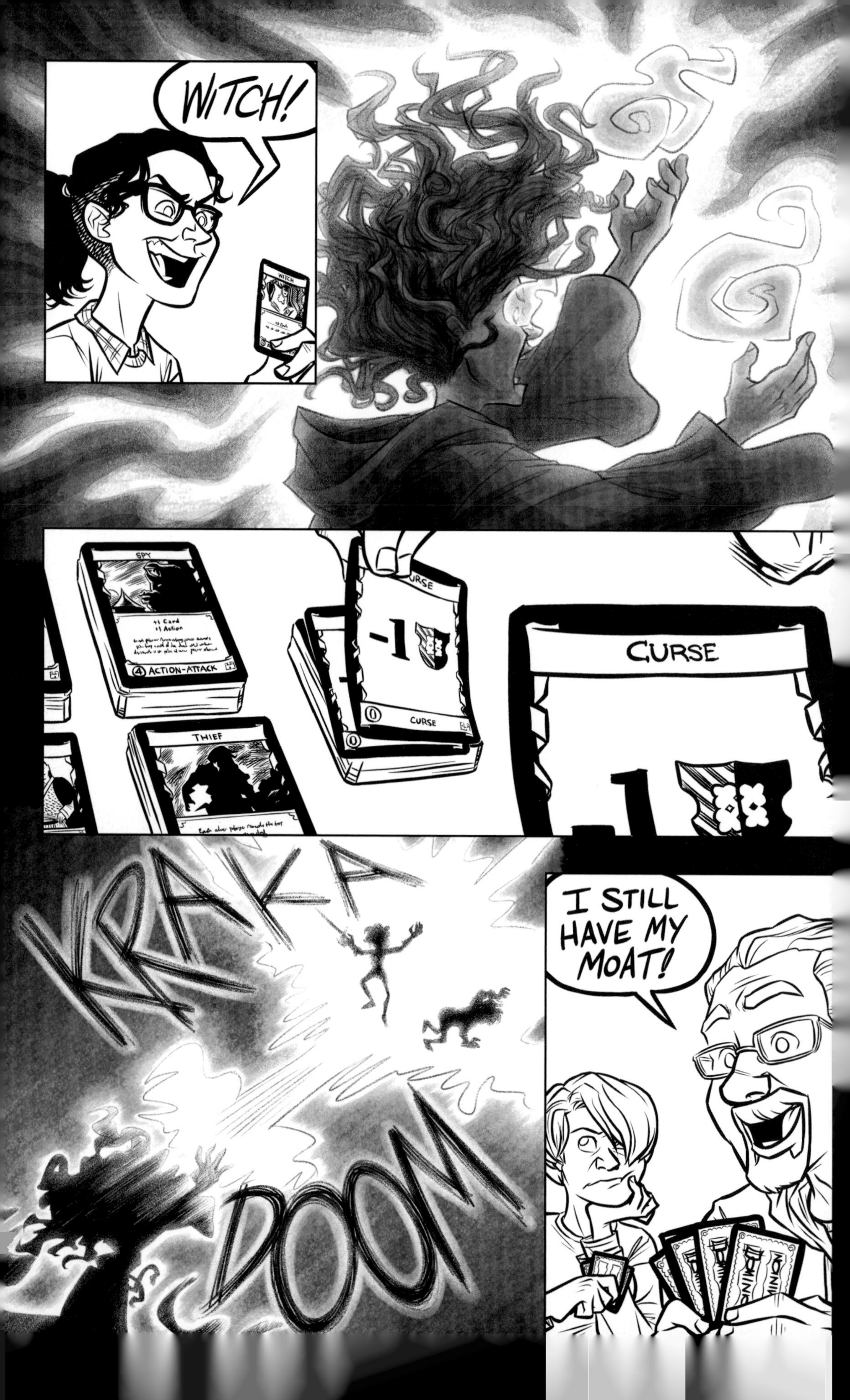
WITCH!
SPY
+1 Card
+1 Action
4 ACTION-ATTACK
CURSE
-1
0 CURSE
THIEF
CURSE
KRAKA
DOOM
I STILL HAVE MY MOAT!

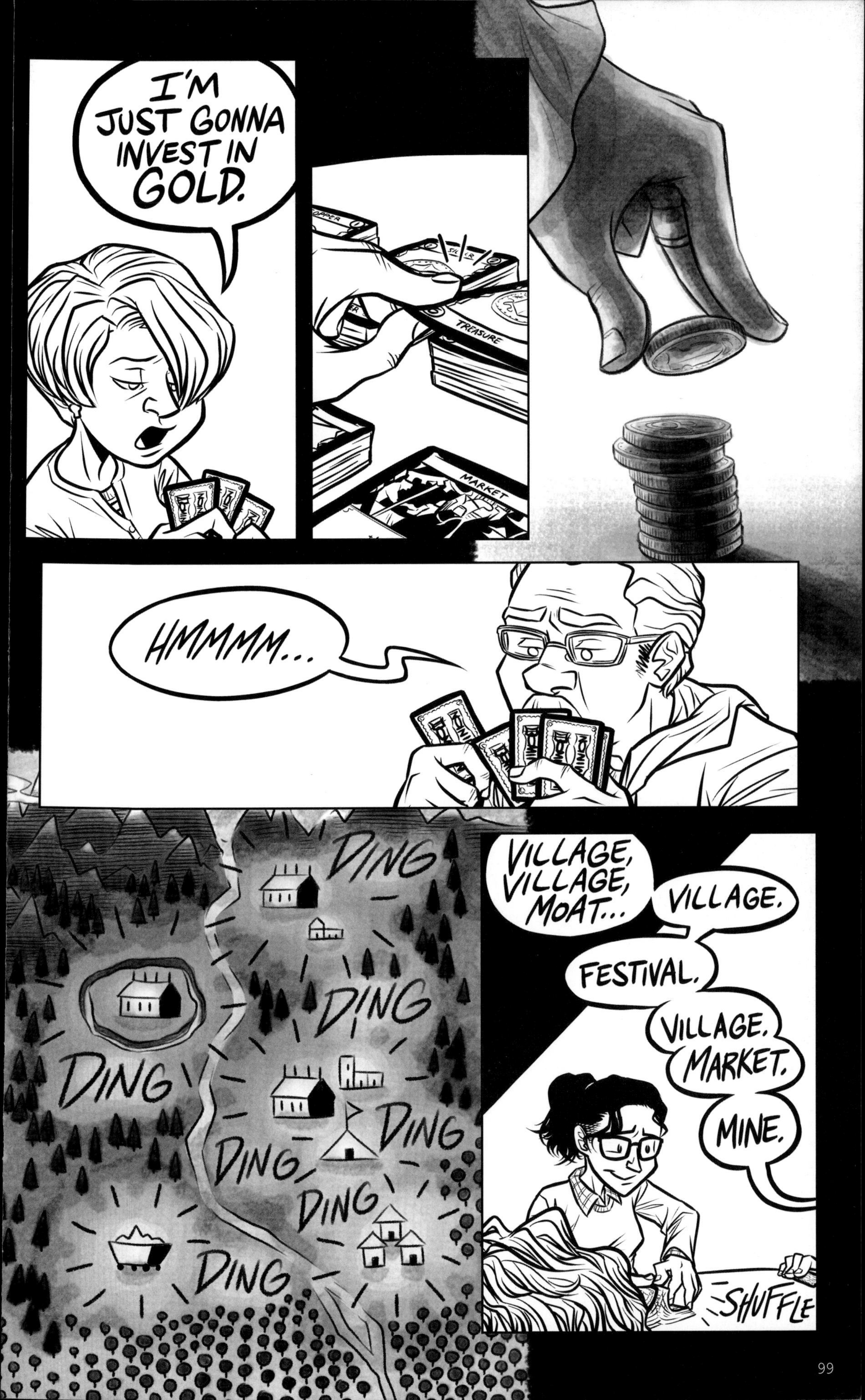
I'M JUST GONNA INVEST IN GOLD.
TREASURE
MARKET
HMMMM...
DING
DING
DING
DING
DING
DING
DING
VILLAGE, VILLAGE, MOAT...
VILLAGE.
FESTIVAL.
VILLAGE. MARKET.
MINE.
SHUFFLE

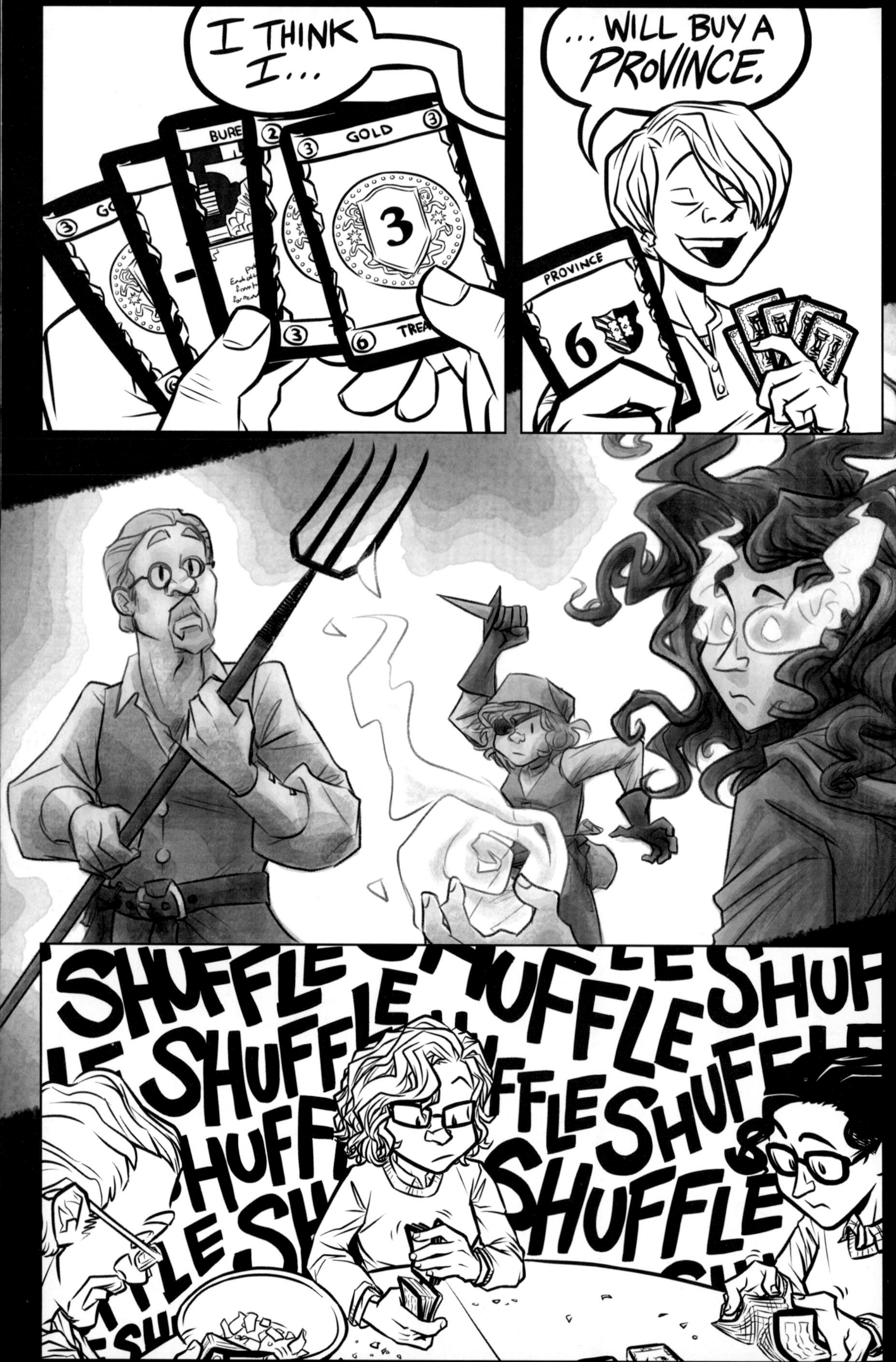
I THINK I...
GOLD
3
...WILL BUY A PROVINCE.
PROVINCE
6
SHUFFLE
SHUFFLE
SHUFFLE
SHUFFLE
SHUFFLE
&
SHUFFLE

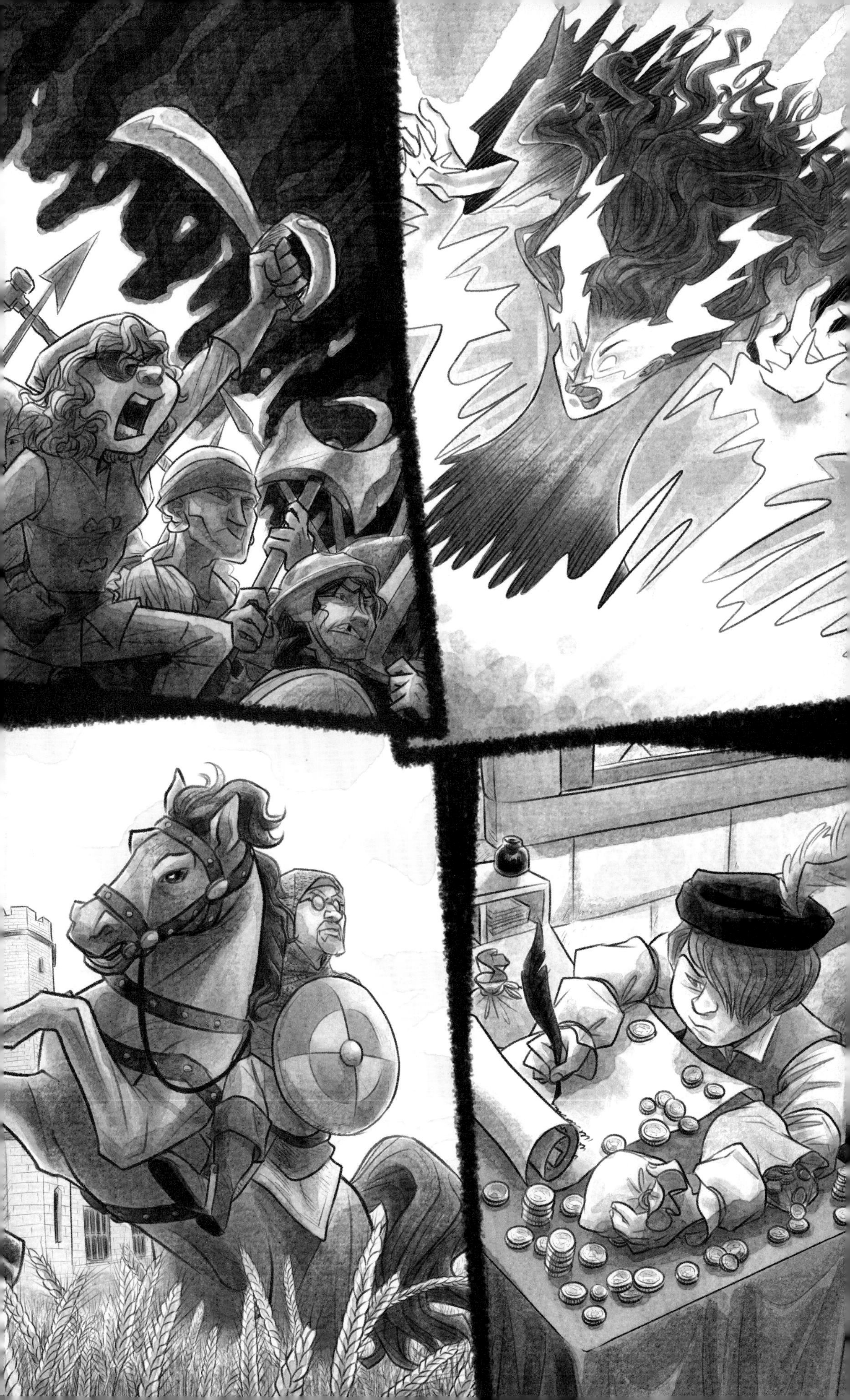

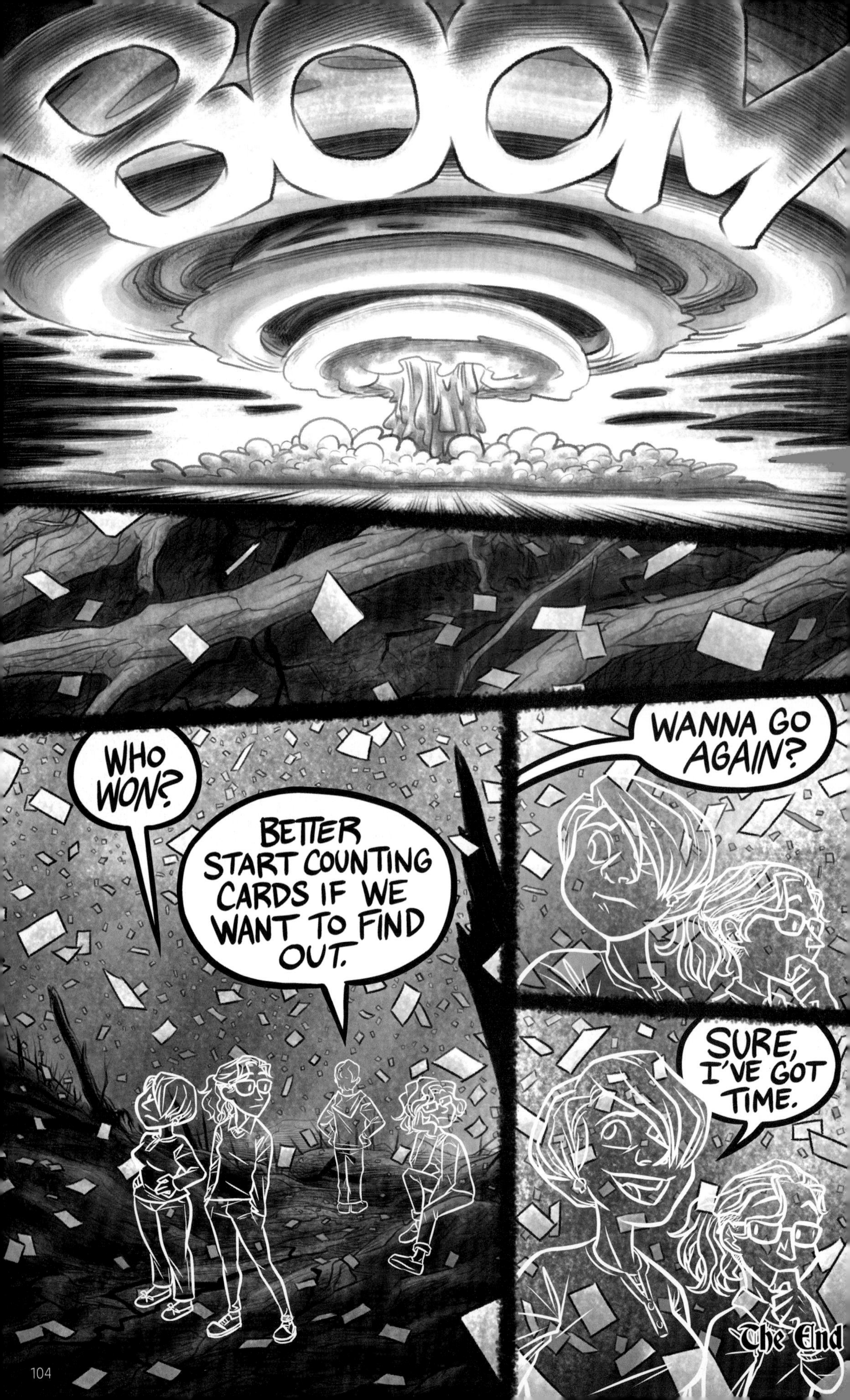
BOOM
WHO WON?
BETTER START COUNTING CARDS IF WE WANT TO FIND OUT.
WANNA GO AGAIN?
SURE, I'VE GOT TIME.
The End

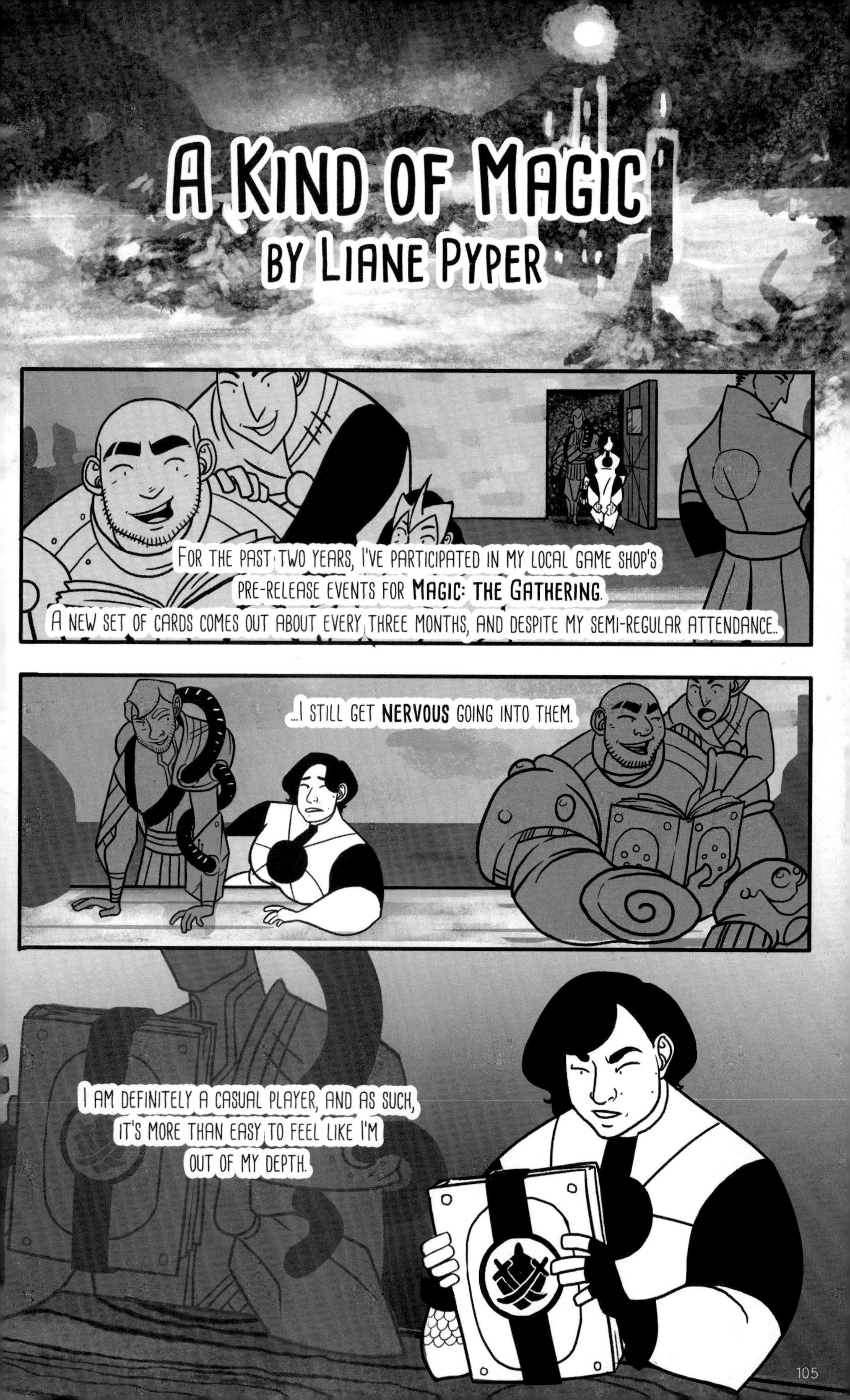
A KIND OF MAGIC
BY LIANE PYPER
FOR THE PAST TWO YEARS, I'VE PARTICIPATED IN MY LOCAL GAME SHOP'S PRE-RELEASE EVENTS FOR **MAGIC: THE GATHERING**. A NEW SET OF CARDS COMES OUT ABOUT EVERY THREE MONTHS, AND DESPITE MY SEMI-REGULAR ATTENDANCE...
...I STILL GET **NERVOUS** GOING INTO THEM.
I AM DEFINITELY A CASUAL PLAYER, AND AS SUCH, IT'S MORE THAN EASY TO FEEL LIKE I'M OUT OF MY DEPTH.

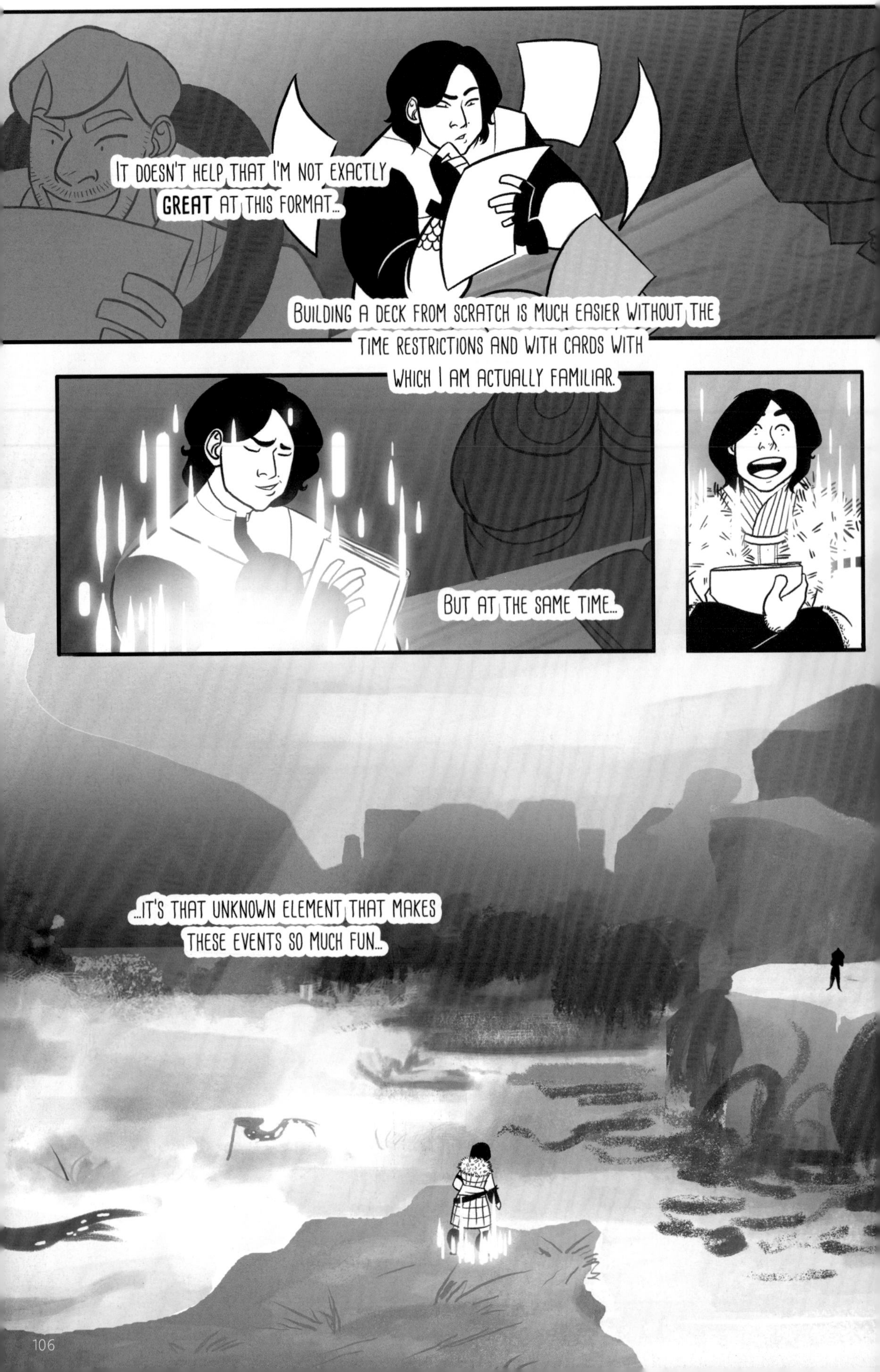
It doesn't help that I'm not exactly **GREAT** at this format...
Building a deck from scratch is much easier without the time restrictions and with cards with which I am actually familiar.
But at the same time...
...it's that unknown element that makes these events so much fun...

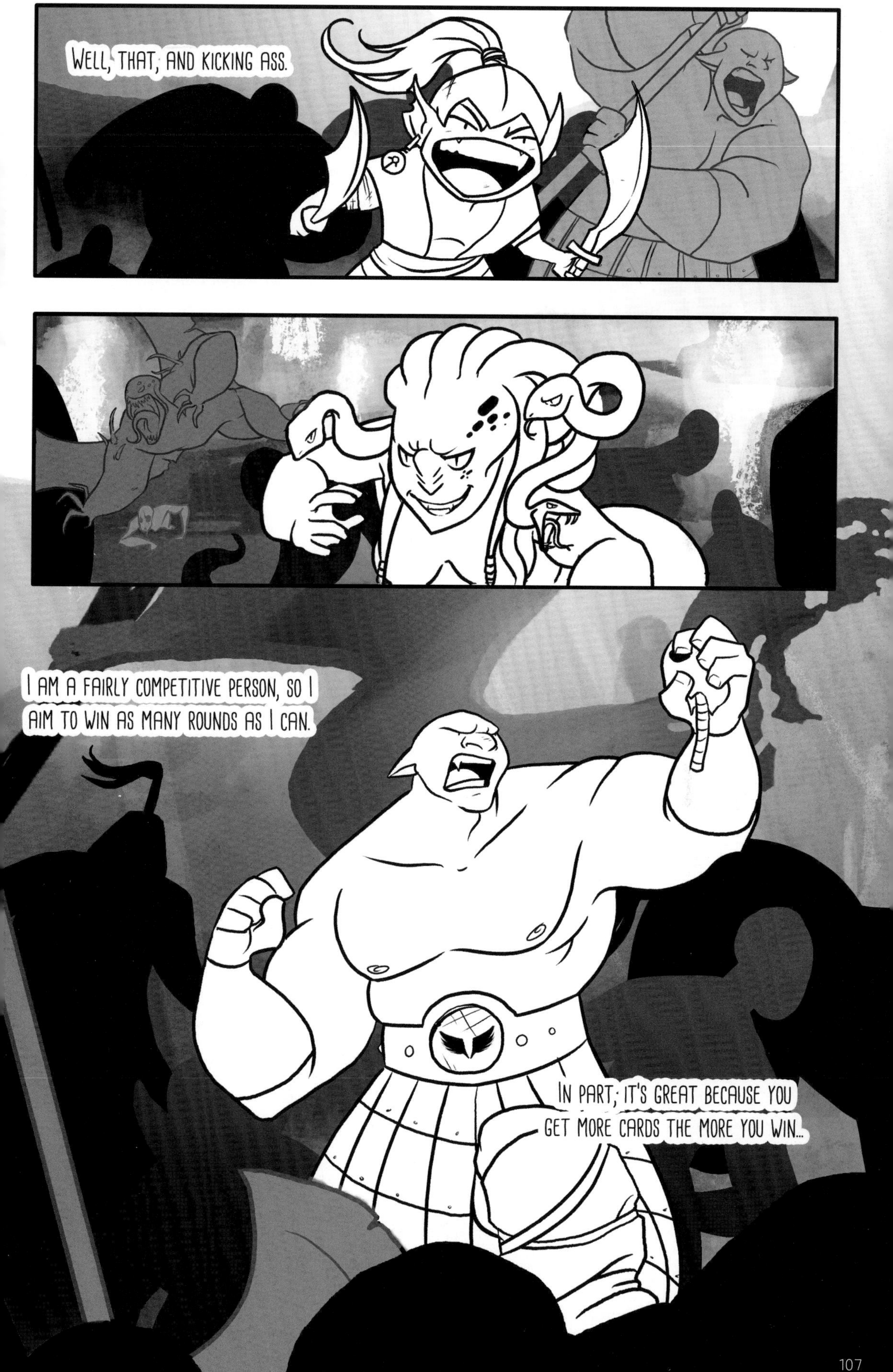
WELL, THAT, AND KICKING ASS.
I AM A FAIRLY COMPETITIVE PERSON, SO I AIM TO WIN AS MANY ROUNDS AS I CAN.
IN PART, IT'S GREAT BECAUSE YOU GET MORE CARDS THE MORE YOU WIN...

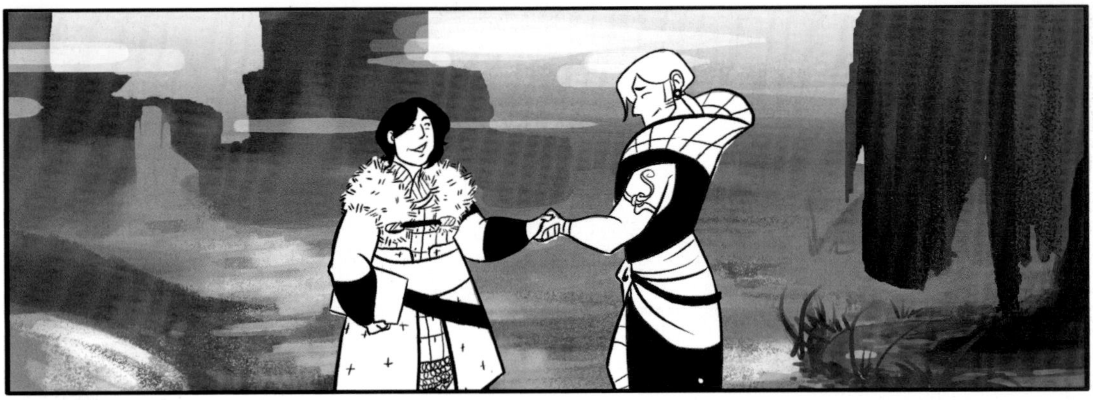

...BUT, IF WE'RE BEING HONEST, IT IS TRULY GRATIFYING TO BE THE ONLY GIRL THERE AND BEATING OUT REGULARS WHO KNOW MUCH MORE ABOUT MAGIC THAN I DO.

UNFORTUNATELY, HOWEVER, THINGS DON'T ALWAYS PLAY OUT THE WAY I'D LIKE.

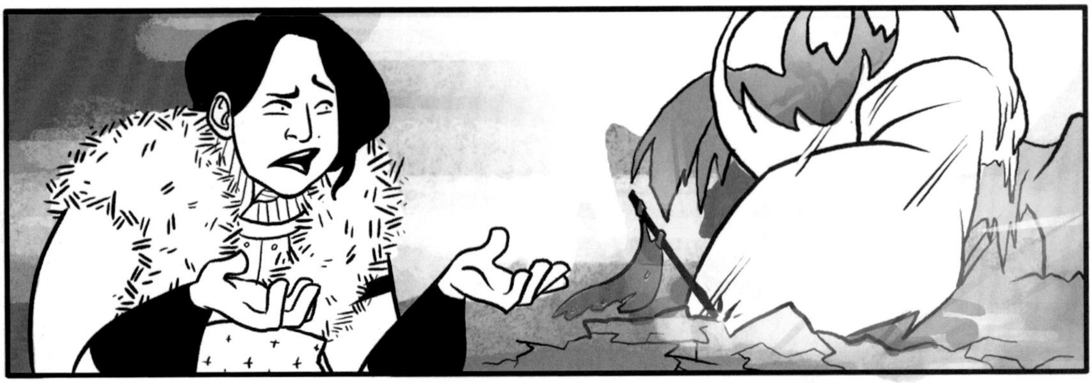

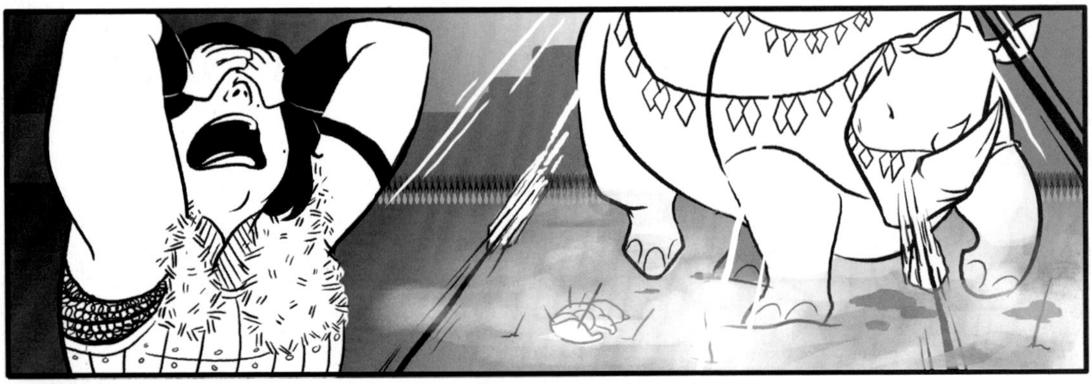

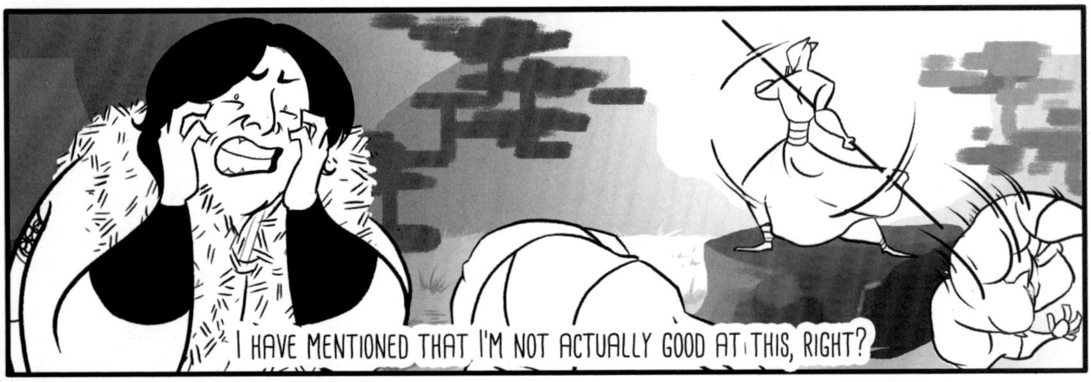
I HAVE MENTIONED THAT I'M NOT ACTUALLY GOOD AT THIS, RIGHT?

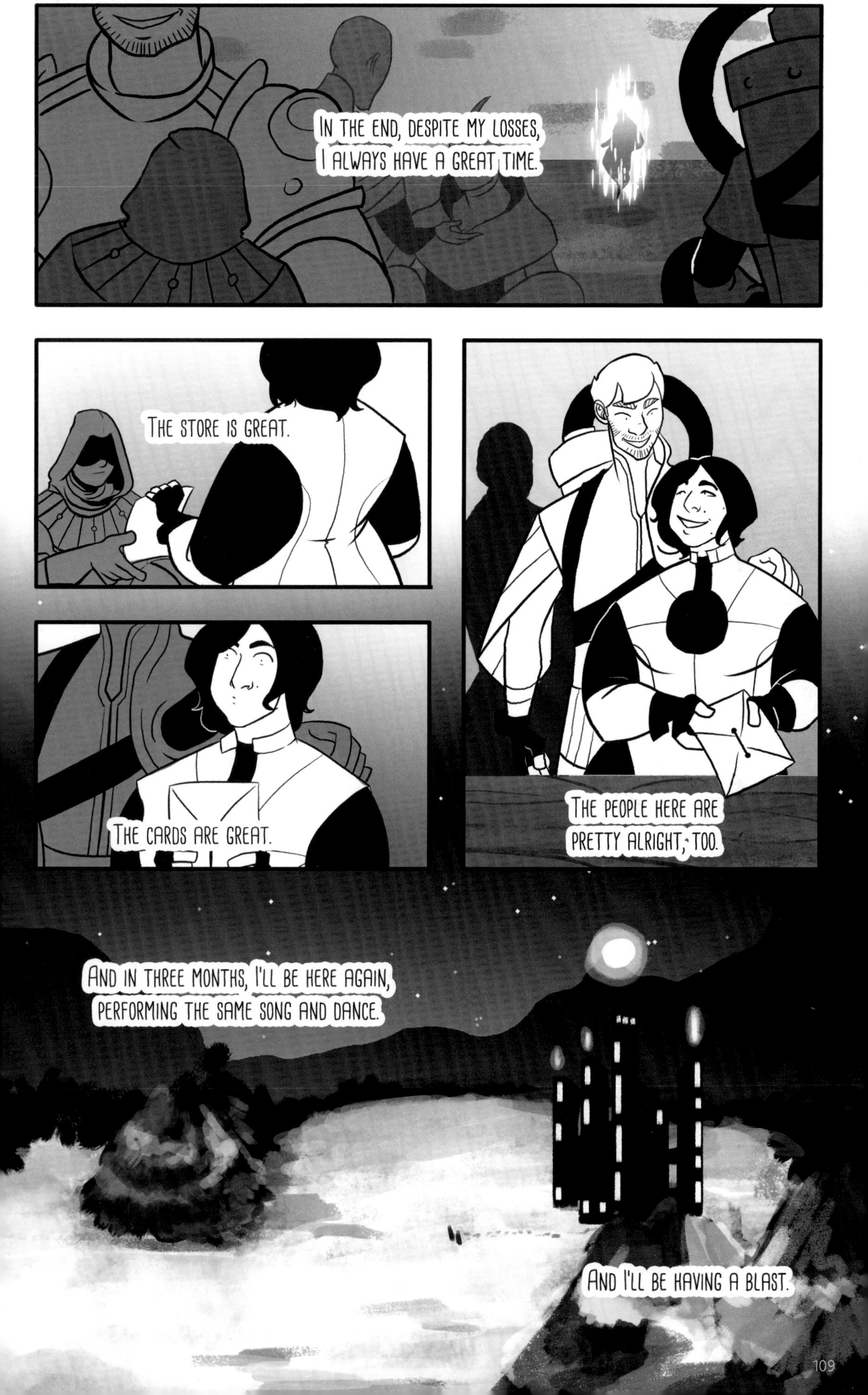
In the end, despite my losses, I always have a great time.
The store is great.
The cards are great.
The people here are pretty alright, too.
And in three months, I'll be here again, performing the same song and dance.
And I'll be having a blast.

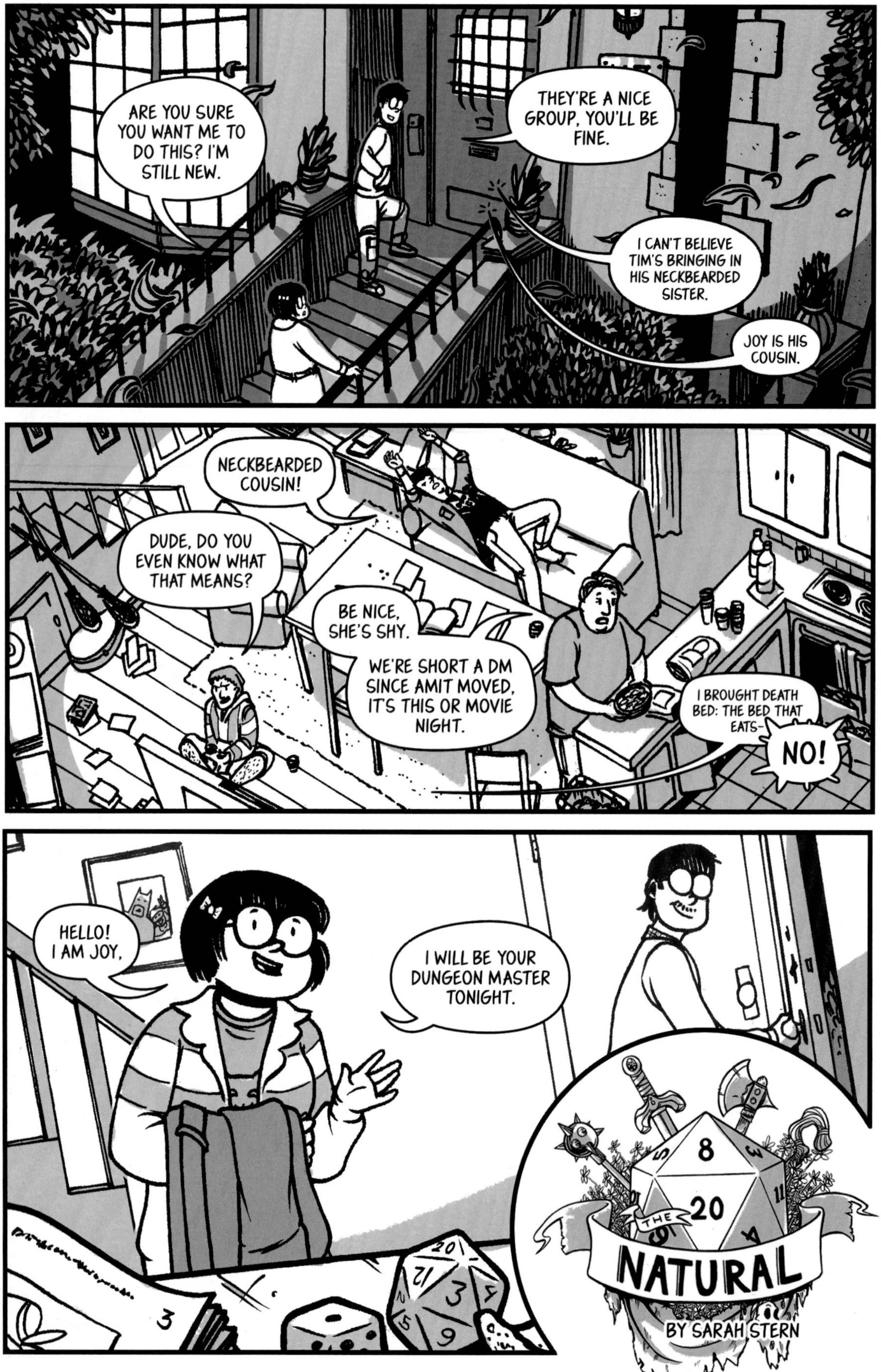
ARE YOU SURE YOU WANT ME TO DO THIS? I'M STILL NEW.
THEY'RE A NICE GROUP, YOU'LL BE FINE.
I CAN'T BELIEVE TIM'S BRINGING IN HIS NECKBEARDED SISTER.
JOY IS HIS COUSIN.
NECKBEARDED COUSIN!
DUDE, DO YOU EVEN KNOW WHAT THAT MEANS?
BE NICE, SHE'S SHY.
WE'RE SHORT A DM SINCE AMIT MOVED, IT'S THIS OR MOVIE NIGHT.
I BROUGHT DEATH BED: THE BED THAT EATS-
NO!
HELLO! I AM JOY,
I WILL BE YOUR DUNGEON MASTER TONIGHT.
THE NATURAL
BY SARAH STERN

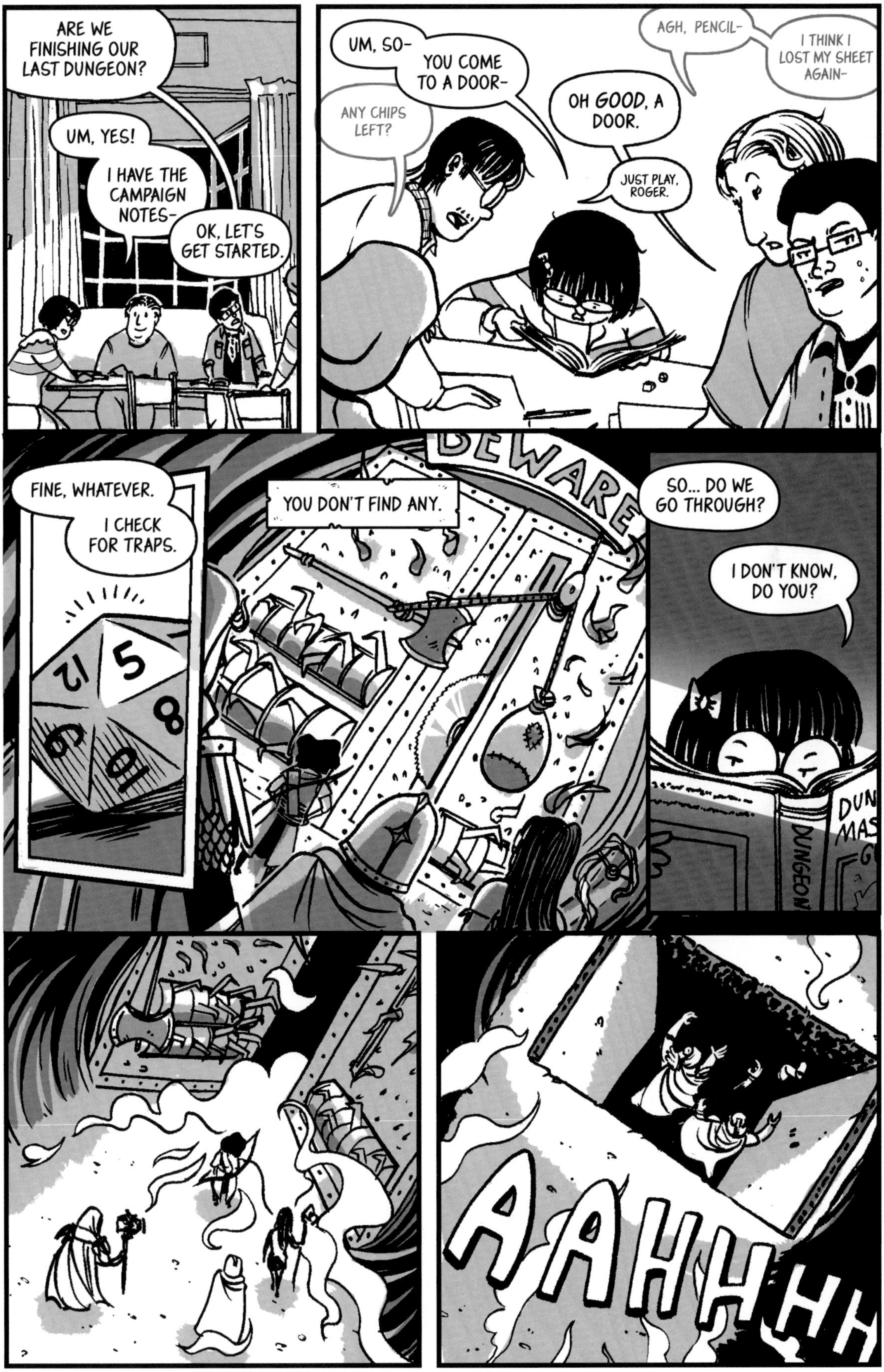
ARE WE FINISHING OUR LAST DUNGEON?
UM, YES!
I HAVE THE CAMPAIGN NOTES-
OK, LET'S GET STARTED.
UM, SO-
YOU COME TO A DOOR-
ANY CHIPS LEFT?
OH GOOD, A DOOR.
JUST PLAY, ROGER.
AGH, PENCIL-
I THINK I LOST MY SHEET AGAIN-
FINE, WHATEVER.
I CHECK FOR TRAPS.
YOU DON'T FIND ANY.
BEWARE
SO... DO WE GO THROUGH?
I DON'T KNOW, DO YOU?
DUNGEON
AAHHHH

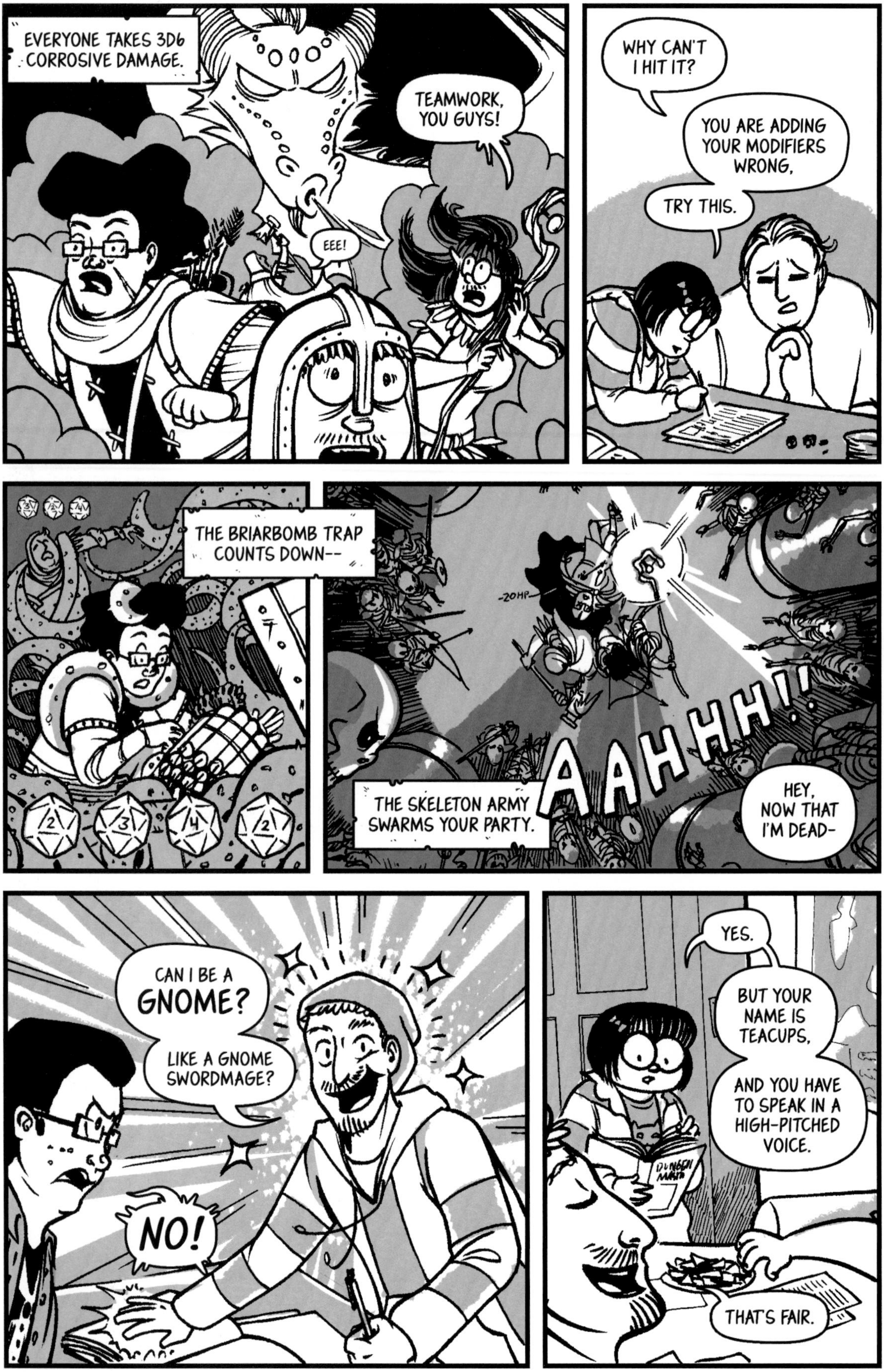
EVERYONE TAKES 3D6 CORROSIVE DAMAGE.
TEAMWORK, YOU GUYS!
EEE!
WHY CAN'T I HIT IT?
YOU ARE ADDING YOUR MODIFIERS WRONG,
TRY THIS.
THE BRIARBOMB TRAP COUNTS DOWN--
-20HP
AAHHH!!
THE SKELETON ARMY SWARMS YOUR PARTY.
HEY, NOW THAT I'M DEAD-
CAN I BE A GNOME?
LIKE A GNOME SWORDMAGE?
NO!
YES.
BUT YOUR NAME IS TEACUPS,
AND YOU HAVE TO SPEAK IN A HIGH-PITCHED VOICE.
THAT'S FAIR.

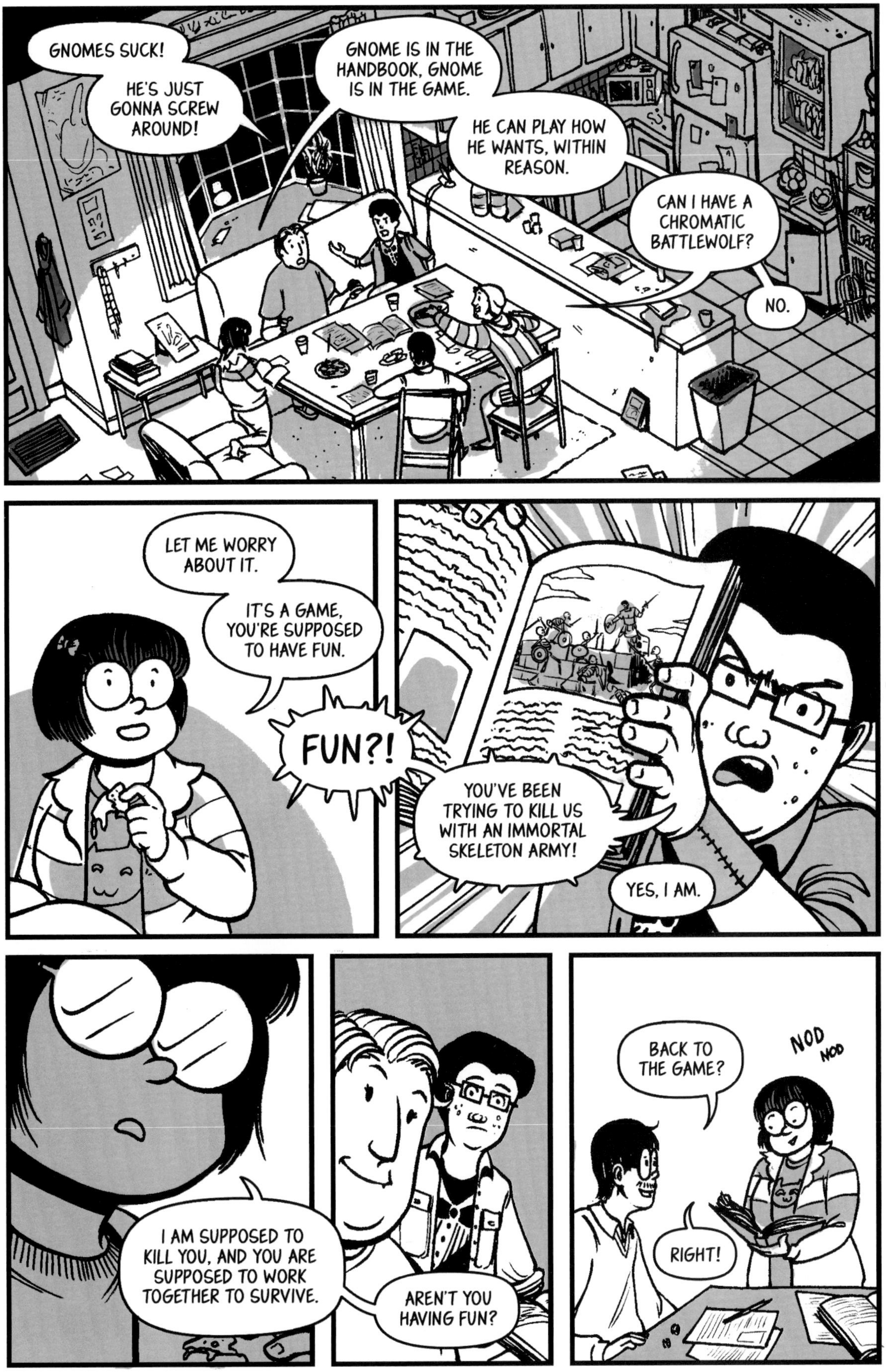
GNOMES SUCK!
HE'S JUST GONNA SCREW AROUND!
GNOME IS IN THE HANDBOOK, GNOME IS IN THE GAME.
HE CAN PLAY HOW HE WANTS, WITHIN REASON.
CAN I HAVE A CHROMATIC BATTLEWOLF?
NO.
LET ME WORRY ABOUT IT.
IT'S A GAME, YOU'RE SUPPOSED TO HAVE FUN.
FUN?!
YOU'VE BEEN TRYING TO KILL US WITH AN IMMORTAL SKELETON ARMY!
YES, I AM.
I AM SUPPOSED TO KILL YOU, AND YOU ARE SUPPOSED TO WORK TOGETHER TO SURVIVE.
AREN'T YOU HAVING FUN?
BACK TO THE GAME?
NOD NOD
RIGHT!

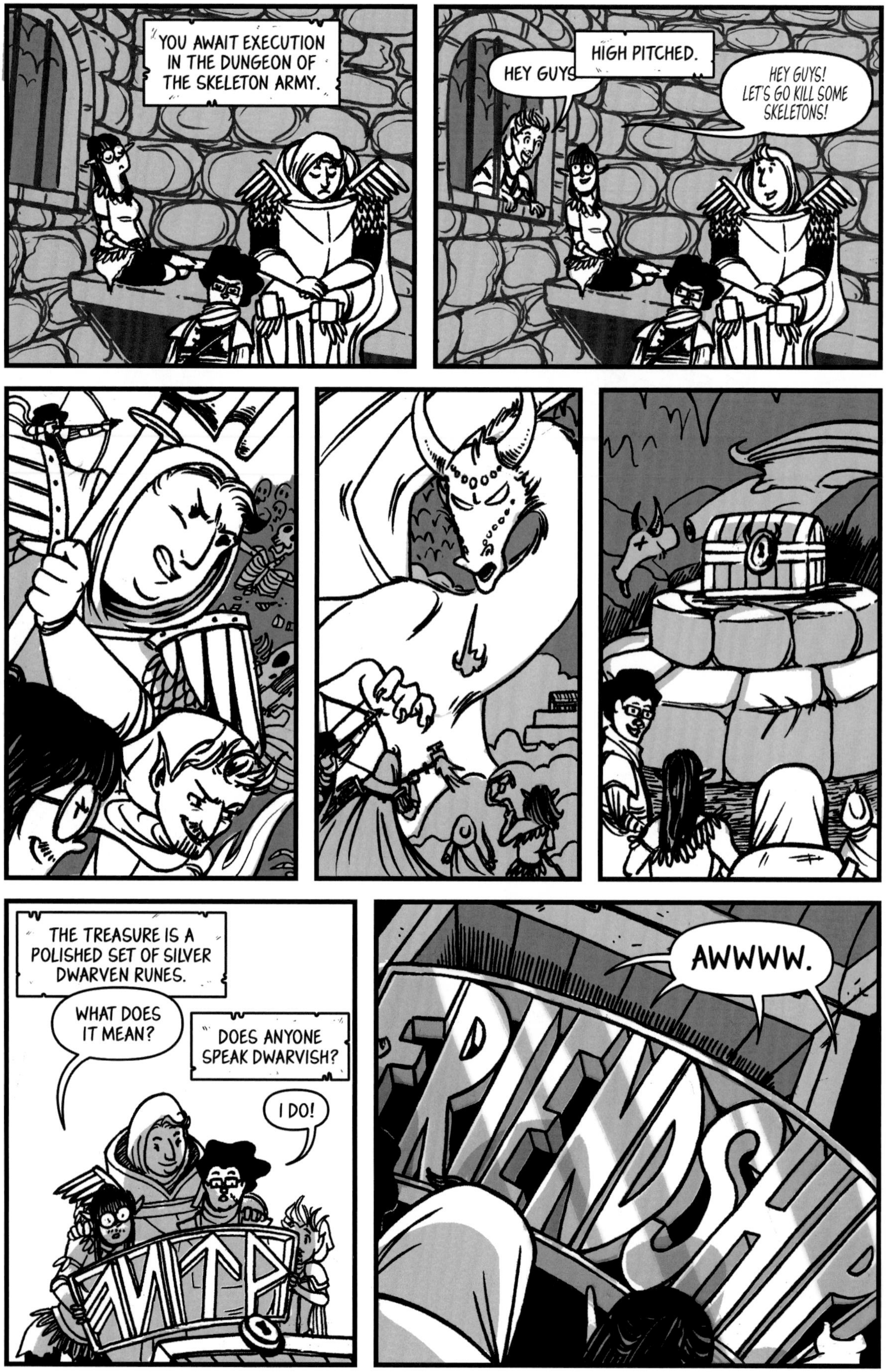
YOU AWAIT EXECUTION IN THE DUNGEON OF THE SKELETON ARMY.
HEY GUYS
HIGH PITCHED.
HEY GUYS! LET'S GO KILL SOME SKELETONS!
THE TREASURE IS A POLISHED SET OF SILVER DWARVEN RUNES.
WHAT DOES IT MEAN?
DOES ANYONE SPEAK DWARVISH?
I DO!
AWWWW.

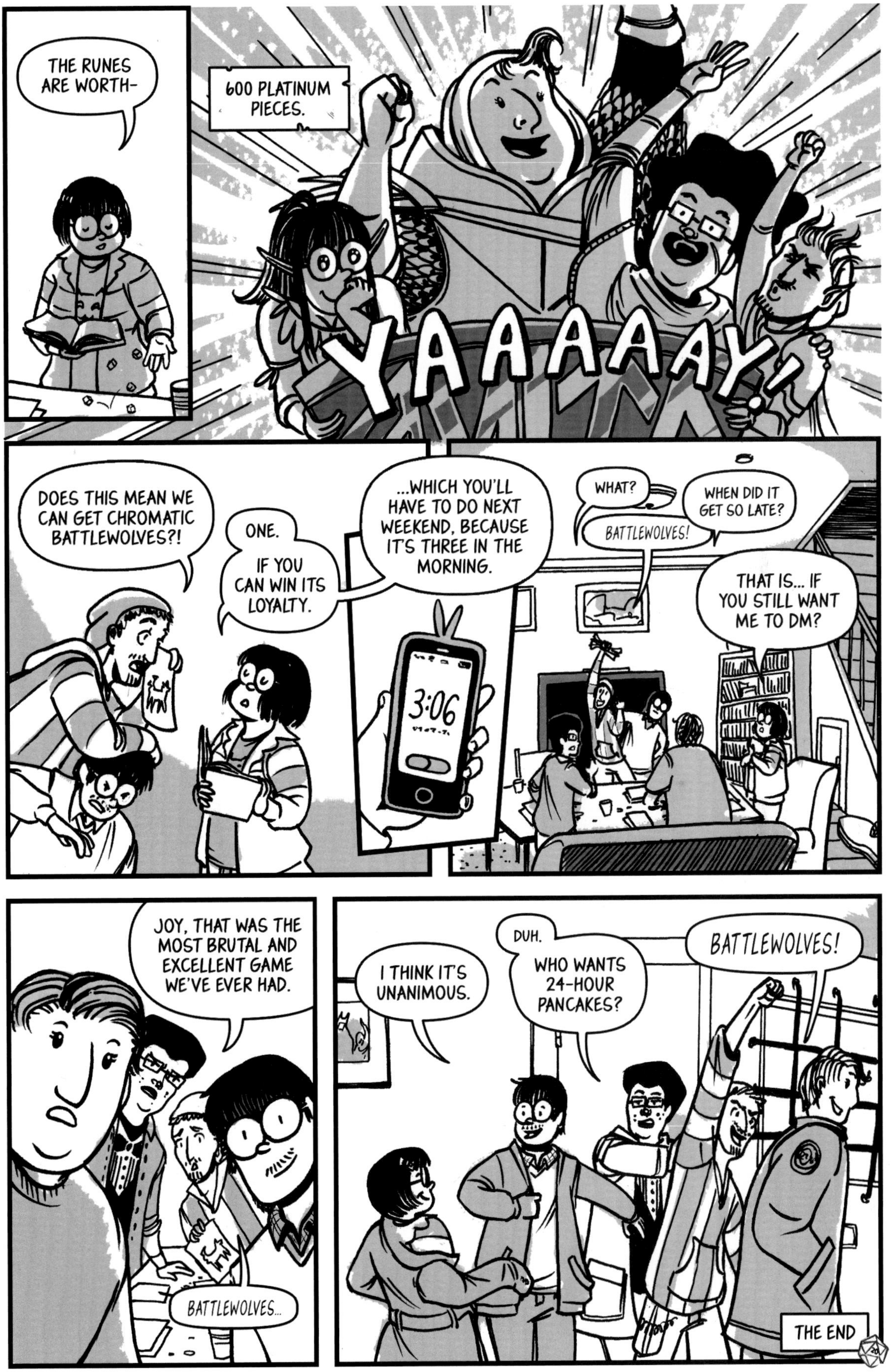

THE RUNES ARE WORTH-
600 PLATINUM PIECES.
YAAAAAY!
DOES THIS MEAN WE CAN GET CHROMATIC BATTLEWOLVES?!
ONE.
IF YOU CAN WIN ITS LOYALTY.
...WHICH YOU'LL HAVE TO DO NEXT WEEKEND, BECAUSE IT'S THREE IN THE MORNING.
3:06
WHAT?
BATTLEWOLVES!
WHEN DID IT GET SO LATE?
THAT IS... IF YOU STILL WANT ME TO DM?
JOY, THAT WAS THE MOST BRUTAL AND EXCELLENT GAME WE'VE EVER HAD.
BATTLEWOLVES...
I THINK IT'S UNANIMOUS.
DUH.
WHO WANTS 24-HOUR PANCAKES?
BATTLEWOLVES!
THE END

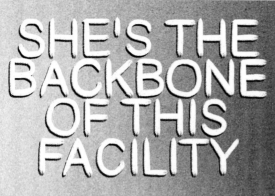

SHE'S THE BACKBONE OF THIS FACILITY

Attention: lots of spoilers ahead.
Dedicated to Hazel, the most patient angel on Earth.

Let's talk about GLaDOS.

She wasn't always an A.I.

First, she was Caroline...

...assistant of Aperture's founder,

Cave Johnson.

We have limited information about Caroline.

The only picture of her is a portrait with Cave.

The two are aged.

CAVE JOHNSON

Her in-game lines aren't much help; they're only five, and in two of them she's saying:

YES SIR, MR. JOHNSON!

Cave tells us a bit about her:

That eager voice you heard is the lovely Caroline, my assistant.

She's the backbone of this facility. Pretty as a postcard, too.

Sorry, fellas. She's married. To science.

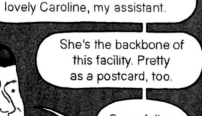

He never talks *about* her again, but he mentions her several times.

Caroline, are the compensation vouchers ready?

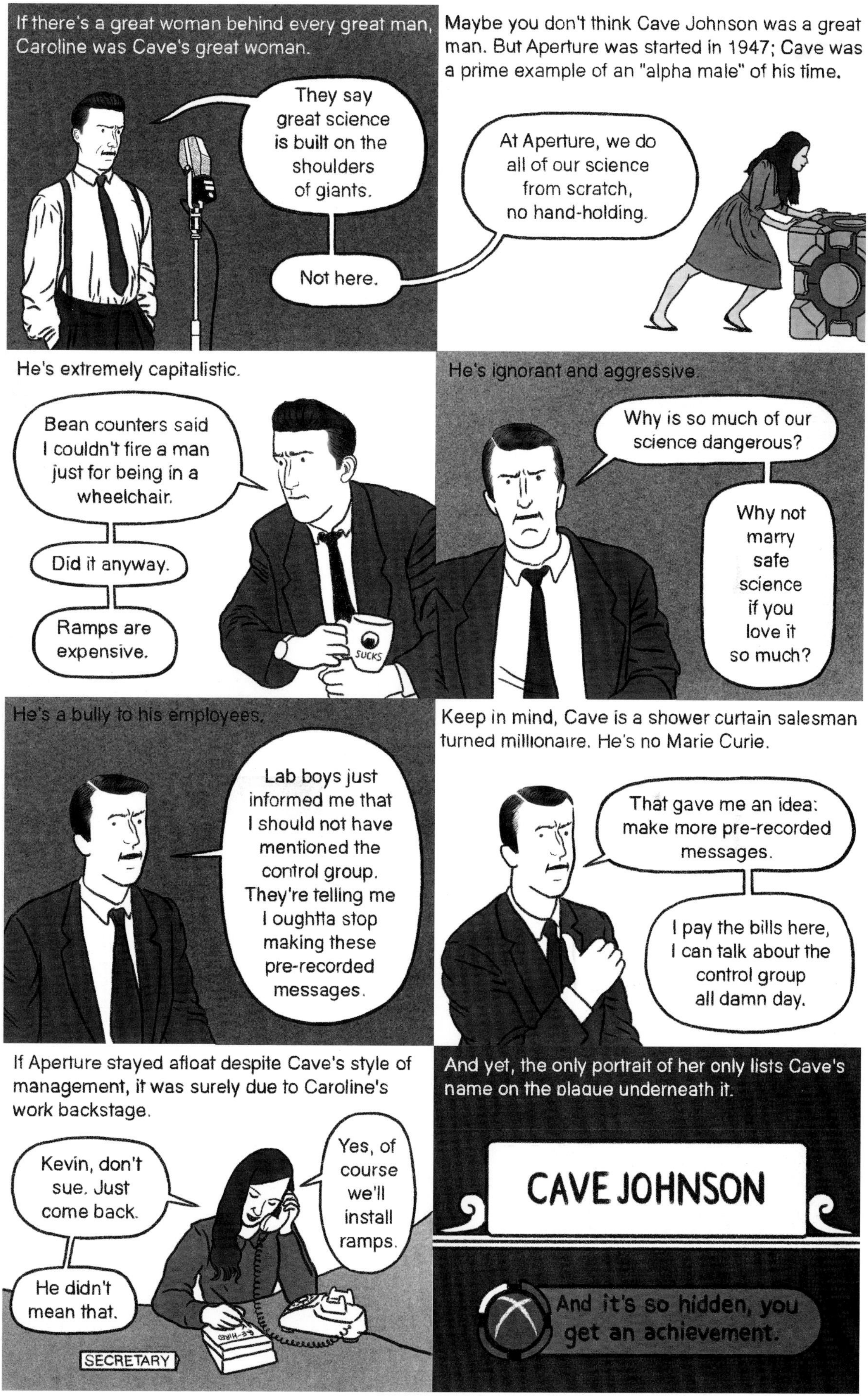

If there's a great woman behind every great man, Caroline was Cave's great woman.
They say great science is built on the shoulders of giants.
Not here.
Maybe you don't think Cave Johnson was a great man. But Aperture was started in 1947; Cave was a prime example of an "alpha male" of his time.
At Aperture, we do all of our science from scratch, no hand-holding.
He's extremely capitalistic.
Bean counters said I couldn't fire a man just for being in a wheelchair.
Did it anyway.
Ramps are expensive.
SUCKS
He's ignorant and aggressive.
Why is so much of our science dangerous?
Why not marry safe science if you love it so much?
He's a bully to his employees.
Lab boys just informed me that I should not have mentioned the control group. They're telling me I oughtta stop making these pre-recorded messages.
Keep in mind, Cave is a shower curtain salesman turned millionaire. He's no Marie Curie.
That gave me an idea: make more pre-recorded messages.
I pay the bills here, I can talk about the control group all damn day.
If Aperture stayed afloat despite Cave's style of management, it was surely due to Caroline's work backstage.
Kevin, don't sue. Just come back.
He didn't mean that.
Yes, of course we'll install ramps.
SECRETARY
And yet, the only portrait of her only lists Cave's name on the plaque underneath it.
CAVE JOHNSON
And it's so hidden, you get an achievement.

In 1974, Cave's bravado causes his destruction.

The bean counters told me we literally could not afford to buy seven dollars worth of moon rocks, much less seventy million.

Bought 'em anyway. Ground 'em up, mixed 'em into a gel.

MOON CURE (?)

And guess what?

Ground up moon rocks are pure poison. I am deathly ill.

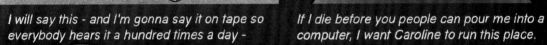

At this point, Caroline's duties have gone beyond assistant and second in command: she's also Cave's nurse.

Caroline, please bring me more pain pills.

Two years later, on his deathbed, Cave left this message for his lab boys:

Brain mapping. Artificial intelligence.

We should have been working on it thirty years ago.

I will say this - and I'm gonna say it on tape so everybody hears it a hundred times a day -

If I die before you people can pour me into a computer, I want Caroline to run this place.

Now she'll argue, she'll say she can't, she's modest like that. But you make her.

Hell, put her in my computer, I don't care.

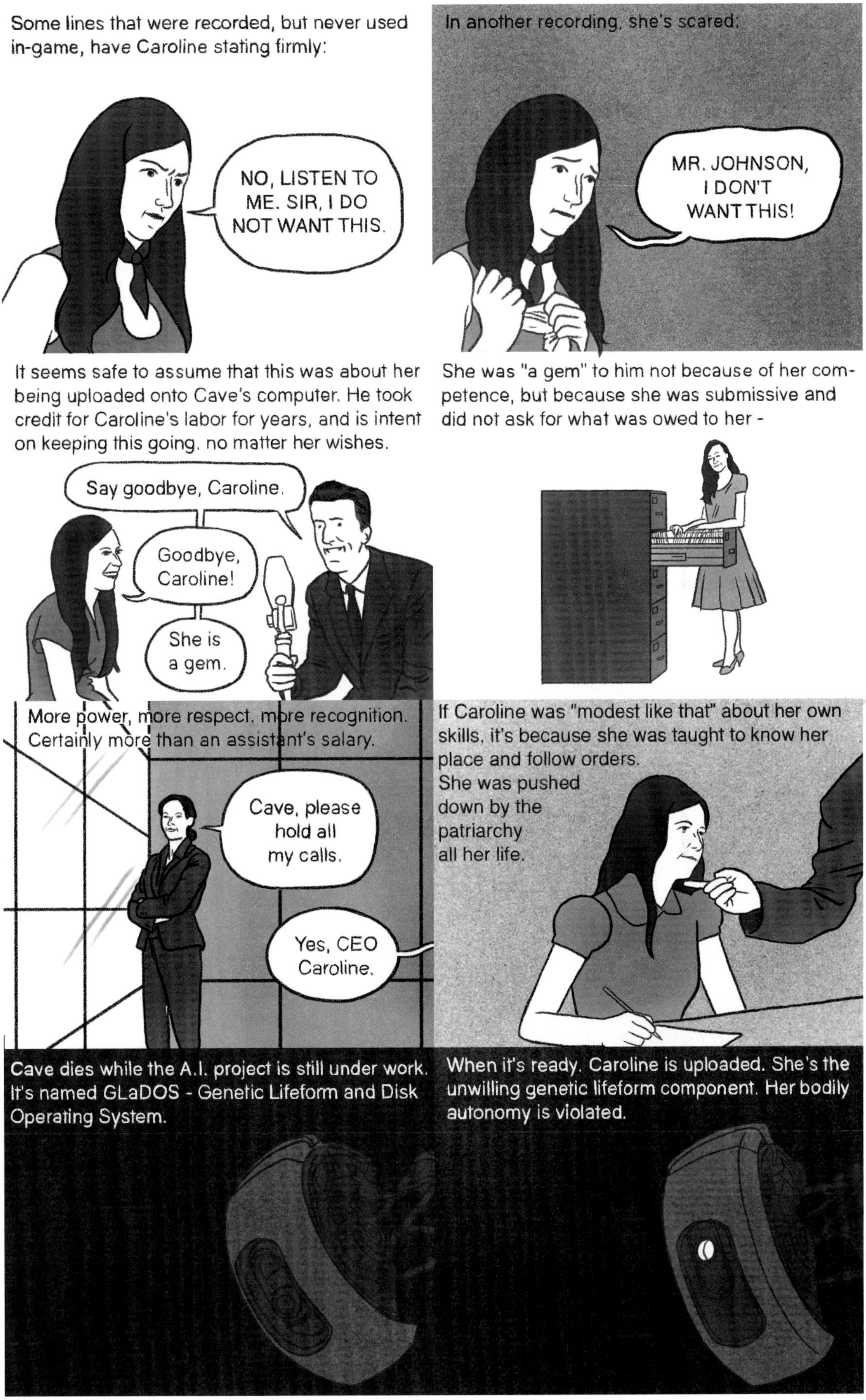
Some lines that were recorded, but never used in-game, have Caroline stating firmly:
NO, LISTEN TO ME. SIR, I DO NOT WANT THIS.
In another recording, she's scared:
MR. JOHNSON, I DON'T WANT THIS!
It seems safe to assume that this was about her being uploaded onto Cave's computer. He took credit for Caroline's labor for years, and is intent on keeping this going, no matter her wishes.
Say goodbye, Caroline.
Goodbye, Caroline!
She is a gem.
She was "a gem" to him not because of her competence, but because she was submissive and did not ask for what was owed to her -
More power, more respect, more recognition. Certainly more than an assistant's salary.
Cave, please hold all my calls.
Yes, CEO Caroline.
If Caroline was "modest like that" about her own skills, it's because she was taught to know her place and follow orders.
She was pushed down by the patriarchy all her life.
Cave dies while the A.I. project is still under work. It's named GLaDOS - Genetic Lifeform and Disk Operating System.
When it's ready, Caroline is uploaded. She's the unwilling genetic lifeform component. Her bodily autonomy is violated.

Caroline was put into GLaDOS by the "lab boys." They also built the body, which resembles a woman in bondage (as has been pointed out many times on the internet).

I think it adds to the story that this was a body built by men, the same men who forced her into it.

Is it any wonder that, upon first activation, GLaDOS tries to kill all the scientists in Aperture? Within 1/16 of a picosecond, in fact?

In response to GLaDOS' attempts at - let's call it what it is - revenge, the lab boys create personality cores.

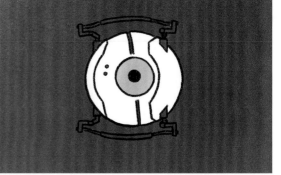

They are meant to override GLaDOS' own personality. So, after violating a woman, they react to her anger by removing her free will.

One of the cores simply lists ingredients for a vanilla cake recipe. Forcing on GLaDOS an interest as domestic as baking is very telling of what kind of men these were.

FOUR
LARGE
EGGS

When in potato form, GLaDOS says:

The scientists were always hanging cores on me to regulate my behavior. I've heard voices all my life.

But now I hear the voice of a conscience, and it's terrifying, because for the first time it's my voice.

While GLaDOS was trapped and brainwashed with cores, Chell was making her escape.

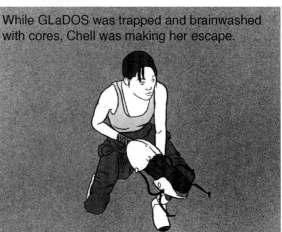

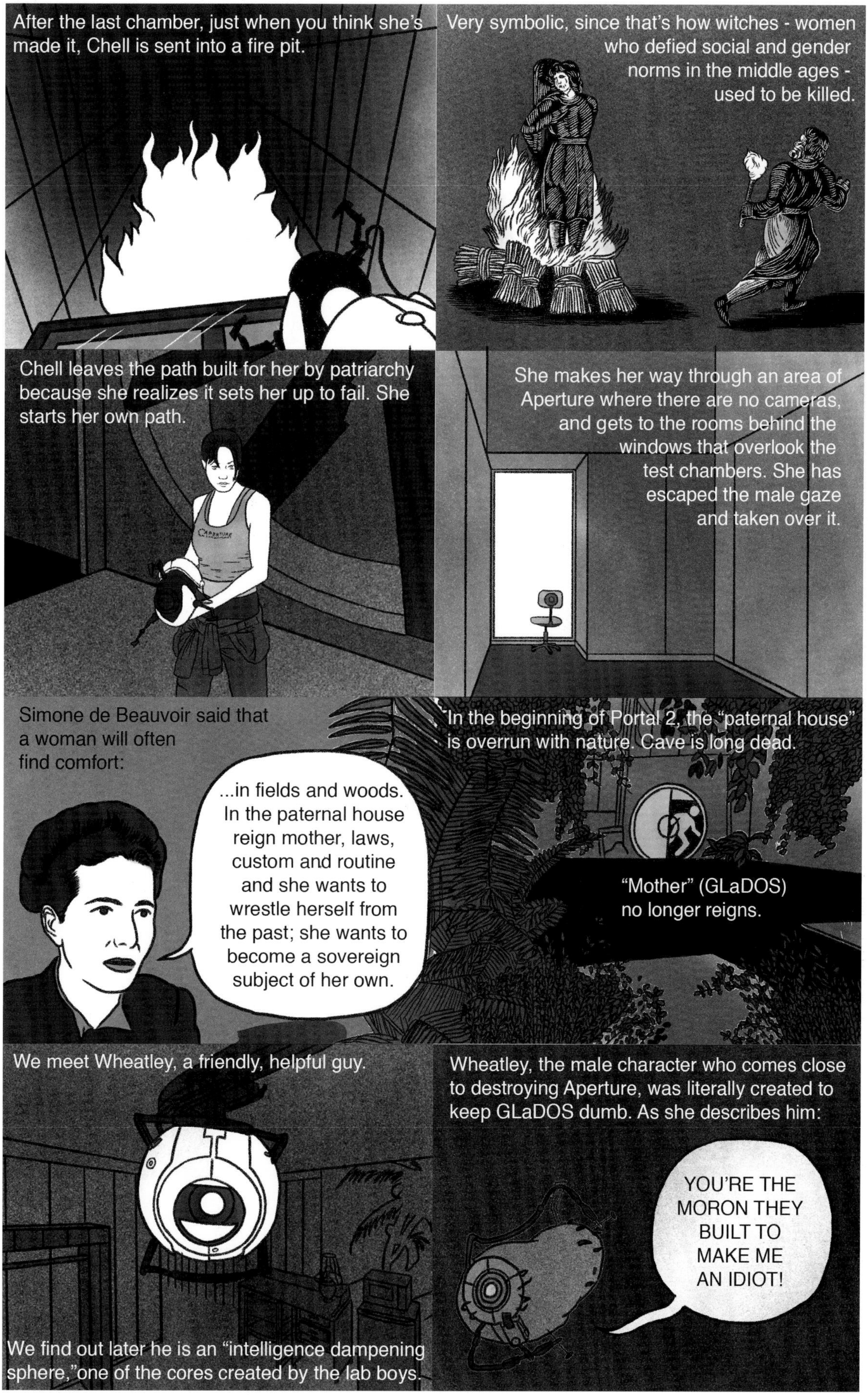

After the last chamber, just when you think she's made it, Chell is sent into a fire pit.
Very symbolic, since that's how witches - women who defied social and gender norms in the middle ages - used to be killed.
Chell leaves the path built for her by patriarchy because she realizes it sets her up to fail. She starts her own path.
APERTURE
She makes her way through an area of Aperture where there are no cameras, and gets to the rooms behind the windows that overlook the test chambers. She has escaped the male gaze and taken over it.
Simone de Beauvoir said that a woman will often find comfort:
...in fields and woods. In the paternal house reign mother, laws, custom and routine and she wants to wrestle herself from the past; she wants to become a sovereign subject of her own.
In the beginning of Portal 2, the "paternal house" is overrun with nature. Cave is long dead.
"Mother" (GLaDOS) no longer reigns.
We meet Wheatley, a friendly, helpful guy.
We find out later he is an "intelligence dampening sphere,"one of the cores created by the lab boys.
Wheatley, the male character who comes close to destroying Aperture, was literally created to keep GLaDOS dumb. As she describes him:
YOU'RE THE MORON THEY BUILT TO MAKE ME AN IDIOT!

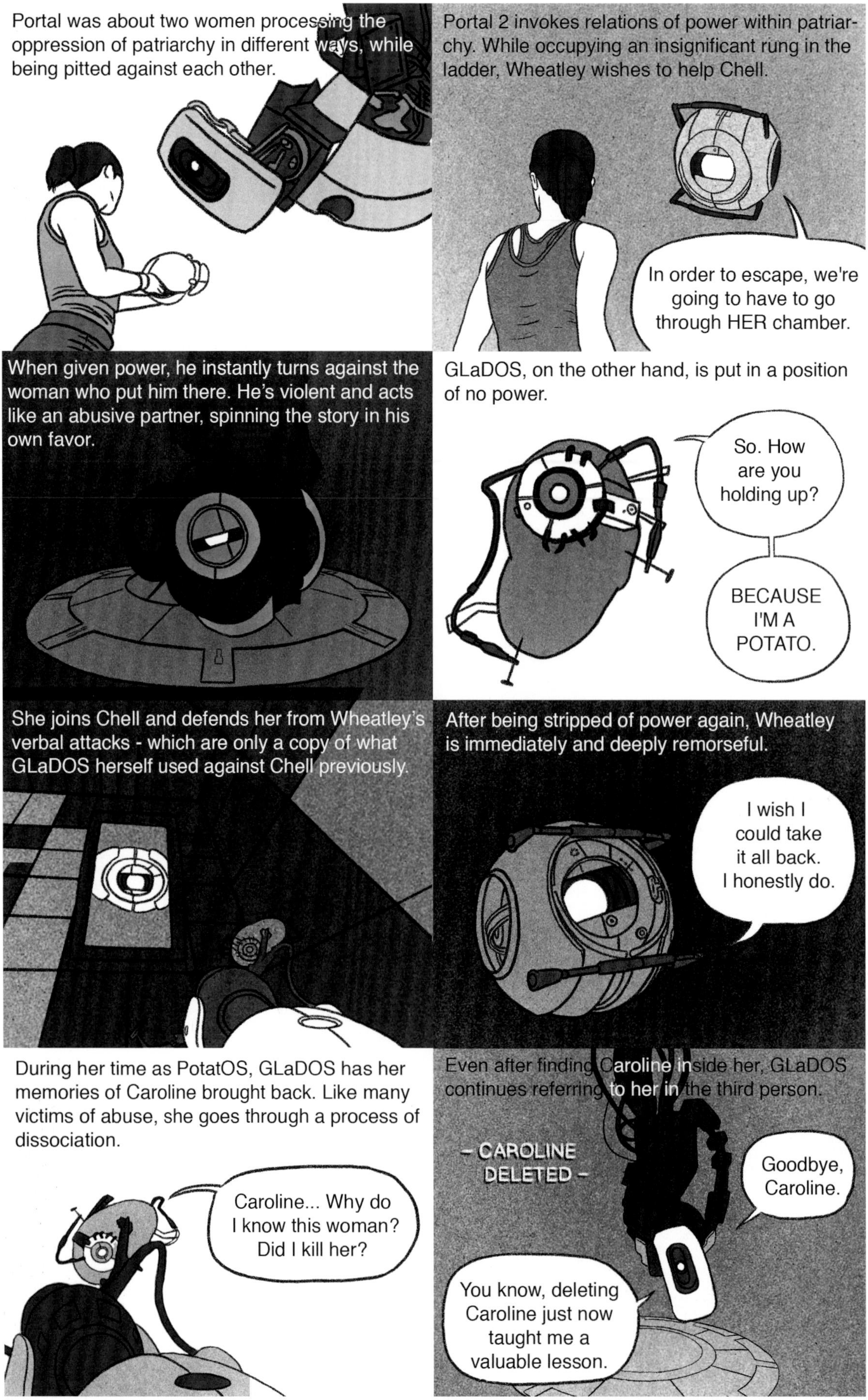
Portal was about two women processing the oppression of patriarchy in different ways, while being pitted against each other.
Portal 2 invokes relations of power within patriarchy. While occupying an insignificant rung in the ladder, Wheatley wishes to help Chell.
In order to escape, we're going to have to go through HER chamber.
When given power, he instantly turns against the woman who put him there. He's violent and acts like an abusive partner, spinning the story in his own favor.
GLaDOS, on the other hand, is put in a position of no power.
So. How are you holding up?
BECAUSE I'M A POTATO.
She joins Chell and defends her from Wheatley's verbal attacks - which are only a copy of what GLaDOS herself used against Chell previously.
After being stripped of power again, Wheatley is immediately and deeply remorseful.
I wish I could take it all back. I honestly do.
During her time as PotatOS, GLaDOS has her memories of Caroline brought back. Like many victims of abuse, she goes through a process of dissociation.
Caroline... Why do I know this woman? Did I kill her?
Even after finding Caroline inside her, GLaDOS continues referring to her in the third person.
- CAROLINE DELETED -
Goodbye, Caroline.
You know, deleting Caroline just now taught me a valuable lesson.

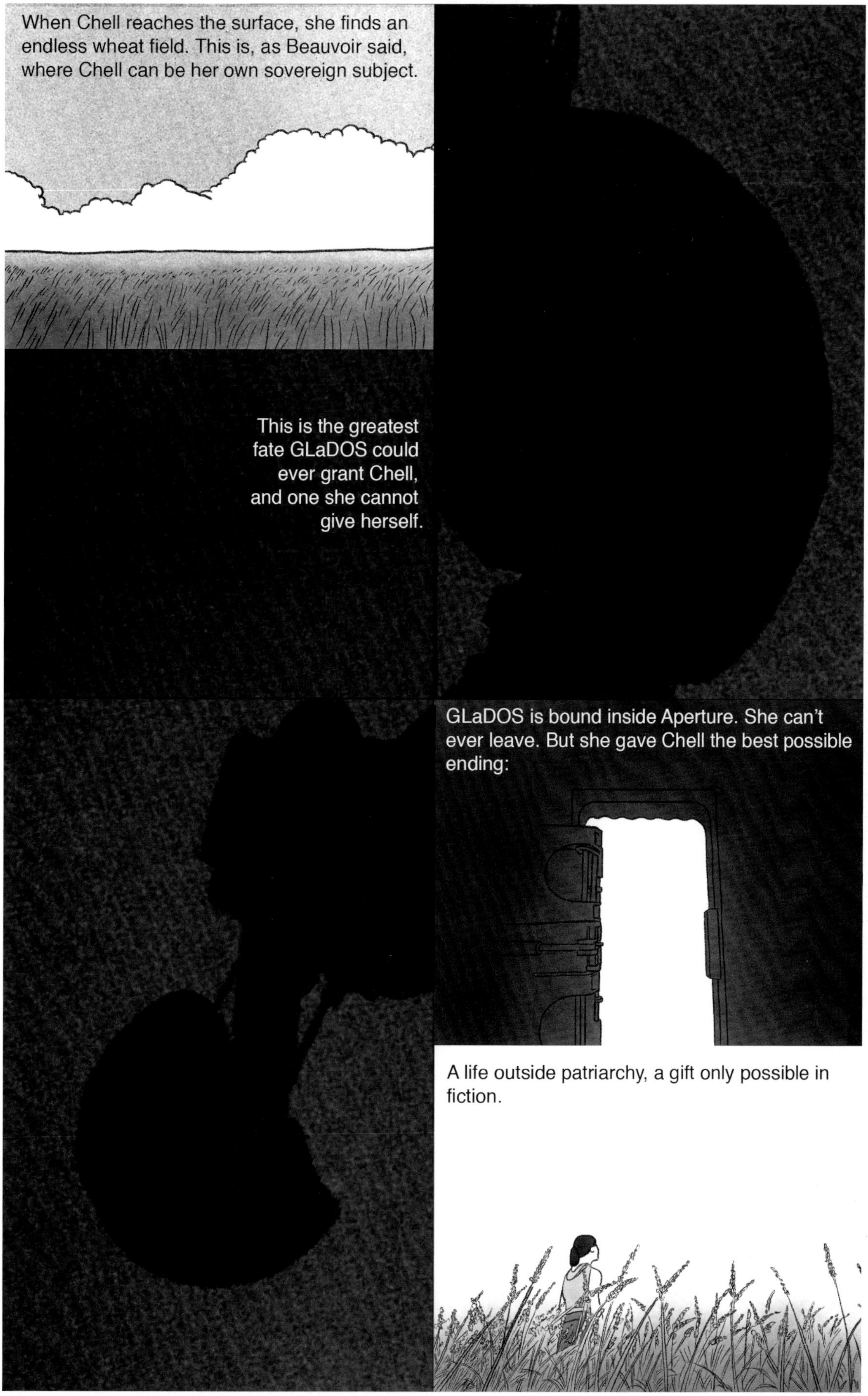
When Chell reaches the surface, she finds an endless wheat field. This is, as Beauvoir said, where Chell can be her own sovereign subject.
This is the greatest fate GLaDOS could ever grant Chell, and one she cannot give herself.
GLaDOS is bound inside Aperture. She can't ever leave. But she gave Chell the best possible ending:
A life outside patriarchy, a gift only possible in fiction.

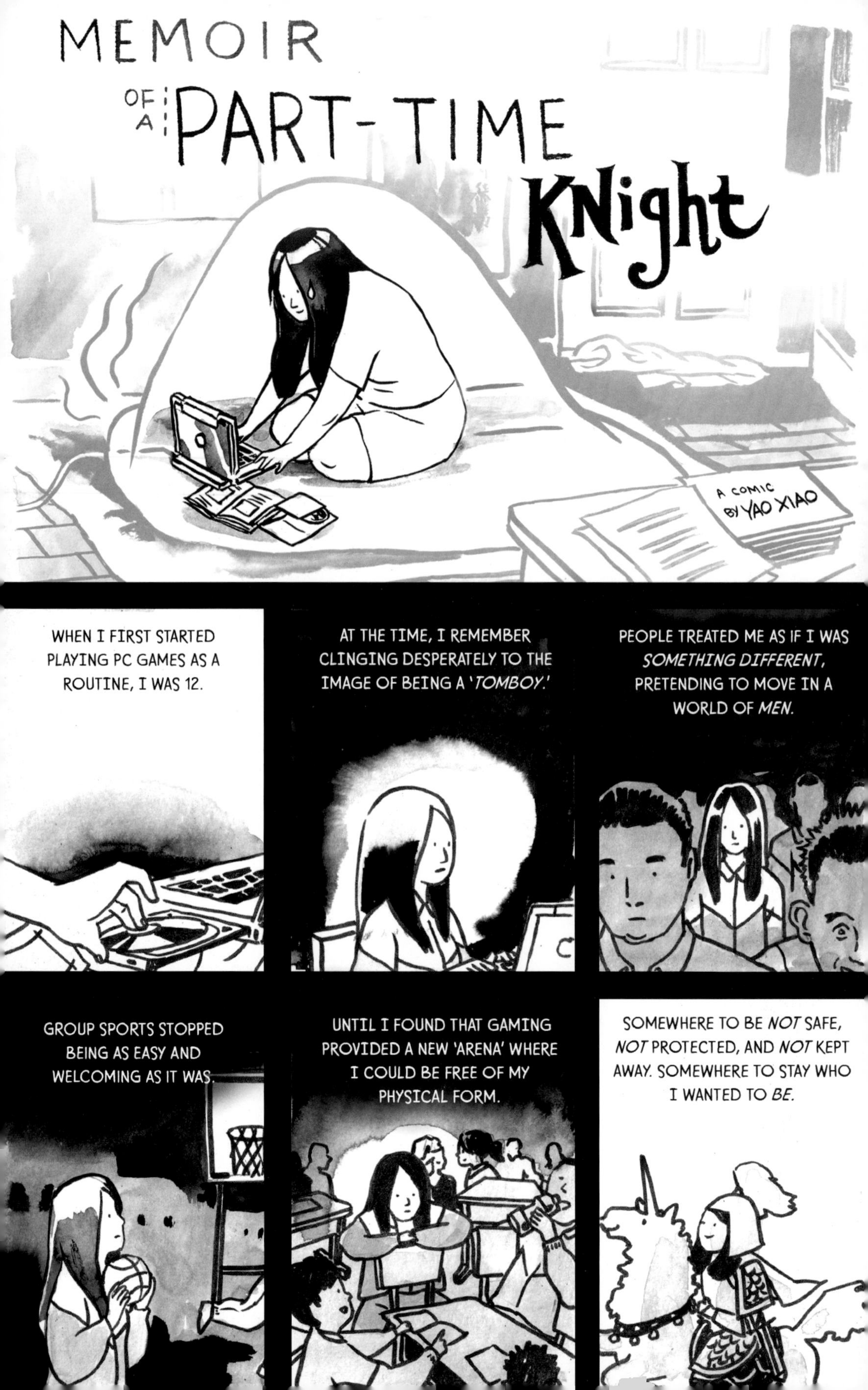
MEMOIR OF A PART-TIME KNIGHT
A COMIC BY YAO XIAO
WHEN I FIRST STARTED PLAYING PC GAMES AS A ROUTINE, I WAS 12.
AT THE TIME, I REMEMBER CLINGING DESPERATELY TO THE IMAGE OF BEING A '*TOMBOY*.'
PEOPLE TREATED ME AS IF I WAS *SOMETHING DIFFERENT*, PRETENDING TO MOVE IN A WORLD OF *MEN*.
GROUP SPORTS STOPPED BEING AS EASY AND WELCOMING AS IT WAS.
UNTIL I FOUND THAT GAMING PROVIDED A NEW 'ARENA' WHERE I COULD BE FREE OF MY PHYSICAL FORM.
SOMEWHERE TO BE *NOT* SAFE, *NOT* PROTECTED, AND *NOT* KEPT AWAY. SOMEWHERE TO STAY WHO I WANTED TO *BE*.

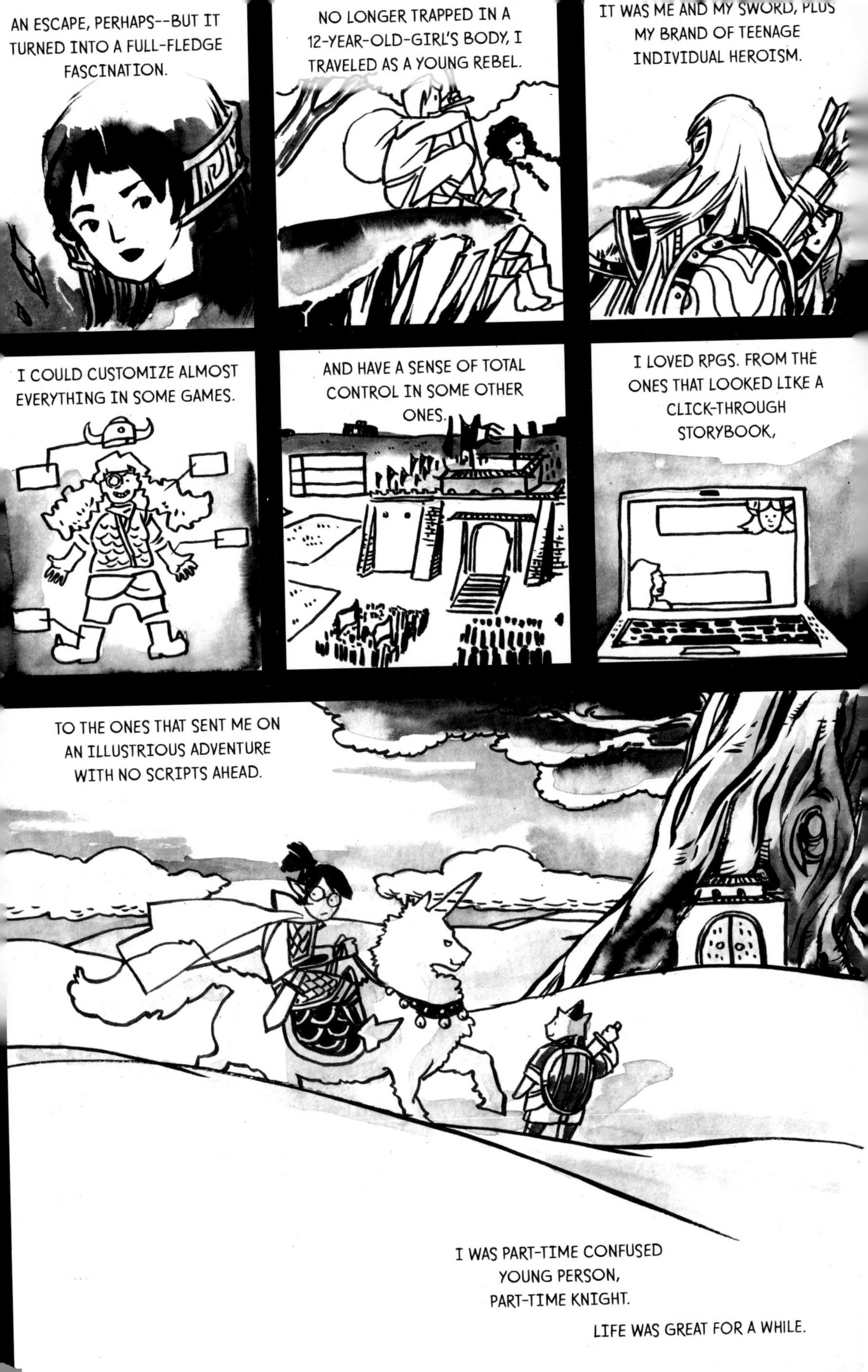
AN ESCAPE, PERHAPS--BUT IT TURNED INTO A FULL-FLEDGE FASCINATION.
NO LONGER TRAPPED IN A 12-YEAR-OLD-GIRL'S BODY, I TRAVELED AS A YOUNG REBEL.
IT WAS ME AND MY SWORD, PLUS MY BRAND OF TEENAGE INDIVIDUAL HEROISM.
I COULD CUSTOMIZE ALMOST EVERYTHING IN SOME GAMES.
AND HAVE A SENSE OF TOTAL CONTROL IN SOME OTHER ONES.
I LOVED RPGS. FROM THE ONES THAT LOOKED LIKE A CLICK-THROUGH STORYBOOK,
TO THE ONES THAT SENT ME ON AN ILLUSTRIOUS ADVENTURE WITH NO SCRIPTS AHEAD.
I WAS PART-TIME CONFUSED YOUNG PERSON, PART-TIME KNIGHT.
LIFE WAS GREAT FOR A WHILE.

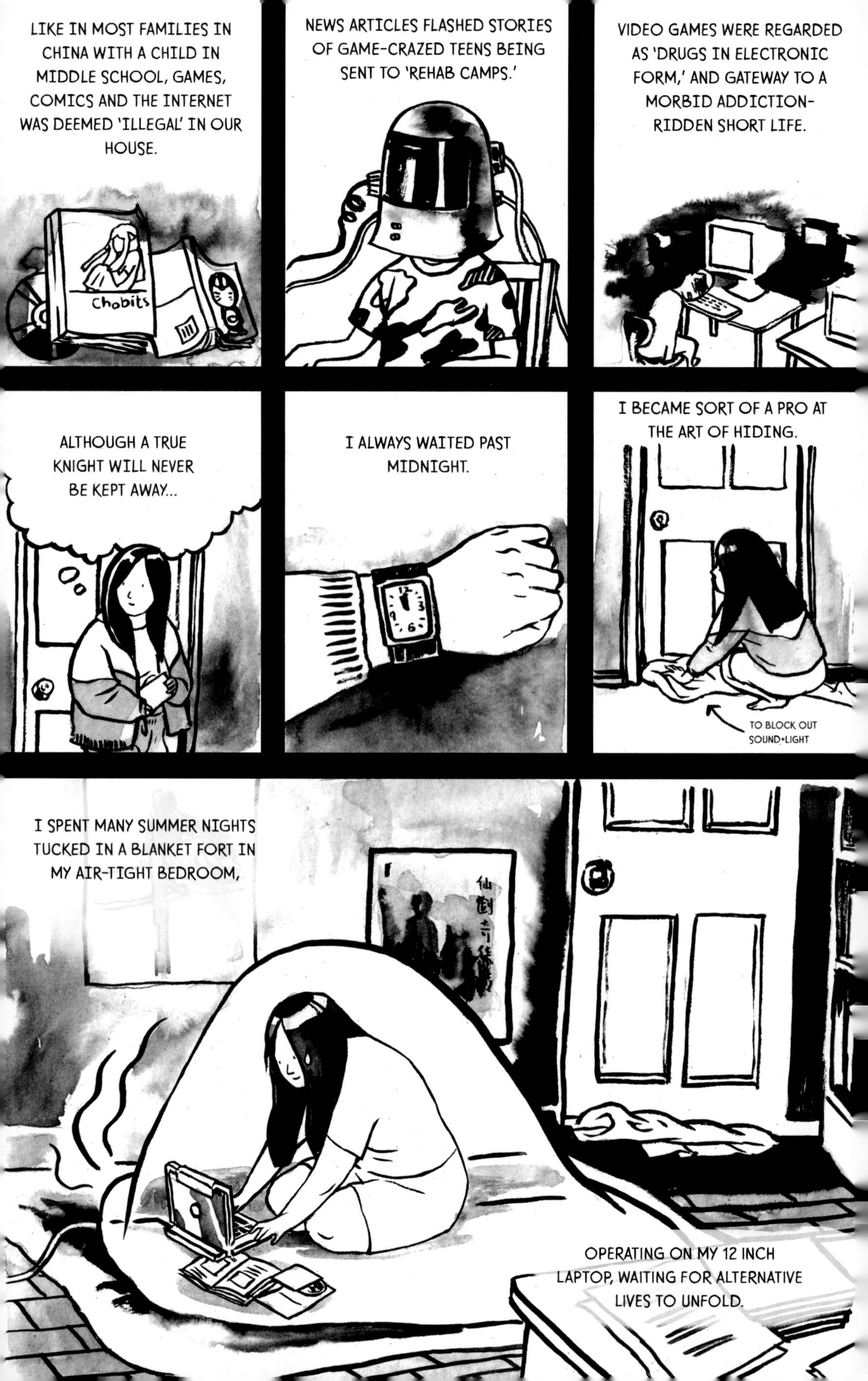
LIKE IN MOST FAMILIES IN CHINA WITH A CHILD IN MIDDLE SCHOOL, GAMES, COMICS AND THE INTERNET WAS DEEMED 'ILLEGAL' IN OUR HOUSE.
Chobits
NEWS ARTICLES FLASHED STORIES OF GAME-CRAZED TEENS BEING SENT TO 'REHAB CAMPS.'
VIDEO GAMES WERE REGARDED AS 'DRUGS IN ELECTRONIC FORM,' AND GATEWAY TO A MORBID ADDICTION-RIDDEN SHORT LIFE.
ALTHOUGH A TRUE KNIGHT WILL NEVER BE KEPT AWAY...
I ALWAYS WAITED PAST MIDNIGHT.
I BECAME SORT OF A PRO AT THE ART OF HIDING.
TO BLOCK OUT SOUND+LIGHT
I SPENT MANY SUMMER NIGHTS TUCKED IN A BLANKET FORT IN MY AIR-TIGHT BEDROOM,
OPERATING ON MY 12 INCH LAPTOP, WAITING FOR ALTERNATIVE LIVES TO UNFOLD.

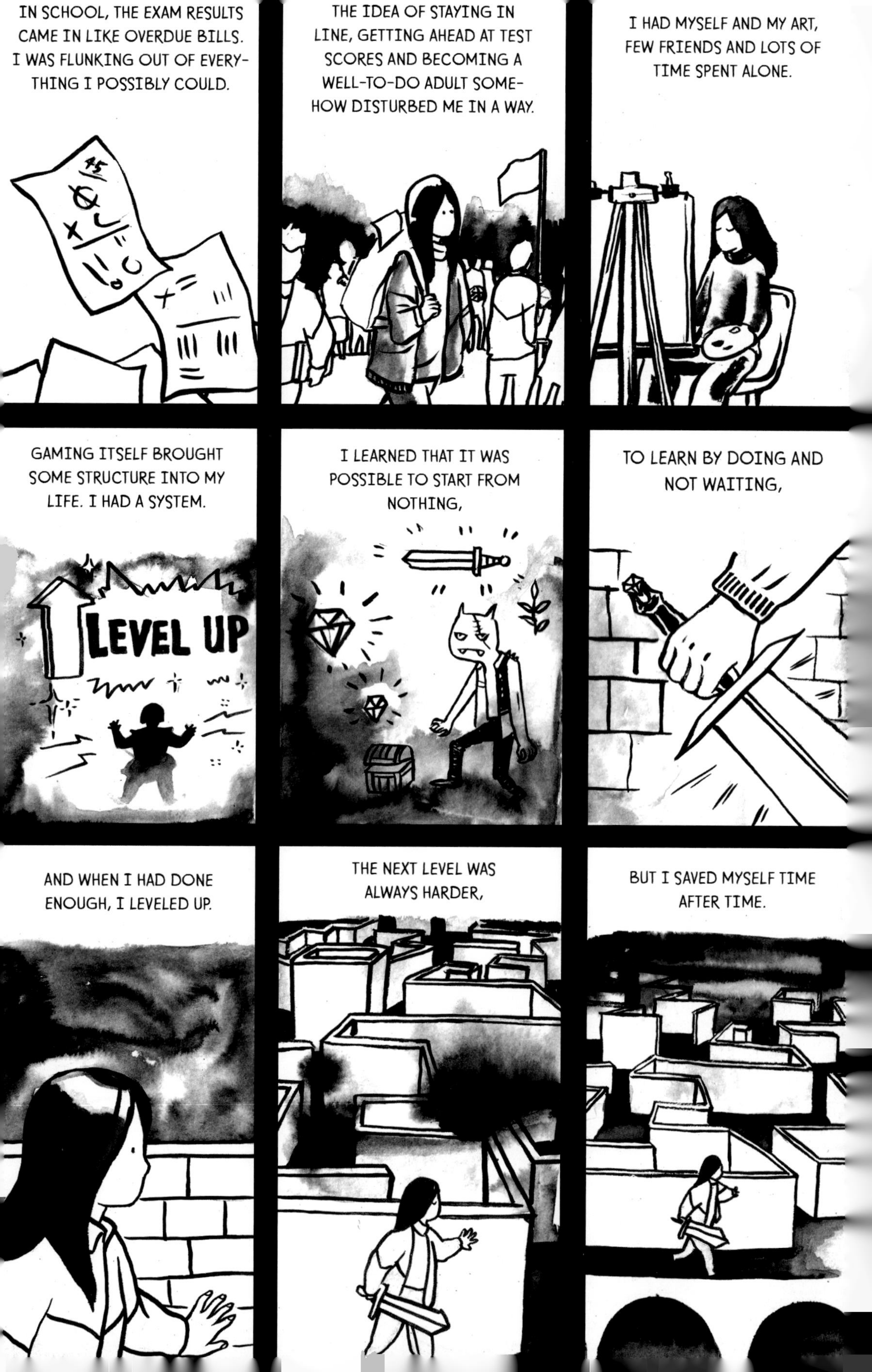
IN SCHOOL, THE EXAM RESULTS CAME IN LIKE OVERDUE BILLS. I WAS FLUNKING OUT OF EVERYTHING I POSSIBLY COULD.
THE IDEA OF STAYING IN LINE, GETTING AHEAD AT TEST SCORES AND BECOMING A WELL-TO-DO ADULT SOMEHOW DISTURBED ME IN A WAY.
I HAD MYSELF AND MY ART, FEW FRIENDS AND LOTS OF TIME SPENT ALONE.
GAMING ITSELF BROUGHT SOME STRUCTURE INTO MY LIFE. I HAD A SYSTEM.
LEVEL UP
I LEARNED THAT IT WAS POSSIBLE TO START FROM NOTHING,
TO LEARN BY DOING AND NOT WAITING,
AND WHEN I HAD DONE ENOUGH, I LEVELED UP.
THE NEXT LEVEL WAS ALWAYS HARDER,
BUT I SAVED MYSELF TIME AFTER TIME.

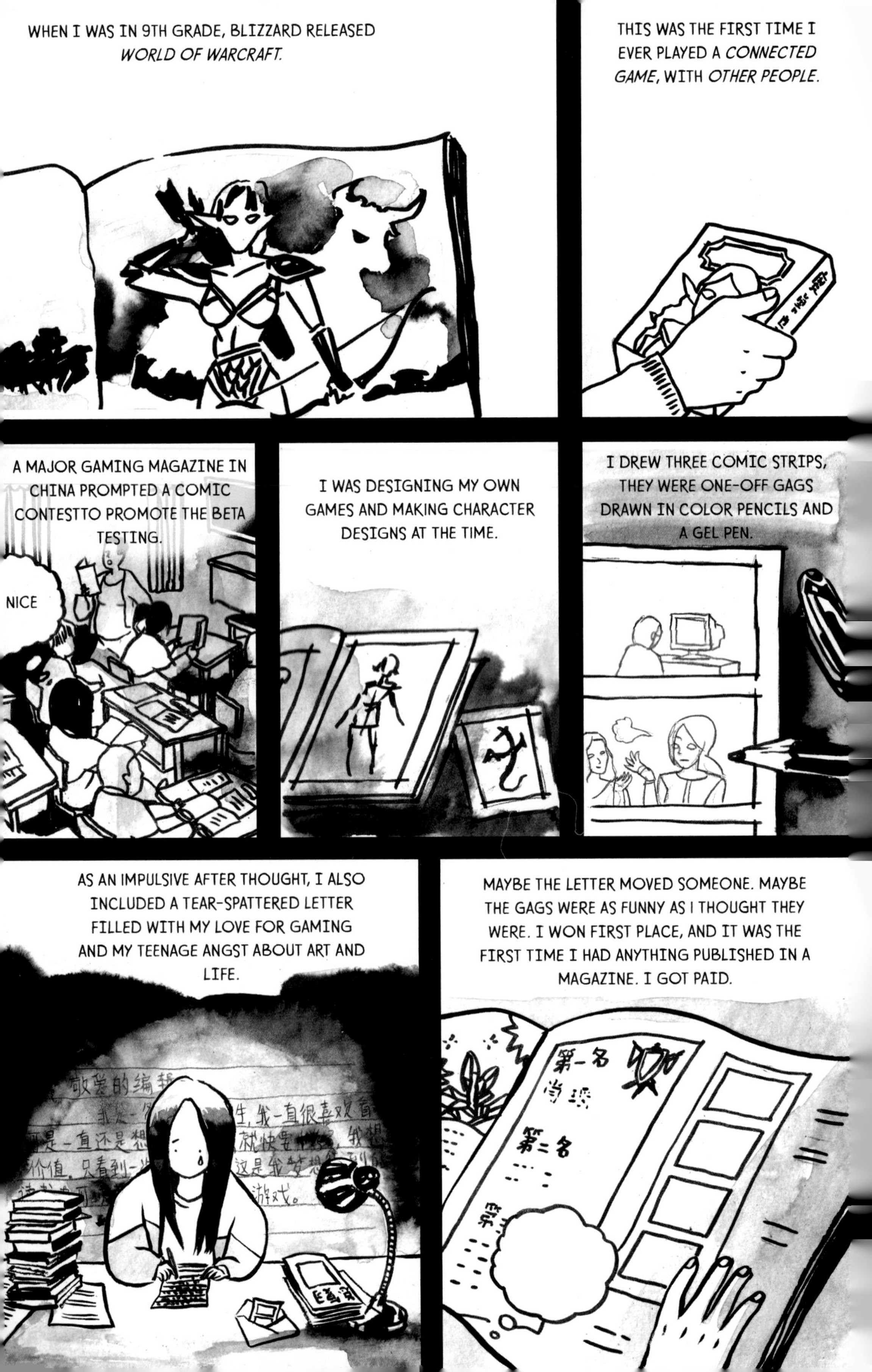

WHEN I WAS IN 9TH GRADE, BLIZZARD RELEASED *WORLD OF WARCRAFT.*
THIS WAS THE FIRST TIME I EVER PLAYED A *CONNECTED GAME*, WITH *OTHER PEOPLE*.
A MAJOR GAMING MAGAZINE IN CHINA PROMPTED A COMIC CONTESTTO PROMOTE THE BETA TESTING.
NICE
I WAS DESIGNING MY OWN GAMES AND MAKING CHARACTER DESIGNS AT THE TIME.
I DREW THREE COMIC STRIPS, THEY WERE ONE-OFF GAGS DRAWN IN COLOR PENCILS AND A GEL PEN.
AS AN IMPULSIVE AFTER THOUGHT, I ALSO INCLUDED A TEAR-SPATTERED LETTER FILLED WITH MY LOVE FOR GAMING AND MY TEENAGE ANGST ABOUT ART AND LIFE.
MAYBE THE LETTER MOVED SOMEONE. MAYBE THE GAGS WERE AS FUNNY AS I THOUGHT THEY WERE. I WON FIRST PLACE, AND IT WAS THE FIRST TIME I HAD ANYTHING PUBLISHED IN A MAGAZINE. I GOT PAID.
第一名
第二名

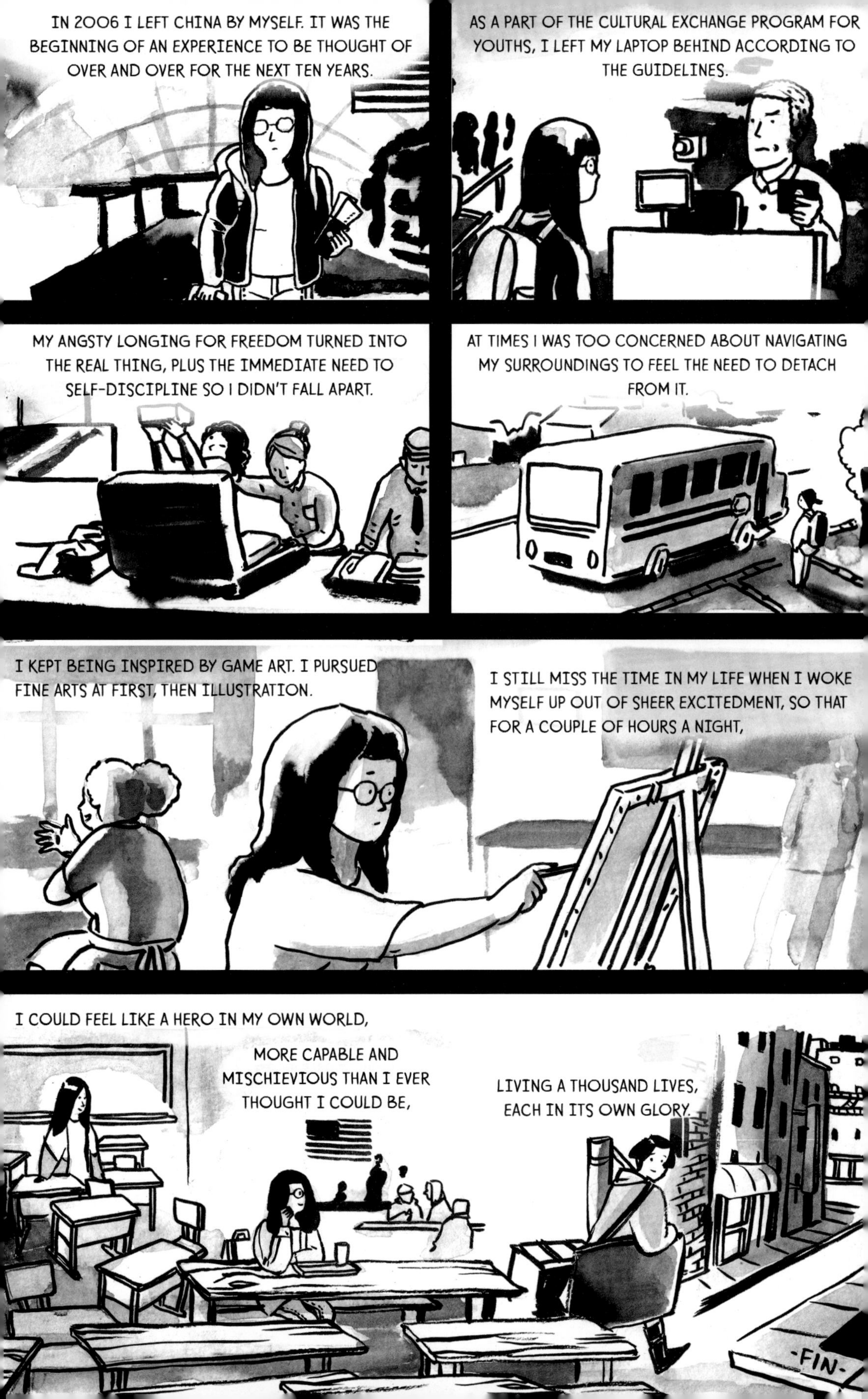
IN 2006 I LEFT CHINA BY MYSELF. IT WAS THE BEGINNING OF AN EXPERIENCE TO BE THOUGHT OF OVER AND OVER FOR THE NEXT TEN YEARS.
AS A PART OF THE CULTURAL EXCHANGE PROGRAM FOR YOUTHS, I LEFT MY LAPTOP BEHIND ACCORDING TO THE GUIDELINES.
MY ANGSTY LONGING FOR FREEDOM TURNED INTO THE REAL THING, PLUS THE IMMEDIATE NEED TO SELF-DISCIPLINE SO I DIDN'T FALL APART.
AT TIMES I WAS TOO CONCERNED ABOUT NAVIGATING MY SURROUNDINGS TO FEEL THE NEED TO DETACH FROM IT.
I KEPT BEING INSPIRED BY GAME ART. I PURSUED FINE ARTS AT FIRST, THEN ILLUSTRATION.
I STILL MISS THE TIME IN MY LIFE WHEN I WOKE MYSELF UP OUT OF SHEER EXCITEDMENT, SO THAT FOR A COUPLE OF HOURS A NIGHT,
I COULD FEEL LIKE A HERO IN MY OWN WORLD,
MORE CAPABLE AND MISCHIEVIOUS THAN I EVER THOUGHT I COULD BE,
LIVING A THOUSAND LIVES, EACH IN ITS OWN GLORY.
-FIN-

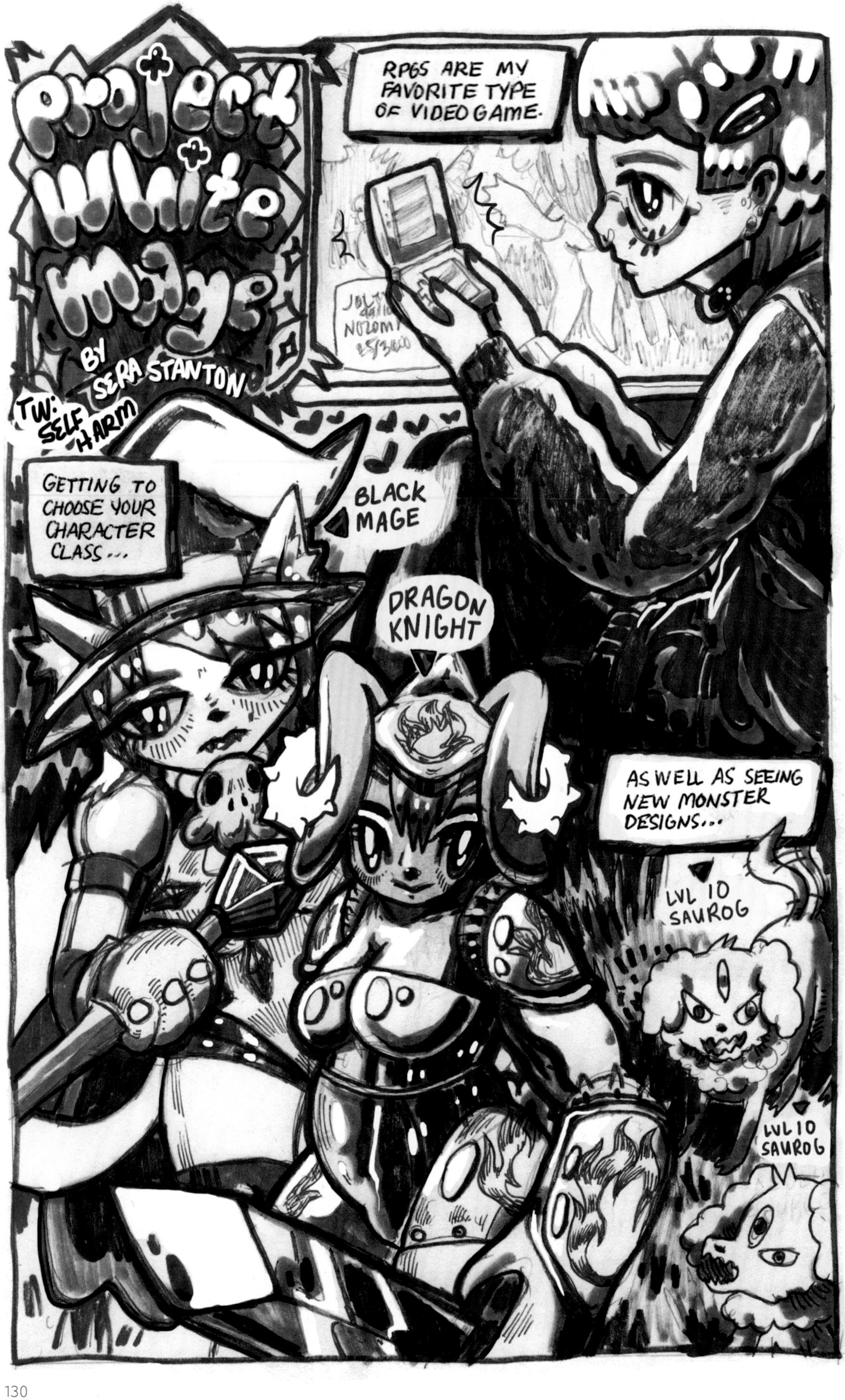
Project White Mage
BY SERA STANTON
TW: SELF HARM
RPGS ARE MY FAVORITE TYPE OF VIDEO GAME.
GETTING TO CHOOSE YOUR CHARACTER CLASS...
BLACK MAGE
DRAGON KNIGHT
AS WELL AS SEEING NEW MONSTER DESIGNS...
LVL 10 SAUROG
LVL 10 SAUROG

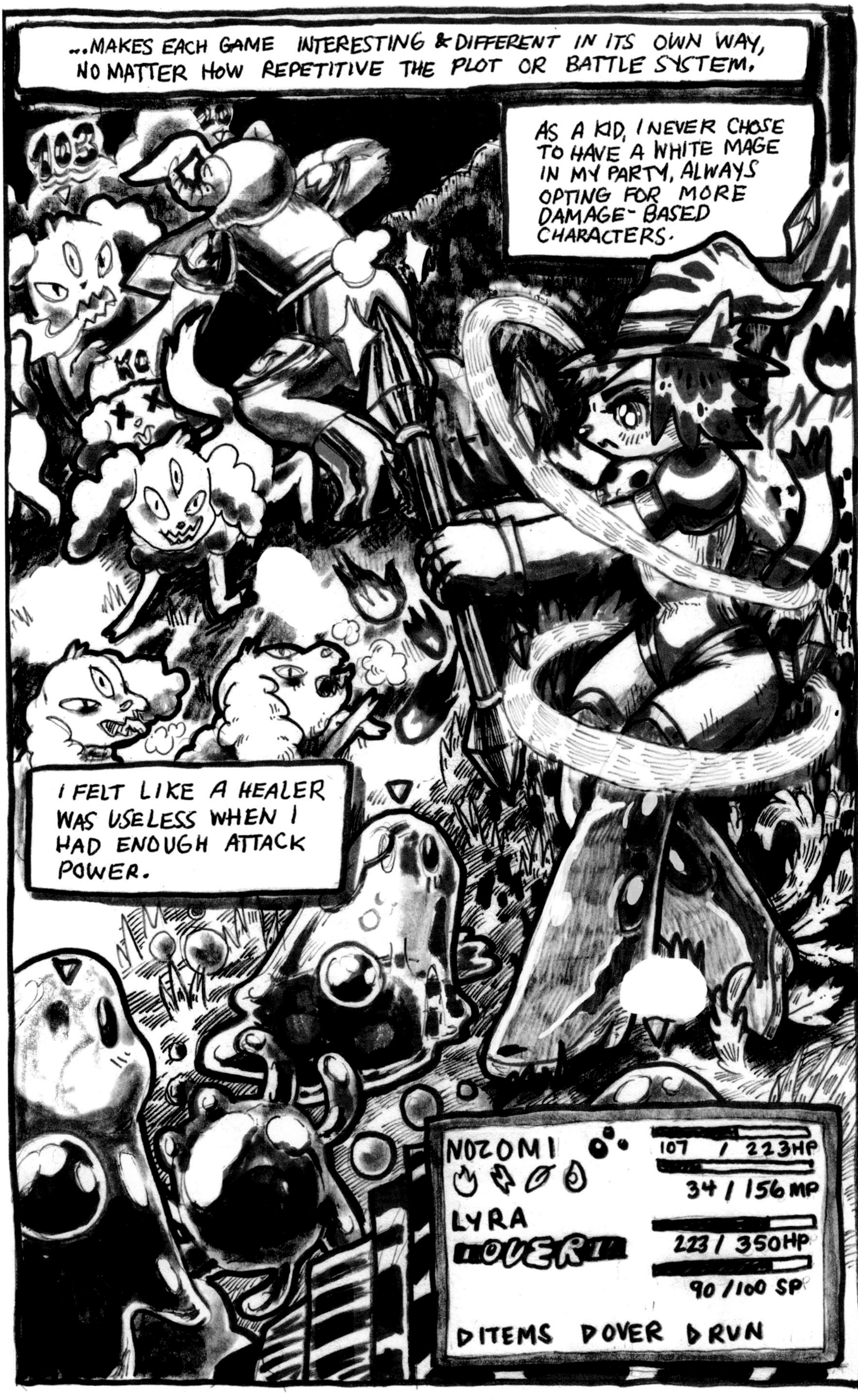
...MAKES EACH GAME INTERESTING & DIFFERENT IN ITS OWN WAY, NO MATTER HOW REPETITIVE THE PLOT OR BATTLE SYSTEM.
AS A KID, I NEVER CHOSE TO HAVE A WHITE MAGE IN MY PARTY, ALWAYS OPTING FOR MORE DAMAGE-BASED CHARACTERS.
103
KO
I FELT LIKE A HEALER WAS USELESS WHEN I HAD ENOUGH ATTACK POWER.
NOZOMI
107 / 223HP
34 / 156MP
LYRA
OVER
223 / 350HP
90 / 100 SP
▷ITEMS ▷OVER ▷RUN

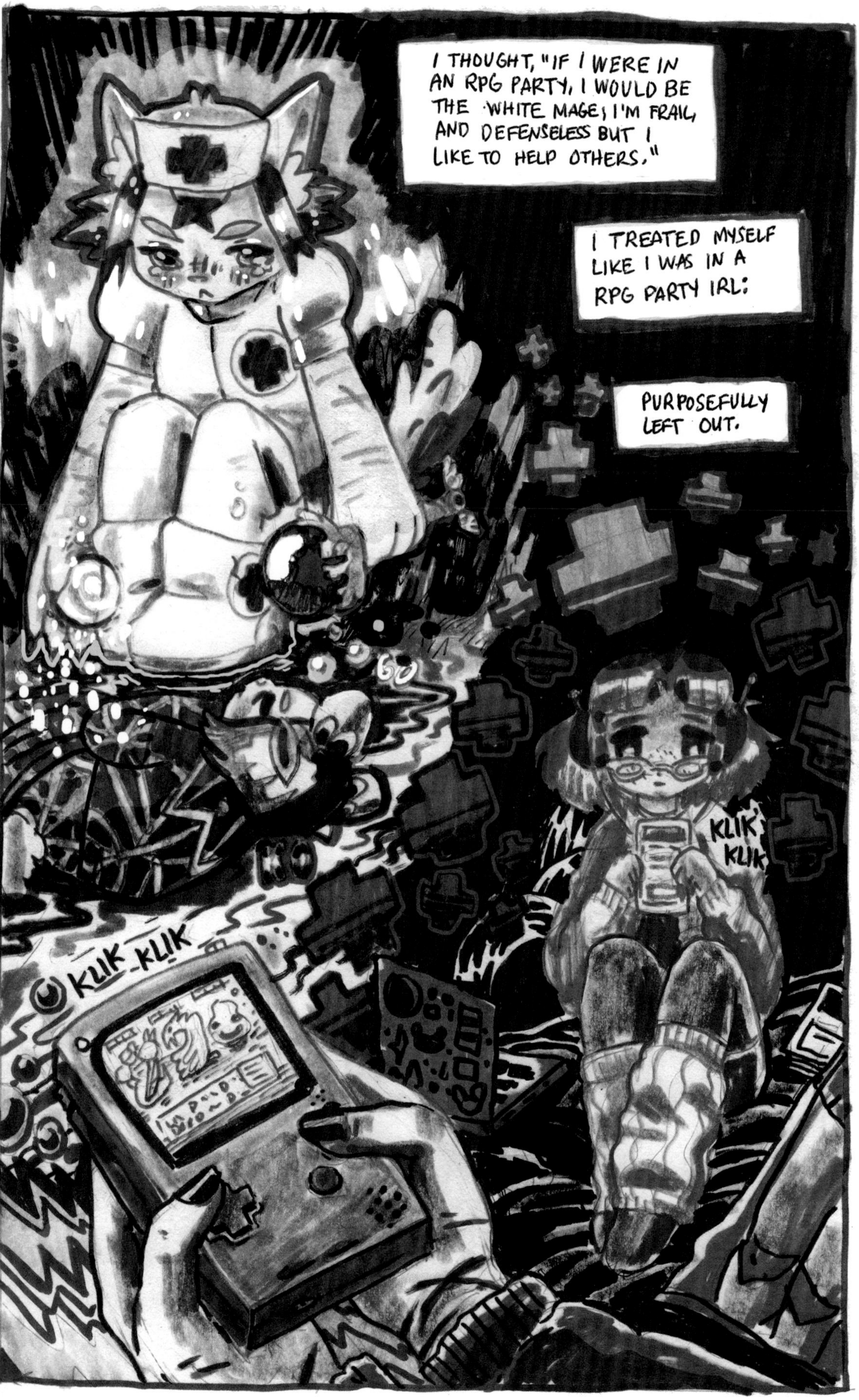
I THOUGHT, "IF I WERE IN AN RPG PARTY, I WOULD BE THE WHITE MAGE; I'M FRAIL, AND DEFENSELESS BUT I LIKE TO HELP OTHERS."
I TREATED MYSELF LIKE I WAS IN A RPG PARTY IRL:
PURPOSEFULLY LEFT OUT.
KLIK KLIK
KLIK KLIK

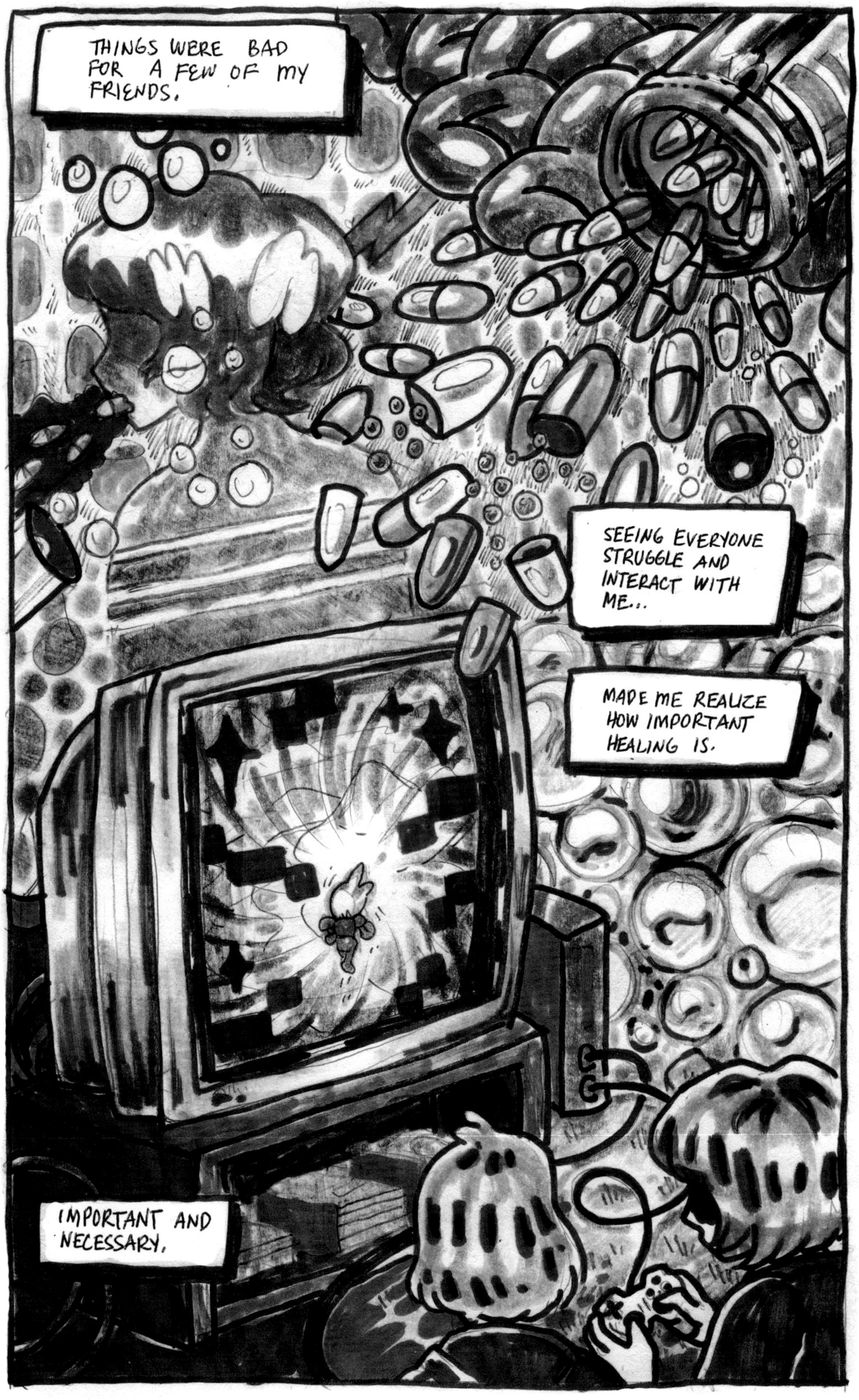
THINGS WERE BAD FOR A FEW OF MY FRIENDS.
SEEING EVERYONE STRUGGLE AND INTERACT WITH ME..
MADE ME REALIZE HOW IMPORTANT HEALING IS.
IMPORTANT AND NECESSARY.

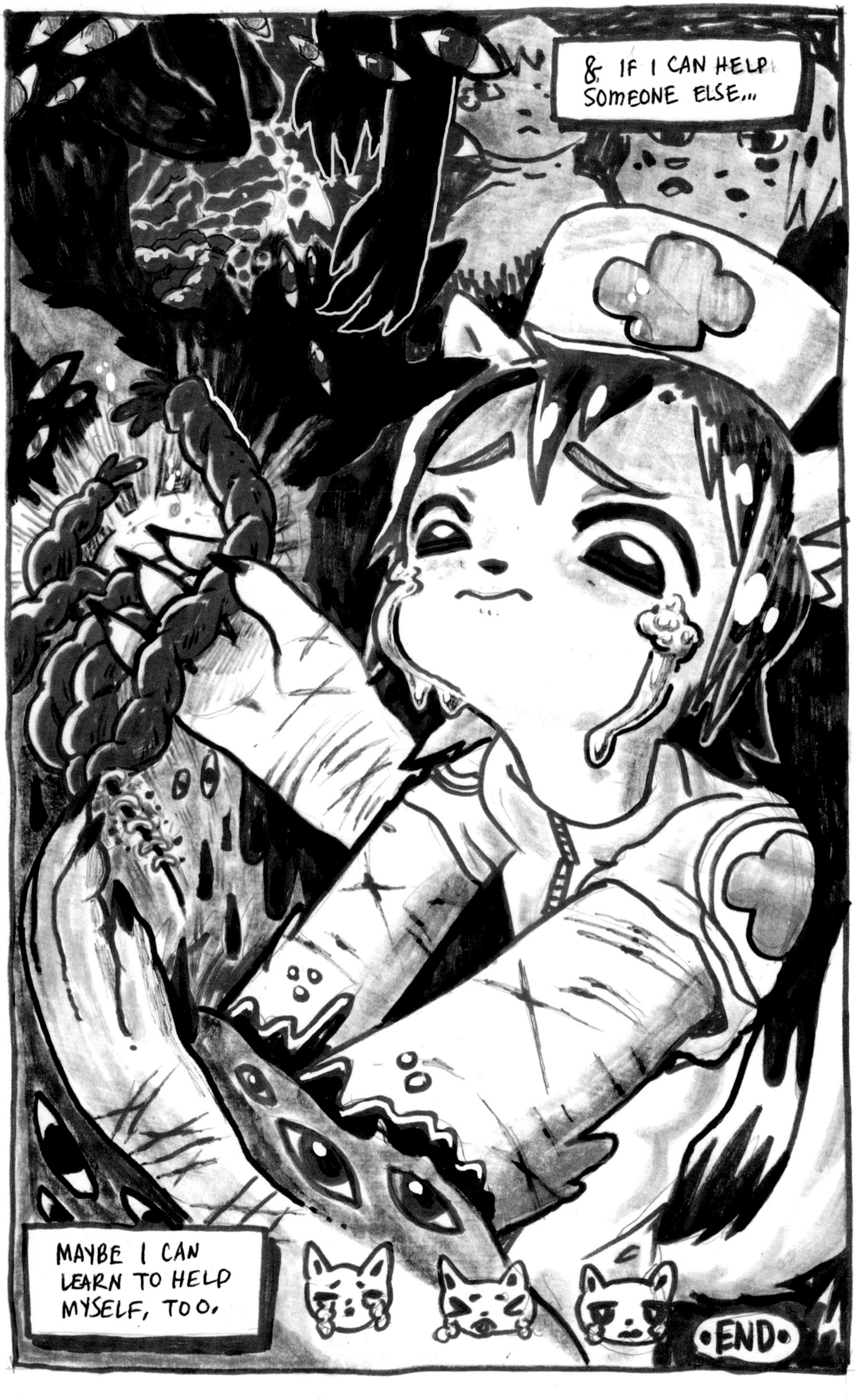
& IF I CAN HELP SOMEONE ELSE...
MAYBE I CAN LEARN TO HELP MYSELF, TOO.
•END•

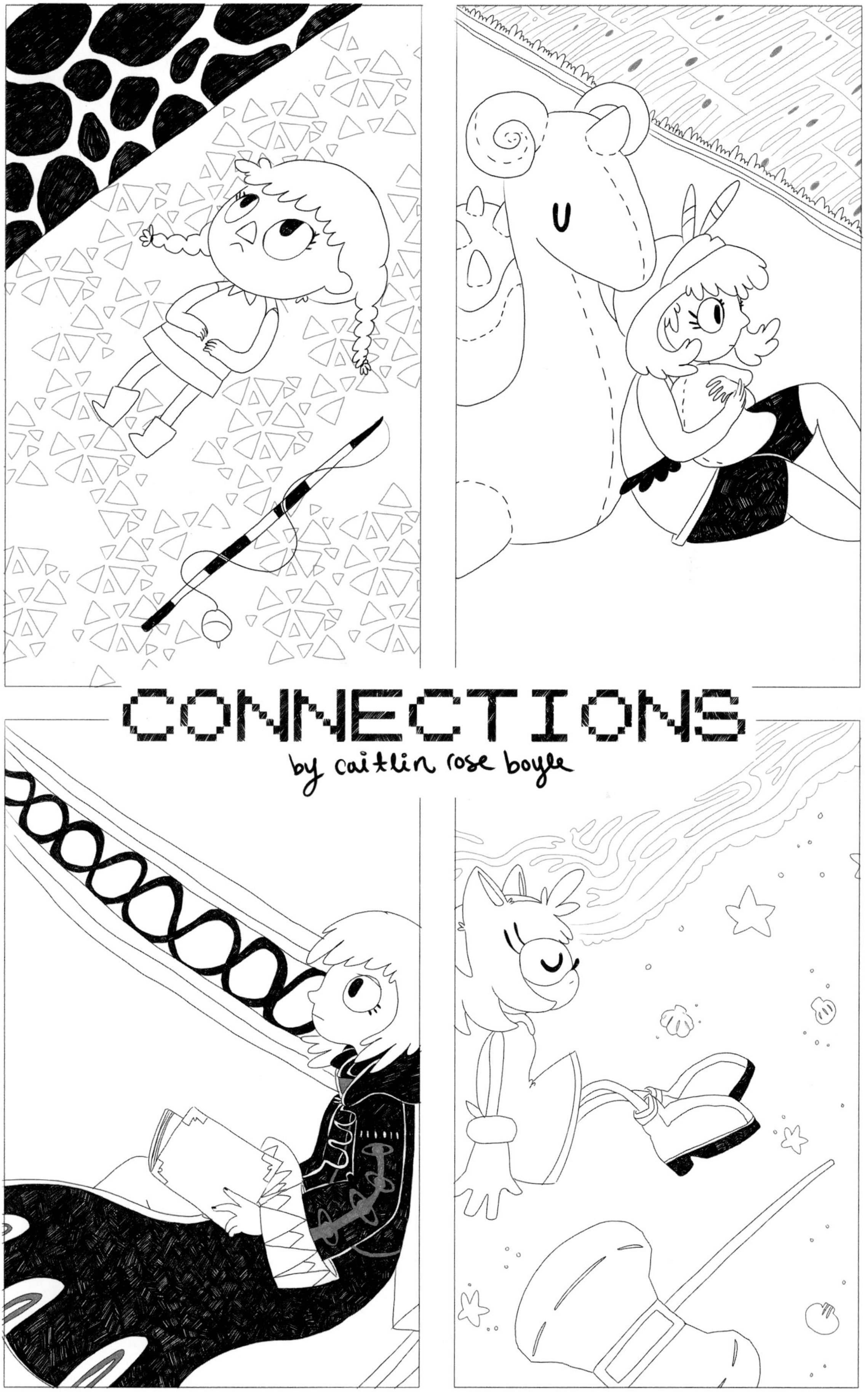
CONNECTIONS
by caitlin rose boyle

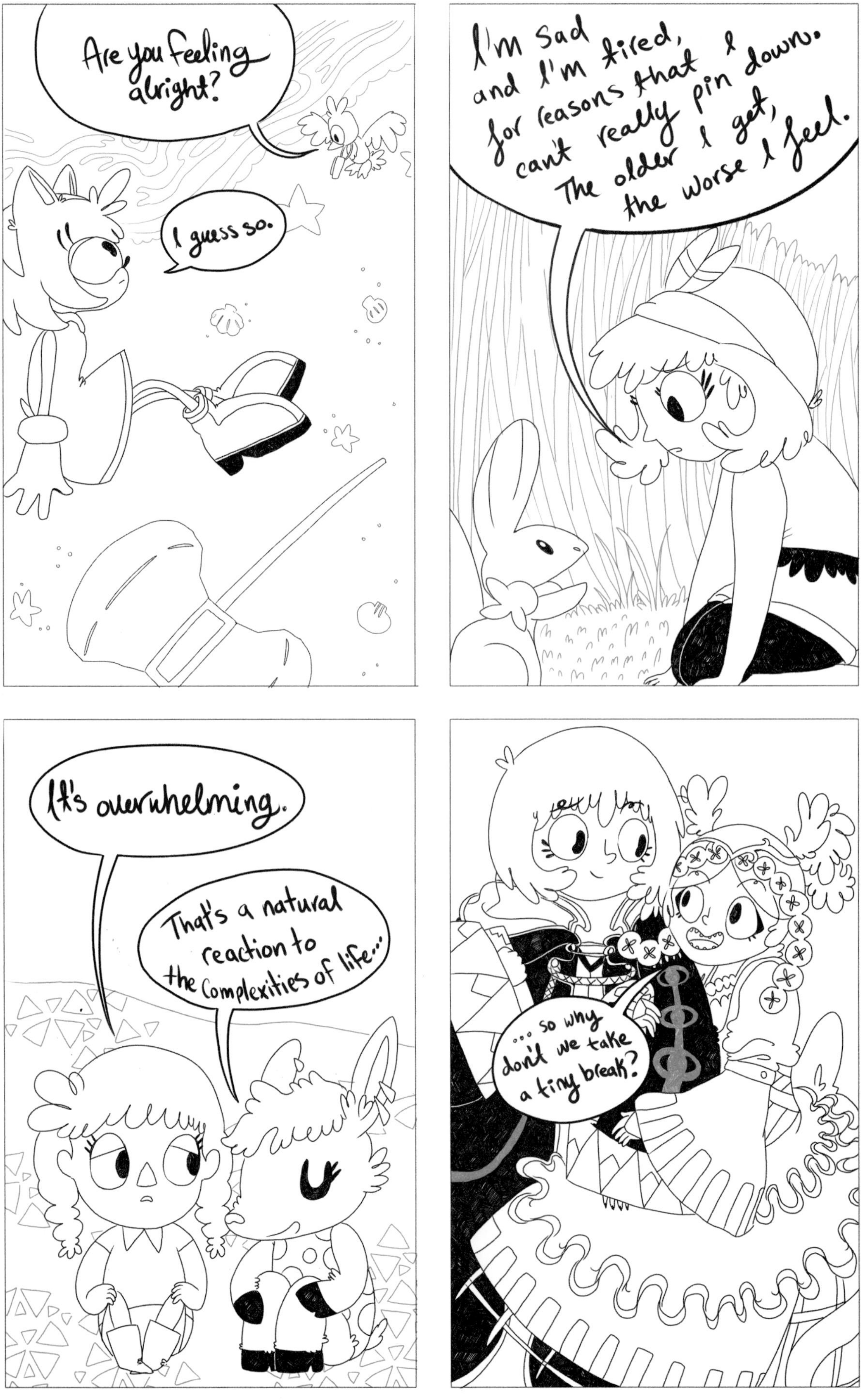
Are you feeling alright?
I guess so.
I'm sad and I'm tired, for reasons that I can't really pin down. The older I get, the worse I feel.
It's overwhelming.
That's a natural reaction to the complexities of life...
...so why don't we take a tiny break?

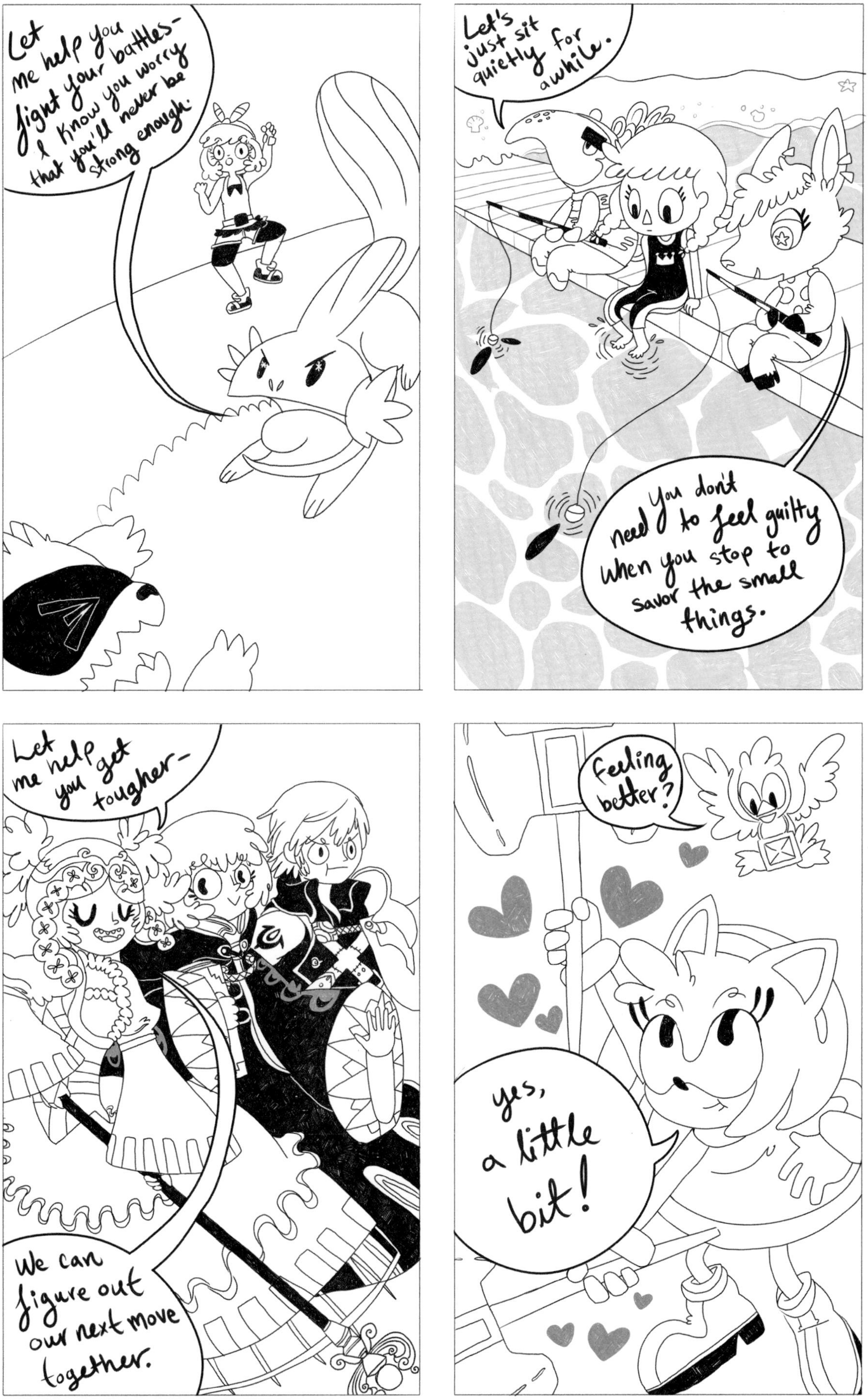

Let me help you fight your battles- I know you worry that you'll never be strong enough.
Let's just sit quietly for awhile.
You don't need to feel guilty when you stop to savor the small things.
Let me help you get tougher-
We can figure out our next move together.
Feeling better?
yes, a little bit!

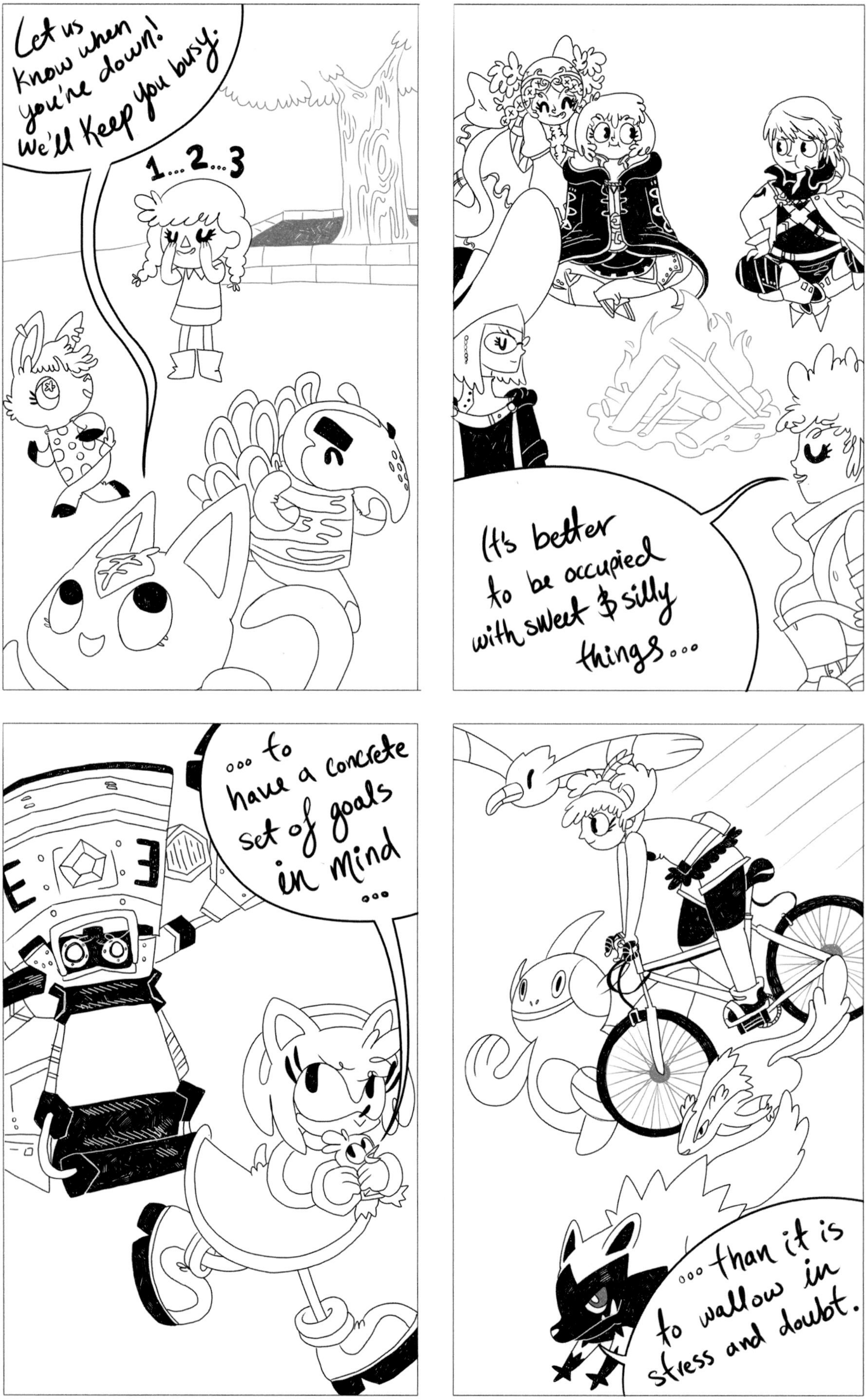
Let us know when you're down! We'll Keep you busy.
1...2...3
It's better to be occupied with sweet $ silly things...
... to have a concrete set of goals in mind ...
... than it is to wallow in stress and doubt.

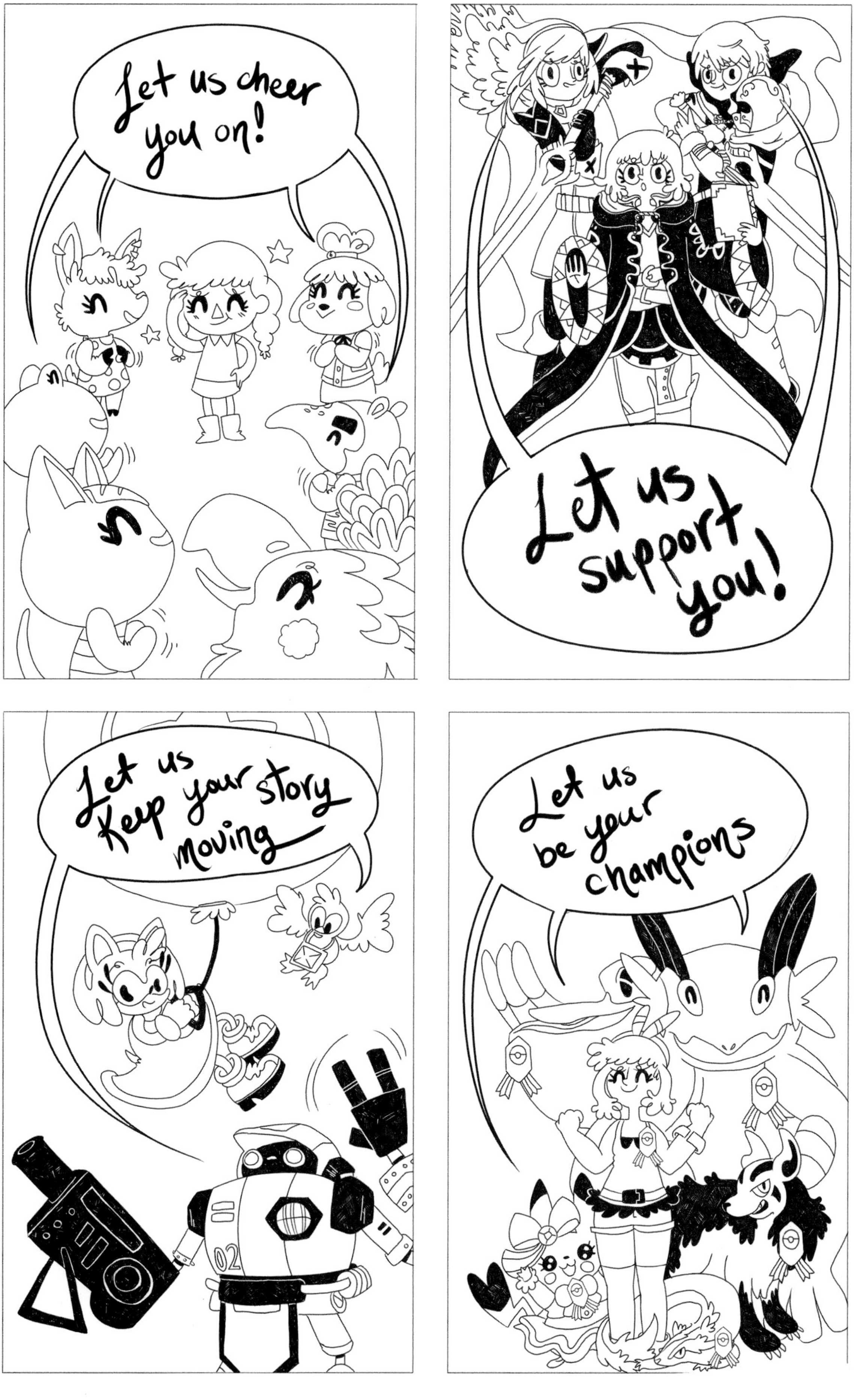
Let us cheer you on!
Let us support you!
Let us Keep your story moving
Let us be your champions

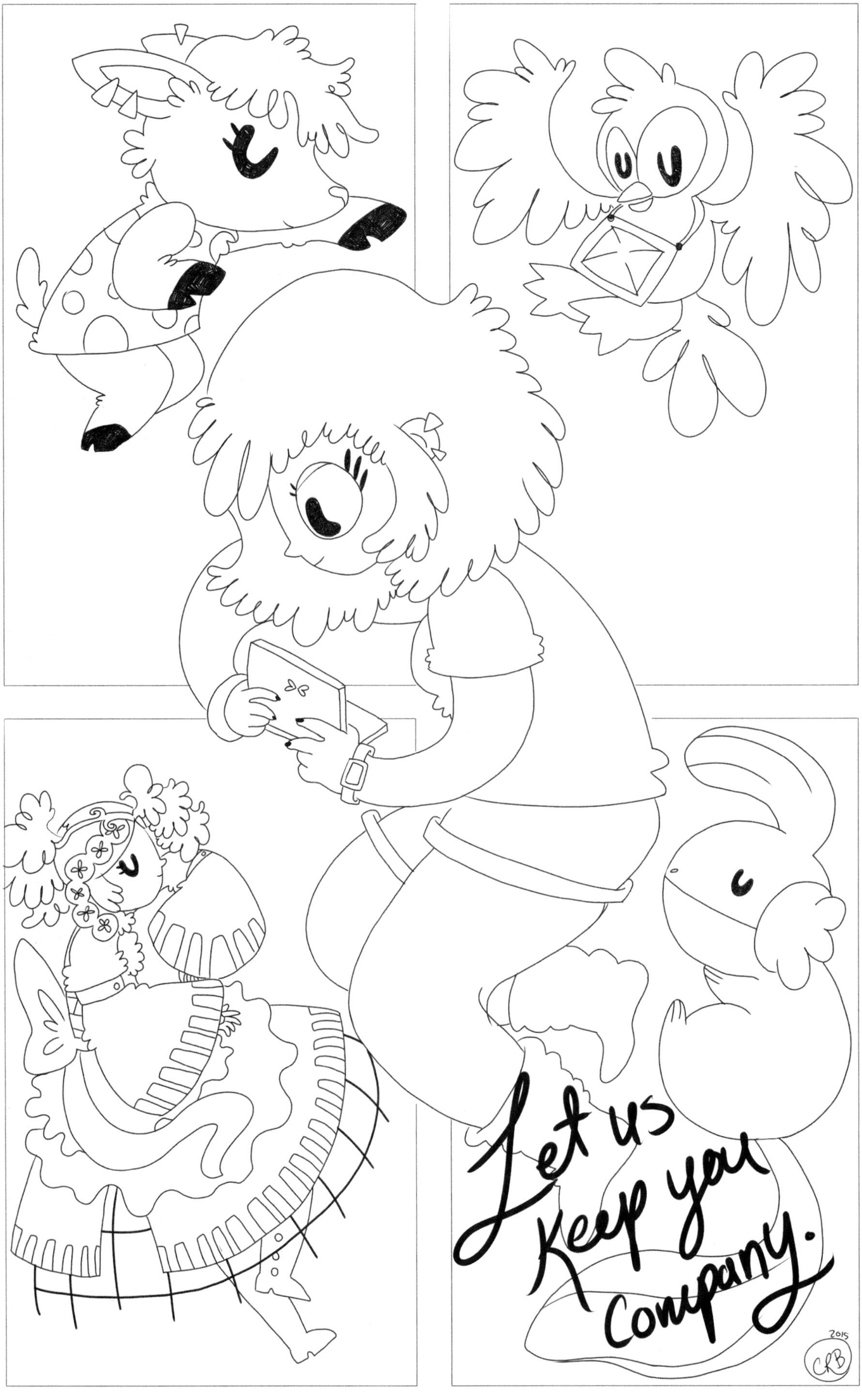
Let us Keep you Company.
2015
CRB

Dream Suite

by Megan Brennan

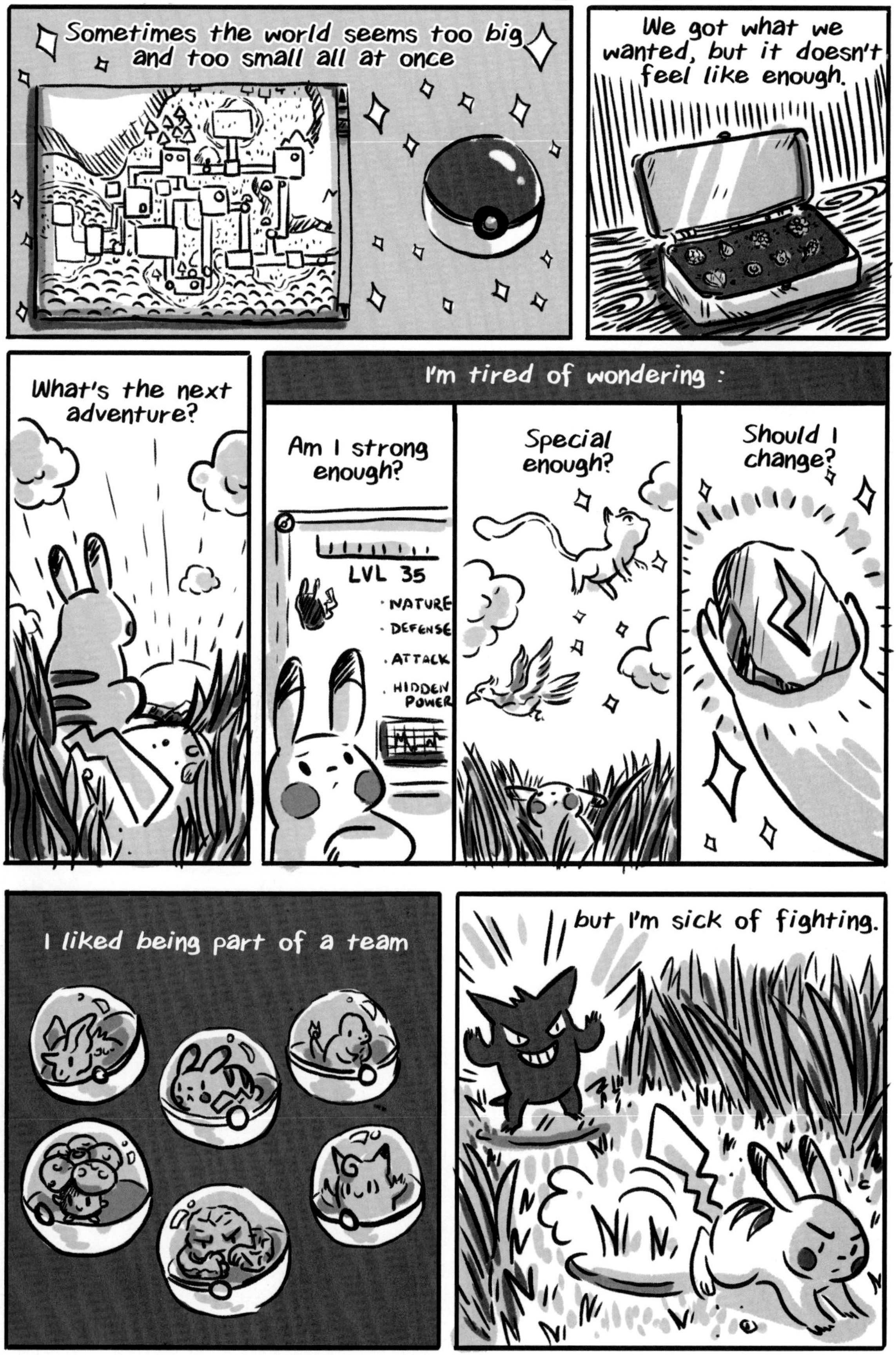

Sometimes the world seems too big and too small all at once
We got what we wanted, but it doesn't feel like enough.
What's the next adventure?
I'm tired of wondering :
Am I strong enough?
LVL 35
· NATURE
· DEFENSE
· ATTACK
· HIDDEN POWER
Special enough?
Should I change?
I liked being part of a team
but I'm sick of fighting.

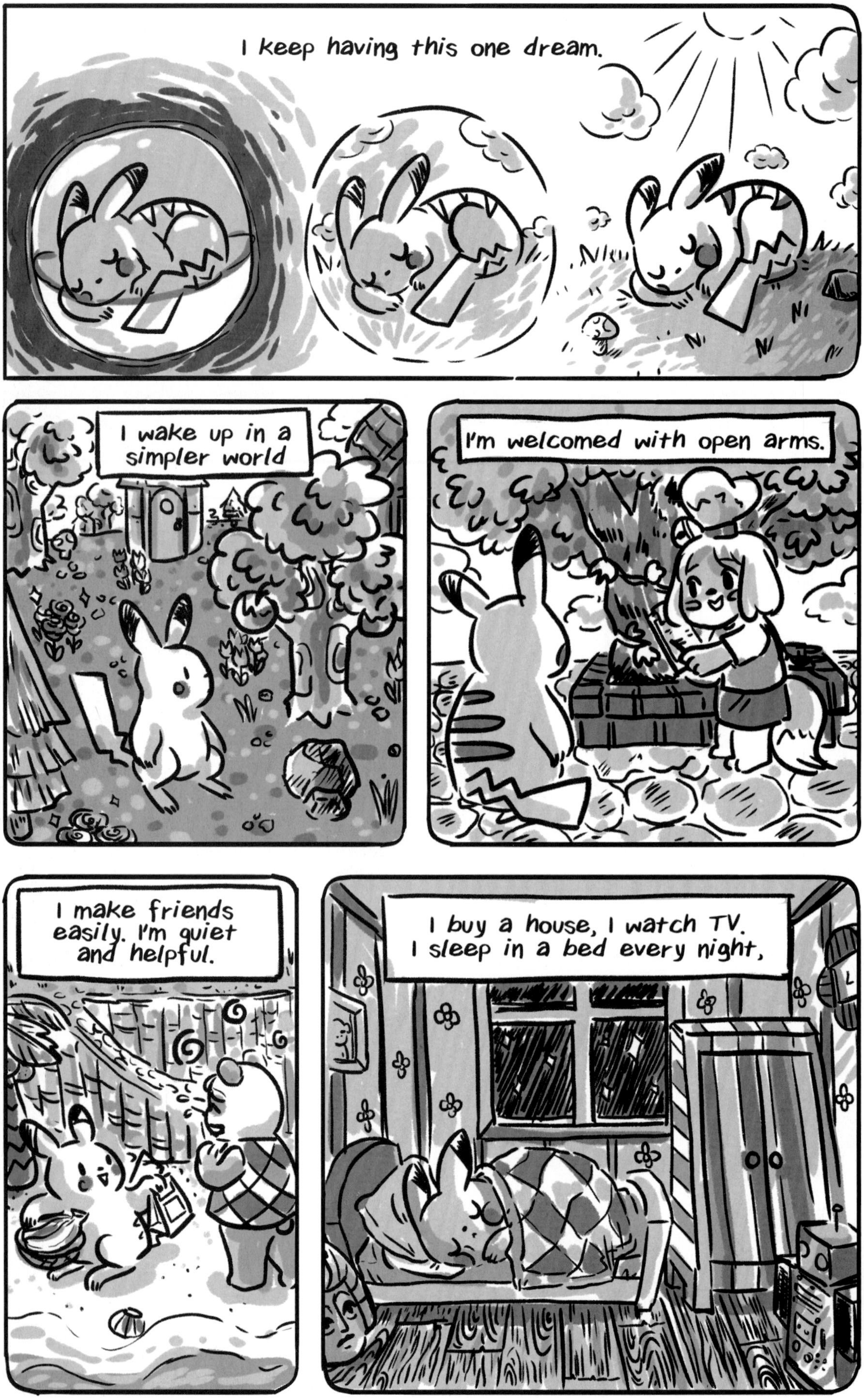
I keep having this one dream.
I wake up in a simpler world
I'm welcomed with open arms.
I make friends easily. I'm quiet and helpful.
I buy a house, I watch TV.
I sleep in a bed every night,

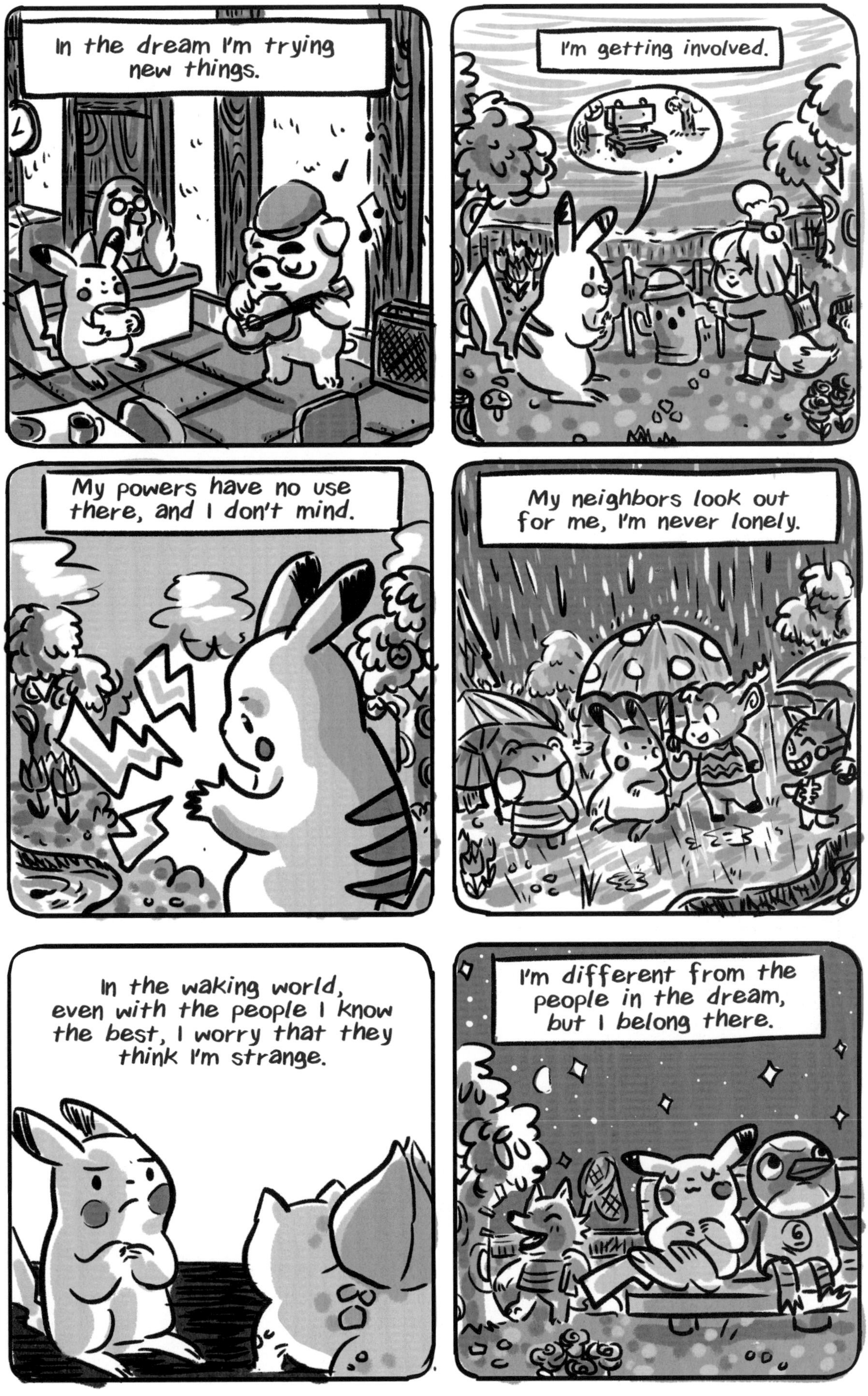
In the dream I'm trying new things.
I'm getting involved.
My powers have no use there, and I don't mind.
My neighbors look out for me, I'm never lonely.
In the waking world, even with the people I know the best, I worry that they think I'm strange.
I'm different from the people in the dream, but I belong there.

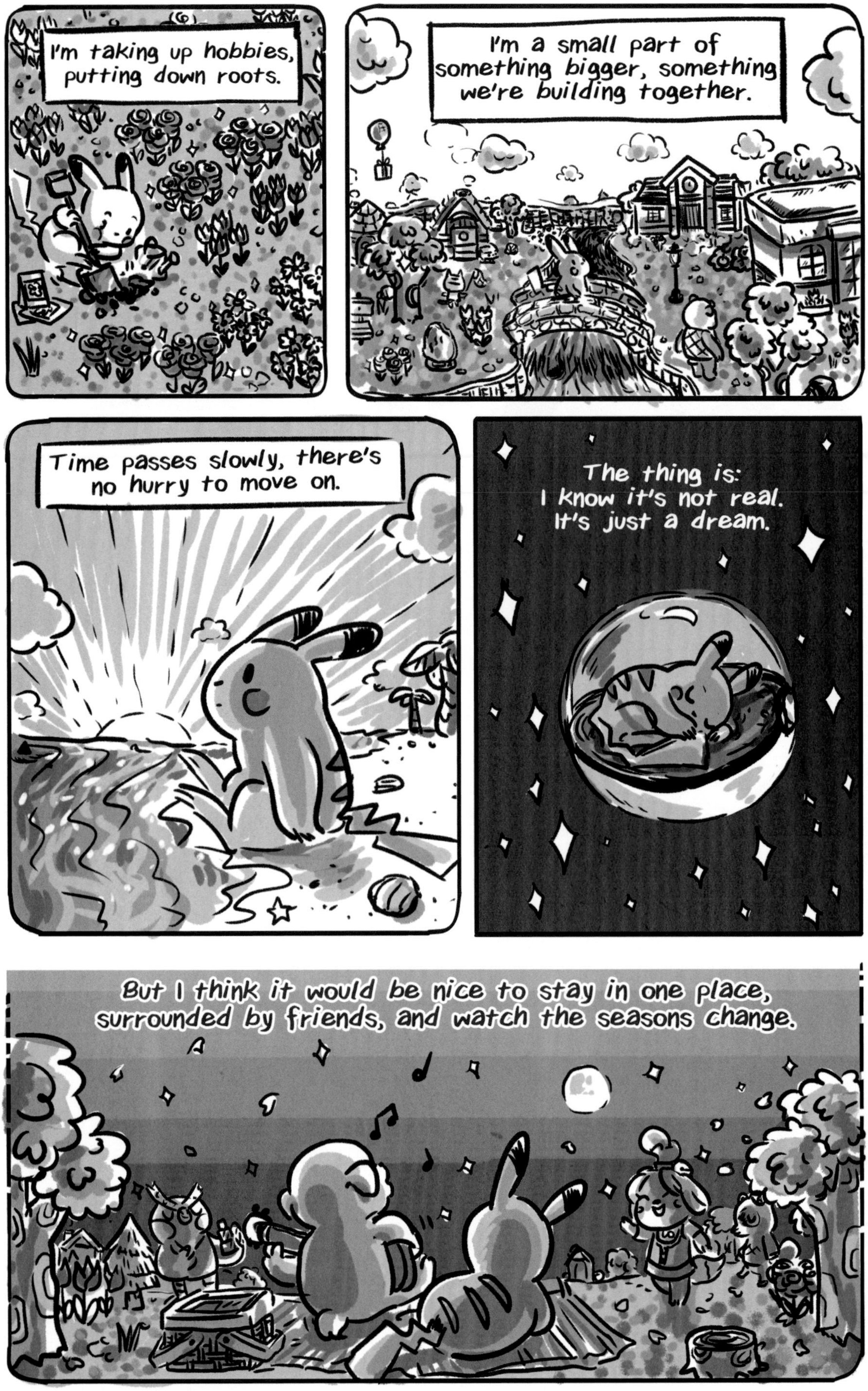
I'm taking up hobbies, putting down roots.
I'm a small part of something bigger, something we're building together.
Time passes slowly, there's no hurry to move on.
The thing is: I know it's not real. It's just a dream.
But I think it would be nice to stay in one place, surrounded by friends, and watch the seasons change.

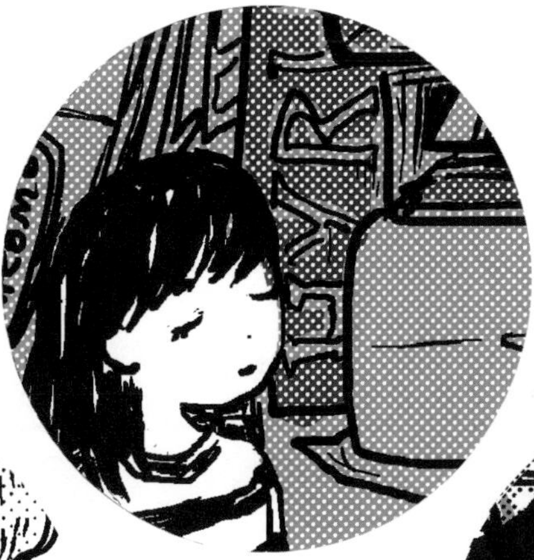

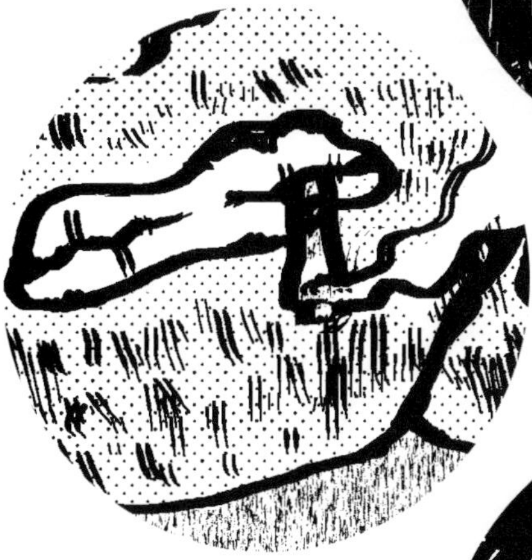

LIFE+1

by BUNTOO

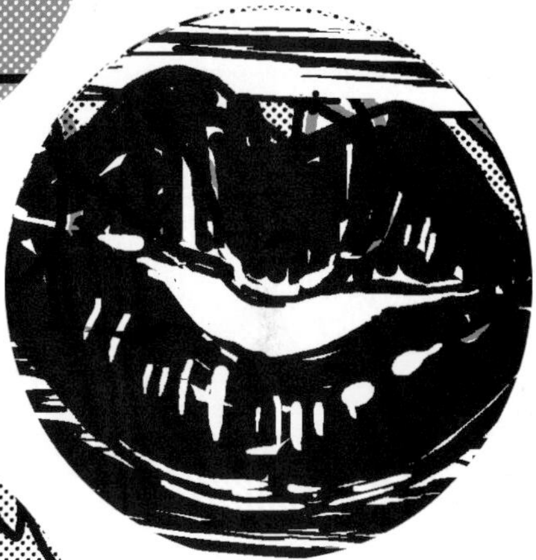

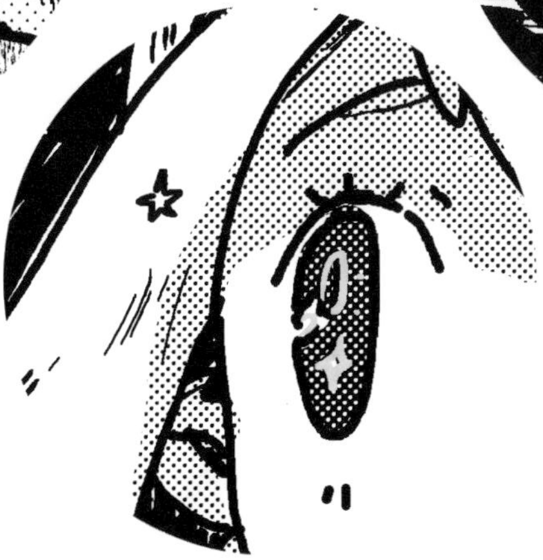

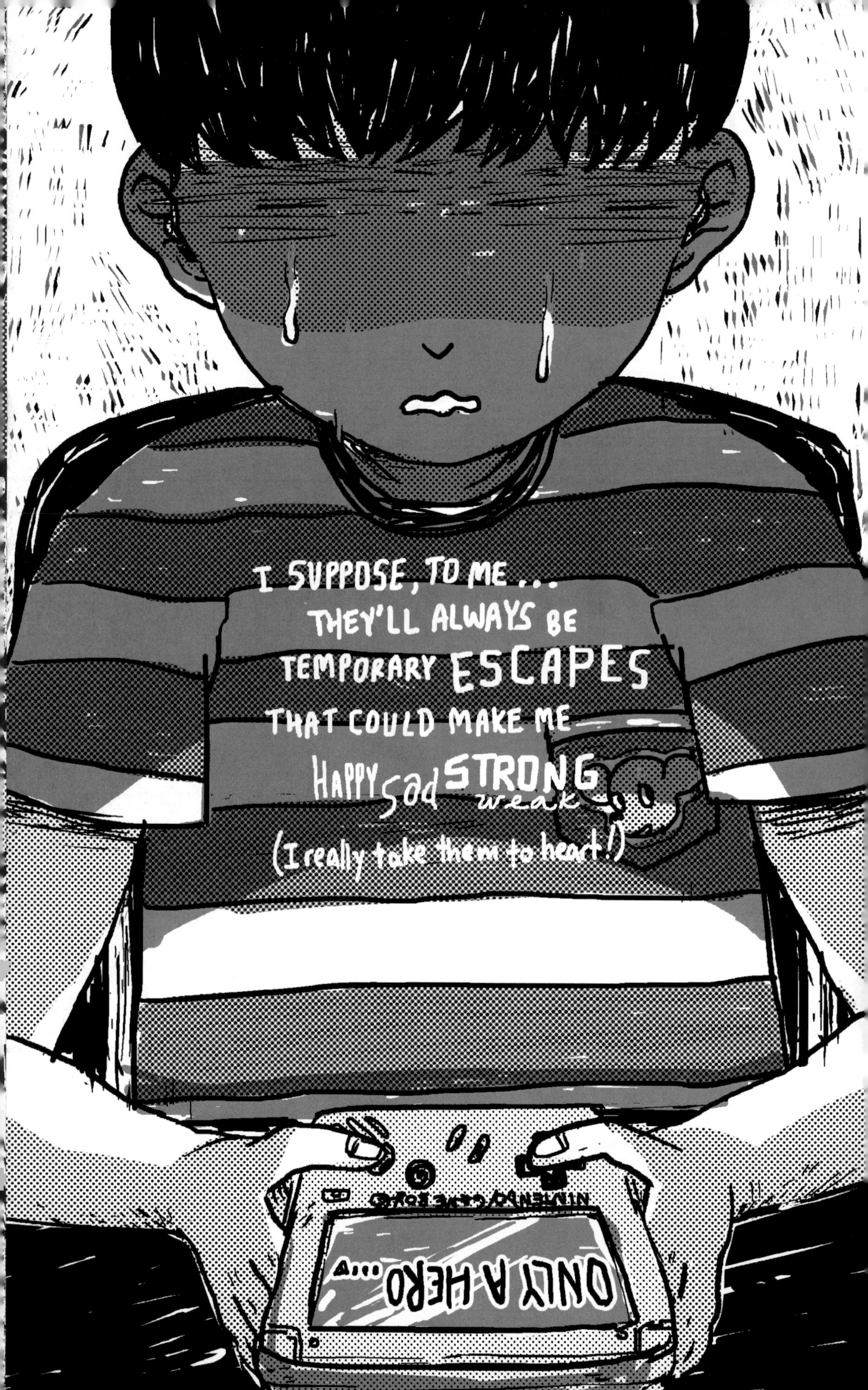
I SUPPOSE, TO ME...
THEY'LL ALWAYS BE
TEMPORARY ESCAPES
THAT COULD MAKE ME
HAPPY sad STRONG weak
(I really take them to heart!)
ONLY A HERO...

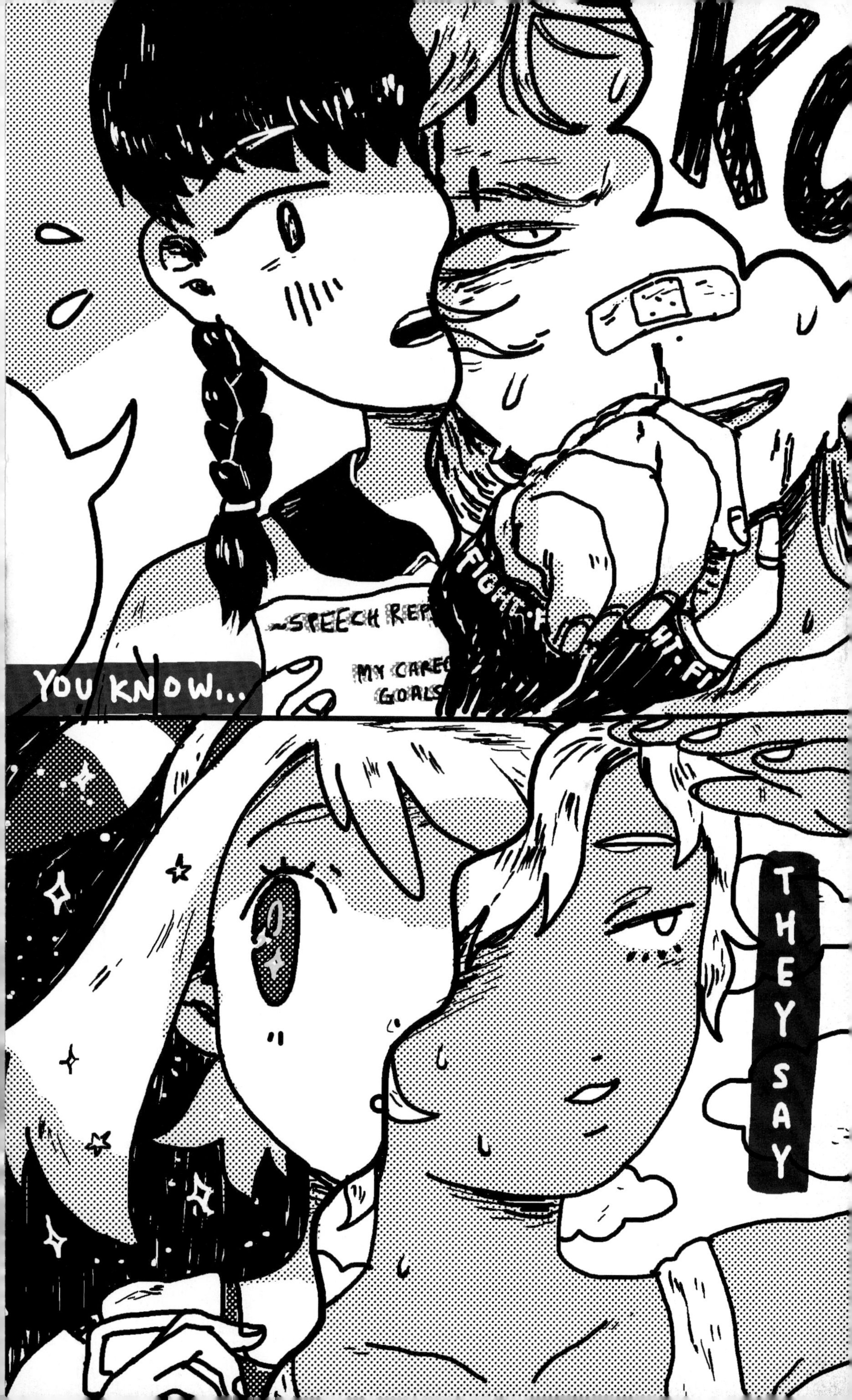
KO
~SPEECH REP
MY CAREE
GOALS
FIGHT·F
HT·F
YOU KNOW...
THEY SAY

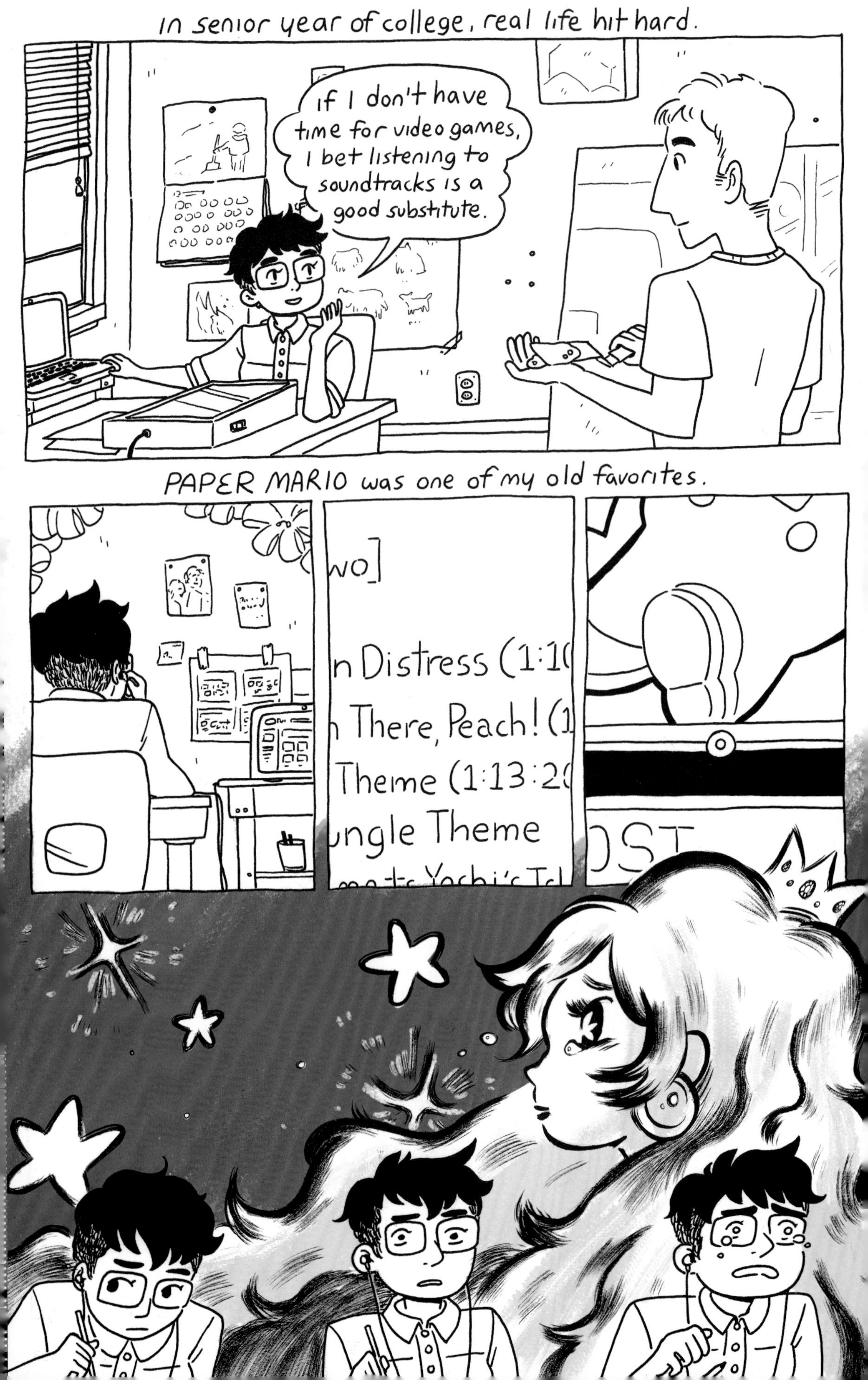
In senior year of college, real life hit hard.
If I don't have time for video games, I bet listening to soundtracks is a good substitute.
PAPER MARIO was one of my old favorites.
wo]
n Distress (1:1
n There, Peach! (1
Theme (1:13:2
ungle Theme
OST

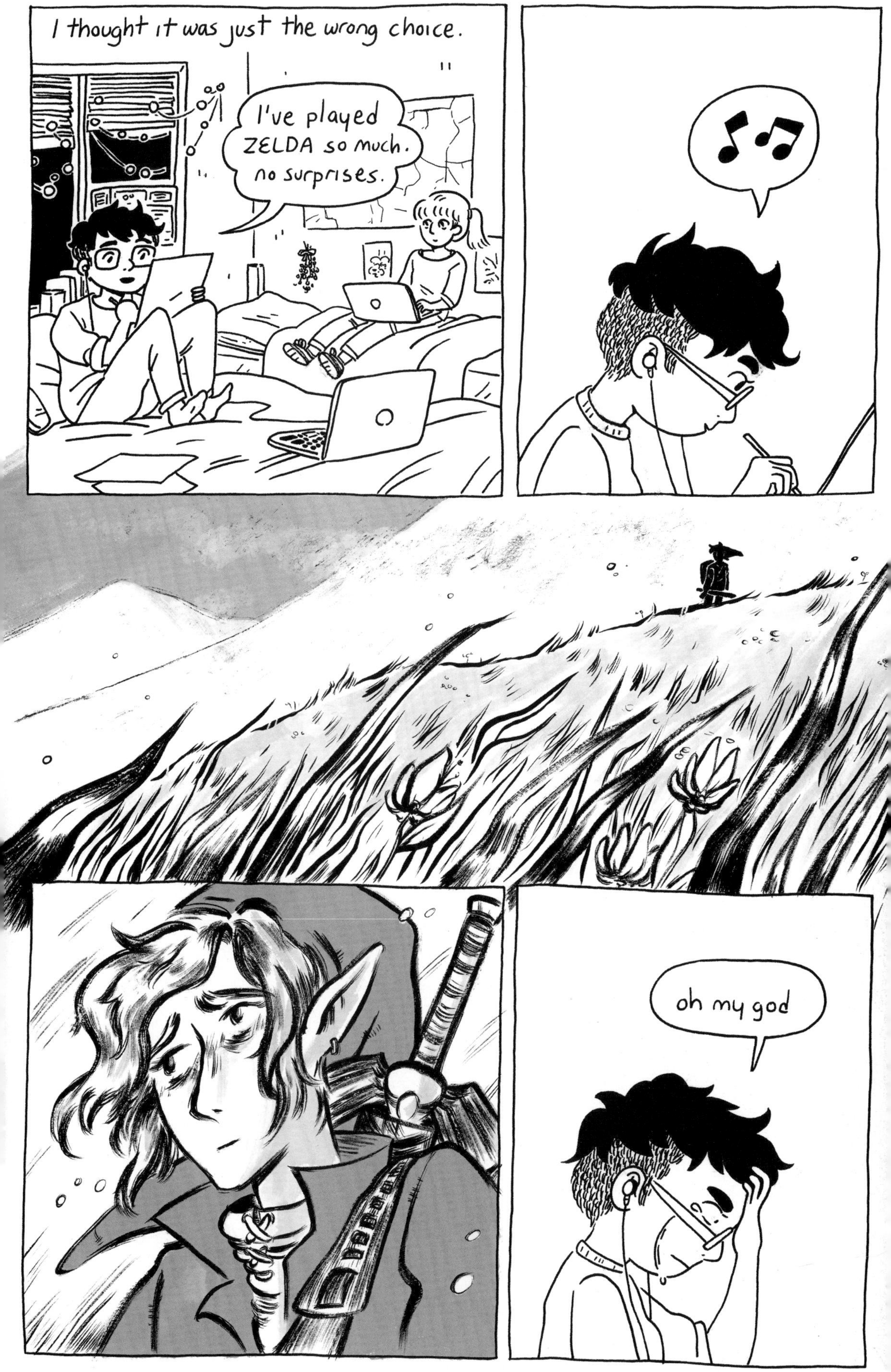
I thought it was just the wrong choice.
I've played ZELDA so much. no surprises.
oh my god

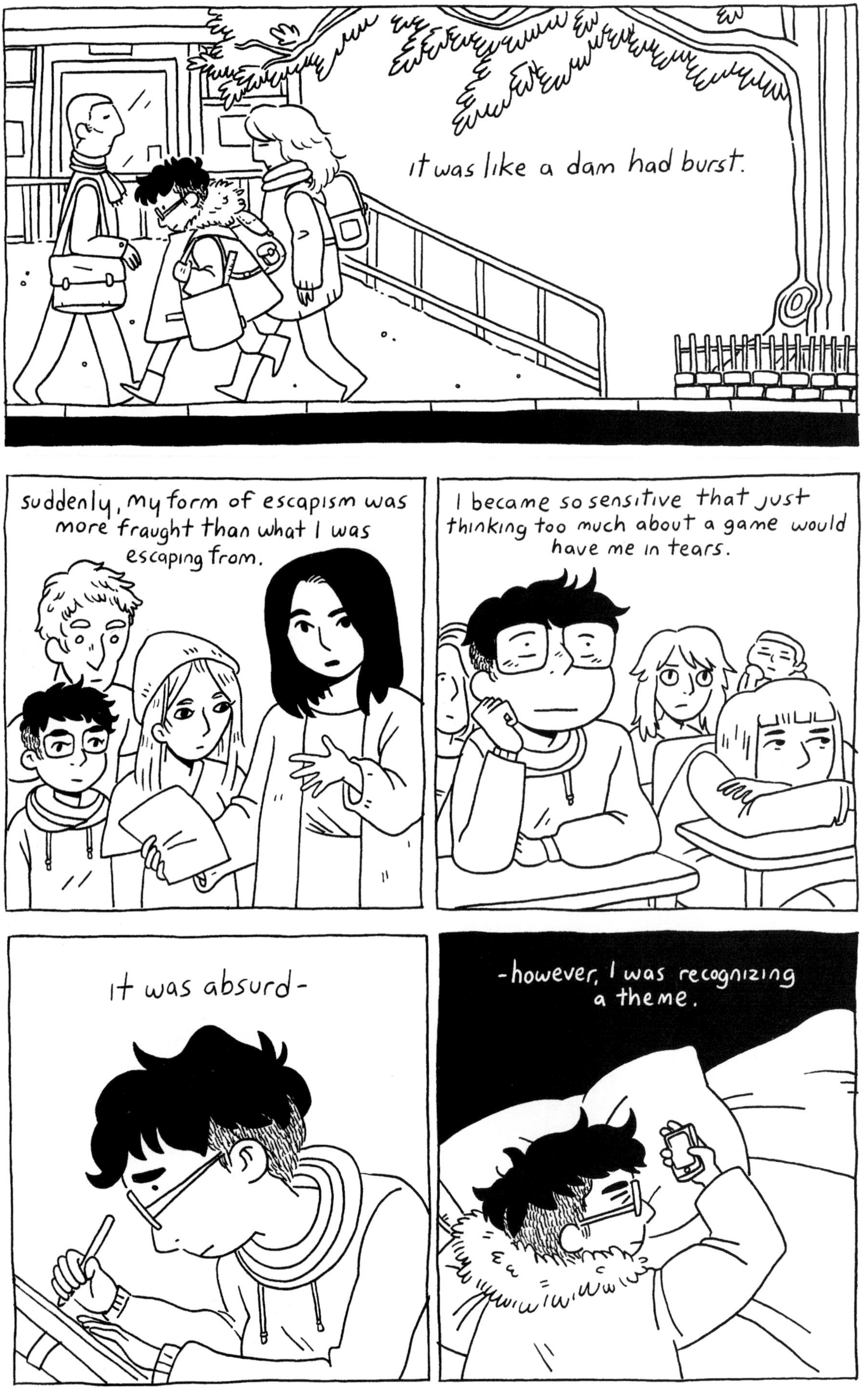

it was like a dam had burst.
suddenly, my form of escapism was more fraught than what I was escaping from.
I became so sensitive that just thinking too much about a game would have me in tears.
it was absurd-
-however, I was recognizing a theme.

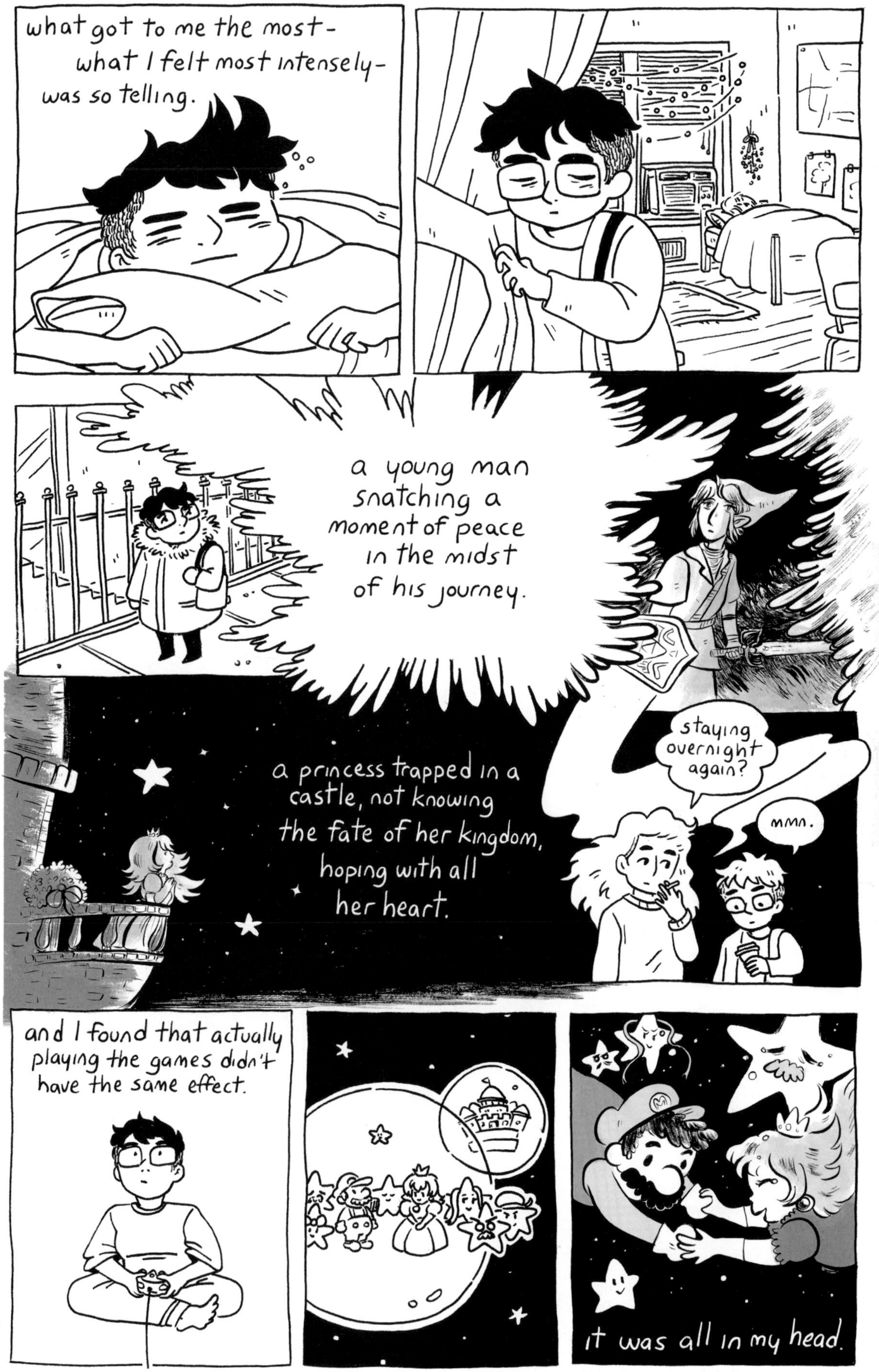
what got to me the most-
what I felt most intensely-
was so telling.
a young man
snatching a
moment of peace
in the midst
of his journey.
a princess trapped in a
castle, not knowing
the fate of her kingdom,
hoping with all
her heart.
staying
overnight
again?
mmn.
and I found that actually
playing the games didn't
have the same effect.
it was all in my head.

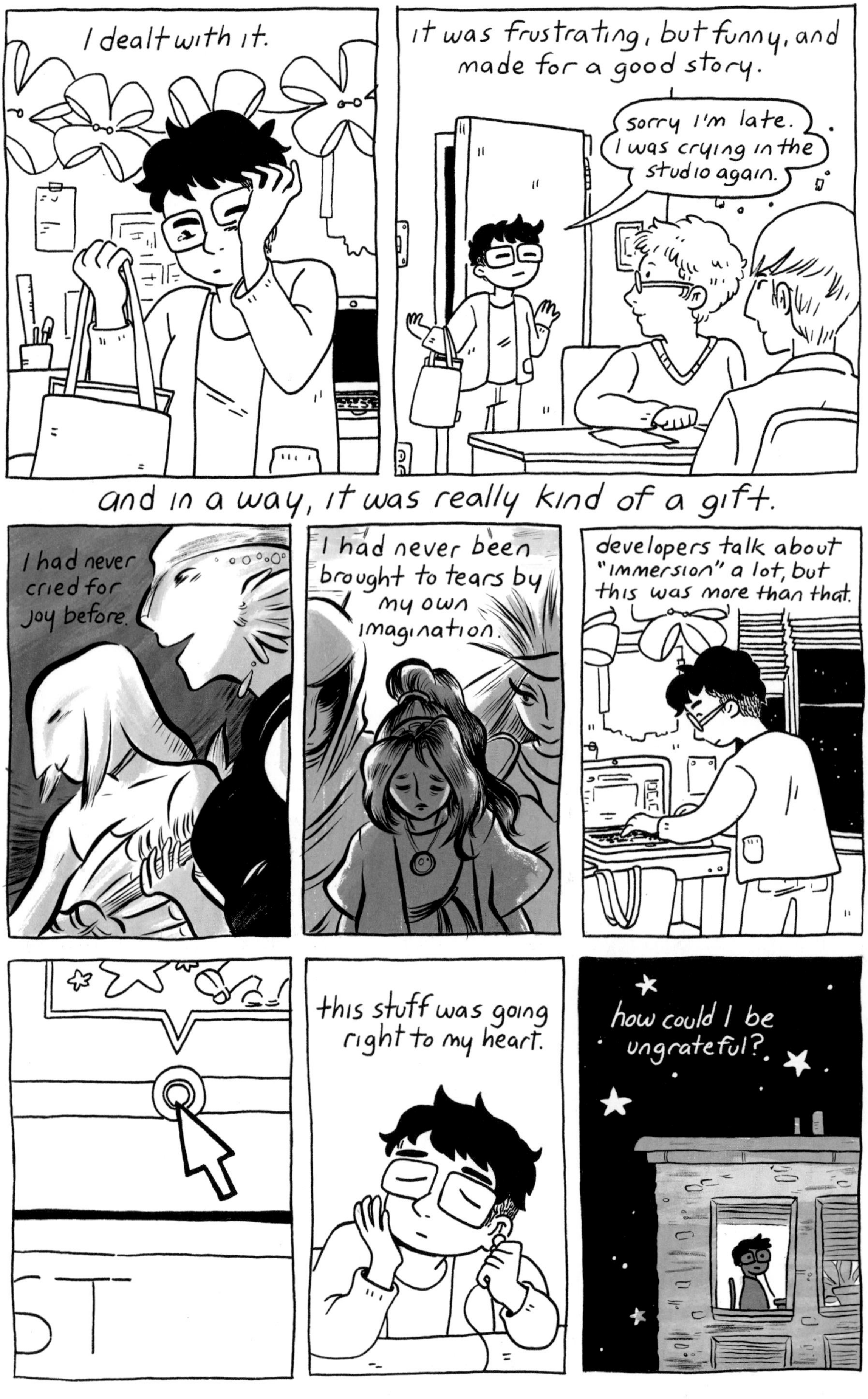
I dealt with it.
it was frustrating, but funny, and made for a good story.
sorry I'm late. I was crying in the studio again.
and in a way, it was really kind of a gift.
I had never cried for joy before.
I had never been brought to tears by my own imagination.
developers talk about "immersion" a lot, but this was more than that.
this stuff was going right to my heart.
how could I be ungrateful?

I don't think playing Guitar Hero 2 was ever in itself a symptom of my Obsessive-Compulsive Disorder. Not like having to make sure the shirts under the one on top were still folded flat, or having to wait until after midnight to cross out the day on the calendar so I wouldn't jinx myself and die.

set you free
I can't be nobody
ell you're kinda lookin at me like I'm
you know what I mean you better listen
she's a woman

I just played it a lot. Until my eyes were bloodshot, until everything I looked at flowed upwards in the middle like the scrolling notes I saw inside my eyelids when I tried to sleep.

MANIC PIXEL DREAM GIRL gaiden: guitar heroine

BY ELIZABETH SIMINS

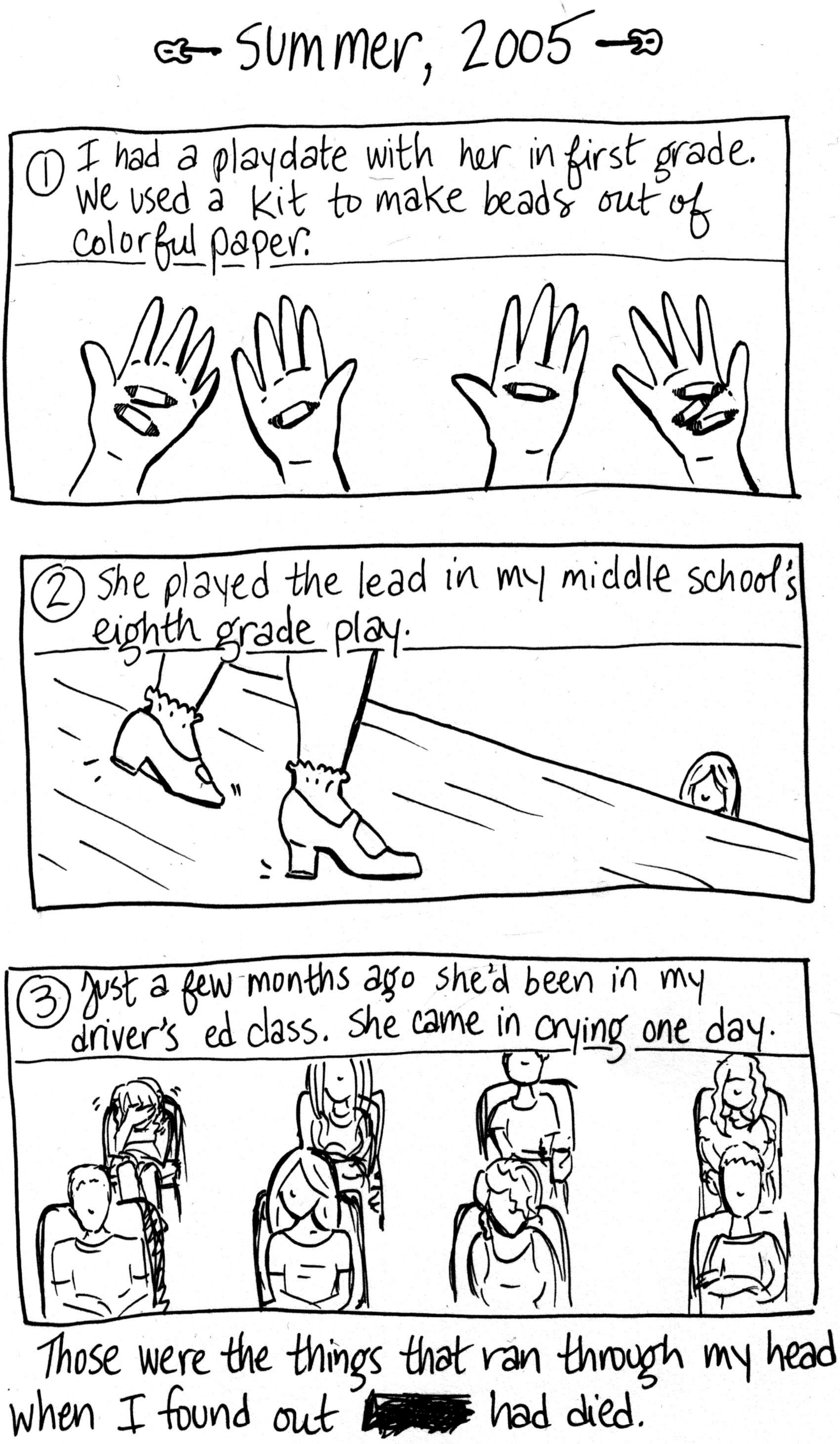
Summer, 2005
① I had a playdate with her in first grade. We used a kit to make beads out of colorful paper.
② She played the lead in my middle school's eighth grade play.
③ Just a few months ago she'd been in my driver's ed class. She came in crying one day.
Those were the things that ran through my head when I found out [redacted] had died.

Kids

those kids over there, just smiling & having fun it's like they don't know yet they're going to die someday I wish I was them I don't want to know this I can

candy bar

I want a candy bar but it's so unhealthy will it make me die sooner if I eat it but WHO CARES I could die at any time I should just enjoy my life and eat the fucking bar I might as well be unhealthy what does it ma

chips / chips / chips

college mailings

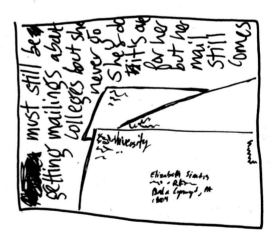

must still be getting mailings about colleges but she never go she do tits are for her but her mail still comes

University

Elizabeth Siatis

nighttime

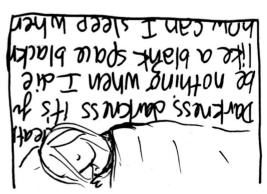

how can I sleep when I die Darkness darkness it's like a black space blackn be nothing when I die

I barely remember my first few months of college. I bought ~~gu~~ Guitar Hero II in January, ~~around the time I finally started therapy~~. I decided I'd get good at it.

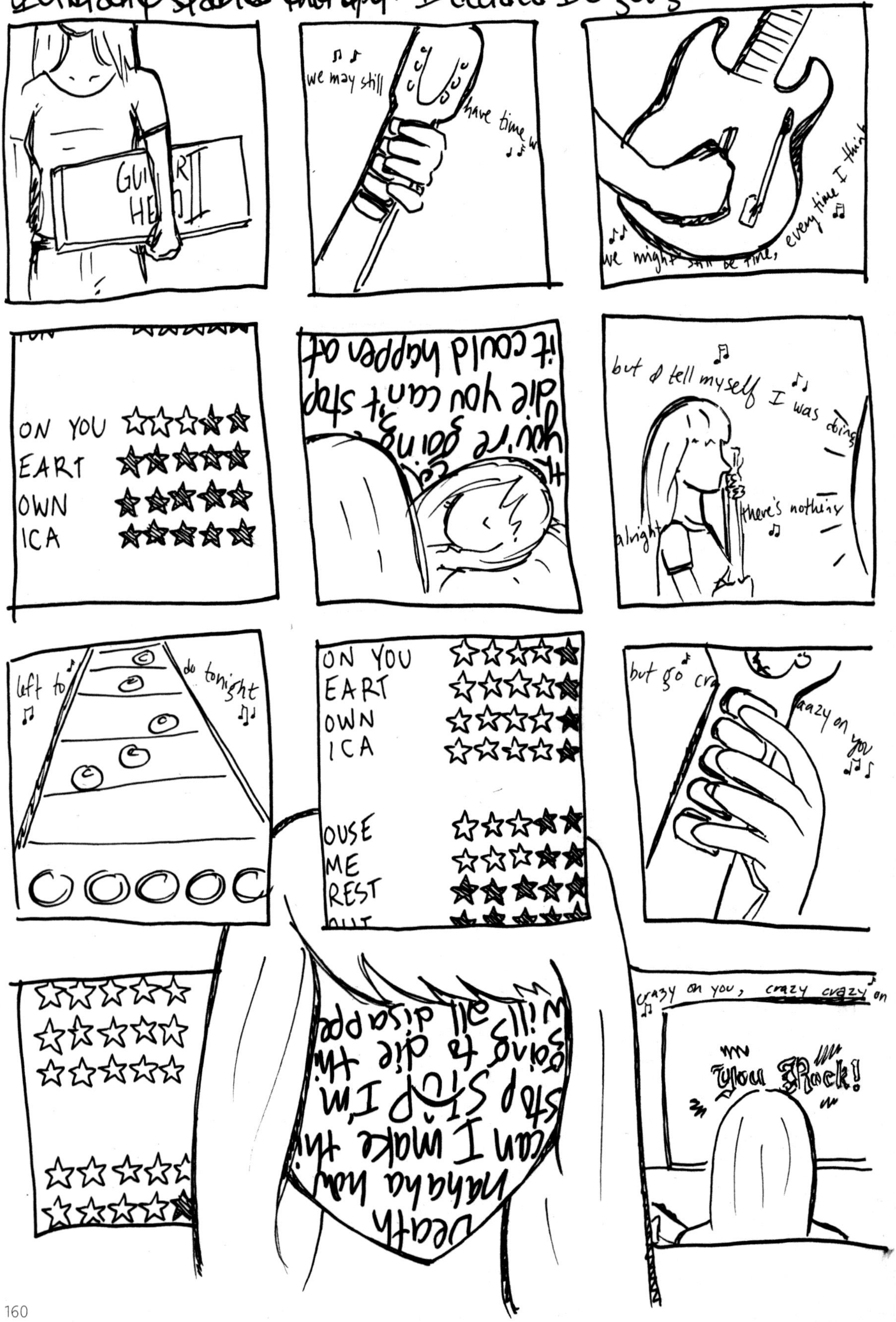

GUITAR HERO II
we may still
have time
we might still be fine, every time I think
ON YOU
EART
OWN
ICA
it could happen at
die you can't stop
you're going to
but I tell myself I was doing
alright
there's nothing
left to
do tonight
ON YOU
EART
OWN
ICA
OUSE
ME
REST
but go crazy on you
Death
hahaha how
can I make this
stop STOP I'm
going to die this
will all disappear
crazy on you, crazy crazy on
You Rock!

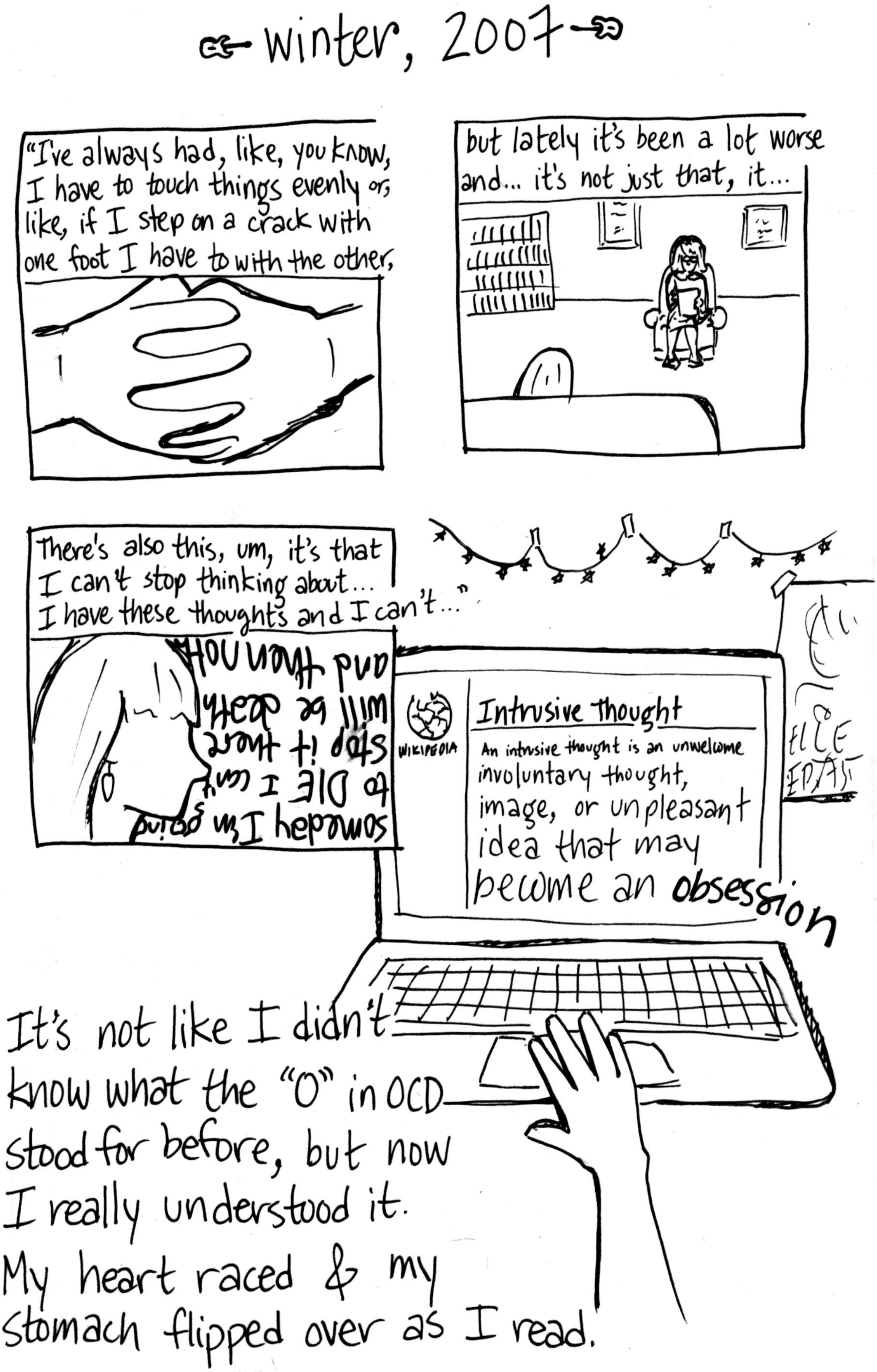
winter, 2007
"I've always had, like, you know, I have to touch things evenly or, like, if I step on a crack with one foot I have to with the other,
but lately it's been a lot worse and... it's not just that, it...
There's also this, um, it's that I can't stop thinking about... I have these thoughts and I can't..."
WIKIPEDIA
Intrusive thought
An intrusive thought is an unwelcome involuntary thought, image, or unpleasant idea that may become an obsession
It's not like I didn't know what the "O" in OCD stood for before, but now I really understood it.
My heart raced & my stomach flipped over as I read.

Knowing what it was didn't make it easier, or better. I felt like a prisoner in my own head, and increasingly in my own room — what with all the constant reminders of my own impending death, there wasn't space in my mind to think about going outside, so I didn't.

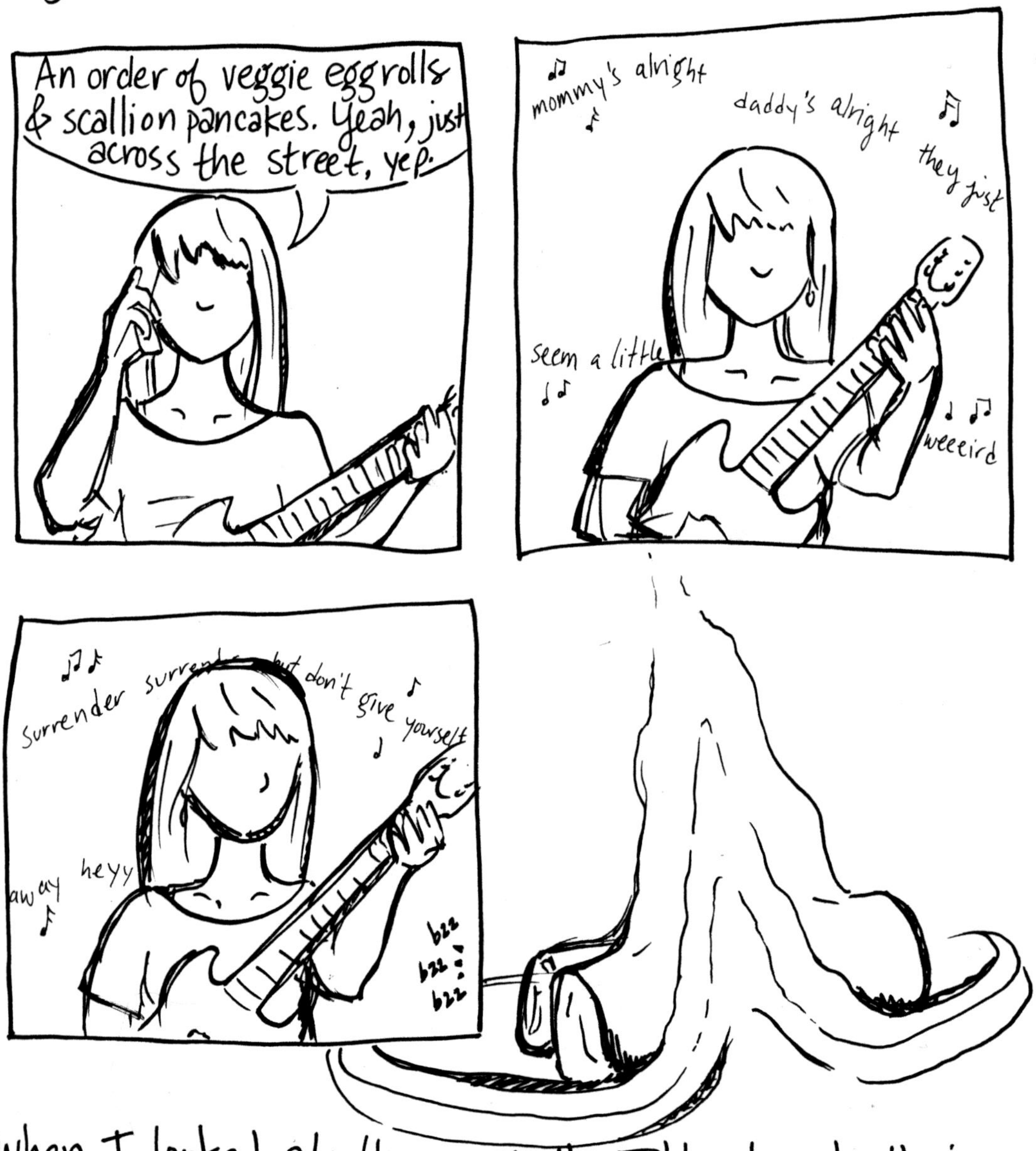
An order of veggie eggrolls & scallion pancakes. Yeah, just across the street, yep.
mommy's alright
daddy's alright
they just
seem a little
weeeird
surrender surrender but don't give yourself
away
heyy
bzz
bzz
bzz

When I looked at the eggrolls I'd ordered, their middles appeared to float upwards.

When I stopped playing Guitar Hero 2, it wasn't because I wanted to; it was because a moving company lost it.

FUCK it was everything! It was like everything I owned I can't fucking believe it

It arrived a few weeks later in a battered box with all my other stuff, apparently found. I don't know why I wasn't interested in it anymore after that. I guess it's just one of those things you can't control.

you remember ▆▆▆?
died yesterday.
hello?

h my gl

Like what news sends us into a tailspin,

or how we learn to cope with that,

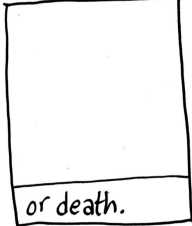

or death.

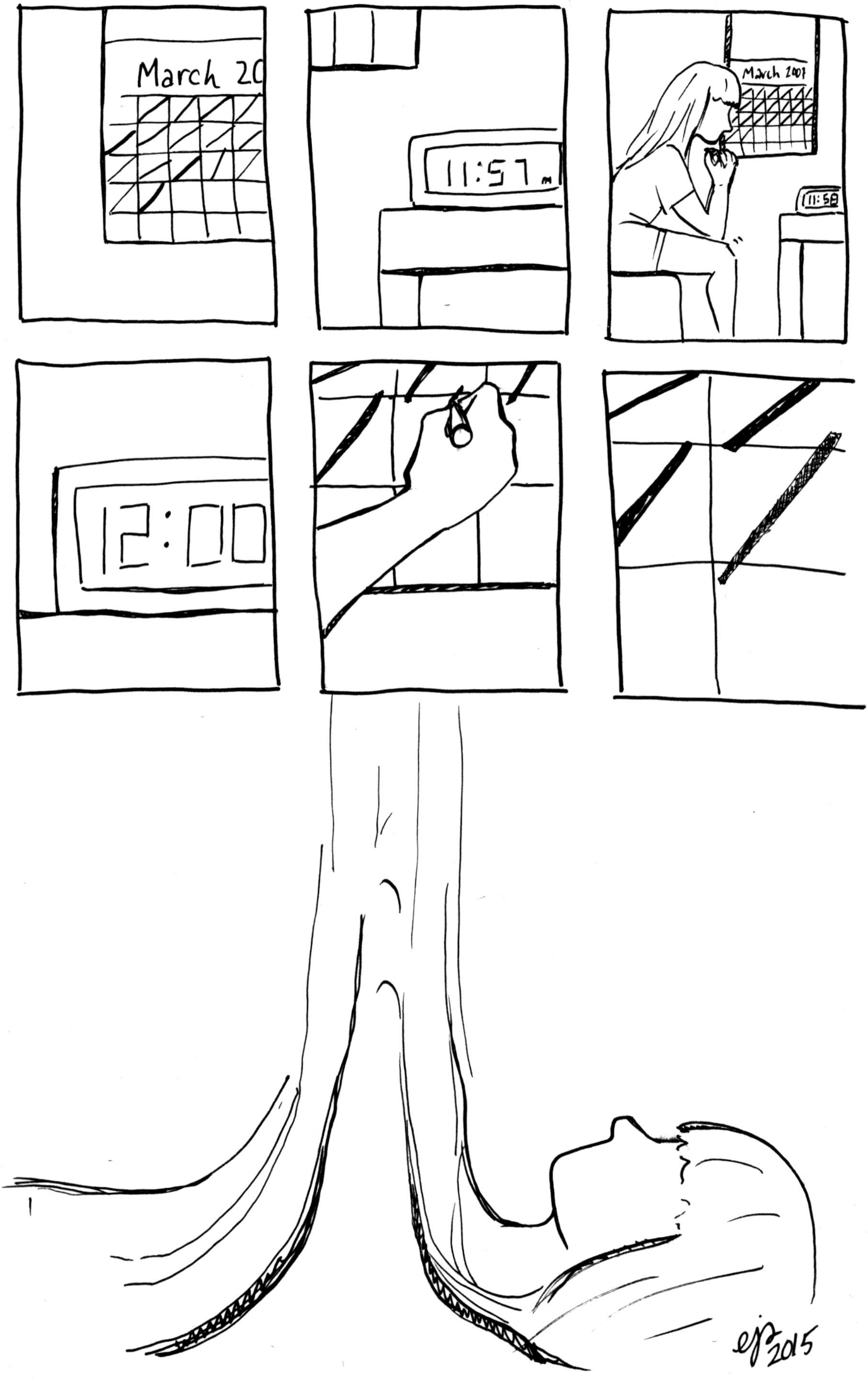
March 20
11:57
March 2007
11:58
12:00
ejp 2015

IKACHAN

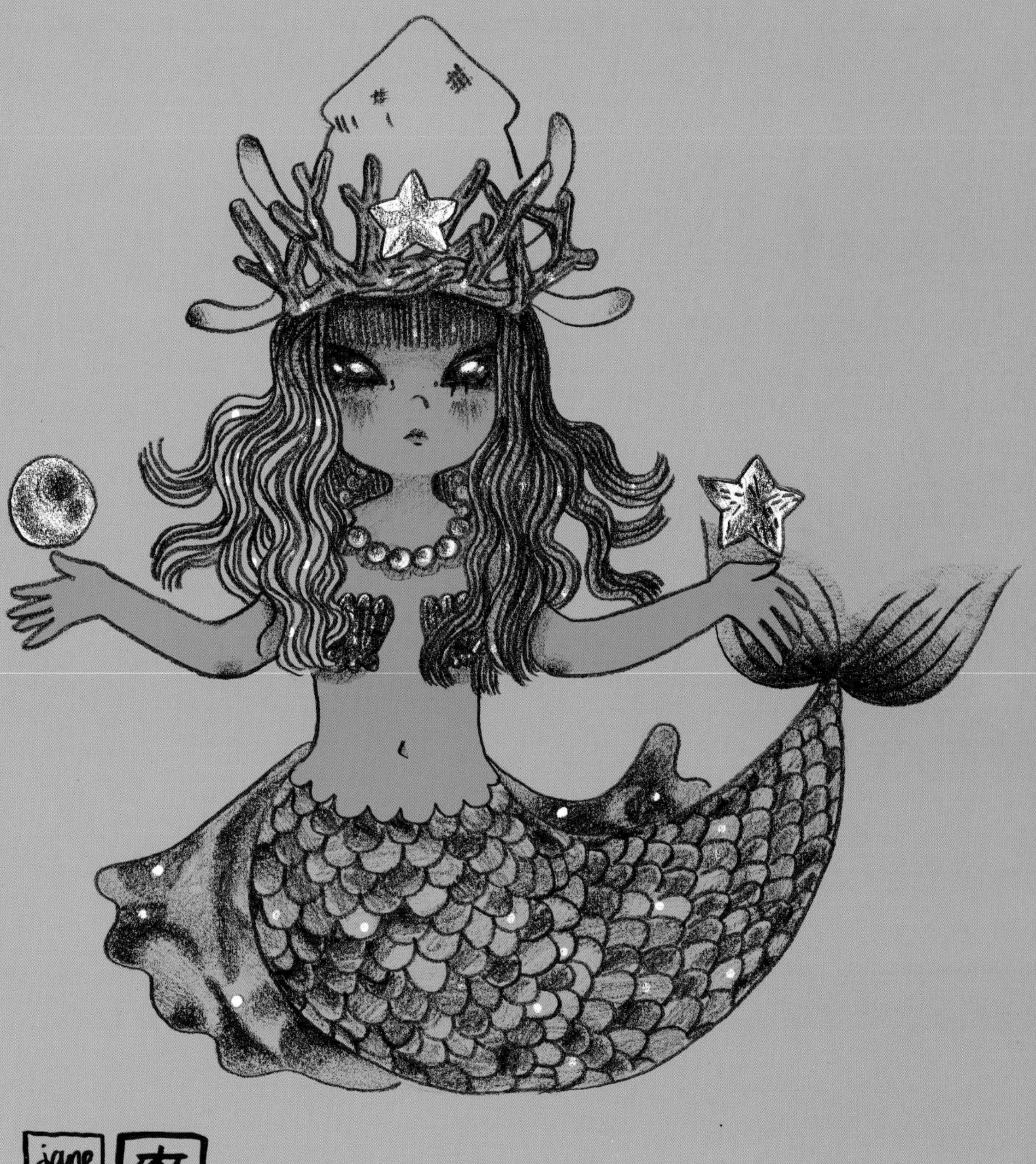

jane mai
麥

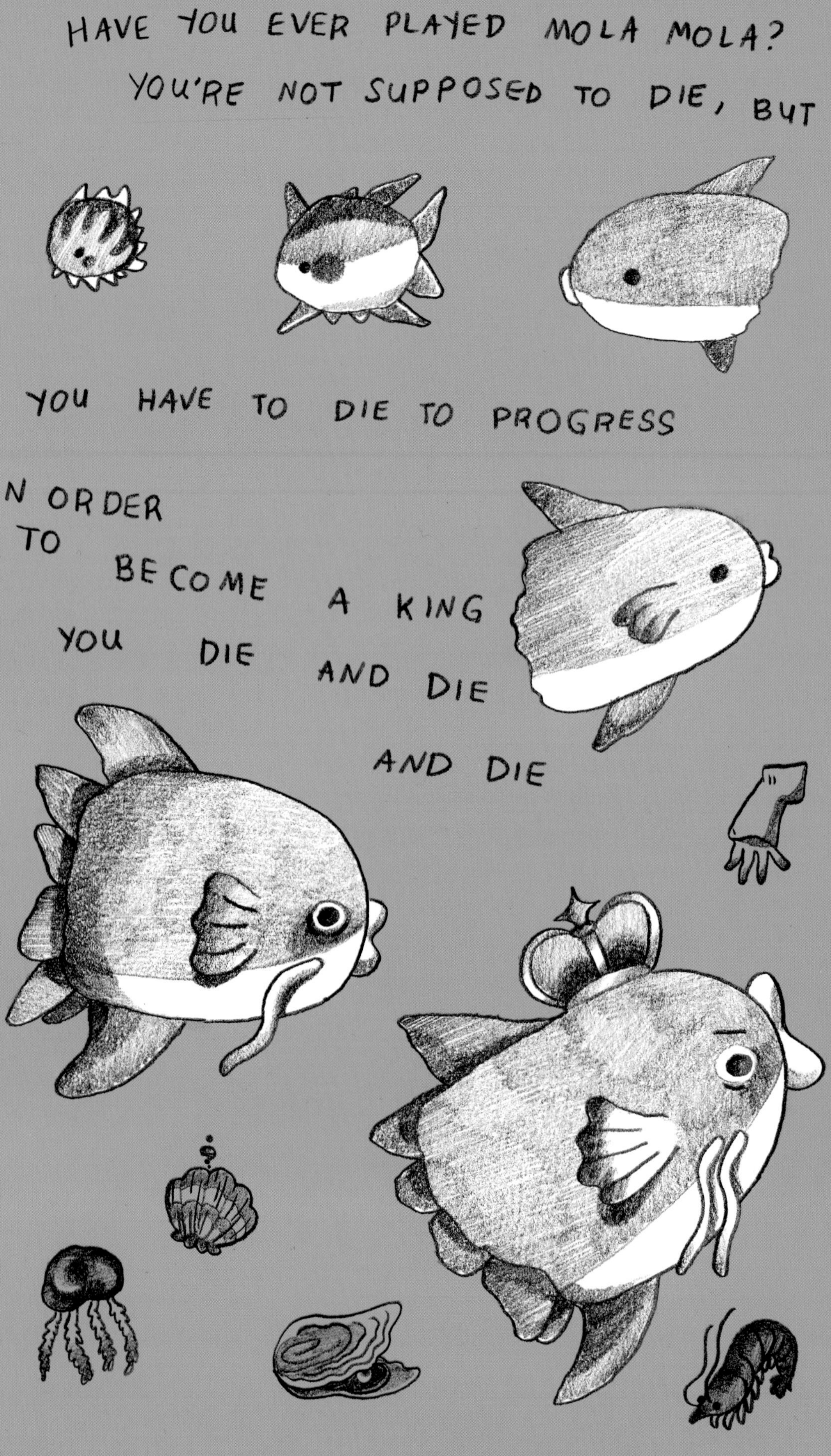
HAVE YOU EVER PLAYED MOLA MOLA?
YOU'RE NOT SUPPOSED TO DIE, BUT
YOU HAVE TO DIE TO PROGRESS
IN ORDER
TO
BECOME A KING
YOU DIE AND DIE
AND DIE

OLD KING MOLA IS
THE MOST POPULAR
ATTRACTION AT THE
AQUARIUM AND
HE WANTS
TO BE FREE, TO
BE A VOYAGER

THAT'S HOW
I FEEL IN THE BATH
IN THE WATER BECAUSE

I REMEMBER WHEN SOMEBODY
I LOVED TRIED TO TEACH ME

TO SWIM

THEY PUSHED MY HEAD UNDER THE WATER AND I THOUGHT I WOULD DIE

I NEVER DID LEARN HOW TO SWIM

IT'S HARD ENOUGH TO FLOAT

IKACHAN, PUT ON YOUR POINTY HAT
AND
PROTECT YOURSELF

IKACHAN, YOU HAVE TO LIVE

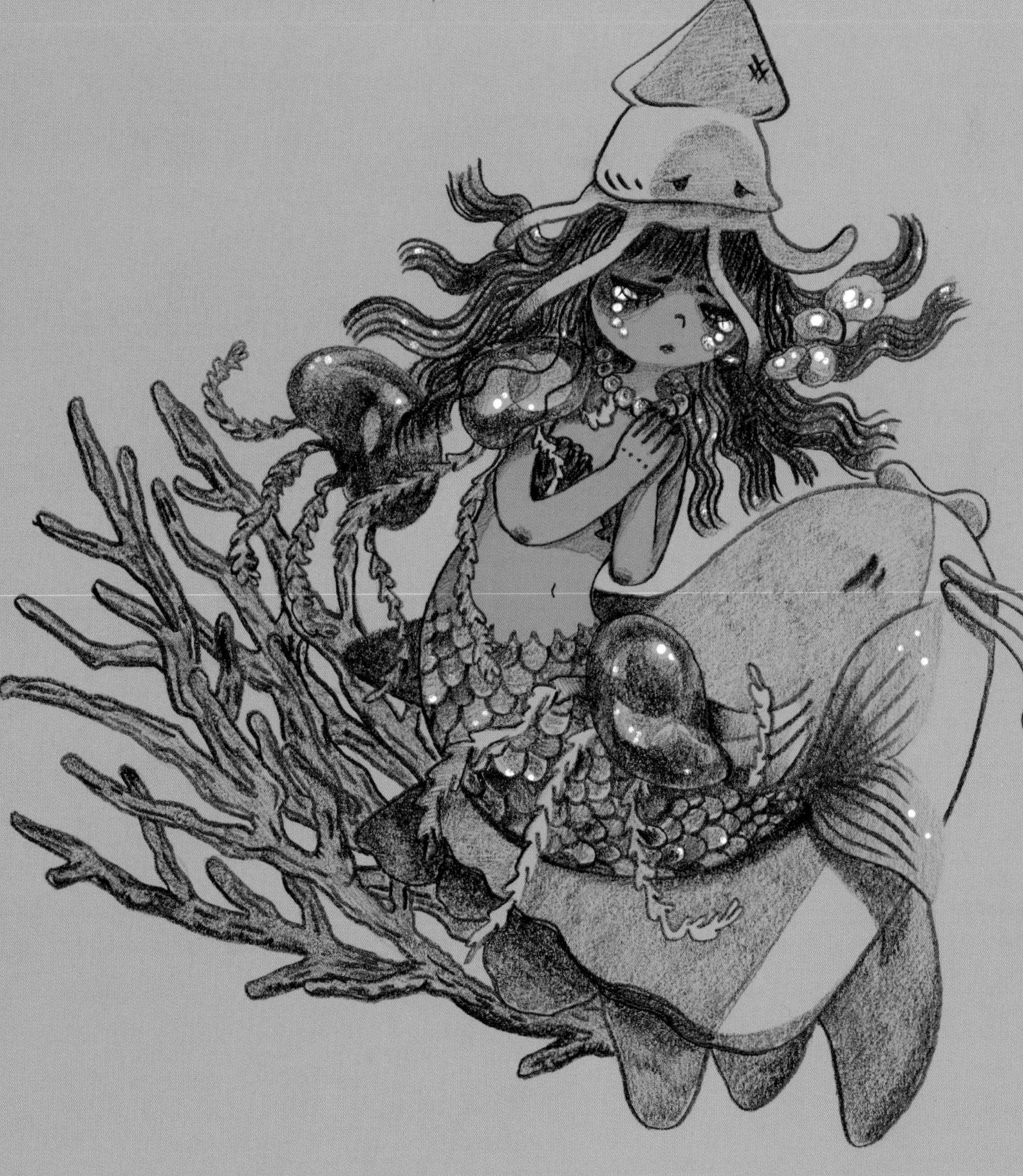

BUT I CAN'T HELP IT

WHEN I REMEMBER

MY LUNGS FILLING UP WITH WATER

WHEN I'D ASK THEM IF THEY LOVED

ME,

AND THEY ONLY GAVE ME

SILENCE

EACH TIME I WOULD DIE
AND DIE AND DIE

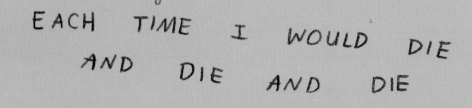

SWIM, IKACHAN, SWIM

GO SAVE SALLY

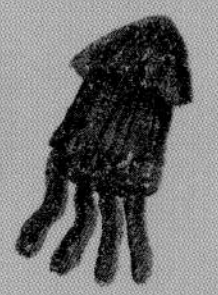

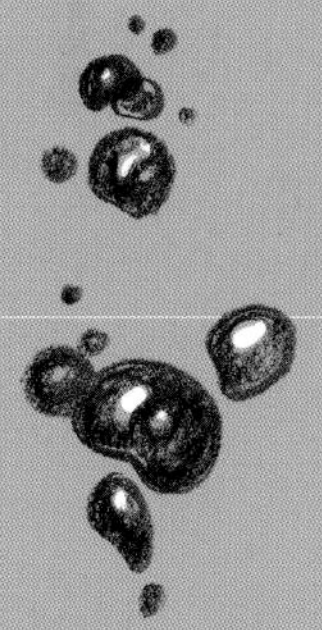

YOU DON'T EVEN NEED A PEARL

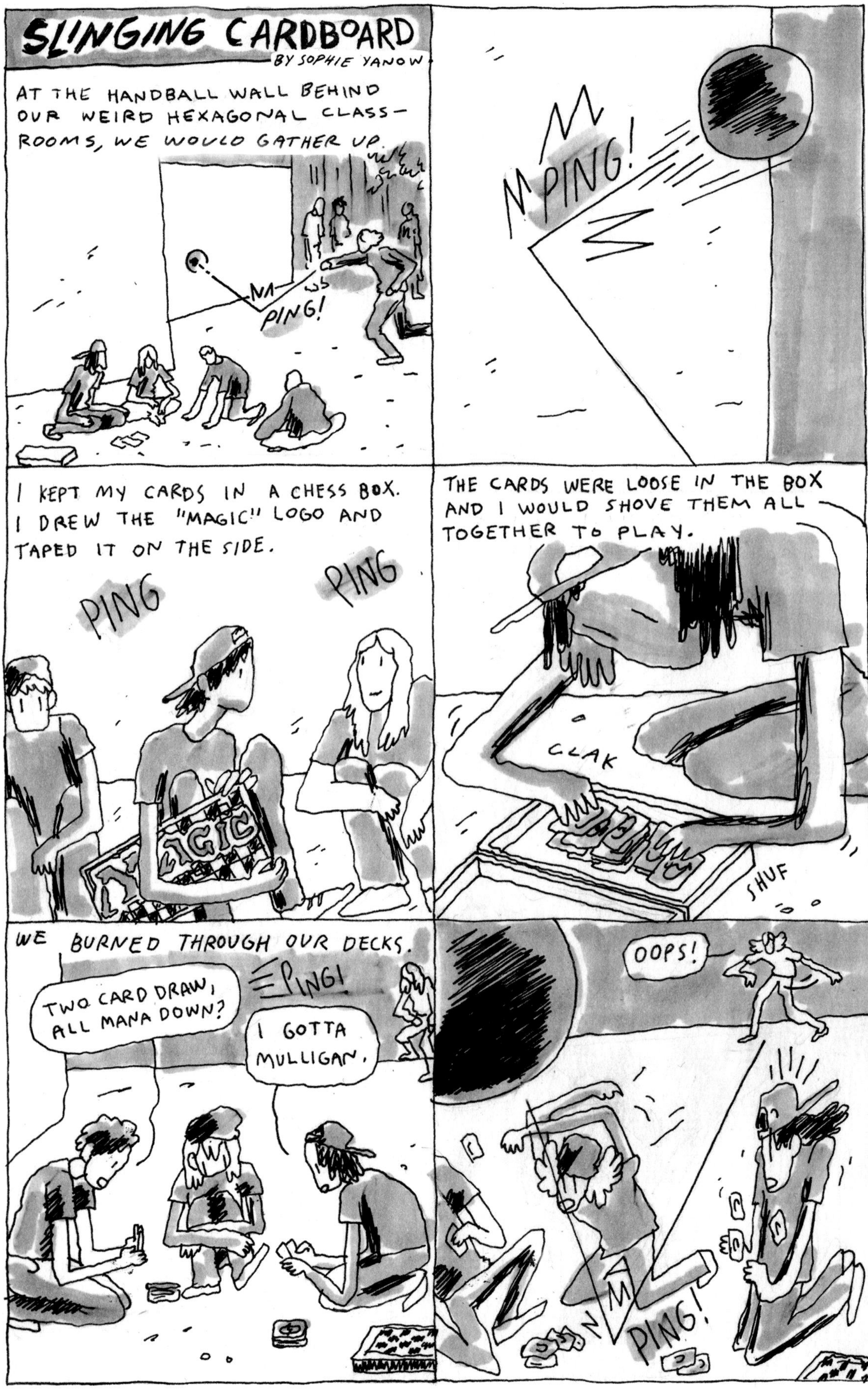
SLINGING CARDBOARD
BY SOPHIE YANOW
AT THE HANDBALL WALL BEHIND OUR WEIRD HEXAGONAL CLASS-ROOMS, WE WOULD GATHER UP.
PING!
PING!
I KEPT MY CARDS IN A CHESS BOX. I DREW THE "MAGIC" LOGO AND TAPED IT ON THE SIDE.
PING
PING
THE CARDS WERE LOOSE IN THE BOX AND I WOULD SHOVE THEM ALL TOGETHER TO PLAY.
CLAK
SHUF
WE BURNED THROUGH OUR DECKS.
PING!
TWO CARD DRAW, ALL MANA DOWN?
I GOTTA MULLIGAN.
OOPS!
PING!

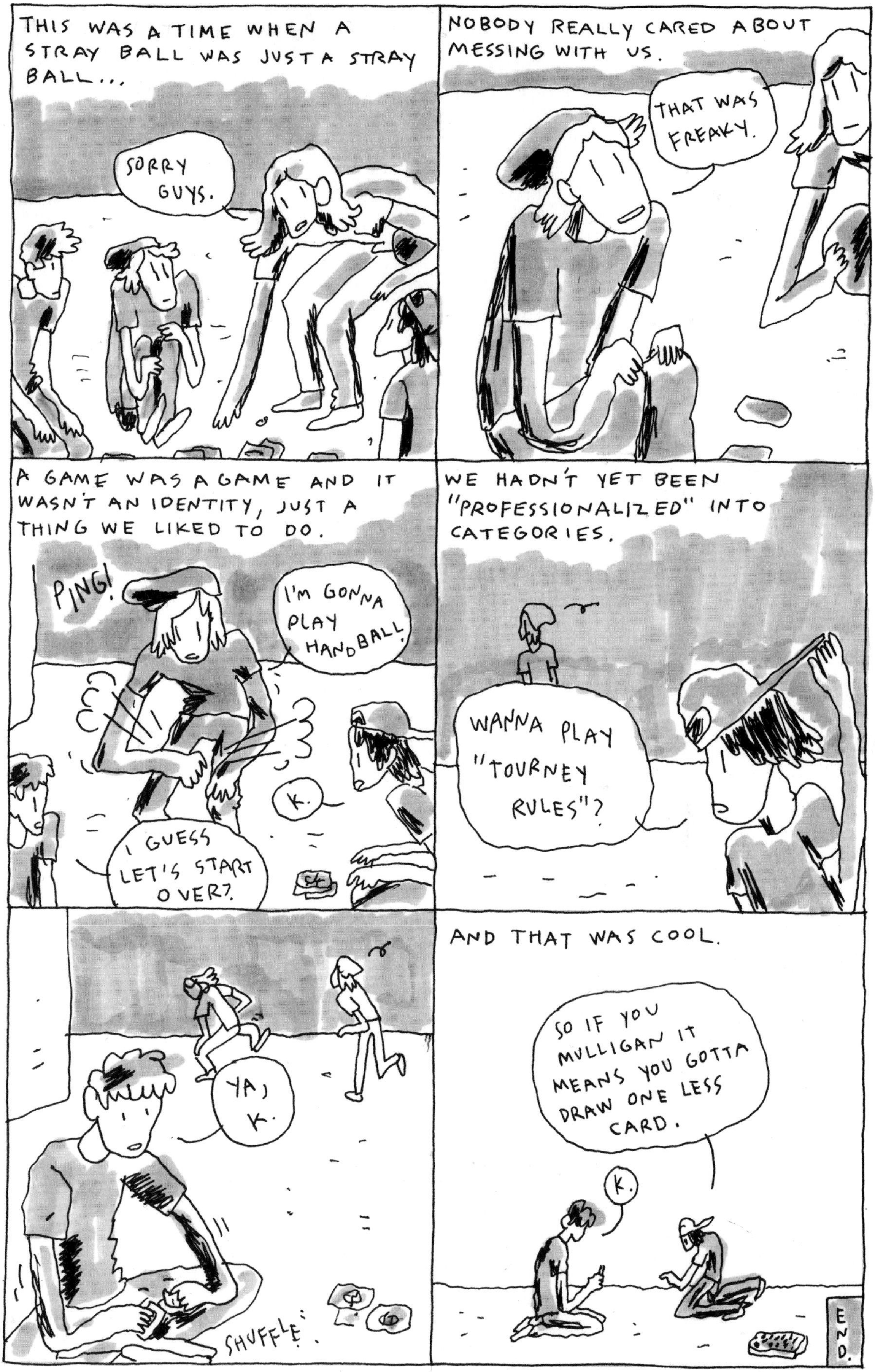
THIS WAS A TIME WHEN A STRAY BALL WAS JUST A STRAY BALL...
SORRY GUYS.
NOBODY REALLY CARED ABOUT MESSING WITH US.
THAT WAS FREAKY.
A GAME WAS A GAME AND IT WASN'T AN IDENTITY, JUST A THING WE LIKED TO DO.
PING!
I'M GONNA PLAY HANDBALL.
K.
I GUESS LET'S START OVER?
WE HADN'T YET BEEN "PROFESSIONALIZED" INTO CATEGORIES.
WANNA PLAY "TOURNEY RULES"?
YA, K.
SHUFFLE
AND THAT WAS COOL.
SO IF YOU MULLIGAN IT MEANS YOU GOTTA DRAW ONE LESS CARD.
K.
END.

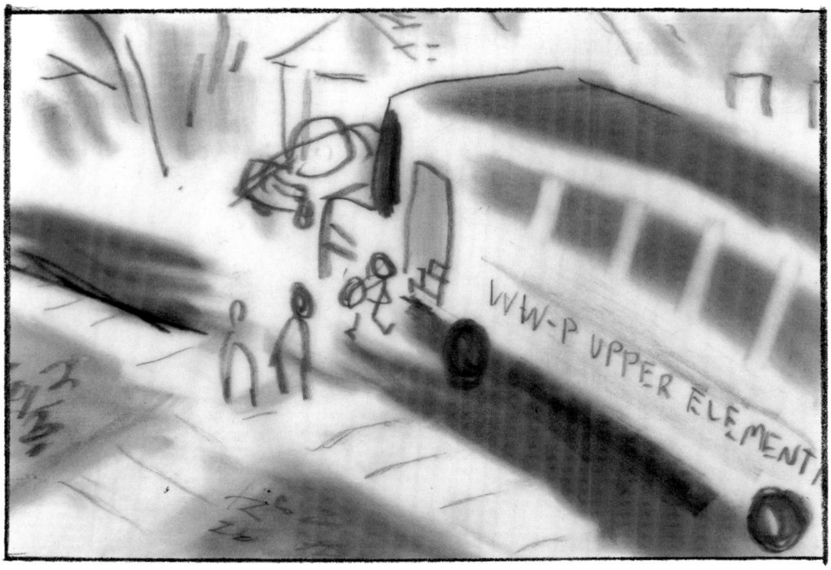
WW-P UPPER ELEMENT

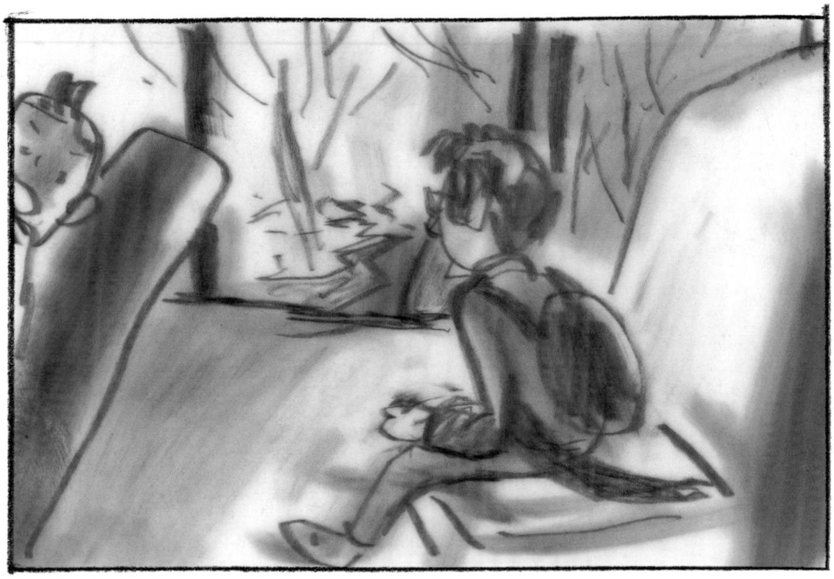

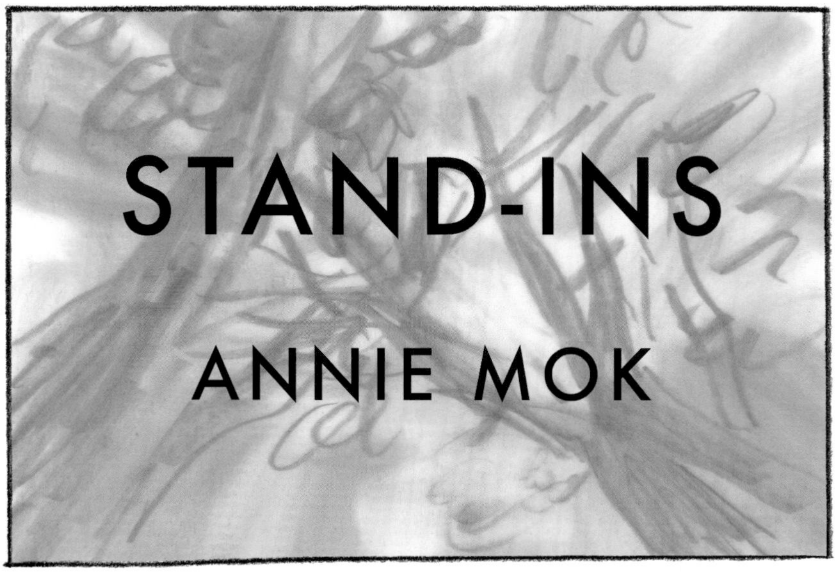

STAND-INS

ANNIE MOK

for Caitlin Rose Boyle.

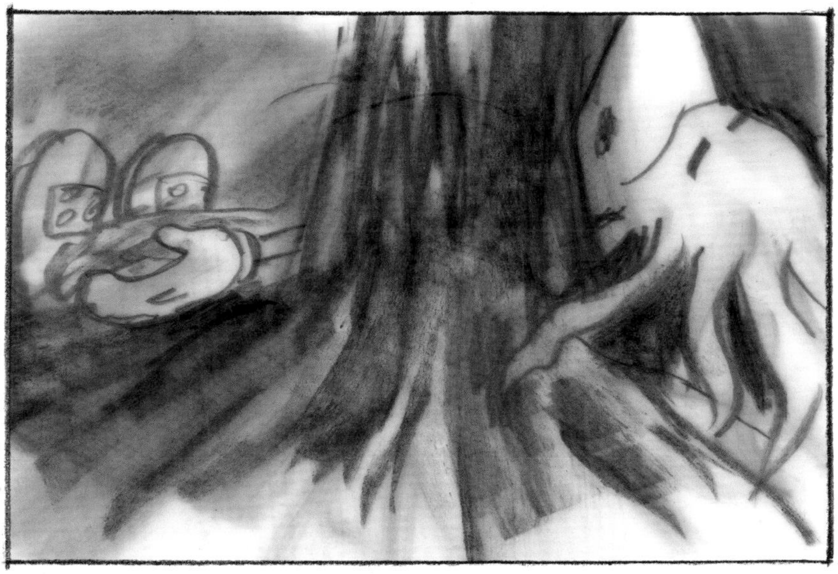

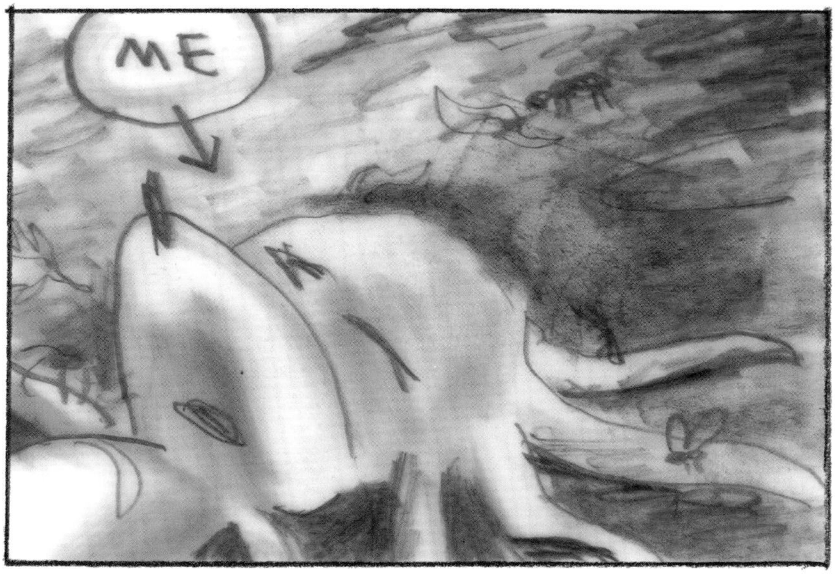
ME

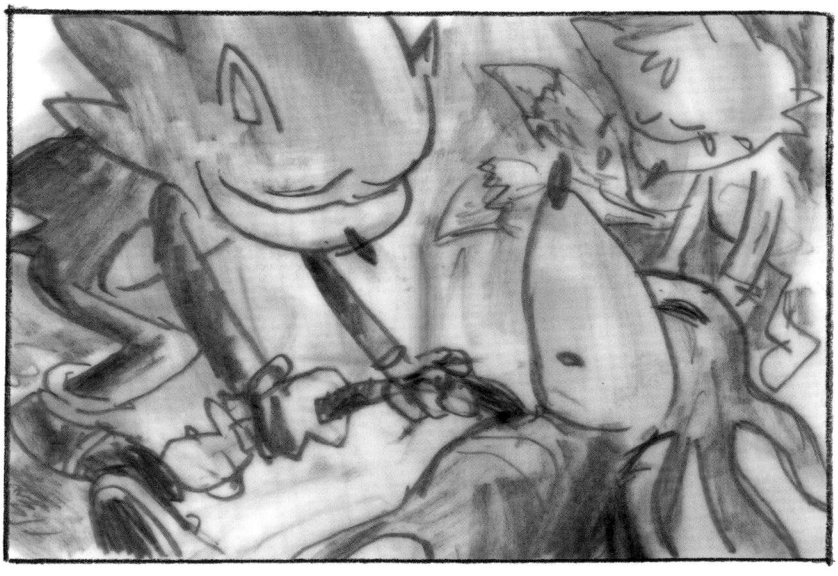

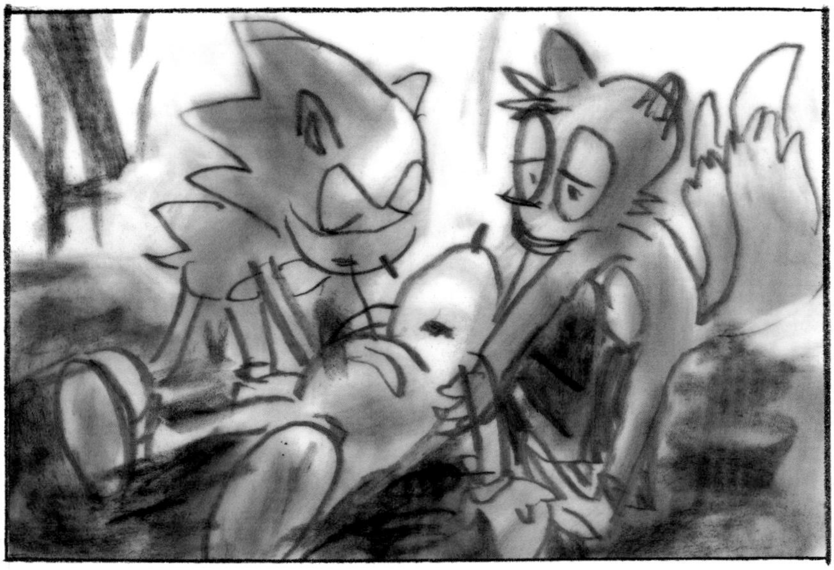

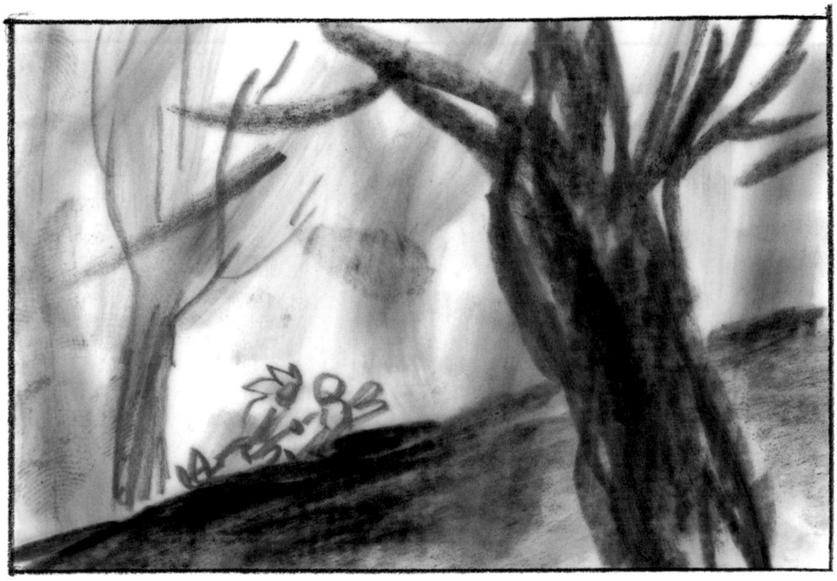

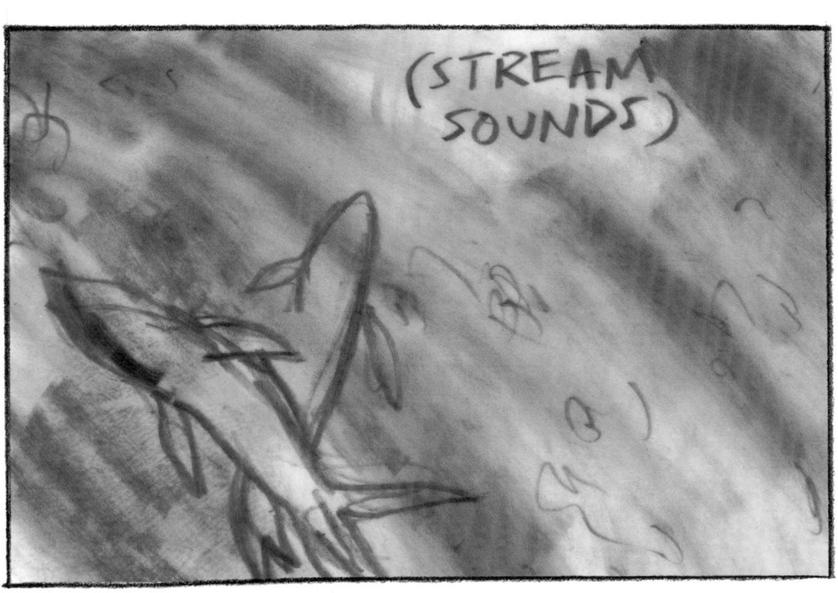
(STREAM SOUNDS)

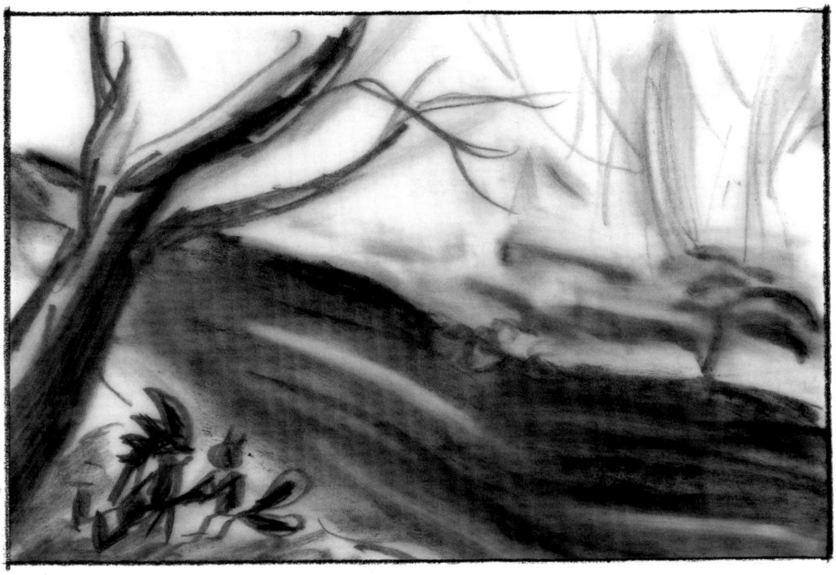

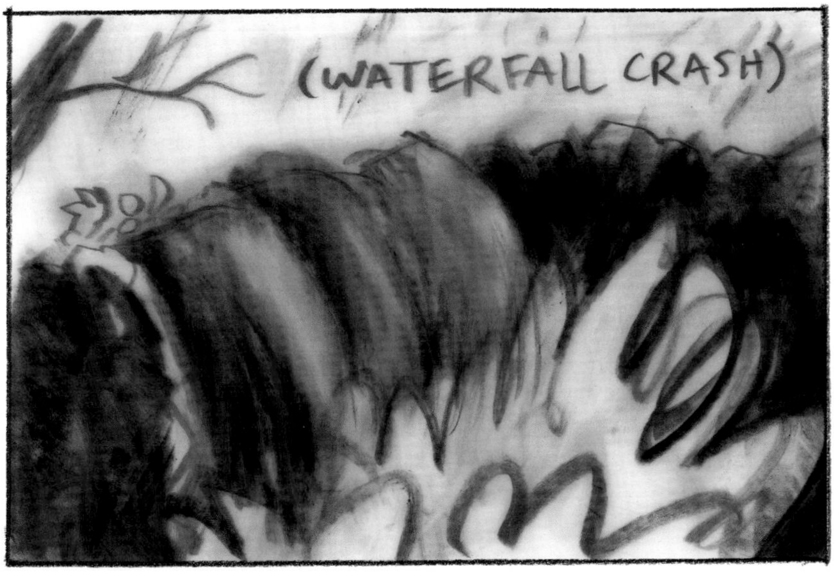
(WATERFALL CRASH)

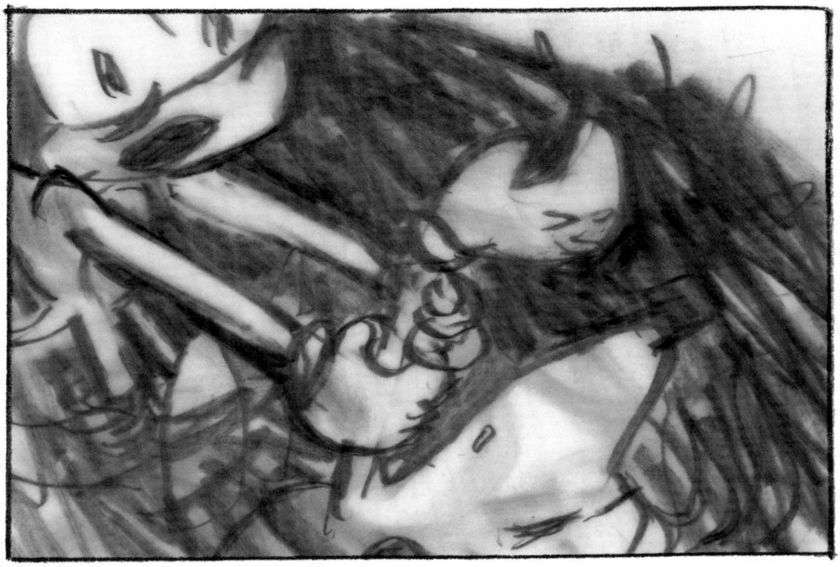

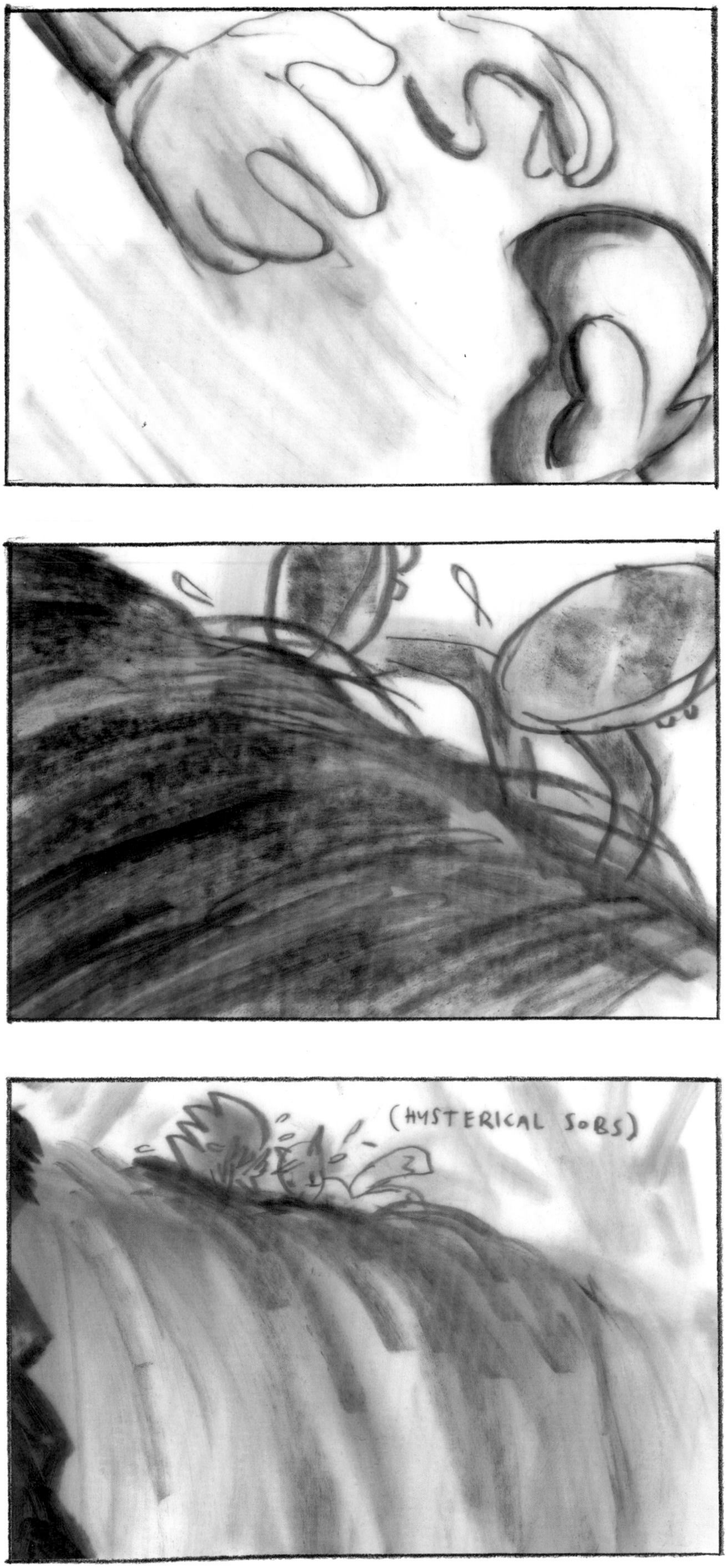
(HYSTERICAL SOBS)

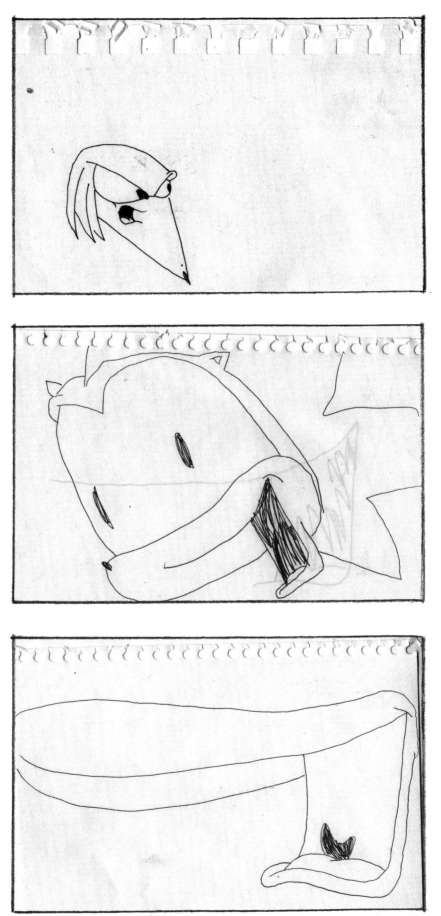

ANNIE MOK 1992(?)+2014

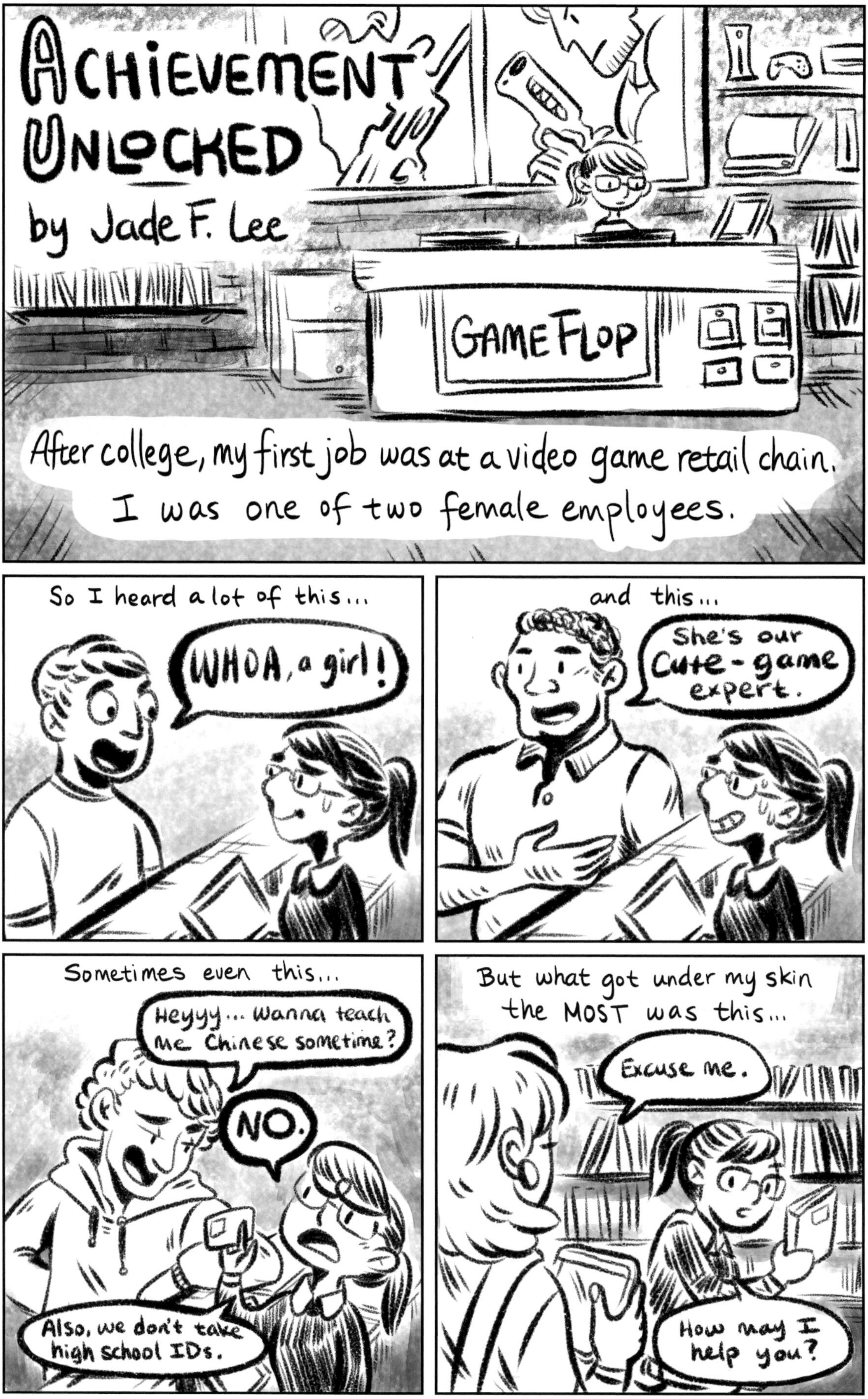
ACHIEVEMENT UNLOCKED
by Jade F. Lee
GAME FLOP
After college, my first job was at a video game retail chain.
I was one of two female employees.
So I heard a lot of this...
WHOA, a girl!
and this...
She's our Cute-game expert.
Sometimes even this...
Heyyy... Wanna teach me Chinese sometime?
NO.
Also, we don't take high school IDs.
But what got under my skin the MOST was this...
Excuse me.
How may I help you?

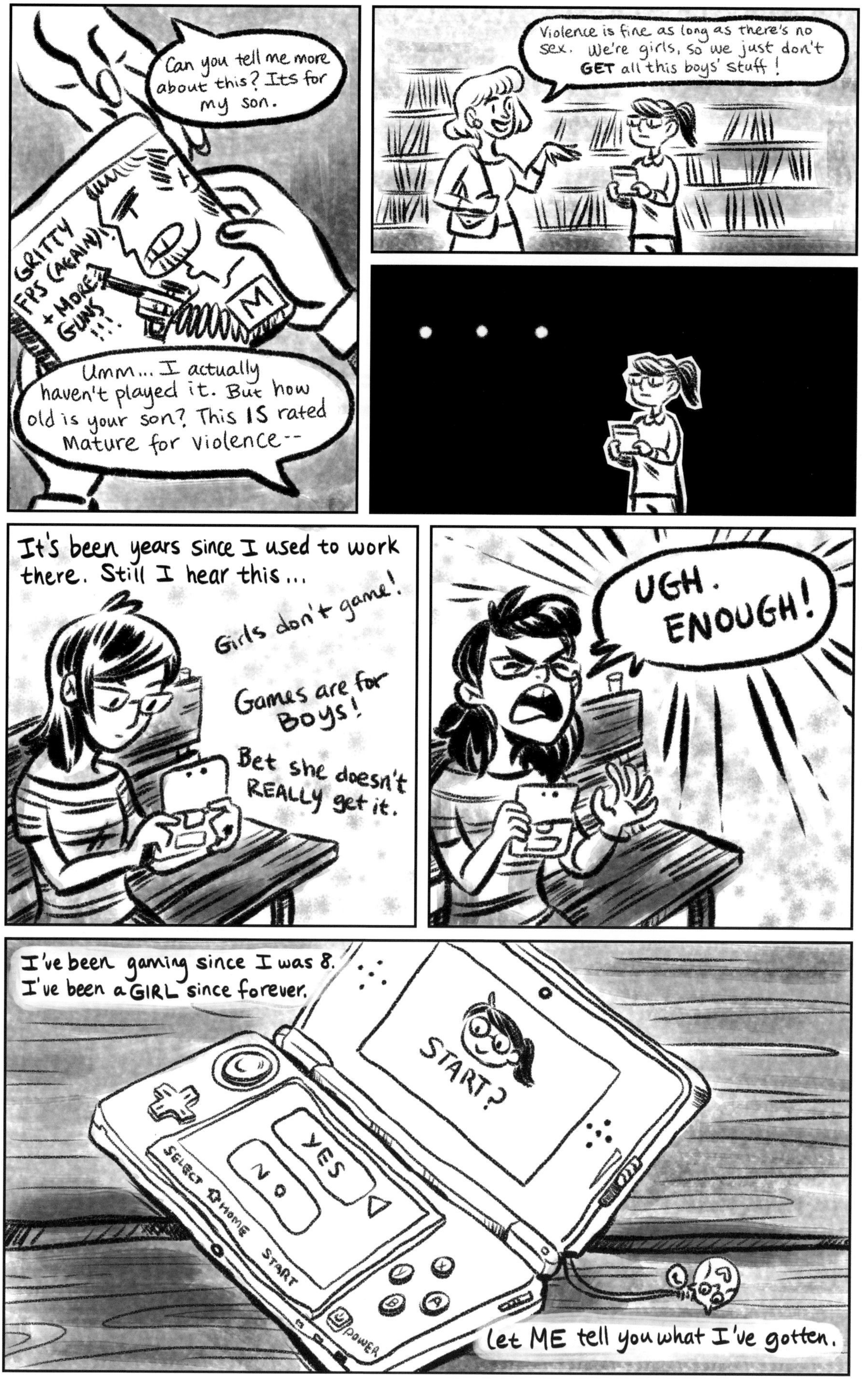
Can you tell me more about this? Its for my son.
GRITTY FPS (AGAIN)! + MORE GUNS !!!
M
Umm... I actually haven't played it. But how old is your son? This IS rated Mature for violence--
Violence is fine as long as there's no sex. We're girls, so we just don't GET all this boys' stuff!
It's been years since I used to work there. Still I hear this...
Girls don't game!
Games are for BOYS!
Bet she doesn't REALLY get it.
UGH. ENOUGH!
I've been gaming since I was 8. I've been a GIRL since forever.
START?
YES
NO
SELECT
HOME
START
POWER
let ME tell you what I've gotten.

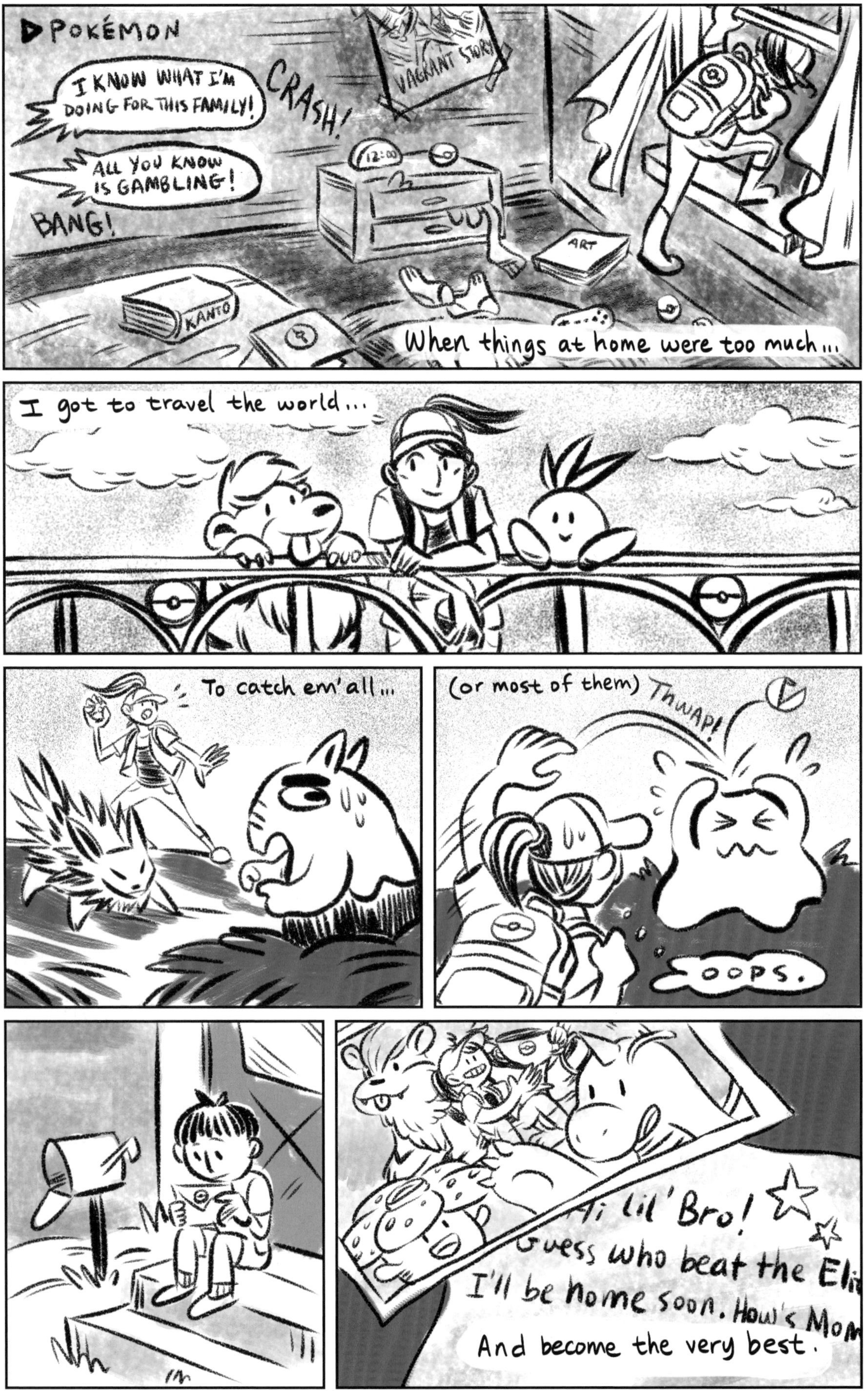
POKÉMON
I KNOW WHAT I'M DOING FOR THIS FAMILY!
ALL YOU KNOW IS GAMBLING!
BANG!
CRASH!
VAGRANT STORY
12:00
ART
KANTO
When things at home were too much...
I got to travel the world...
To catch em'all...
(or most of them)
THWAP!
OOPS.
Hi lil' Bro!
Guess who beat the Eli
I'll be home soon. How's Mom
And become the very best.

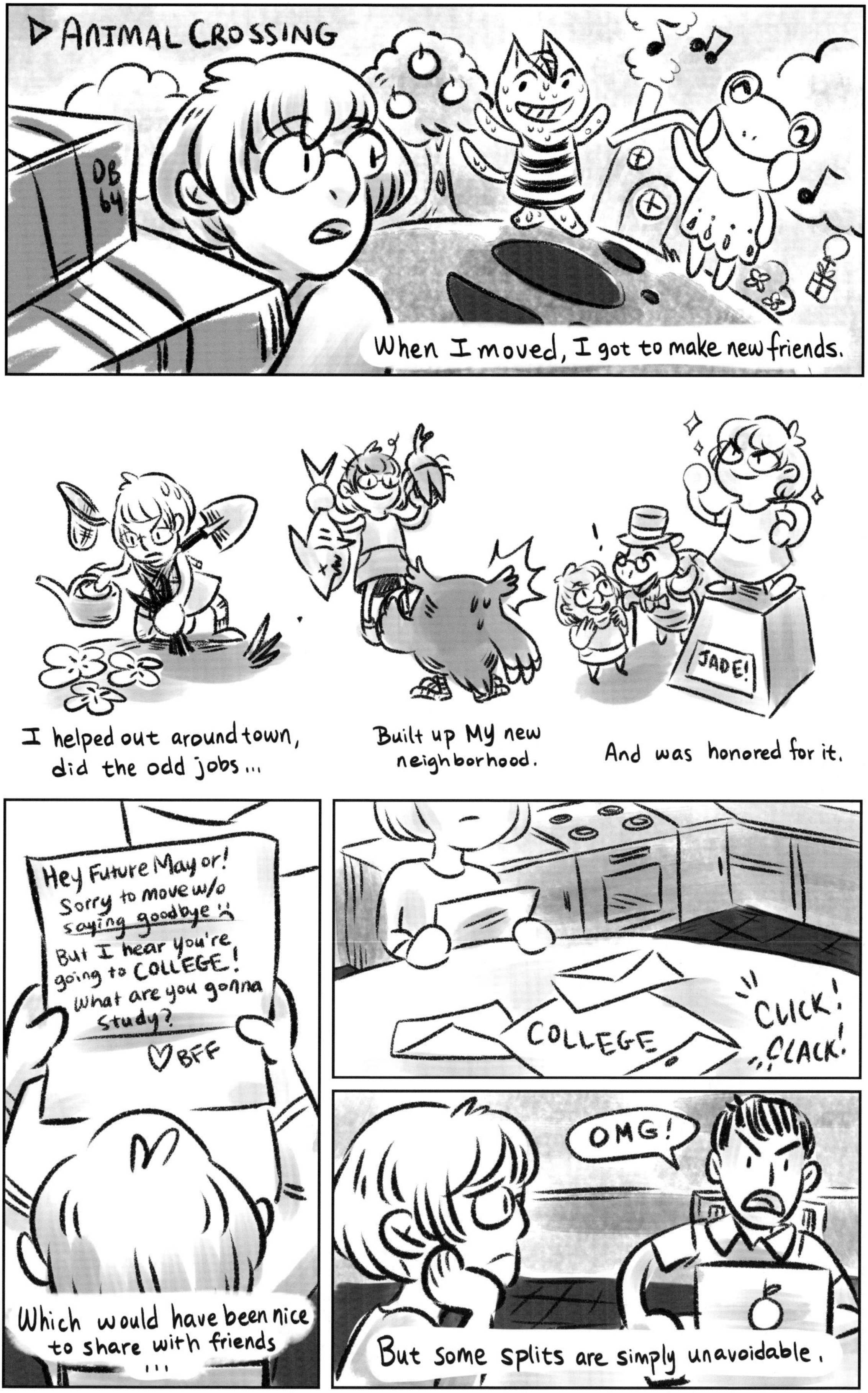

ANIMAL CROSSING
DB 64
When I moved, I got to make new friends.
I helped out around town, did the odd jobs...
Built up my new neighborhood.
And was honored for it.
JADE!
Hey Future Mayor! Sorry to move w/o saying goodbye :(But I hear you're going to COLLEGE! What are you gonna study? ♡BFF
Which would have been nice to share with friends ...
COLLEGE
CLICK! CLACK!
OMG!
But some splits are simply unavoidable.

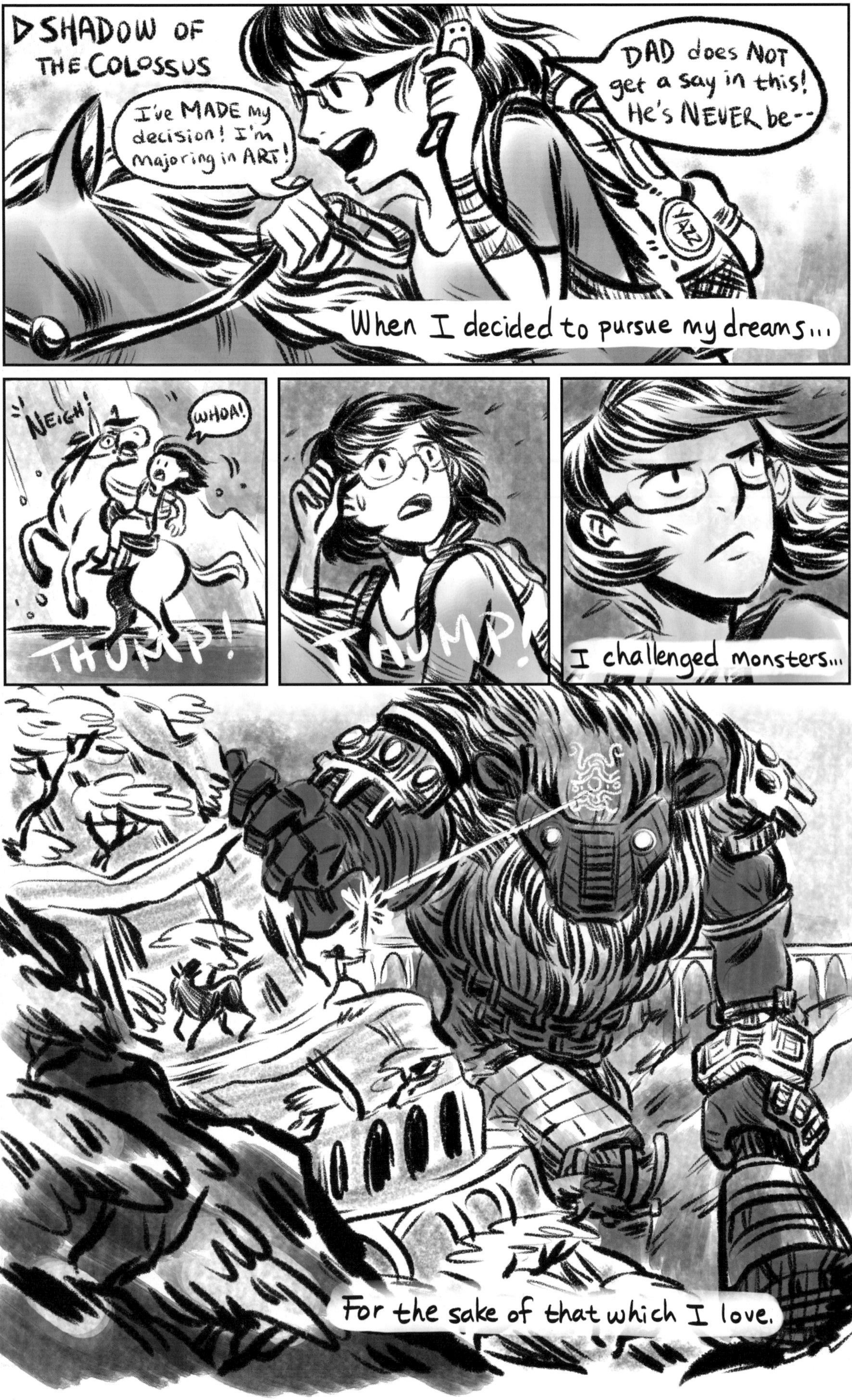

SHADOW OF THE COLOSSUS
I've MADE my decision! I'm majoring in ART!
DAD does NOT get a say in this! He's NEVER be--
YAZZ
When I decided to pursue my dreams...
NEIGH!
WHOA!
THUMP!
THUMP!
I challenged monsters...
For the sake of that which I love.

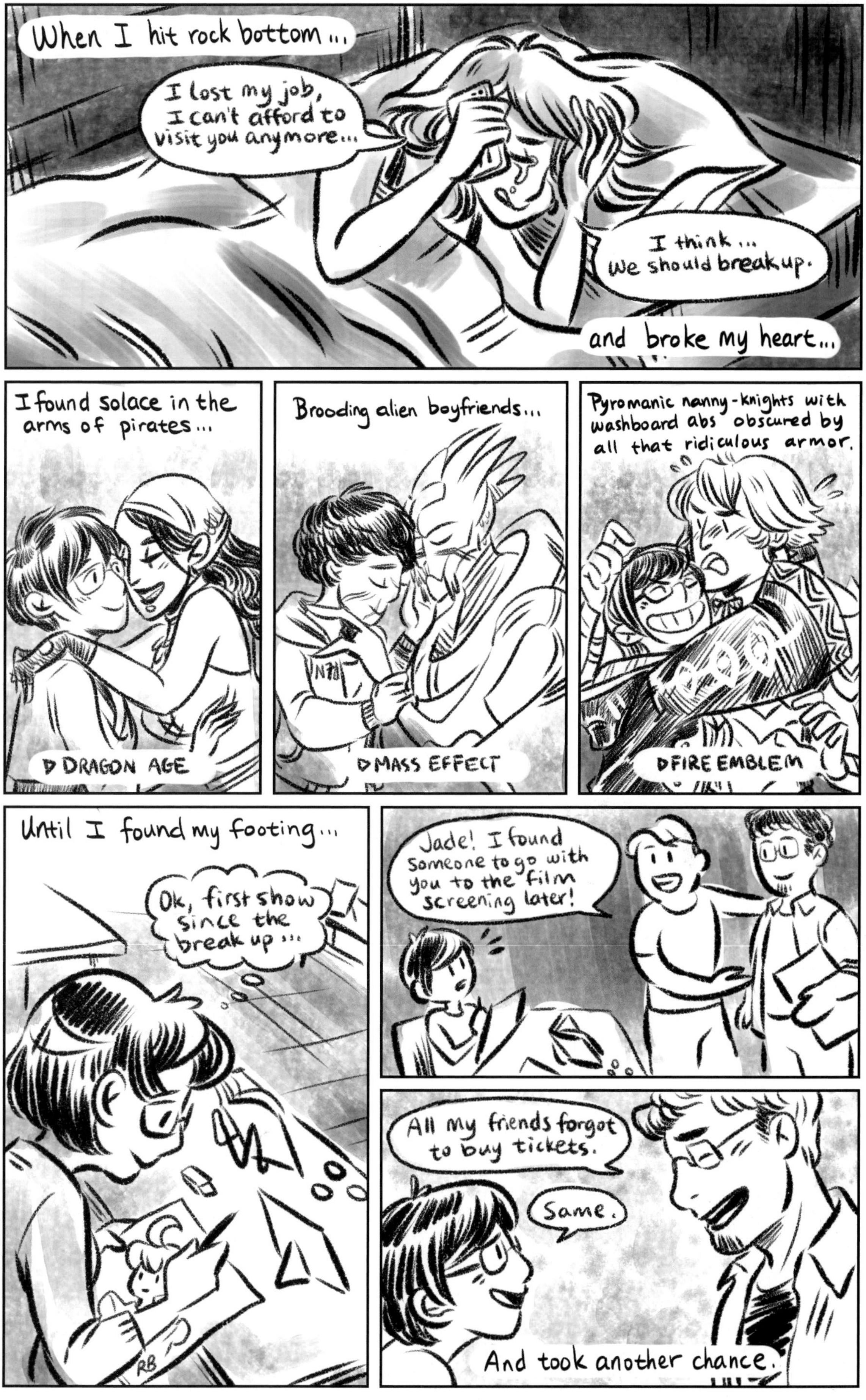
When I hit rock bottom...
I lost my job, I can't afford to visit you anymore...
I think... we should break up.
and broke my heart...
I found solace in the arms of pirates...
DRAGON AGE
Brooding alien boyfriends...
N7
MASS EFFECT
Pyromanic nanny-knights with washboard abs obscured by all that ridiculous armor.
FIRE EMBLEM
Until I found my footing...
Ok, first show since the break up...
RB
Jade! I found someone to go with you to the film screening later!
All my friends forgot to buy tickets.
Same.
And took another chance.

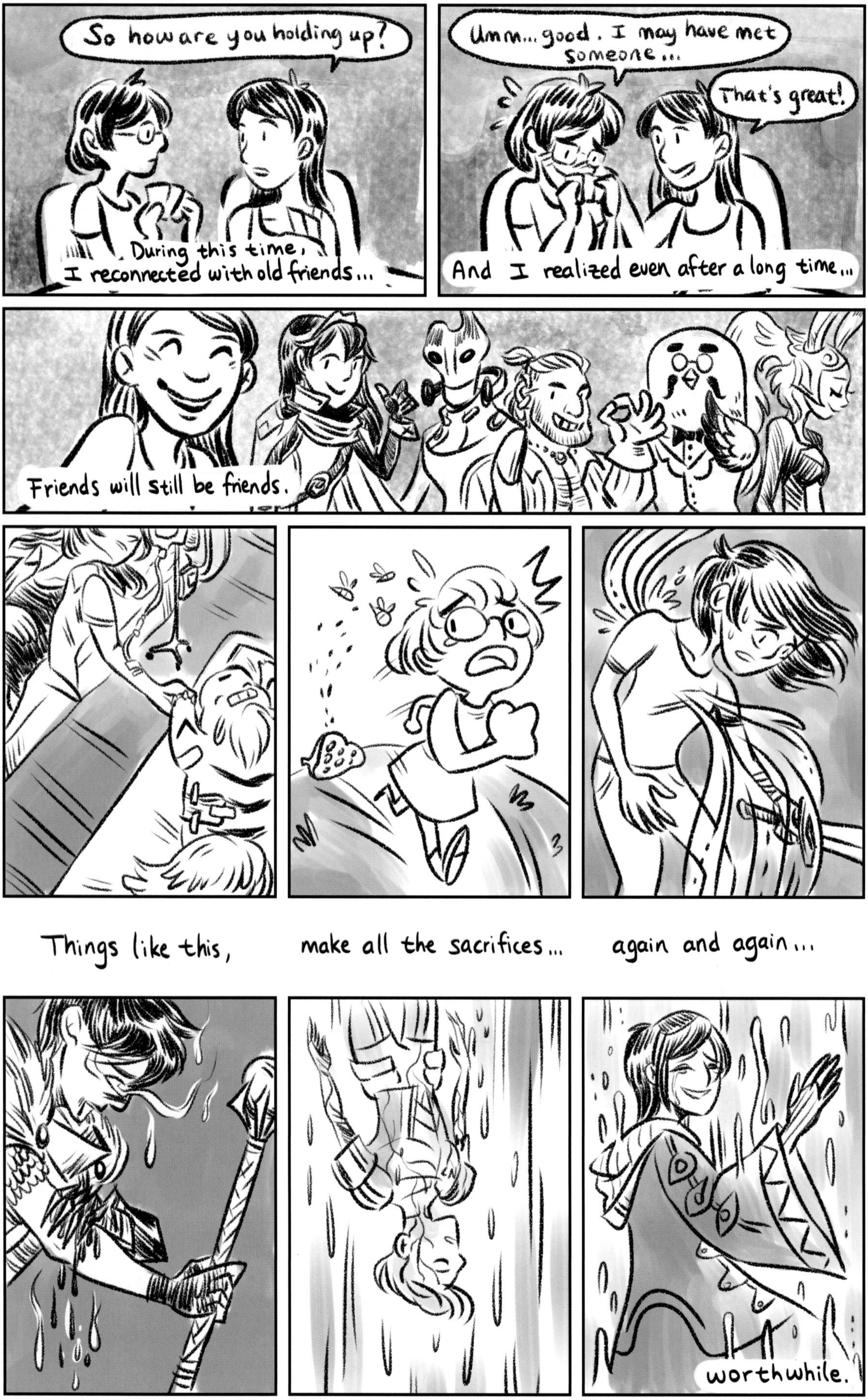

So how are you holding up?
During this time, I reconnected with old friends...
Umm... good. I may have met someone...
That's great!
And I realized even after a long time...
Friends will still be friends.
Things like this,
make all the sacrifices...
again and again...
worthwhile.

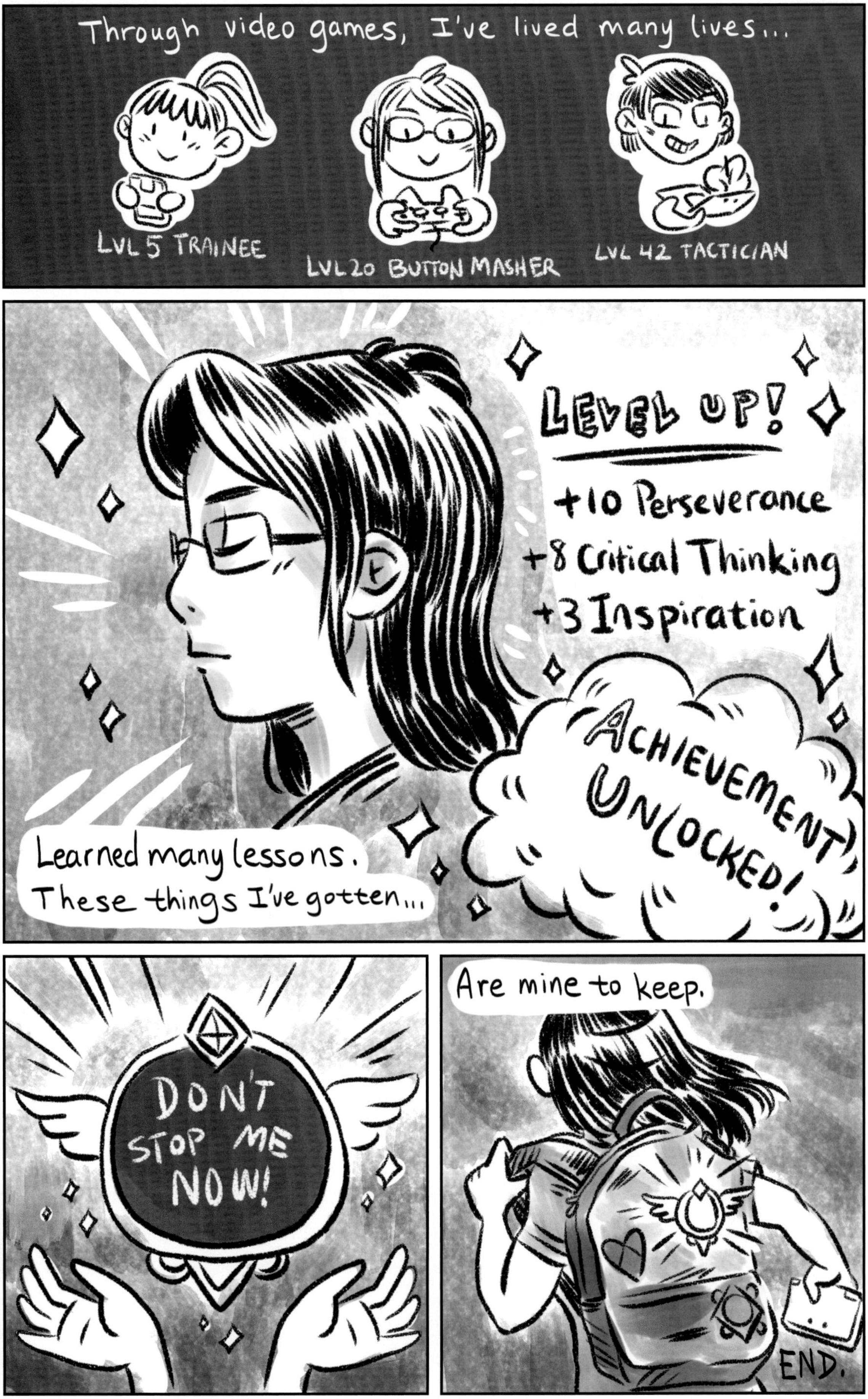
Through video games, I've lived many lives...
LVL 5 TRAINEE
LVL 20 BUTTON MASHER
LVL 42 TACTICIAN
LEVEL UP!
+10 Perseverance
+8 Critical Thinking
+3 Inspiration
ACHIEVEMENT UNLOCKED!
Learned many lessons.
These things I've gotten...
DON'T STOP ME NOW!
Are mine to keep.
END.

HERMIA

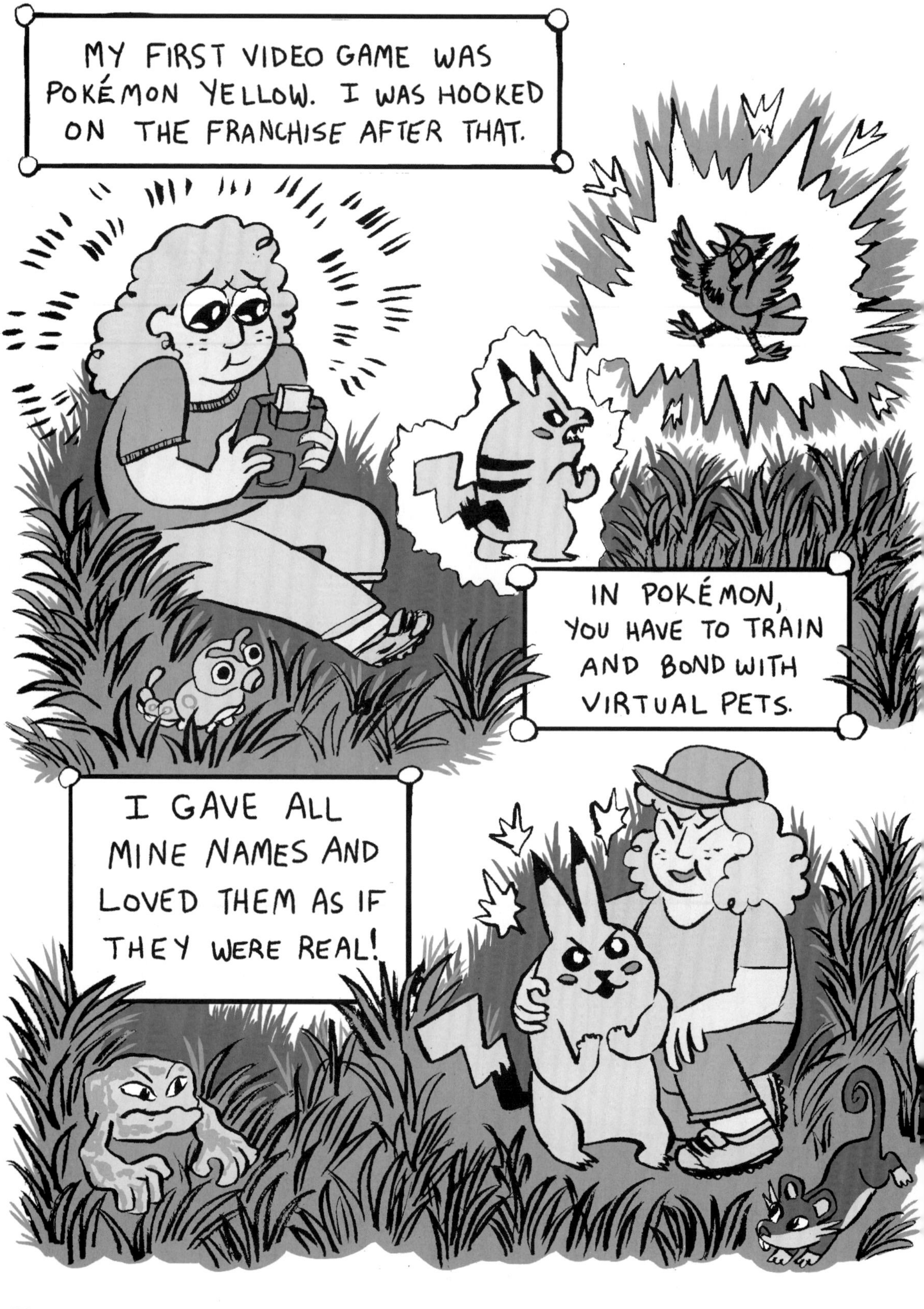
MY FIRST VIDEO GAME WAS POKÉMON YELLOW. I WAS HOOKED ON THE FRANCHISE AFTER THAT.
IN POKÉMON, YOU HAVE TO TRAIN AND BOND WITH VIRTUAL PETS.
I GAVE ALL MINE NAMES AND LOVED THEM AS IF THEY WERE REAL!

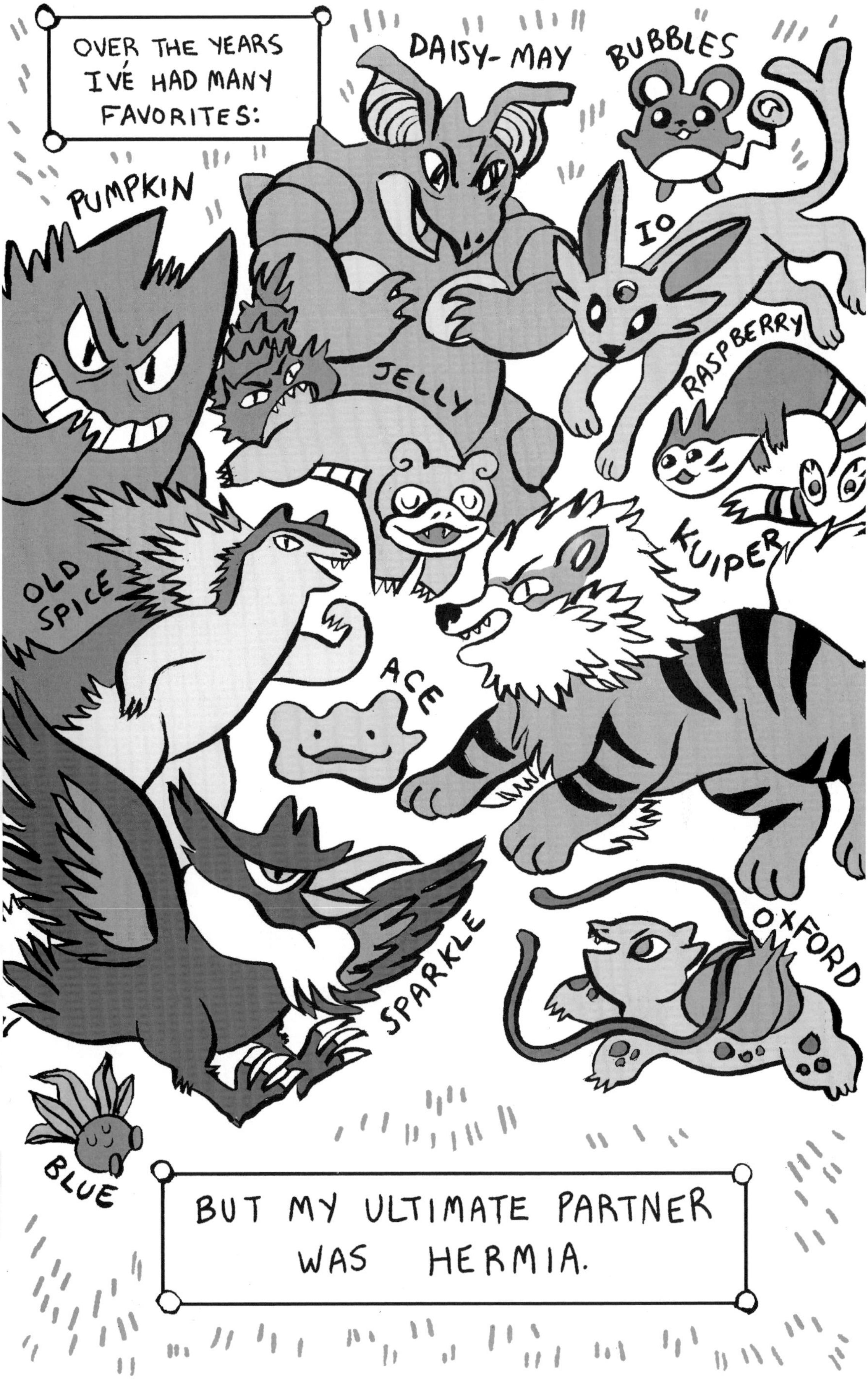
OVER THE YEARS I'VE HAD MANY FAVORITES:
DAISY-MAY
BUBBLES
PUMPKIN
IO
JELLY
RASPBERRY
KUIPER
OLD SPICE
ACE
OXFORD
SPARKLE
BLUE
BUT MY ULTIMATE PARTNER WAS HERMIA.

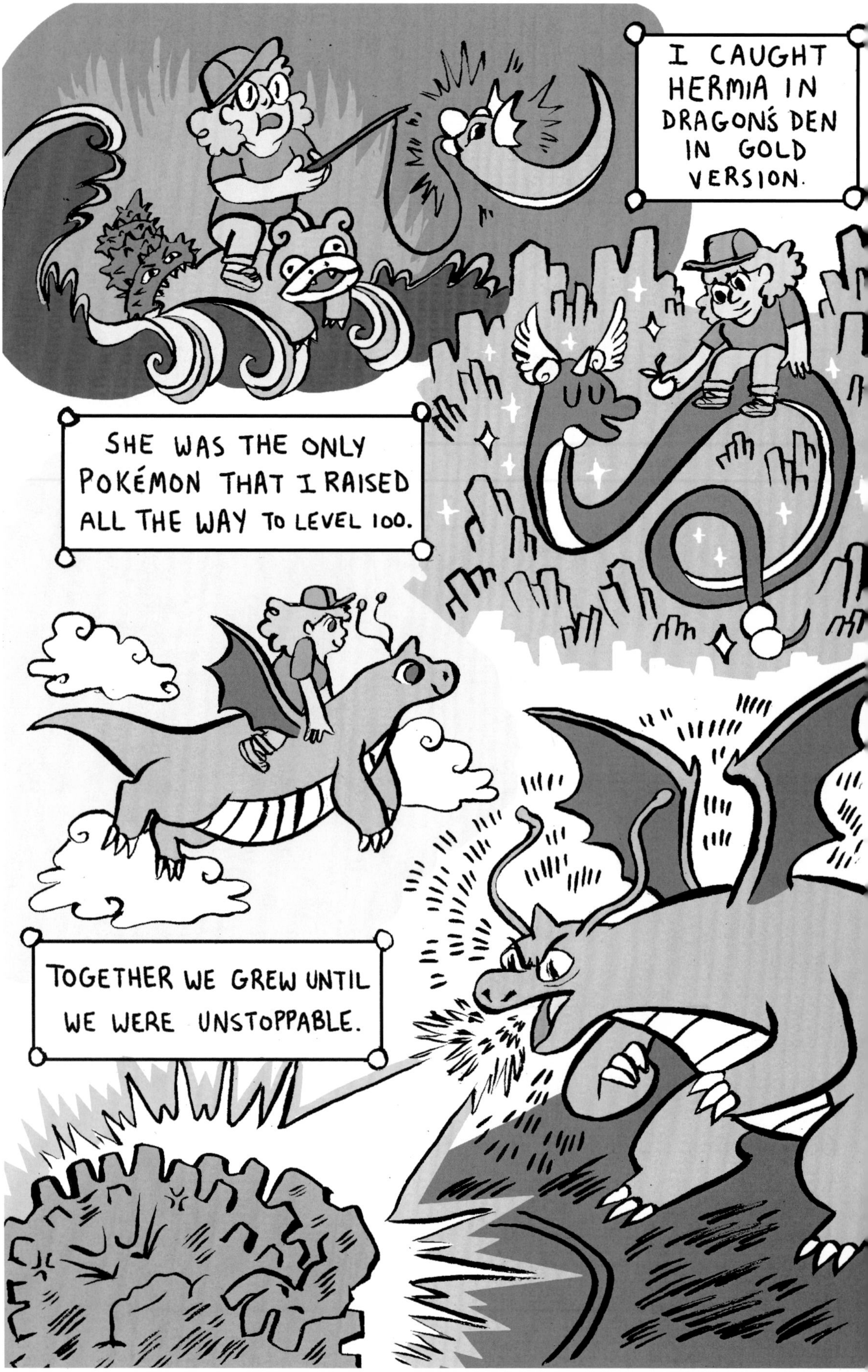
I CAUGHT HERMIA IN DRAGON'S DEN IN GOLD VERSION.
SHE WAS THE ONLY POKÉMON THAT I RAISED ALL THE WAY TO LEVEL 100.
TOGETHER WE GREW UNTIL WE WERE UNSTOPPABLE.

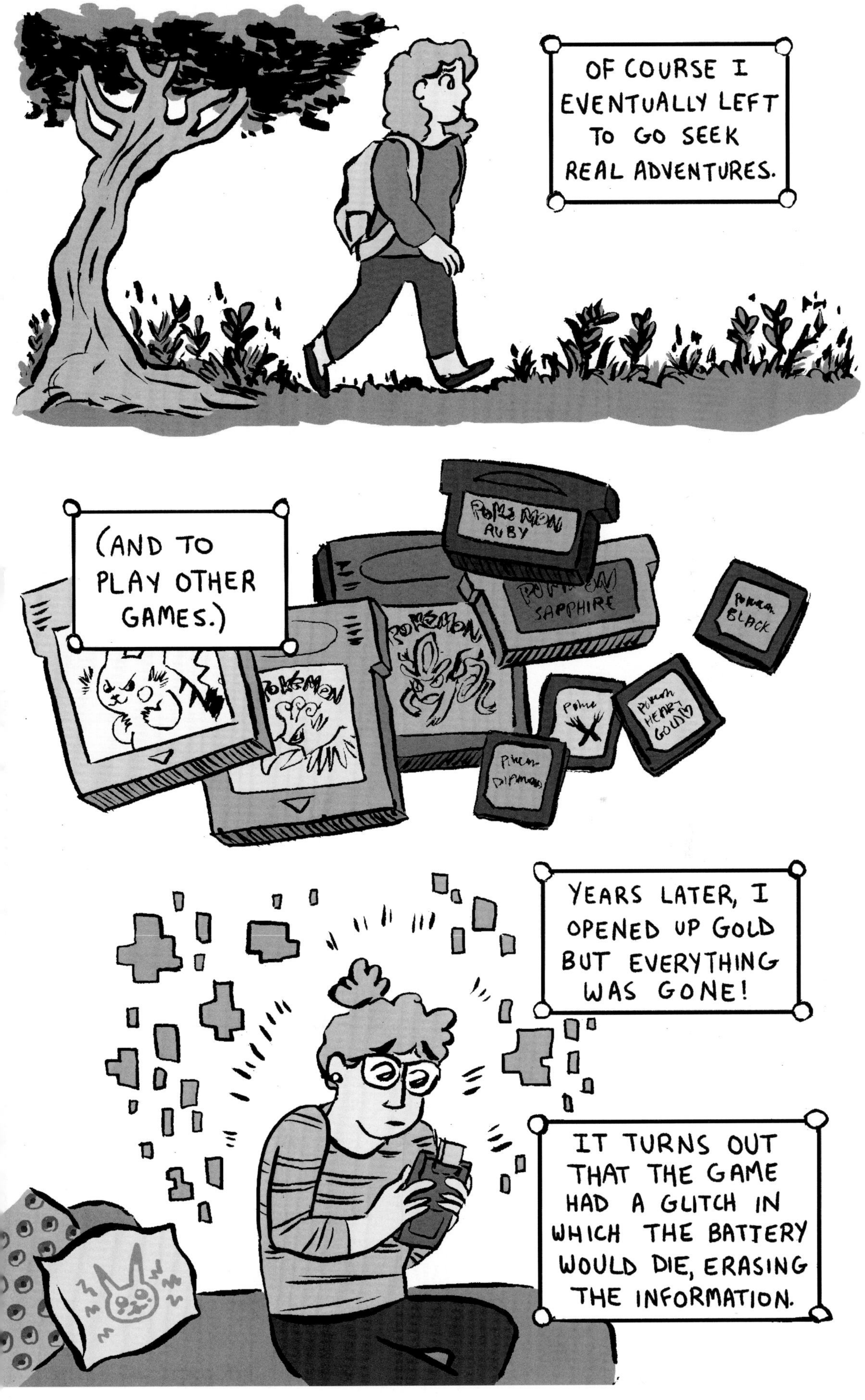
OF COURSE I EVENTUALLY LEFT TO GO SEEK REAL ADVENTURES.
(AND TO PLAY OTHER GAMES.)
RUBY
SAPPHIRE
POKEMON
POKEMON
BLACK
YEARS LATER, I OPENED UP GOLD BUT EVERYTHING WAS GONE!
IT TURNS OUT THAT THE GAME HAD A GLITCH IN WHICH THE BATTERY WOULD DIE, ERASING THE INFORMATION.

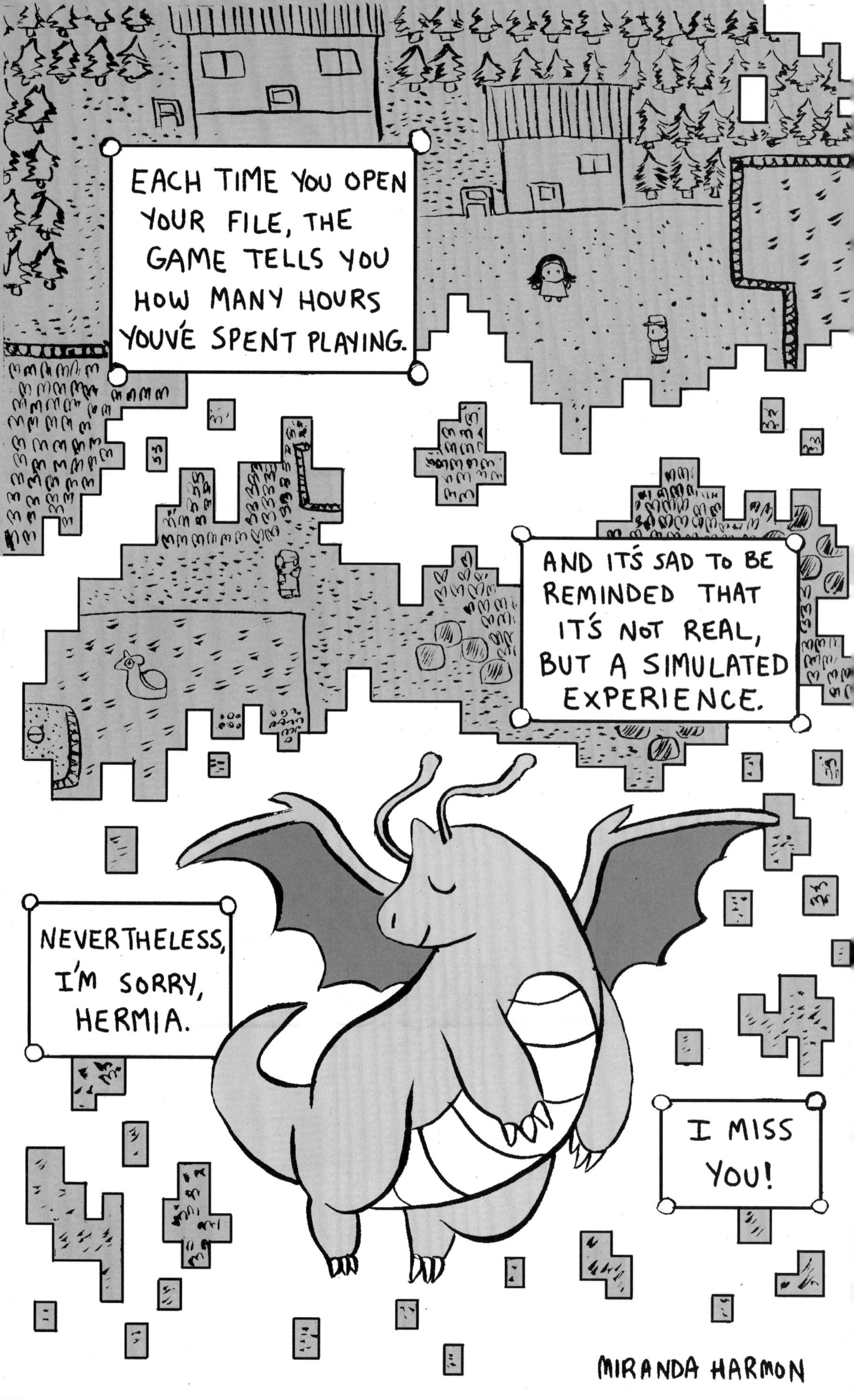
EACH TIME YOU OPEN YOUR FILE, THE GAME TELLS YOU HOW MANY HOURS YOU'VE SPENT PLAYING.
AND IT'S SAD TO BE REMINDED THAT IT'S NOT REAL, BUT A SIMULATED EXPERIENCE.
NEVERTHELESS, I'M SORRY, HERMIA.
I MISS YOU!
MIRANDA HARMON

pocket

by carey pietsch

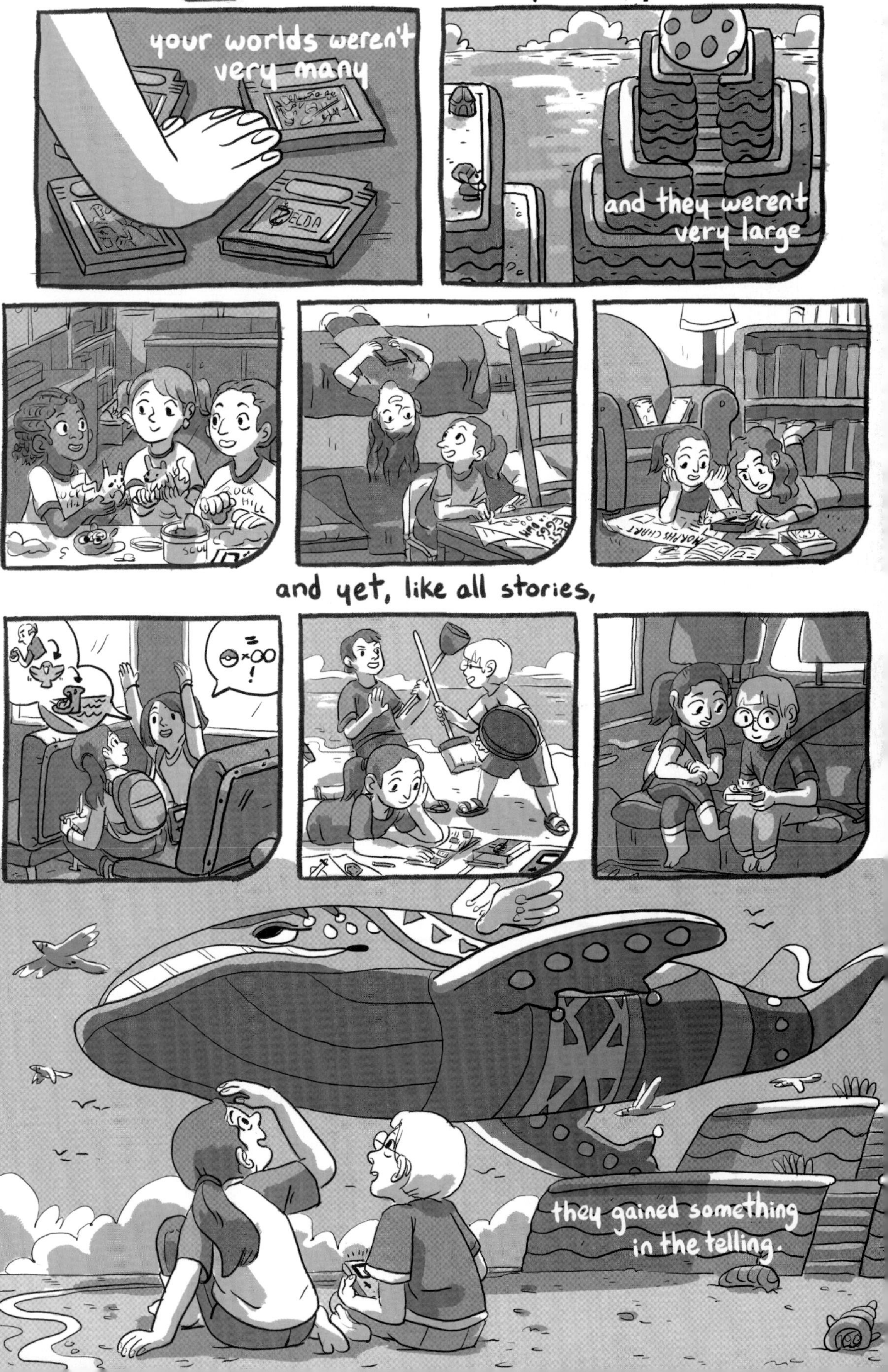
your worlds weren't very many
and they weren't very large
and yet, like all stories,
they gained something in the telling.

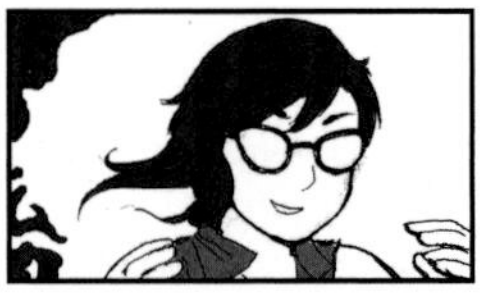

anna anthropy
auntiepixelante.com
anna anthropy is a play designer, historian, and thirty-year-old teenage witch.

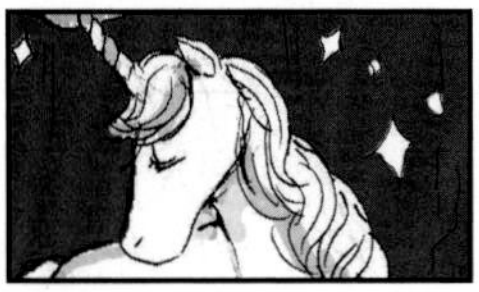

Jeremy Boydell
slimgiltsoul.tumblr.com
Jeremy Boydell is a freelance illustrator and comic book artist working in London.

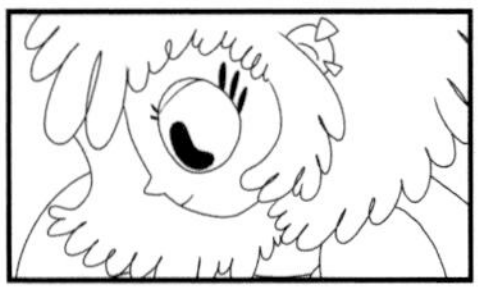

Caitlin Rose Boyle
sadsadkiddie.com
Caitlin Rose Boyle makes comics, illustrations, tiny video games, & short animations whenever she manages to put down her 3DS. She's currently developing an animated short for Nickelodeon.

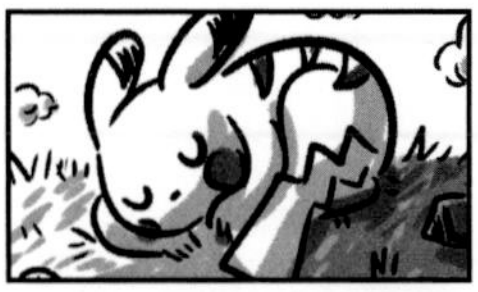

Megan Brennan
megan-brennan.com
Megan Brennan is an artist from New Jersey who draws a bunch of comics for the internet. As a kid, she thought Pikachu was pretty annoying.

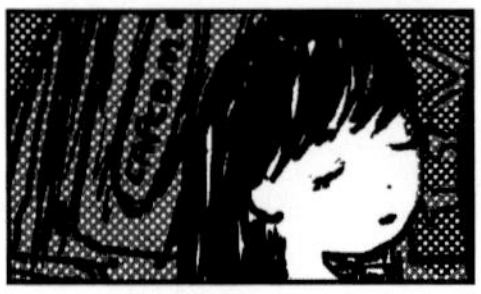

Buntoo
bun-too.tumblr.com
Drawing and gaming since childhood.
"You know the down in Phoenix Down? It's DOWN... like feathers! Wow!!"

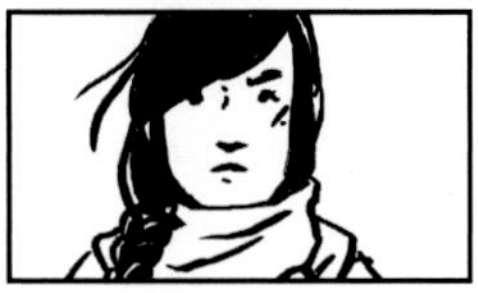

Kate Craig
katecraig.net
Kate Craig lives in Canada and makes game art, short comics, and grows raspberries.

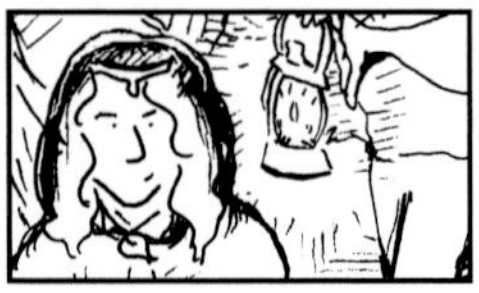

Natalie Dupille
thefeministbakery.com
Natalie Dupille is a cartoonist who hails from Seattle but calls her backpack home. Her most current project is an illustrated travelogue of her adventures through Oceania and beyond.

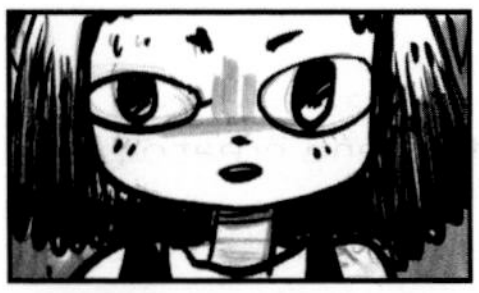

Kinoko Evans
kinokogallery.com
Kinoko Evans is an illustrating, cartooning printmaker in love with research and drawing.

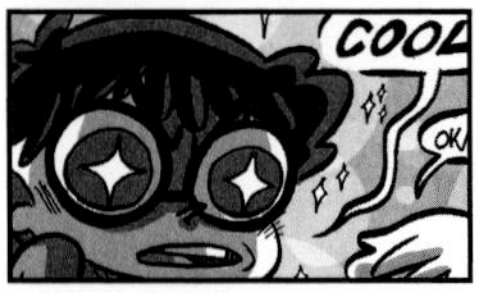
COOL
OK

Sara Goetter
sgoetter.com
Sara Goetter currently lives in Pennsylvania. She loves drawing comics about monsters and magic and getting into adventures.

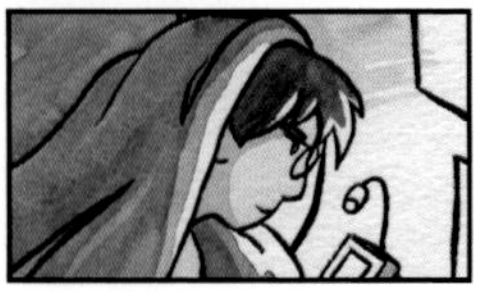

Kori Michele Handwerker
korimichele.com
Kori Michele is a watercolorist & the author of the *Prince of Cats* webcomic. Their current work, which includes various anthology comics & zines, focuses on transgender & nonbinary identities.

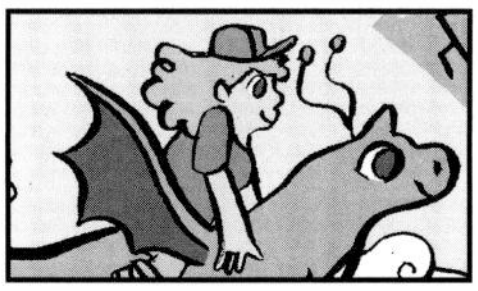

Miranda Harmon
mirandaharmon.com
Miranda Harmon is 22 years old and has spent most of her life in Florida. She currently studies at the Sequential Artists Workshop in Gainesville, where she makes comics and hangs with alligators.

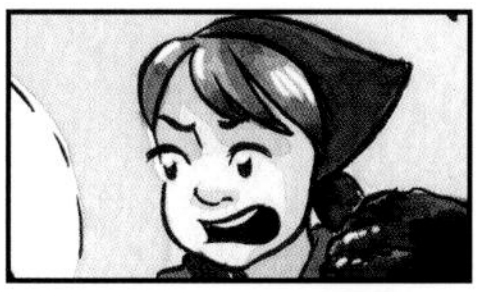

Becca Hillburn
nattosoup.tumblr.com
Becca Hillburn is a comic artist and illustrator living in Nashville, TN. When not behind the artist alley table, she's drawing comics.

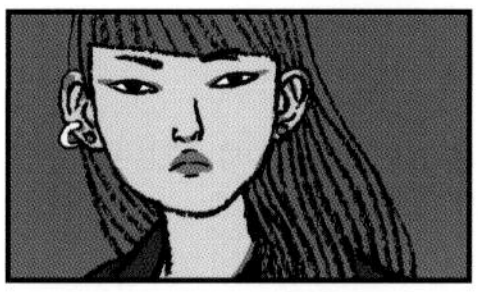

Hellen Jo
helllllen.org
Hellen Jo is a cartoonist, illustrator, and Bay Area native living in Los Angeles, California.

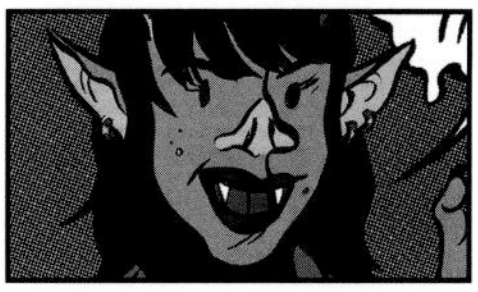

Kae Kelly-Colon
spacewrite.tumblr.com
Kae Kelly-Colon is a twenty-two year old femmegender writer & musician. "Gamer Grrrl" is just one of the many pieces Kae has worked on that focus on newer gender identities.

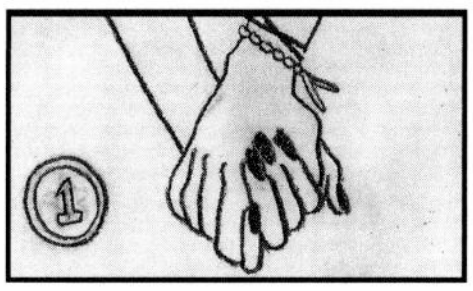

merritt kopas
mkopas.net
merritt kopas is a designer dreaming of more compassionate & human forms of digital play. She runs the alternative games website forest ambassador & is the editor of *Videogames for Humans*.

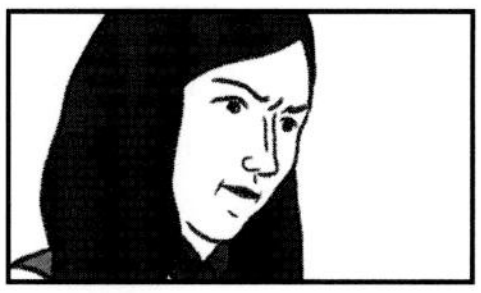

Laura Lannes
lauralannes.com
Laura is an illustrator and cartoonist from Rio de Janeiro, Brazil, living in New York City. She studied illustration at the School of Visual Arts. Her comic got a good review on The Comics Journal.

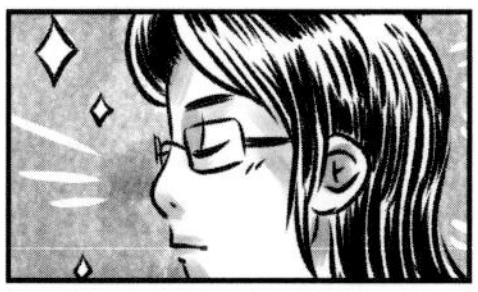

Jade F. Lee
www.jadefenglee.com
Jade often draws from childhood experiences. Video games were an important part of that childhood, and a big influence on her artistic style. She is currently playing and loving Child of Light.

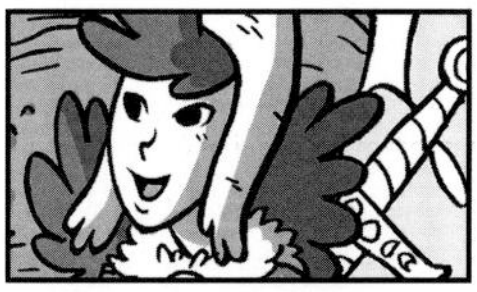

Katie Longua
klongua.com
Katie Longua is an illustrator, Pokémon master, and creator of the award-winning mini-comic series RÖK. She has played the role of Poppy with her D&D group for over 3 years.

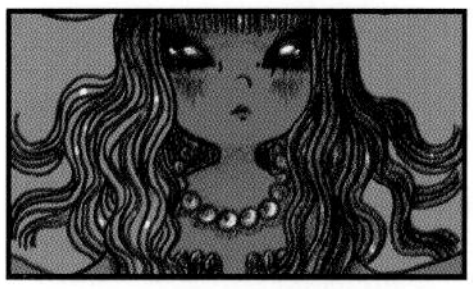

Jane Mai
janemai.com
Nobody knows who or what Jane Mai is.

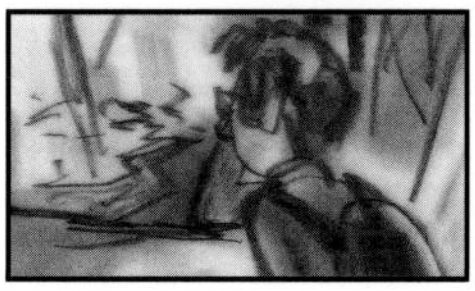

Annie Mok
heyanniemok.tumblr.com
Annie Mok studied comics at the Minneapolis College of Art and Design and lives in West Philly. She received a 2014 Transformation Award from the Leeway Foundation.

Hazel Newlevant

newlevant.com

Hazel draws and publishes comics about cuties, music, and gender. Her work has been awarded the Xeric Grant and the Prism Comics Queer Press Grant.

Diana Nock

intrepidgirlbot.com

Diana is a reclusive cartoonist, typically found hunched over her drawing tablet in her Minneapolis burrow. She somehow makes a living on comics, which is lucky, since she went to art school.

Rachel Ordway

rachelordway.com

A freelance cartoonist and SCAD alum who enjoys drawing more than eating, to her stomach's dismay. She self-publishes minicomics and is a regular contributor to "The Line It Is Drawn."

Molly Ostertag

mollyostertag.com

Molly Ostertag graduated from the School of Visual Arts in 2014. She makes comics with a focus on powerful women of all kinds, and draws the webcomic *Strong Female Protagonist*.

Aatmaja Pandya

aatmajapandya.com

Aatmaja Pandya is a cartoonist & illustrator from New York! Her favorite game is The Legend of Zelda: Majora's Mask, but the Paper Mario soundtrack will always be her greatest weakness.

Carey Pietsch

careydraws.com

Carey Pietsch is a cartoonist & illustrator based out of Philadelphia, currently illustrating the Adventure Time comic Marceline Gone Adrift. She's into stories about magic and empathy.

Liane Pyper

leepart.tumblr.com

A recent graduate of Northern Michigan University's Illustration program, Liane hails from the peninsula of Michigan that's just like Skyrim, except without the dragons.

MK Reed

mkreed.com

MK Reed is the author of *Americus* & *The Cute Girl Network*, from First Second. She writes & draws *About A Bull*, a comic adaptation of the Táin Bó Cúailnge. MK plays 1eAD&D & is a 5th level cleric.

Anna Rose

astralrejection.com

Anna Rose is an illustrator. Her favorite game is is Harvest Moon: Back to Nature and her favorite food is a cheeseburger.

Mia Schwartz

super-villain.org

Mia graduated from SVA recently and now lives in Queens. She asked for Harvest Moon 64 for her 10th birthday expressly because your character could date girls.

Amanda Scurti

amandascurti.com

Amanda Scurti is an illustrator, cartoonist, and colorist from Long Island, NY. She has been a casual gamer since childhood, and still wishes for a life cheat as valuable as rosebud;!;!;! (ad infinitum).

Sarah Winifred Searle

swinsea.com

Sarah hails from spooky New England, where she makes comics and lives with the love of her life, Kitty.

Maggie Siegel—Berele

maggiesiegelberele.com

Maggie is a Brooklyn based cartoonist and gamer. She has been a part time Druid for the last decade. She graduated from the School for Visual Arts in 2011 and currently works at Marvel.

Jasmine Silver

oohsilver.com

Although hand-lettering is her first love, Jasmine's practice is influenced by permaculture traditions because designing with dirt can help change the world.

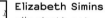

Elizabeth Simins

eliz.abeth.net

Elizabeth Simins is an artist & illustrator living in Portland with her two fluffy cats, Link & Zora. She makes comics about games, girlhood, and the apocalypse (usually not at the same time).

Sera Stanton

serastanton.tumblr.com

Sera Stanton is an illustrator, printmaker, comics artist and editor and living in Portland, Oregon. Her work reveals a not-so-faraway land of daydreams and challenges.

Sarah Stern

sarahstern.com

Sarah Stern is an artist and writer from New York. She is completing an MFA in Sequential Art at SCAD, and spends most of her time making stories about teamwork and wizards.

June Vigantes

junerevolver.tumblr.com

June Vigants is a comic artist, illustrator & musician who graduated from the School of Visual Arts in 2014. June loves ren fairs, D&D, and monsters—an enduring theme of their work.

Yao Xiao

yaoxiaoart.com

Yao Xiao is a New York-based artist. A native from Tianjin, China, Xiao has been living in the States for 9 years. Her work explores foreigner identity, adolescent memories & surreal fantasies.

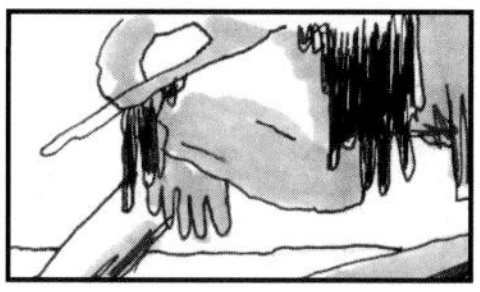

Sophie Yanow

sophieyanow.com

Sophie Yanow grew up in Northern California. Then she moved to a place where they actually have winter and realized how good she had it.

Special thanks to Anita Sarkeesian for being an inspiration to this project with her thought-provoking criticism and tireless work in support of gaming gender equality, to Robin Enrico for the fantastic Kickstarter video, to Molly Ostertag for her support and sage advice, to George O'Connor for being the #1 fan, to Charles Mudd for sharing his love of gaming with the next generation, and to all our backers on Kickstarter, who trusted in our vision and made this book possible.

Chainmail Bikini: The Anthology of Women Gamers
First Printing, Fall 2015
ISBN 978-1-5136-0012-3

Edited by Hazel Newlevant
Cover illustration by Hellen Jo
Layout & logo by Jasmine Silver

PropCourier Sans font by Manufactura Independente
manufacturaindependente.org/propcourier-sans/

Printed in China

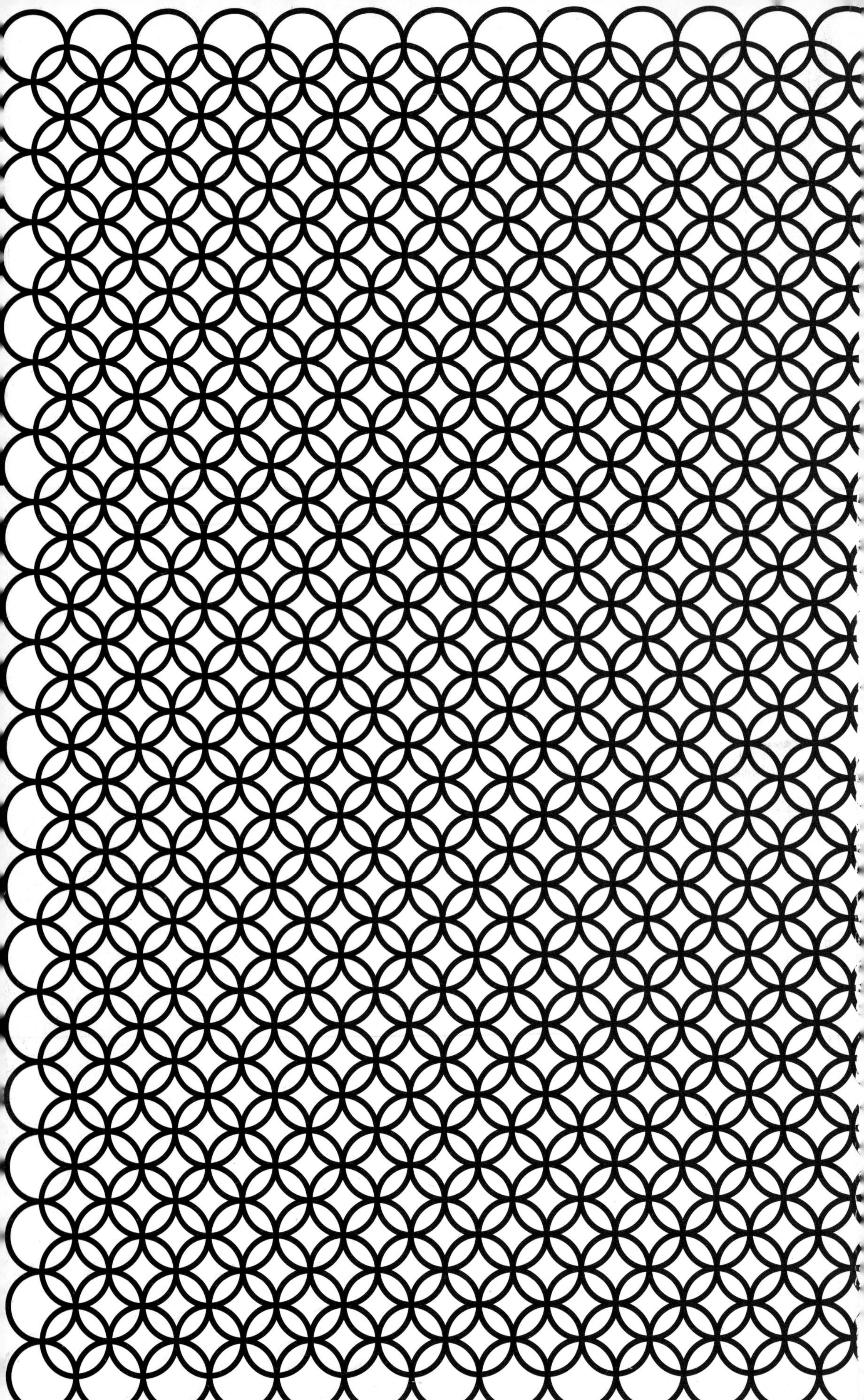